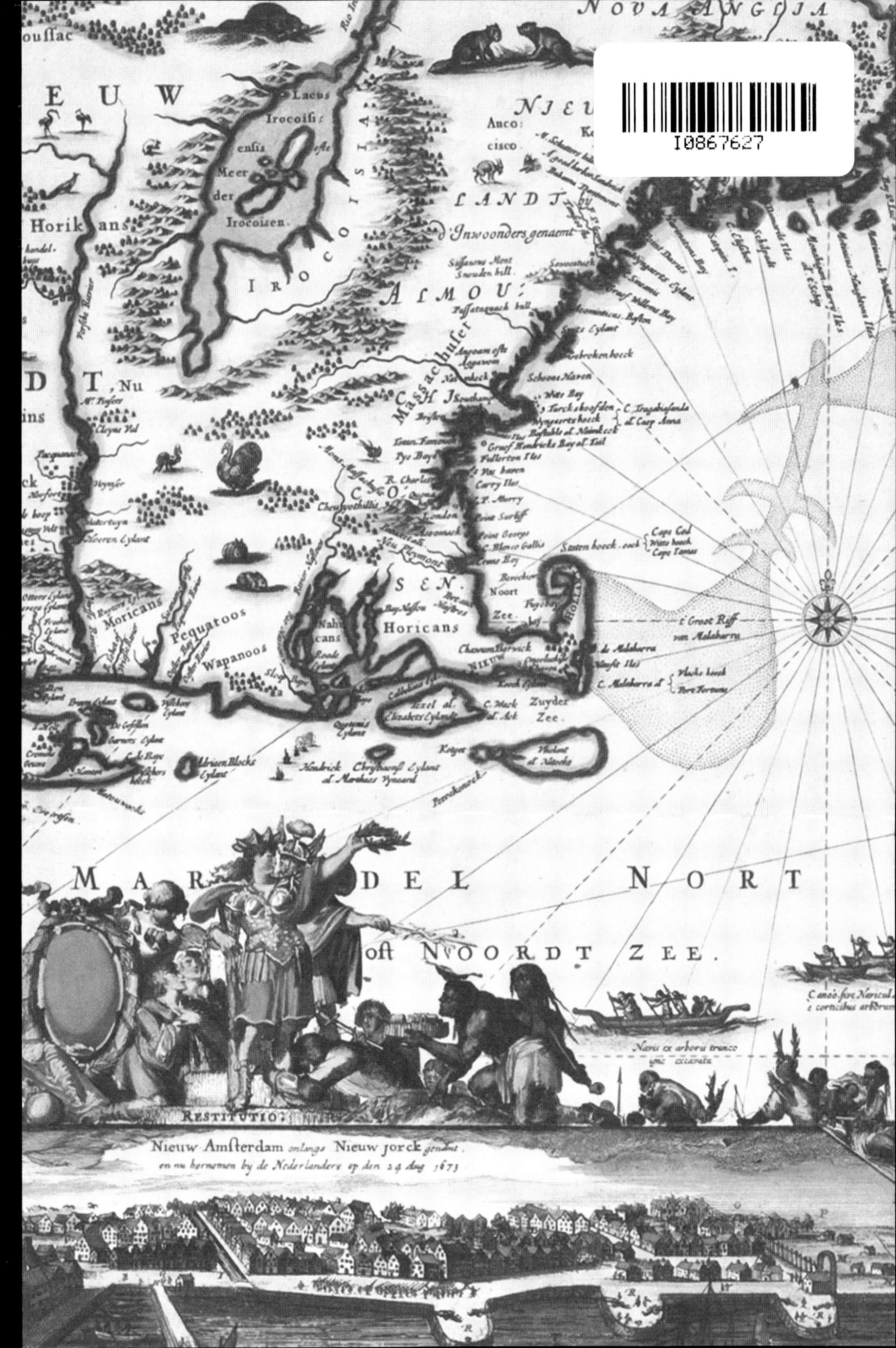
NOVA ANGLIA
NIEUW
LANDT
Lacus Irocoisi: ensis ofte Meer der Irocoisen
IROCO
ALMOU
Massachuset
Horikans
Moricans
Pequatoos
Wapanoos
Horicans
Noort Zee
Zuyder Zee
MAR DEL NORT
oft NOORDT ZEE.
RESTITUTIO
Nieuw Amsterdam onlangs Nieuw Jorck genaemt,
en nu hernomen by de Nederlanders op den 24 Aug 1673

Opening Statements

Mural painted by Attilio Pusterla (1862–1941) in the ceremonial courtroom in the New York County Courthouse at 60 Centre Street, as photographed by Teodors Ermansons.

Opening Statements

Law, Jurisprudence, and the Legacy of Dutch New York

edited by

Albert M. Rosenblatt and Julia C. Rosenblatt

ee
excelsior editions
AN IMPRINT OF STATE UNIVERSITY OF NEW YORK PRESS

and

THE HISTORICAL SOCIETY OF THE COURTS OF THE STATE OF NEW YORK

Published by
State University of New York Press, Albany

Printed in the United States of America

Excelsior Editions
is an imprint of State University of New York Press

For information, contact State University of New York Press, Albany, NY
www.sunypress.edu

Production and book design, Laurie Searl
Marketing, Kate McDonnell

Library of Congress Cataloging-in-Publication Data

Opening statements : law, jurisprudence, and the legacy of Dutch New York /
Edited by Albert M. Rosenblatt and Julia C. Rosenblatt.
p. cm.
Includes bibliographical references and index.
ISBN 978-1-4384-4657-8 (hardcover : alk. paper)
1. Law—New York (State)—History. 2. New York (State)—History—Colonial period, ca. 1600–1775.
3. Dutch—New York (State)—History—17th century. I. Rosenblatt, Albert M. II. Rosenblatt, Julia C.
KFN5078.O64 2012
349.74709'032—dc23 2012023547

10 9 8 7 6 5 4 3 2 1

To the scholars who for decades unearthed and studied New Netherland history, enabling today's historians and commentators to expand upon the earlier writings and present fresh insights to a receptive public.

Contents

Illustrations

Acknowledgments
with thanks

For us, as with so many others, our interest in the field began not long after we started to read Russell Shorto's book *The Island at the Center of the World*. He transported us to a place of which we had been only dimly aware. Rightfully, he reveals that Charles Gehring's translations of old Dutch language records have made much of this possible. Charly, as he is known and to whom all New Netherland paths lead, is the ultimate mentor, and that is how we gratefully regard him.

At the Historical Society of the Courts of the State of New York, we were planning the 2009 calendar of events, and it seemed appropriate to dedicate at least one program to our Dutch legacy, considering it was the year of the Henry Hudson Quadricentennial. Plans were shaped by ideas, which gave way to research, and, eventually, familiarity with an array of scholars who had been laboring in the vineyards for decades.

From the outset, we received encouragement from Marilyn Marcus, Executive Director of HSCSNY, who has been with us through every stage of this work. Her input, ideas, and initiative go well beyond the hundreds of conversations and e-mails with her in planning and developing the volume. We also thank her administrative assistants, Olivia Green and Michael Benowitz, for their considerable help.

We love pictures. The essays in this volume—by world-level scholars—are themselves stirring, but imagery enhances them. Collecting and allocating pictures has been an ongoing enterprise, and we thank Evan Friss, who arranged and stored selections we made from libraries, archives, and museums. Hearty thanks also to Teodors Ermansons of the New York State Court System. He is a creative photographer, and his work is reflected throughout this book.

In finding articles, books, and images, we had a great deal of help from several sources. Mary Collins at the Holland Society Library smiled cheerfully at our "lists of must-haves," as did Jay Shuman, the New York University Law School Librarian, and Jean Ashton at the New-York Historical Society. We appreciate also the courtesies shown us at the New York Public Library and the Museum of the City of New York.

Mary Ellen Pelzer, Director of the South Street Seaport Museum in New York, has been generous in her time and her cooperation, personally, and through her assistant, Molly Nora.

Sue Kriete of the New-York Historical Society painstakingly assembled for us the images the society had in its relevant collections, a sumptuous menu. We chose several, including one of her favorites and ours, a picture of elementary school girls learning a Dutch dance.

How rewarding it is to deal with the New York State Library, Archives, and Museum staffers in Albany. The facilities are well maintained by energetic and talented people, such as Fred Bassett and Vicki Weiss, Senior Librarians in the Manuscripts and Special Collections Department of the State Library. Christine W. Ward, the State Archivist, and James D. Folts, Head of Reference Services at the State Archives, led the way to many interesting items. Their suggestions were always on the mark, and they made our visits to Albany delightful.

Not much time passed between calls and e-mails from us to Frances Murray, Chief Legal Reference Attorney at the New York Court of Appeals. She has been at the receiving end of numerous "Fran, can you help us locate . . ." appeals for help.

Try as we may to be meticulous in our own writing, vexing questions of grammar and style arise, and we have regularly consulted our friend Susan McCloskey. She has repeatedly helped us triumph over syntax, but played no role in whatever miscues appear.

Getting the manuscript into shape was sometimes arduous, but we had help from Karen Grant, who could always be counted on, especially to resolve the conflicts between Microsoft Word and Word Perfect.

Thanks also to Joep de Koning for the use of his extensive private map collection and help, and to Charles Gehring, Jaap Jacobs, David Voorhees, Willem Frijhof, Martha Shattuck, and Leo and Marcia Hershkowitz for their encouragement and suggestions, particularly in the early stages of this project.

We have saved our final acknowledgment for the members of the Board of Trustees of the HSCSNY, with special thanks to Judge Judith S. Kaye, Roy Reardon, and John Gordan III, for their lasting support.

We gratefully acknowledge the generosity of the William Nelson Cromwell Foundation in funding the publication of this volume, with thanks as well to the Historical Records of the New York County Clerk, Inc., for its contribution.

Albert and Julia Rosenblatt
Pleasant Valley, New York

Acknowledgments
of Previous or Prospective Appearances

Portions of "Real Estate or Political Sovereignty? The Dutch, Munsees, and the Purchase of Manhattan Island," by Paul Otto, first appeared as part of chapter 3, "Trade and Settlement, 1624–1638," in Paul Otto, *The Dutch Munsee Encounter in America: The Struggle for Sovereignty in the Hudson Valley* (New York: Berghahn Books, 2006) and are used here by permission of the author and the publisher.

Earlier versions of "A Flourishing City—Jews in New Amsterdam, 1654," by Leo Hershkowitz, appeared as "By Chance or by Choice," *American Jewish Archives Journal,* LVII, nos. 1&2 (2005): 1–13, published by the Jacob Rader Marcus Center of the American Jewish Archives; and "By Chance or Choice: Jews in New Amsterdam 1654," *de Halve Maen* 77 (Summer 2004): 23–30, published by the Holland Society of New York. Permission has been granted by the respective publishers for the present revised and expanded essay.

"The Souls of New Amsterdam's African America Children," by Joyce D. Goodfriend, originally appeared in the online journal *Common-Place* (www.common-place.org) in 2003. Used here by permission.

"The Declaration of Independence and the Dutch Legacy," by Wijnand W. Mijnhardt, was first presented as a part of the panel *Declarations of Independence and Rights,* at the 11th Conference of the International Society for Eighteenth-Century Studies at UCLA, August 3–10, 2003.

"*Crimen Læsæ Maiestatis* or Abuse of Power? The 1647 Trial of Cornelis Melijn and Jochem Pietersz Kuijter," by Jaap Jacobs, is an adaptation of parts of chapter 6 of his work in progress, a full biography of Petrus Stuyvesant.

Foreword

It gives me great pleasure to write a foreword to this book, which provides a useful and telling picture of life in New Netherland. Until recently, Americans generally thought of the Dutch settlement in the New World (when they thought of it at all) in terms of caricatures—the authoritarian director general with a wooden leg, Petrus Stuyvesant, whose name adorns a cigarette brand and a beautiful memorial stone in St. Mark's Church-in-the-Bowery in lower Manhattan; the trade of the island of Manhattan from Indian tribes for goods with a calculated value of $24. All this attention gave happy meaning to the lyrics of another day: "Even old New York was once New Amsterdam." But as we know, some of this history is at once over-romanticized and underappreciated.

Recent books, as well as this collection of essays, have been aided immeasurably by an extraordinary scholar, Charles Gehring, who translated the seventeenth-century Dutch records, which had been stored silent and little used for countless years in the New York State Library in Albany. Gehring has given more than three decades to the painstaking effort to translate the papers, diaries, records, and books, written in seventeenth-century Dutch script and faded by time. The New Netherland Project, with which Gehring is associated, and other groups, have greatly expanded our knowledge of and fascination with the Dutch era. The within volume is edited by Albert and Julia Rosenblatt, two New Yorkers who live in the Hudson Valley where the history of patroons, adventurous seafaring, and a very Dutch sense of a well-ordered society was marked by the quadricentennial celebration of Henry Hudson's voyage in 1609, which opened the New World to European settlement. We are indebted to Judge Rosenblatt, retired from New York State's highest court, and his wife Julia Rosenblatt, a retired Vassar College professor, for selecting and editing these essays, which surround the reader with information, facts, anecdotes, and graphic word pictures of an era worthy of study and recollection. And best of all, there is a uniformity of good writing, along with wonderful pictorial representation, which makes for pleasurable reading.

When arriving on these shores long before our nation was born, the new settlers had brought with them the laws of Holland, which gave a solid structure to the governance of New Amsterdam. The Dutch Republic was governed by civil law and jurisprudence based on written law and statutes, as Martha Shattuck's essay points out. This system did not define processes of petition and redress against alleged wrongs, nor did it grant the freedom and liberties that Americans associate with our Bill of Rights. The settlers of Manhattan had to struggle for the liberal values of freedom that government is arguably established to secure and of which the courts are the ultimate protectors. These essays recount the arduous journey toward freedom that had its beginning in New Amsterdam, a journey that brought ideas and inspiration to the Continental Congress and to the deliberations of the Constitutional Convention in Philadelphia. In fact, as Russell Shorto wrote, and as this book certainly supports, Americans owe an important debt to the culture of the Netherlands and its development of Manhattan.

Was the Netherlands, not England, the mother of America as Edward Bok asserted? Bok came to America as a fourteen-year-old Dutch immigrant and transformed our twentieth-century reading habits as the publisher of the *Ladies Home Journal* and the *Saturday Evening Post*. He cited four institutions that were brought from Old to New Amsterdam: free public education, freedom of religion, freedom of the press, and the secret ballot (one hears the echoes of the famous Four Freedoms speech by Franklin Delano Roosevelt, another American who honored his Dutch heritage). This book helps us understand what Bok was talking about and gives credibility to his argument. In his essay, Wijnand Mijnhardt shows the striking similarities of our Declaration of Independence to the Act of Abjuration of 1581 (Plakkaat van Verlatinge), with which the Dutch declared their independence from Spain, becoming the first country in history to win its freedom from a dominant world empire. To read Charles Gehring's account of the 1657 Flushing Remonstrance is to understand the Dutch commitment to freedom of worship and conscience. Perhaps the fervor of these proud Dutch assertions could be qualified by broader historical analysis, but it should be remembered that the Pilgrims who landed at Plymouth Rock in 1620 began their fateful voyage from Leiden, the university town in Holland where they had been given Dutch protection for years as they escaped religious persecution by the English.

An excellent essay by Troy McKenzie and Wilson Freeman tells how arbitration as a means of dispute resolution was firmly established in New Amsterdam. Arbitration—a growing and significant part of American legal processes—reflected Dutch values of pragmatism, common sense, and reconciliation rather than the often endless confrontation of modern courtroom litigation.

The legendary City Hall of New Amsterdam, the *Stadt Huys*, once the subject of archeological digs in lower Manhattan, is re-created in an imaginative essay that demonstrates how the courtroom that commanded its entire second floor was understood to be at the center of a civil society that respected law and justice as fundamental to its governance.

Dutch rule in New Amsterdam lasted less than fifty years. With the English takeover in 1664, most of the Dutch settlers elected to stay in what its new rulers renamed New York. There must have been a sense of quiet pleasure among the descendants of those settlers when the Netherlands in 1782 became the first country to recognize the independence of the Thirteen Colonies.

Opening Statements: Law, Jurisprudence, and the Legacy of Dutch New York addresses only a short chapter in the long history of America. Its judgments will not be without dispute, but then, as the eminent Dutch historian Pieter Geyl once wrote: "History is an argument without end." There can be no doubt, however, as to the value of those seeds of freedom that were deeply planted in New Netherland. They produced a revolutionary harvest that causes us to appreciate what the Dutch inspired. A small country, the Netherlands—yes—but always a powerful ally for America in the unending struggle for a well-ordered society where freedom and justice prevail.

William J. vanden Heuvel

Introduction

Albert M. Rosenblatt and Julia C. Rosenblatt

We may call England our "mother country," but our culture, political system, and jurisprudence have a more varied heritage. Each state with its own settlement history has a unique flavor. Our nation's lineage, and New York's in particular, has an often-overlooked Dutch component. Scholars differ as to how much of New Netherland, or Dutch New York, survived in present-day institutions. Some commentators say that the heterogeneous, commerce-oriented

Figure I.1. "Light on the Past," postcard from the 1909 Hudson-Fulton Celebration. New York: A. C. Bosseman & Co., c. 1909. New York State Library Postcard Collection QC16510.

nature of the forty years or so of Dutch settlement gave New York a character that persists to this day. Others contend that little, if anything, survives.

By the beginning of the seventeenth century, Western Europe had a long-established trade relationship with the East, from which it desired luxuries such as spices and precious stones. In exchange, the East valued European goods, silver, and manufactured articles.

Europeans had few trade routes. One was across the desert and mountains to the Caspian and Black Seas; another from the Arabian and Red Seas into the Indian Ocean; still another

Figure I.2. "The Entrance of the *Half Moon* into New York Harbor," postcard ([S. l.: P. Sander], c. 1909). Hudson River Steamboat and Navigation Ephemera Collection, 1866–1964, William S. Clark, collector. New York State Library call number SC23080.

around the Cape of Good Hope. Because these routes were long and controlled by rival countries, each sought alternate passageways to the East, including a "Northeast passage" to Asia.

The Netherlands, at the time a center of trade and commerce, hoped to find such a route. In 1609, the Dutch East India Company engaged Henry Hudson, an Englishman, for the venture. He did not find the route and is best known for exploring the river that now bears his name.

Not long after Hudson's exploration, the Dutch sent others to examine the territory. Adriaen Block explored the coast all the way to Cape Cod and mapped the region. When in 1613 his ship burned near the shore of lower Manhattan, he and his crew built a new one on the spot.

Although the Dutch never found the hoped-for "Northeast passage," they found a land teeming with resources to trade, especially a wealth of beavers, whose pelts found favor in

FIGURE I.3. Figurative Map, by Adriaen Block, the first European to circumnavigate Manhattan and Long Island. Parchment, 1614. Collection Nationaal Archief (National Archives of the Netherlands) 4.VELH 520.

European fashion. From 1624 through 1664, the Dutch colonized and controlled a large area—"New Netherland," including "New Amsterdam" as its nerve center. For that near half-century, the Dutch established government, trade, and institutions that helped shape the future of what would become New York.

For years, the history of New York under Dutch rule languished in what Washington Irving called "the regions of doubt and fable." He used this phrase in his preface, "an author's apology," to the 1848 edition of his whimsical history of New York as told by an imaginary Diedrich Knickerbocker.

Irving penned his fictional history in 1809, the bicentennial year of Hudson's exploration of the river so vital to New Netherland. Irving never intended his writing to substitute for true historical scholarship, merely using the gap in recorded history to write something entertaining. Indeed, he was one of the citizens who banded together in 1804 to form the New-York Historical Society, which took steps to acquire and preserve New York's historical record. Ironically, his "history" plunged the Dutch epoch even deeper into the shadowy realm of legend.

Figure I.4. Washington Irving's depiction of Wouter van Twiller's administration is reflected in "Van Twiller and Council Met in Debate," drawn by O. Steeden, published by T. A. Palser, 67 Fleet Street, London, June 21, 1830. PR 058 Printmaker File, Q-V; negative no. 83110d. Collection of The New-York Historical Society.

FIGURE I.5. To advertise its Water Route through the Hudson River Valley, the New York Central Line used a romantic view of Dutch New York. New York State Library call number BRO5973+.

The Dutch period would have remained in Washington Irving's land of doubt and fable were it not for people who had a passion to preserve and study documents from the era. Many records, letters, diaries, and the like have perished through neglect or disaster. Others have been spared. The saga of the archives is an adventure story in itself.[1]

The Dutch records, along with British colonial records, had survived years on board ship during the Revolutionary War, followed by multiple moves, mutilation, theft, periods of neglect, and two fires. In the meantime, New York took some positive steps to enlarge and protect its archives. In 1895, it established the Office of the State Historian, and in 1950, it ordered a systematic management of Executive Branch records. In 1975, the state hired its first archivist, and three years later opened its storage and research facility on the eleventh floor of the Cultural Education Center in Albany.

Historians know that record retention is chancy. Documents take up space, and those who covet that space will seek to dispose of the papers. If we are lucky, records will go to a willing archive, but too often end up in the trash. Several contributors to this volume can be numbered among those who cared enough to collect and preserve important materials.

Historian Leo Hershkowitz has rescued many valuable documents, in some cases moments before they were on the way to the shredder. He has climbed into dumpsters to retrieve unappreciated items. He tells of hearing, "You want these things? Take 'em." That is why Queens College, where he is a history professor, held several valuable archives for a time. Hershkowitz has since distributed the Queens archives to the care of various institutions. The City of Kingston wanted the Dutch documents related to Ulster County, and he furnished them. Hershkowitz has sent records of New York's Court of Chancery and Supreme Court of Judicature—a huge collection of pre-1847 court records—to the State Archives, where they are tended carefully under the direction of archivist Christine W. Ward.

Fortunately, the paper of the Dutch colonial era was acid free; unfortunately, the ink was not. Some records suffered from clumsy efforts to reconstruct or preserve them. Today, the State Archives cares for its records in a pristine laboratory. As conservation has become a science, conservators now know exactly what solutions will lessen stains without disturbing the ink or compromising the paper. They know what substances will mend torn paper to prevent further damage without adverse consequences years later.

Storing papers in a library or archive does not always ensure safety. In 1911, fire swept through the New York State Library, destroying much of the state's historical records. The Dutch documents, considered of lesser importance, occupied the bottom shelves. As the English records burned, the debris fell to the bottom, protecting much of what lay below. A photo of the 1911 fire occupies a prominent place on the bulletin board of the conservation laboratory, a cautionary reminder of past disasters.

These records are, of course, in seventeenth-century Dutch, a language difficult even for those who speak modern Dutch. In the early 1970s when four volumes, already translated, remained unpublished, Ralph de Groff Sr., a trustee of the Holland Society of New York, wanted to see these published and have the remaining volumes translated. He contacted his acquaintance, then-vice president Nelson Rockefeller, who got in touch with his successor as governor, Malcolm Wilson, asking him to make money available in his discretionary budget to hire a translator. Wilson agreed. Peter Christoph, Curator of the Manuscripts and History section of the New York State Library, did not have to look far for the right person. Charles Gehring had done research at the library for his PhD dissertation. Gehring started work in

FIGURE I.6. New York State Capitol Fire, March 29, 1911. New York State Library Photograph Collection.

September 1974. The state funds lasted one year. After that, the New Netherland Project has been kept alive by private funding.

Much of the contemporary writing about New Netherland shows the place to be rife with drunkenness, brawling, and adultery—truly disorderly. Disorder endows writing with the dramatic tension that makes exciting reading, and many primary sources lead directly to this aspect of life. A significant part of New Netherland documents comes from court records, which by their very nature chronicle crime and conflict.

Although we can expect a young frontier community to have a bit of the "wild west" about it, there surely must have been families who lived simple, god-fearing lives, going about their business and family rearing without making trouble. We have little information about them. If diaries ever existed, they have been lost. Few letters home to Holland survived generations of Dutch house cleaning. A new cache, however, has come to the attention of Charles Gehring, from of all places, the British Admiralty. During wartime, ships of opposing nations commonly

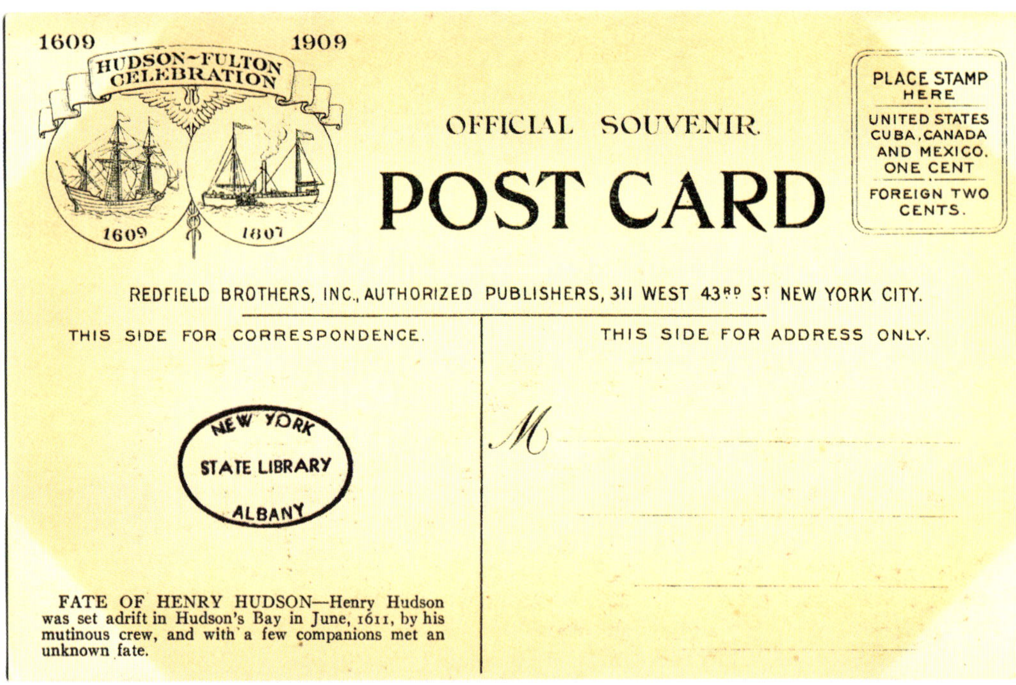

Figure I.7. Float—"Fate of Henry Hudson." Hudson-Fulton Celebration Commission Official Post Card no. 15. New York: Redfield Bothers, c. 1909. New York State Library Postcard Collection call number QC16510.

confronted each other and confiscated correspondence entrusted to the ships' captains. Some letters home never reached their intended recipients, but reposed in the Admiralty files all these years—more than three centuries.

Some students at Leiden University have begun a project called *Brieven als Buit,* or letters as loot, drawn from the British Admiralty records, some of which pertain to New Netherland. Each month the students select a letter to post on the project's Web site. A student brought one in particular to Gehring's attention. In 1664, when New Netherland was transferred to the English, Hendrick Meessen Vrooman in Schenectady wrote to his brother Jacob in Leiden. He discussed his crops and his reaction to the English takeover. He did not think it was so bad. With the English soldiers present, the Indians were less of a threat, he believed.[2]

Interest in New Netherland comes in waves. The last peaked a hundred years ago, around 1909, the year of the Hudson-Fulton celebration, which included parades, floats, library and museum displays, and an exhibit at the Metropolitan Museum of Art. A so-called Dutch Mania led up to the Hudson tercentennial and persisted for about a decade or two afterward.

The recent quadricentennial of Henry Hudson's 1609 exploration has brought renewed interest in the period and new scholarly accounts. The recent flurry of interest comes from more than the current century marker. Several events have brought the study of this period to light: First, scholars have access to more primary source material than ever before, owing to the work of the New Netherland Project under the direction of Charles Gehring. Second, the best-selling *The Island at the Center of the World* by Russell Shorto has brought this facet of our history to public attention. Examining Dutch influence on America is too interesting to be a once-a-century phenomenon. Many avenues of research lie before future scholars. Let us hope they maintain a steady stream of new information and further illumination from historians.

In the present volume, a broad spectrum of eminent scholars treat the legal heritage New Netherland bequeathed to New York. This volume covers a number of issues that speak to that heritage, including concepts of governance, liberty, women's rights, and religious freedom. In many ways, those fundamental concepts resonate in today's legal culture. Not all our authors agree with each other about everything, and that is fine. Controversy advances scholarship.

NOTES

1. For a full account, see Charles Gehring, "New York's Dutch Records: A Historiographical Note—Updated," *The Hudson River Valley Review* 25, no. 2 (Spring 2009): 12–19; and Christine W. Ward, "The New York State Archives—25 Years Old This Year," *New York Archives* 3, no. 2 (Fall 2003): 34–36.

2. "De Nieu Nederlanse Marcurius," 25, no. 4 (December 2009): 4. Online at http://www.nnp.org/nni/Marcurius/marc25-4.pdf.

Chapter One

"... a well regulated country where justice and government prevail"

Martha Dickinson Shattuck

Martha Shattuck treats a subject that is an important part of the jurisprudential landscape: the right of petition. Our own right to petition the government for redress of grievances is embedded in the Constitution's First Amendment. It grew up in New Netherland as part of an unwritten Old World Dutch legacy.

The magistrates of local courts, and on occasion New Netherland's colonial council, often used the title of this essay when dealing with slanderous language used against them and their decisions, or behavior that violated the laws. Such behavior could result in "serious consequences" which not only could not be suffered but also was promptly punished by making the defendant publicly apologize and pay a steep fine.[1] The laws that regulated New Netherland, and were to be upheld, were those that regulated Holland, and were brought over with the first colonists. Once the Amsterdam Chamber of the West India Company was given sole oversight of New Netherland, the laws and ordinances of the city of Amsterdam were added to the list. Moreover, as stated in the instructions to the first director, any new laws or ordinances that the director and colonial council wished to enact had to be approved by the Company. Since many of these ordinances dealt with the living conditions in a new world, such as relations with the Indians, regulations for baking bread, and taxes, they needed immediate attention and were usually issued before receiving the Company's approval and apparently did not cause a negative response from the Company. This was, therefore, a highly regulated country governed firmly by the written laws of Holland and its own laws and ordinances.

There was one action, however, that did not appear in the law—the right of the public to petition the courts to achieve their rights and privileges they felt had been denied; to demand changes within the community; to ask for a particular job not delegated by the courts; or to try to depose the magistrates or directors not abiding by the known laws. This seldom discussed aspect of public participation in government was not part of the established and written jurisprudence, but quite likely, as it was never contested in either Holland or New Netherland, part of customary law.[2] This chapter will discuss the background of petitioning in Holland and its use and effect in New Netherland.

The law by which the Dutch governed was civil law, a jurisprudence based on written laws and statutes, as opposed to common law employed by the English, which was based on

INLEIDING TOT

DE HOLLANDSCHE

RECHTS-GELEERTHEYD.

Beſchreven by

Hugo De Groot

IN 'sGRAVEN-HAGE

By de Weduwe van Hillebrant

Iacobſz van Wou. 1631.

NIEUWE UITGAVE

DOOR

MR. S. J. FOCKEMA ANDREÆ.

Te Arnhem, bij S. GOUDA QUINT.

1910.

FIGURE 1.1. Image of court scene, from a book by Hugo Grotius. Inleidinge tot de Hollandsche rechtsgeleerdheid / beschreven bij Hugo de Groot; met aanteekeningen van S. J. Fockema Andreae. Arnhem: S. Gouda Quint, 1910. New York State Library call number N,347.492,G881,93-18921,1910.

custom and precedents established by the courts. Dutch law is often called Roman-Dutch law, a term that originated with Dutch lawyer Simon van Leeuwen who first used it as a subtitle of a book he published in 1652.[3] If any ordinances, statutes, local laws, customs, or privileges granted in charters or otherwise to towns did not apply to a specific situation the "common written law," essentially Roman law, was applied. As the Dutch Republic, lacking a strong central government, had a decentralized political system, the legal system was not identical in each of its seven provinces.[4] Thus, it was only the jurisprudence of Holland that was required by the West India Company in its instructions for New Netherland. It is therefore the petitioning in Holland that we will look at first.

The decentralized aspect of the republic's government also meant that petitions from the people were aimed at any and all levels of government, including the States General, depending on what they were asking for. In his detailed description of petitioning, Dutch historian Henk van Nierop has outlined the process. For example, the petitions were to be "written on a standard-size sheet of paper, with a stamp costing a few stuivers affixed to discourage idle requests." The petitioners called themselves "supplicants," followed by their names, and then went on to state their problem, its causes, and their suggestions for correcting the problem. According to Van Nierop, petitioners "were never allowed to present their cases in person." As a result, the petitions were often written by solicitors and agents, as they knew the proper formats.[5]

The petitions, of which there are thousands in Amsterdam's municipal archives, were submitted under two circumstances: when a petition was requested for such things as a "printer asking for a license to publish a particular book"; and by individuals whose requests were related to personal matters that needed attention, such as "inheritances, bankruptcies, wardship, and other matters where property rights were involved." Van Nierop notes that the authorities treated the peoples' affairs "with care and scrutiny."[6] The petitions from either individuals or groups regarding a request for certain legislations affecting or adding to the laws of the city, were sent to Amsterdam's court, consisting of the burgemeesters, *schouts,* and *schepenen*. Legislation requests were read by an appointed committee that drafted an opinion, on which, if necessary, the views of the groups involved were solicited. A draft was then made of a new law and sent to the burgemeesters by the *schepenen* for their approval and ultimately the bylaws were enacted on the petitions that were granted. Criminal laws, however, remained untouched by the commonalty.[7]

We do not know how far back in the history of the Low Countries petitioning was used. But certainly the Dutch were not strangers to the process, considering that they submitted a petition on April 5, 1566. On that day about three hundred nobles appeared before the court of Margaret of Parma in Brussels with what is called the famous *Petition*. The object was to have the governess, who was appointed by Philip II in 1559, suspend the Inquisition in the Netherlands which, if maintained, would "destroy all old privileges, freedoms and immunities." They also asked Philip "to seek the advice and consent of the assembled States General for new ordinances and other more suitable and appropriate ways to put matters right." Needless to say, he did not.[8]

As they knew that petitioning was an active ingredient in the governance of Holland and that all but fanciful requests were carefully attended, it is no surprise that the colonists who immigrated to New Netherland were accustomed to the idea of petitioning for a variety of conditions and complaints, or that the local courts and the colonial council responded quickly to the petitions. If the governments of Dutch Republic and its provinces were decentralized, New Netherland was just the opposite as it was firmly centralized. The director and council made all the laws and ordinances and received and distributed the laws sent from the Amsterdam

Figure 1.2. L. F. Tantillo, *A View of Fort Orange, 1652*. Reproduction courtesy of the artist.

Chamber. They chartered new villages, appointed their magistrates and reviewed and approved—or not—the local ordinances that villages might make. Major criminal behaviors, such as killing and sodomy, were sent to the colonial council for handling.

Accustomed to appealing their cases to the West India Company or even the States General when they felt particularly aggrieved, the people eventually could only appeal to the director and the council by order of the Company. Unlike the local towns in Holland, the commonality had no voice in their village appointments, nor did the village magistrates have any say in the appointment of their *schout*. And not even the director and council members had any say in

the appointment of those positions as they were appointed by the Company. However, mindful of the care of their rights and privileges, the public knew to use petitioning and, as we shall see, knew to whom and when and what to petition.

Without extant court records for the first three directors, Willem Verhulst, Pieter Minuit, and Wouter van Twiller, it is impossible to determine whether or not the small amount of early settlers of those times ever needed to petition the council. Nor is it recorded at any time whether petitioners employed the certain sized paper that Van Nierop described or whether the petitioners could not appear in person. Certainly the fact that people did appear in court with their petitions is evidence that appearance was not prohibited. Moreover, I doubt that a stamp on a petition written in Beverwyck (present-day Albany) and sent down to the council in New Amsterdam, either by an Indian courier or on one of the ships that plied the river between the capital and the village, would have any restriction on the petition's contents even if stamps existed in New Netherland. A look at some of the existing petitions—which would have been kept in a box, as were all records—may tell us something of the needs, concerns, and influence of the New Netherland population.[9]

Fortunately, the colonial council's records and the laws and ordinances promulgated by the director and council for the period of 1638–1647 when Willem Kieft was director still survive. The Secretarial Registers for his term, which lasted until he was replaced by Petrus Stuyvesant in 1647, are full of declarations, deeds, leases, powers of attorney, wills, agreements, complaints, settlements, appointments, contracts, debts, indentures, mortgages, affidavits, but nary a petition until one appears in the council minutes for 1646. Deacon Oloff Stevensen petitioned the court for "four referees to be appointed to settle the difficulty which he has with Domine Everardus Bogardus, minister here." As Bogardus agreed to this in writing the court appointed four referees, one of whom was the Domine Megapolensis, and "authorized and empowered them to decide and settle the aforesaid question." In a unanimous decision, the referees "concluded" that Stevensen was not guilty and that the question between the two "shall be from now on finally settled, disposed of and extinguished without hereafter being in any way revived on either side." Since the parties agreed to the decision of the referees, the director and council approved and affirmed the decision.[10] This detailed report gives some idea of how personal petitions may have been handled in Kieft's court.

There was, however, some difference in the petition that came to Stuyvesant's attention soon after his ordinance establishing a board of nine men was issued in September 1647. Stuyvesant and council apparently had instructions from the Company, "to solicit the cooperation of the commonalty, as this tends mostly to their own welfare and protection and is customary in all well administered government, colonies and places"[11] Actually, what the growing commonalty of New Amsterdam really wanted since Kieft's time was the appointment of a municipal court with its own burgemeesters, *schout,* and *schepenen* to handle the city's affairs as would have been done in Holland. What they got under Kieft were two short-lived boards, which got cancelled when they decided to point out the government's problems. What they got under Stuyvesant was a board of nine men comprised of three each from the merchants, burghers, and farmers and a long list of rules that they were to obey—including not holding private meetings.[12]

In February 1648, the selectmen, which is what the board of nine men was called, petitioned the director and council on a subject not detailed in the minutes. Whatever it was, they approved of it "for the present what the selectmen propose from a sense of well meant duty and, as they claim, for the promotion of the public interest, and will take the same into further consideration and make and issue such order thereon as they shall consider to be to the public benefit and advantage." The director and council followed with a warning to the selectmen "to keep within the bounds of their commission, to hold no meetings or assembly except with the knowledge and consent of the director, and not to draw up any propositions, much less to pass any resolutions, except in the presence of and before a deputy from the honorable council." The petition undoubtedly offered some ideas for the government, as the final comment in the response was that in "future petitions they must observe more respect in submitting their requests, that is that they must not presume to dictate to the director and council what they ought to do."[13]

The director and council continued to receive other petitions such as the burgemeester guards of the city protesting the regulation about musketry as there was a lack of guns among

FIGURE 1.3. Bronze bust of Petrus Stuyvesant in the churchyard of St. Mark's in-the-Bowery. It was sculpted by Dutch sculptor Toon Dupuis and given by Queen Wilhelmina of the Netherlands in 1915. Photo by Teodors Ermansons.

the citizens so the burghers had to provide "themselves with fire arms." Those with no guns were given some from the Company's magazine with the understanding that they keep them in good condition. Then the crew of the *Valckenier* presented a petition in which they requested "permission to sell, without hinderance, their personal freight." Stuyvesant and the council promptly agreed to the request, given the small amount of freight under consideration, but did forbid the sale of the guns, which they appropriated and planned to pay for.[14]

By February 1653, New Amsterdam finally had its municipal government, a court of burgemeester, *schout,* and *schepen.* Some of the petitions they dealt with were requests for offices, such Adriaen Dircksen Coen's petition which asked to be "favored with the office of Carrier of Beer and wine on such orders and wages as in their Worships discretion, shall be found proper." The magistrates put this aside to attend to "at the earliest opportunity." The same day, Johannes Withart presented the court with his petition asking that there be an end to a suit that had been examined. The court decided to have commissioners appointed "to examine the papers and reconcile the parties." Later in the day, the burgemeesters and *schepenen* petitioned Stuyvesant and the council asking that since they had been in office for a year they needed the councils' consent to their nominating a double number for them to select a single number of burgemeesters and *schepenen.*[15]

Many of the petitions were requests for jobs, which required the court's permission, such as tapping. Often two or more petitioners would appear before the court on the same day.

Figure 1.4. Insert of a map of Rensselaerswyck, showing the mapmaker, by Gillis van Scheyndel (1631–32). New York State Library call number 7474 (1631–1632).

For example on Monday, September 7, 1654, seven cases were dealt with in court, followed by four petitions. One requested permission to "act again as a tapster"; another petitioned to tap "half a hogshead of Brandy by the small measure"; and the written petition from the "sworn Beer and Wine Carriers" requested attention to the fact that others unloaded the wine brought in ships, which affected their business. Jacques de la Motthe, master of the bark *St. Charles,* submitted a petition written in French, requesting "payment of the freight and board of the Jews whom he brought here from Cape St. Anthony according to the agreement and contract in which each is bound *in solidum*."[16]

Looking through the volumes containing municipal court minutes, several things become apparent. Unlike Holland, people in New Netherland presented the petitions in person. The petitions were not always written but more often presented verbally. Moreover, the court did not have the advantage of the Amsterdam court where "three of the nine judges" alternated "special duty for one week to read petitions and dispose of them at once if they were of

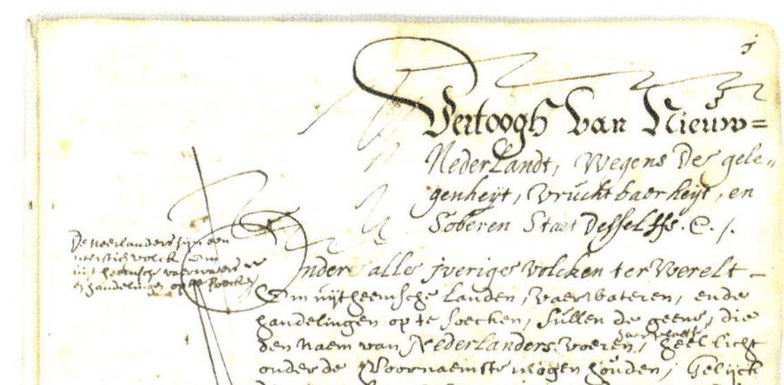

FIGURE 1.5. "Petition of New Netherland," by Adriaen van der Donck, paper, 1649. Collection Nationaal Archief (National Archives of the Netherlands) 1.01.07, inv.nr. 12564.30A.

small importance."[17] Lack of time to address the petition requests may explain why some of the decisions on the petitions were delayed a day or so, and even longer when the more complicated petitions required meeting with the director general. Yet by and large, the court dealt directly and as quickly as possible. Petitions, even those simply petitioning for a minor job, were never considered too small to warrant the court's attention. As the size of the population was miniscule compared to Amsterdam, the court hardly had the stacks of petitions that faced the Amsterdam judges.

Once the villages and towns were chartered the people could petition directly to their own court. The village of Beverwyck, which was the entrepôt of the fur trade and became the second largest town in the colony, probably had the most examples of petitioning. Chartered by Stuyvesant in 1652, the opening session of the court on April 15, 1652, dealt with two petitions. Rut Arentz petitioned to have a lot near his house, which the court referred to a committee to be appointed to look into the situation, and Harmen Bastiaensz Timmerman petitioned for permission to erect a house that he had started and which he was sure would not crowd the fort. The court gave him permission to proceed with the building.[18] Many of the people in Beverwyck had been a part of the Rensselaerswyck patroonship and thus were acquainted with one another. They also had a working knowledge of the jurisprudence and were quick to utilize petitioning to serve their needs. Their requests were quite varied and ranged from the personal requests for exclusive rights, such as running a horsemill, to petitions from the fighting neighbors, the Van Hoesem and Wesslesz, who asked the court for restraining orders against each other. There were group petitions based on community concerns, such as the petition of some burghers for an ordinance to have the playing of golf on the streets stopped as it broke their windows. The profits from the fur trade were particularly important and problems concerning them led forty-five small and large fur traders, one of whom was a woman, to sign a petition that was sent to the colonial council requesting that the Manhattan merchants be forbidden to sell retail in Beverwyck during the trading season.[19] The petition was granted.

Clearly, the Dutch continued the practice of petitioning in the New World with the confidence that through its use they could protect their rights and even correct personal or community problems or needs, and that the ruling powers would, indeed had to, listen to them and provide fair answers or solutions. With the takeover of the colony in 1664 by the English, the articles of surrender allowed the Dutch to keep two rights—their religion and to "enjoy their own customes, concerning their inheritance."[20] While petitioning did not make much of an appearance in the early English records of the colony, in Beverwyck, then called Albany by the English, the Dutch continued to run things in the Dutch manner, using mainly Dutch jurisprudence and keeping records in the Dutch language. They also petitioned on the usual subjects, such as for lots on the hill. The church masters presented a petition about the repairs that were needed "with the request where they are to find the money?" The court said that the windows could be repaired and that they would look further into the means for handling the rest of their request. Widow Lysbeth Brower presented a petition asking for permission to renounce the estate, and "that she may receive the same favor and mercy as other oppressed persons." Aware of her circumstances the court granted her petition, provided she declared that she was keeping nothing from the estate. And some burghers petitioned to have the recent ordinance on selling brandy repealed; after consultation, Governor Lovelace and the magistrates decided to grant the petition as it would be in the best interest of the community.[21]

The use of petitions in New Netherland may not have completely followed the patterns

FIGURE 1.6. "Belgii Novi, Angliae Novae et Partis Virginiae," by Johannes Janssonius, 1650. This plate was engraved in 1650 based on a 1648 manuscript map that accompanied a 1649 petition on behalf of the New Netherland Commonalty delivered by Adriaen van der Donck to the States General. It urged the Dutch Republic to negotiate with England the exact borders between New Netherland and New England. Van der Donck delivered this manuscript map to the States General in order to support Adriaen Block's original 1614 claim to New Netherland. The presentation of this map also illustrates an exercise of a right to seek redress of grievance from the highest governmental authority. From the collection of Joep de Koning.

established in Amsterdam. Nevertheless, they did work to the advantage of the needs of the Dutch in the New World. While the Dutch records for the court of Albany, Rensselaerswyck, and Schenectady from 1668–1685 show minimal use of petitions, usage by the Dutch for granting their rights and privileges was not forgotten.

This became apparent on July 30, 1673, when during the Third Anglo-Dutch War, a Dutch squadron anchored a musket shot away from Fort James and demanded its surrender. The fort and the city surrendered to the Dutch and the new government only took four days to get established in the Dutch manner. A ship was soon sent up the Hudson to demand the surrender of Fort Albany and the villages in the Esopus area.[22] In short order, the delegates from Albany and the villages of Kingston, Hurley, and Marbeltown in the Esopus area headed down the river, petitions in hand. On September 1, 1673, the magistrates from the Esopus presented their petition first. The details are not spelled out in the extant records, but the eight

Figure 1.7. L. F. Tantillo, *Manhattan, 1660*. Reproduction courtesy of the artist.

points were addressed by the Council of War and allowed. Then it was Fort Orange's turn to "deliver in a writing" nine articles in their petition "for the maintenance and preservation of the rights of the Town of Beverwijck and Fort Orange." The War Council answered by writing their decisions opposite the articles, and ended by saying that "[t]he petitioners shall enjoy the same privileges as they did in the time of the previous Dutch government."[23] And until the colony was returned to the English in the peace of Westminster on February 19, 1674 and formally surrendered to Governor Edmund Andros on November 10, 1674, they did.

NOTES

1. For an example, see the case against Juriaen Jansz who was accused of denouncing "in scandalous, villainous and contemptuous terms the ordinance against going into the woods to trade . . . and to speak of it in such a way as if the magistrates of this court were thereby trying reserve the entire trade to themselves" and ultimately making them out to be "incapable louts." *Fort Orange Court Minutes, 1652–1660,* ed. and trans., Charles T. Gehring (Syracuse: Syracuse University Press, 1990), 195.

2. Henk van Nierop. "Popular Participation in Politics in the Dutch Republic," in *Resistance, Representation, and Community,* ed. Peter Blickle (NewYork: Oxford University Press, 1997), 284.

3. The use of Roman-Dutch law dominated the title of Van Leeuwen's next book, *Commentaries on Roman-Dutch Law,* published in 1664. See H. W. Lee, *An Introduction to Roman-Dutch Law* (Oxford: Clarendon Press, 1953), 2. Lee further notes that Roman-Dutch law, while part of the law in the province of Holland, was not necessarily in other provinces of the Dutch Republic, as "the laws of no two provinces were precisely the same," although he suggests that legal systems of the principal provinces may have had a "general resemblance" (5).

4. According to J. L. Price, the towns of Holland had considerable autonomy as well as "a wide range of administrative powers and competence," which made it difficult for the States of Holland to act against them. J. L. Price, *The Dutch Republic in the Seventeenth Century* (New York: St. Martin's, 1998), 72.

5. Van Nierop, "Popular Participation," 285. On the same page Van Nierop says that petitioning "gave rise to a vast professional lobbying circuit of solicitors and agents, particularly in The Hague with its many government agencies."

6. Ibid., 286.

7. Ibid., 286–87.

8. Martin van Gelderen, *The Political Thought of the Dutch Revolt, 1555–1590* (Cambridge: Cambridge University Press, 1992), 110–11, 114.

9. There is a reference in the documents to a "Book of Petitions," which has been lost along with the "Book of Resolutions." There are, fortunately, uncounted numbers of petitions of every sort that appear in village and municipal court records.

10. *Council Minutes, 1638–1649,* trans. A. J. F.van Laer (Baltimore: Genealogical Publishing, 1974), 318–20.

11. Ibid., 438.

12. Ibid., 438–42.

13. Ibid., 482.

14. Ibid., 520, 527–28.

15. *Records of New Amsterdam from 1653 to 1674,* ed. Berthold Fernow. 7 vols. (Baltimore: Genealogical Publishing, 1976), I: 155, 156.

16. Ibid., 240.

17. Van Nierop, "Popular Participation," 284.

18. *Fort Orange Court Minutes,* 4. The concern of Stuyvesant had been that the director of the Rensselaerswyck patroonship had moved their nonagricultural people across the river, where they began putting up buildings too close to the fort and on a piece of land that Stuyvesant felt they had no right to use.

19. See the New York Colonial Manuscripts at the New York State Archives, vol. 10, part 3, docs.187, 189, 191. The council resolution is in doc. 193.

20. *General Entries, 1664–1673,* ed. Peter R. Christoph and Florence A. Christoph (Baltimore: Genealogical Publishing, 1982), 36.

21. *Minutes of the Court of Albany, Rensselaerswyck, and Schenectady, 1668–1673,* ed. and trans. A. J. F. van Laer. 3 vols. (Albany: The University of the State of New York, 1926), I: 47, 170, 247–48, 305.

22. Donald G. Shomette and Robert D. Haslach, *Raid on America: The Dutch Naval Campaign of 1672–1674* (Columbia: University of South Carolina Press, 1988), 178.

23. *Documents Relative to the Colonial History of the State of New York*, vol. 2, trans. E. B. O'Callaghan (Albany: Weed, Parson, and Company, 1858), 502–505.

Chapter Two

The Souls of New Amsterdam's African American Children

Joyce D. Goodfriend

New York's early history with respect to slavery makes us uncomfortable, and rightfully so. Slavery likely made many of the Dutch uncomfortable as well during the colonial era, but its economic advantages overcame moral qualms. What began with a few African slaves captured from Spanish or Portuguese ships had expanded appreciably by 1664. New York began to phase out slavery in 1799 and 1817, but the state did not rid itself of the institution until 1827.

Once in the New World, everyone, slave and free, faced the difficulties of making a life in a frontier society, and all contributed to its vitality and character. Most Europeans came voluntarily and could leave if they found the venture unsuitable. Few, if any, Africans had a choice about either arrival or departure. This made them all the more valuable when reliable labor was scarce. Some Africans were free, but unlike the Europeans, they had to contend with diminished status.

Joyce Goodfriend's essay describes the conflicts over the baptism of African children as it related to the possibility of their emancipation.

On March 31, 1647, an African father brought his newborn twins to be baptized by a Dutch minister in New Amsterdam's Reformed church. With other members of the city's sizeable African community serving as godparents, the boy and girl were baptized with the names Adam and Eva. "Emanuel Neger," as he was called in the baptismal register, had chosen to cast his family's lot with the city's Protestant Christians.[1] Though most likely a slave of the Dutch West India Company, Emanuel must have nurtured the hope that he soon would join the ranks of the score of Africans who, after laboring for the Company in New Amsterdam for nearly two decades, had recently been granted conditional freedom.

New Amsterdam had begun its history in 1626 as a frontier settlement under the control of the West India Company, a Dutch commercial enterprise whose ventures included slave trading posts in Africa and colonies in Brazil and New Netherland.[2]

Occupying the tip of Manhattan Island, New Amsterdam was strategically located, with a harbor that was ideal for oceangoing commerce. Though it had languished during its early years, despite the profits of the fur trade with the natives, by the late 1640s New Amsterdam had taken on the shape of a settled community. Fort Amsterdam, the Reformed Church, and the Stadt Herbergh, a tavern that was later converted into the City Hall, were surrounded by farms, windmills, warehouses,

Figure 2.1. Luanda, in present-day Angola, which the Dutch held from 1641 to 1648, was the place of origin of many enslaved Africans who toiled in the sugar plantations of Brazil. Some were brought to New Amsterdam. Watercolor by Johannes Vingboons, c. 1665, Collection Nationaal Archief (National Archives of the Netherlands) 4.VELH 619-064.

and private dwellings. Still sparsely populated, it already was distinguished by its diverse array of residents from Europe and Africa.

African men and women formed an essential component of the local labor force, though their status as slaves had never been defined with precision or codified in law.[3] Emanuel, along with his fellow Africans in New Amsterdam, had concluded that Christianization would be a potent weapon in their struggle to emerge from enslavement. They turned to Dutch religious rituals to sanctify their marriages and to validate their babies as Christians to enhance their chances for emancipation. Adam and Eva were just two of the more than sixty infants of African origin who were baptized in the city's Dutch church between 1639 and 1655.[4]

Why would clergymen of the Reformed church use their office to baptize the offspring of men and women claimed as property by the Dutch West India Company, the premier slave trading company of the seventeenth century? One might expect a Dutch minister stranded in a colonial outpost to exhibit an attitude toward slaves resembling that of Jonas Michaëlius, New Amsterdam's first minister, who in 1628 described the Angola slave women he encountered as "thieving, lazy and useless trash."[5] Everardus Bogardus, who was sent to New Amsterdam as a minister in 1633, had earlier served as a *ziekentrooster* (comforter of the sick) on the Guinea

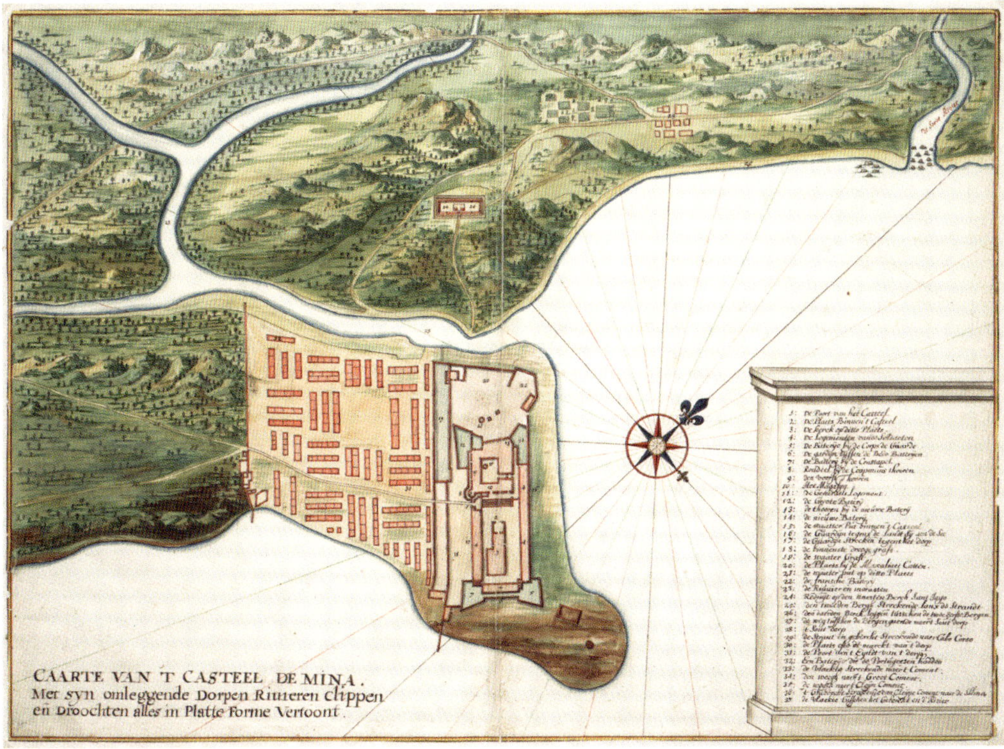

Figure 2.2. Elmina Castle in Ghana, built by the Portuguese in 1482 and taken by the Dutch in 1637, was a center of Dutch slave trade for many years. "Map of Elmina Castle" by Johannes Vingboons, watercolor, c. 1665. Collection Nationaal Archief (National Archives of the Netherlands) 4.VELH 619-077.

coast.[6] While there, he apparently developed a genuine concern for the spiritual condition of Africans that carried over into his dealings with the tiny city's West Africans. In 1636, Bogardus pleaded for a schoolmaster to be sent from Holland "to teach and train the youth of both Dutch and blacks in the knowledge of Jesus Christ."[7] By 1641, he was convinced that good hopes existed for the conversion of the negroes, a judgment corroborated by the elders and deacons who reported that "the negroes living among the colonists come nearer [to the right knowledge of God]" than the Indians.[8] Most important, Bogardus acted on his convictions. During his tenure as New Amsterdam's minister, he routinely married African men and women and baptized their children, and once served as a godparent for an African infant.[9] From October 1639, when the extant church records commence, until August 1647, when he departed for the Netherlands, he baptized thirty-nine children of African descent.[10] Bogardus took pains to welcome Africans into New Amsterdam's Reformed Protestant church, most likely because he suspected that people with surnames such as Angola, Congo, and Portugies had been exposed to Catholic doctrines in the course of their travels in the Atlantic world.[11] He saw it as his duty to counteract these erroneous teachings and adverse influences.

FIGURE 2.3. "New Amsterdam, or New York, in America" by Pieter Mortier, colored engraving, c. 1700. Image and border $7^{3}/_{8}$ x $9^{1}/_{2}$ in.; sheet $7^{3}/_{4}$ x $10^{3}/_{8}$ in; negative no. 7613. Collection of The New-York Historical Society.

Yet no matter how much credit we assign Domine Bogardus for promoting the Christianization of New Amsterdam's Africans, his actions alone cannot explain the flood of African baptisms in New Amsterdam's church. Over the first few decades of Dutch rule, a procession of fathers (mothers only occasionally were present), accompanied by other Africans who stood as godparents, willingly stepped before a Dutch man of God to cement the good standing of their children in the eyes of the European majority. Certifying their children's membership in the Christian community was a matter of vital concern to the city's adult Africans, who, in essence, were engaged in a tug of war with the Dutch West India Company for control of their numerous children. From the outset, the Company had condoned the formation of families by captured Africans, and by 1644, Company officials acknowledged that their African slaves "are burdened with many children."[12] As the city's forced laborers wrestled with the tribulations of life in a society that defined them as slaves, they fixed their hopes on the next generation. They aimed to supply their boys and girls with armament to protect themselves from people determined to exact as much as they could from them. Tendering these children for baptism in the Dutch

Reformed church was the central strategy in a multipronged effort to achieve a secure niche for the African American children of this North American Dutch city.

Their primary adversary was the Dutch West India Company, whose officers envisioned Africans born in New Amsterdam as a fresh and continuously available source of labor. Such children would make especially desirable slaves, since they would be acculturated and would have roots in the city. With their kinfolk nearby, they would not pose a risk of flight. Company administrators did not hesitate to exert their authority over these youngsters.

The beneficiaries of the 1644 law that gave conditional freedom to the Company's longest serving male slaves and their wives were confronted with an excruciating dilemma. Though placed "on the same footing as other Free people . . . in New Netherland," and granted plots of land on the outskirts of the city that enabled them to become productive agriculturalists who could easily pay the mandatory annual tribute of wheat, maize, peas or beans, and a fat hog to the Company, they were compelled to honor the law's proviso that their children "at present born or yet to be born shall be bound and obligated to serve the Honorable West India Company."[13] The motives of the Company officers who crafted the law were transparent. They sought to relieve themselves of the burden of supporting aging slaves, yet wished to reserve the right to command the labor of young and vigorous African youth. But the African parents, whose dreams for their baptized sons and daughters had rested on the indeterminacy of their status, could not reconcile themselves to a principle they regarded as illegitimate.

Their hopes may have been raised in 1649, when critics of the provincial administration, in the course of a lengthy Remonstrance to the Directors of the Dutch West India Company, complained that the children of the emancipated Africans "have remained slaves, though it is contrary to the laws of every people that any one born of a free Christian mother should be a slave and be compelled to remain in servitude."[14] The response from Amsterdam was anything but comforting. Company officials minimized the impact of the law—they boasted that only three children currently were in the service of the company and emphasized that these slave children were treated as Christians.[15] More importantly, they implicitly upheld the principle of commandeering the labor of the children of the former company slaves, even as they condoned the release of more laborers from bondage in succeeding years. New Amsterdam's free Africans had no alternative but to try and capitalize on the liberties they had gained to weaken the power of Europeans over them and their progeny. Their task was made more difficult by the influx of immigrants from Europe and the emergence of a consensus that slavery was the appropriate status for people of African origin.

In the 1650s, as the second generation reached maturity, New Amsterdam attained both stability and prosperity. Regulations on subjects ranging from sanitation and fire prevention to observance of the Sabbath were imposed by Director General Petrus Stuyvesant, bringing order to the burgeoning community, while improving the conditions of everyday life. Commercial opportunities expanded as local merchants engaged in trade along the North American coast, in the Caribbean, and over the ocean to Europe and Africa. A merchant elite emerged and, with the backing of small traders and artisans, successfully pressed for a city government that would promote local interests and temper the authoritarianism of Company rule.

New Amsterdam's incorporation as a municipality in 1653 accelerated its transformation into a city consciously modeled on Dutch prototypes. Its houses with the gable end turned toward the street and tiled roofs were only the most visible manifestation of the cultural heritage that was selectively reproduced in the colonial city. Once installed, New Amsterdam's burgemeesters and *schepenen*, as representatives of the merchants and artisans, set about implementing their conception of Dutch urban life. The streets were surveyed, canals were dug, a weighhouse built, and court procedures elaborated. Most important, city leaders gained Stuyvesant's approval to institute the Burgher Right, which restricted the privilege of conducting business to local property owners. The civic customs of Amsterdam, modified to suit local conditions, had taken root in what municipal leaders deliberately called the City of Amsterdam in New Netherland.

The enhancement of the power of Euro-Americans under burgemeester government did not bode well for New Amsterdam's Africans. Now, not only Company officials but also individual slaveholders and city officials were in a position to make decisions that would shape the course of young Africans' lives. African parents did not wish to yield control over their children's lives to Europeans, but, as one mother learned in 1661, her little girl was vulnerable and she lacked any means to protect her. Ten-year-old Lysbet Anthony admitted to the burgemeesters of New Amsterdam that she had been stealing from her mistress, the wife of Domine Drisius. Given the option of chastizing her own child or having a public servant do it, Lysbet's mother, Mary, chose to do it, and, with the assistance of another African woman, "severely punished and whipped her daughter with rods in [the] presence of the [city] Magistrates."[16] To inflict physical harm on her daughter while Dutch officials looked on with satisfaction must have been unbearable for this mother, who could not shield her child from the pain and public humiliation.

Well aware of the unpredictability that shadowed the lives of non-Europeans in the Dutch city, free Africans attempted to safeguard their children through labor contracts, such as the one made by Maria Portugies for her daughter to be a household servant, and apprenticeships.[17] Susanna Anthony Roberts, a free African, acting as guardian of her minor brother negotiated an apprenticeship agreement for him that mandated that he be taught reading and writing.[18] Unable to write herself, she yearned to equip her brother with the tools of literacy.

Having managed to extricate themselves from slavery, the members of New Amsterdam's free African community kept a watchful eye on the enslaved children still embedded in the interstices of the society, and, at opportune moments, contrived ways to liberate them from the control of Euro-Americans. Anthony Matysen, a free African, had made a contract with ferrymaster Egbert van Borsum to rear "his negro's child," which involved Matysen's wife's nursing the baby.[19] The deal had been consummated by Van Borsum's wife, who had "bargained with [Matysen's] wife for the child for one year at least, and has not refused her payment of what she promised her in the presence of other negroes." Matysen went before the city court in March 1655, claimed that he had not been paid by Van Borsum, and "request[ed], therefore, that the child be declared free, when [*sic*] he promises to rear the same at his own expense." Anthony Matysen was the father of four children baptized in the Reformed Church between 1651 and 1655, but it was not just parental affection for the infant entrusted to him and his wife that explains why they invented a pretext for adopting the baby and raising it as a free person. Their commitment to the future of the city's African community played a major part as well.

Though the court ruled against Anthony Matysen, they did take his suit seriously. Perhaps the fact that Matysen had baptized his twin sons with the Old Testament names Abraham and Isaacq elevated his standing among New Amsterdam's Christians.[20] By the time Matysen brought his case against Van Borsum, free Africans were certain that the best way to narrow the distance between themselves and the city's Europeans was to identify themselves as Christians. Two separate petitions composed in the 1660s by free Africans who wished to secure the freedom of a boy and a girl, each on the verge of adulthood, made a point of identifying the parties as Christians. When Domingo Angola requested the manumission of Christina Emanuels, a Company slave, he mentioned that she was the baptized orphan daughter of Manuel Trumpeter and Anthonya his wife.[21] Emmanuel Pietersen and Dorothe Angola, a free couple who wished to adopt Dorothe's godson, also framed their petition in a way that established their credentials as Christians. They noted that Dorothe had stood "godmother or witness at the Christian baptism of a little son of Kleyn Anthony of Angola, begotten by his wife Louwize [both free Negroes]" and that after the boy's parents died, she had, "out of Christian affection," adopted and reared him as her own child.[22]

Claiming ties to the Christian community gave Africans leverage as they pressed for greater control over the lives of the city's African children. Skeptical of the Dutch West India Company's rationalization for holding the children of Christian mothers in bondage, they sensed that the enslavement of baptized individuals rested on a flimsy foundation. With good reason, they had come to believe that the path to freedom ran through the baptismal font of the Reformed Church. Anxious to perpetuate the practice of baptizing Africans initiated by Everardus Bogardus, they found that, after 1655, access to the ritual that had emboldened them was foreclosed to their offspring. New Netherland's Reformed ministers, following church dictates, had inaugurated a policy of restricting baptism to people knowledgeable in the faith. This clerical decision may well have been influenced by the growing aversion of the burghers to participating in a biracial religious community.

Yet African parents continued to seek baptism for their infants. In the 1660s, the forty enslaved workers who resided at Director General Stuyvesant's bouwery north of the city, at times importuned Domine Henricus Selijns, who had been hired by the devout Stuyvesant to preach at his chapel every Sunday night, to baptize their children. Selyns's refusal to do so was grounded in church policy—the "negroes . . . lack of knowledge and faith"—but the minister felt impelled to impugn their motives, stressing "the material and wrong aim on the part of [these negroes] who sought nothing else by it than the freeing of their children from material slavery, without pursuing piety and Christian virtues."[23] Discovering the mainspring of their actions did not deter Selyns from spreading Christian gospel among these people "whose country of origin is the Negro-Coast." He engaged in private and public catechizing, which, he claimed "bore little fruit among the old people, who do not understand, but gave more hope with regard to the young, who have improved reasonably well."[24] The old people, he neglected to mention, had managed to grasp the centrality of baptism to the prospects of freedom.

Selyns's injunctions against baptizing slave infants did not prevent Judith Stuyvesant, the director's wife, from proceeding with the baptism of African children in her own household. But the imperatives of slavery as an economic institution trumped the pious designs of Mrs. Stuyvesant. An official on Curaçao, the great slave trading entrepôt of the Dutch West India Company, apologetically wrote Petrus Stuyvesant of the "serious mistake that has been committed here in the sale of your Slaves; especially of the little children, since with great forethought on the part of Madam Stuyvesant . . . they were presented at the baptismal Font."[25]

Should the sad fate of Judith Stuyvesant's baptized slave children stand as the symbolic end of the contest over the souls of New Amsterdam's African American children? Only if we believe that the African men and women who were shrewd enough to name their babies after figures from the Old Testament would stop searching for ways to deliver their heirs from slavery.

NOTES

This essay was originally published in the online journal COMMON-PLACE [www.common-place.org] in 2003. References to more recent scholarship appear in the notes. For further thoughts on this topic, see Joyce D. Goodfriend's "Slavery in Colonial New York City," *Urban History* 35 (2008): 485–96; and "Why New Netherland Matters," in *Explorers, Fortunes, and Love Letters: A Window on New Netherland,* ed. Martha Dickinson Shattuck (Albany: New Netherland Institute/Mount Ida Press, 2009).

1. "Baptisms from 1639 to 1730 in the Reformed Dutch Church, New York," in *Collections of the New York Genealogical and Biographical Society,* Vol. II (New York: The Society, 1901), 22.

2. For a comprehensive history of New Netherland, see Jaap Jacobs, *New Netherland: A Dutch Colony in Seventeenth-Century America* (Leiden/Boston: Brill, 2005).

3. On African Americans in New Amsterdam, see Joyce D. Goodfriend, "Burghers and Blacks: The Evolution of a Slave Society at New Amsterdam," *New York History* 59 (1978): 125–44; Ira Berlin, "From Creole to African: Atlantic Creoles and the Origins of African-American Society in Mainland North America," *William and Mary Quarterly,* 3rd series, 53 (1996): 251–88; and Linda M. Heywood and John K. Thornton, *Central Africans, Atlantic Creoles, and the Foundation of the Americas, 1585–1660* (New York Cambridge University Press, 2007).

4. Baptisms from 1639 to 1730 in the Reformed Dutch Church, New York.

5. "Letter of Reverend Jonas Michaelius, 1628," in *Narratives of New Netherland 1609–1664,* ed. J. Franklin Jameson (New York: Charles Scribner's Sons, 1909), 129.

6. For an illuminating biography of Bogardus, see Willem Frijhoff, *Fulfilling God's Mission: The Two Worlds of Dominie Everardus Bogardus 1607–1647* (Leiden, Boston: Brill, 2007).

7. "Letters of Wouter van Twiller and the Director General and Council of New Netherland to the Amsterdam Chamber of the Dutch West India Company, August 14, 1636," *The Quarterly Journal of the New York State Historical Association* 1 (1919): 48. Reprinted as a supplement to *New York History* 50 (1969).

8. E. T. Corwin, ed., *Ecclesiastical Records of the State of New York,* 7 vols. (Albany: J. B. Lyon Company, Printers, 1901–1916), vol. 1, 142.

9. On May 8, 1644, D. Everardus Bogardus is listed as a witness at the baptism of Anna, daughter of Philppe Swartinne along with Emanuel Congo, Anthony van Angola, Negers; 't Wyf. Van Anthony, trompetter, Negrinne. Baptisms from 1639 to 1730 in the Reformed Dutch Church, New York, 17.

10. Baptisms from 1639 to 1730 in the Reformed Dutch Church, New York.

11. On the prior religious experiences of African migrants to New Netherland, see Heywood and Thornton, *Central Africans, Atlantic Creoles, and the Foundation of the Americas, 1585–1660.*

12. E. B. O'Callaghan, *Laws and Ordinances of New Netherland, 1638–1674* (Albany: Weed, Parsons and Company, Printers, 1868), 36.

13. Ibid., 36–37.

14. "The Representation of New Netherland, 1650," in *Narratives of New Netherland 1609–1664,* 330.

15. "Answer to the Representation of New Netherland, by Cornelis van Tienhoven, 1650," in *Narratives of New Netherland 1609–1664,* 364–65.

16. Berthold Fernow, ed., *The Records of New Amsterdam from 1653 to 1674,* 7 vols. (New York: The Knickerbocker Press, 1897), vol. 3, 315. On parental punishment of children in New Amsterdam, see Mariah Adin, "'I Shall Beat You, So That the Devil Shall Laugh At It': Children, Violence and the Courts in New Amsterdam," in *Children in Colonial America,* ed. James Marten (New York and London: New York University Press, 2007), 90–103.

17. *Records of New Amsterdam,* vol. 3, 232, 242.

18. *New York Historical Manuscripts: Dutch. The Register of Salomon Lachaire, Notary Public of New Amsterdam 1661–1662,* trans. E. B. O'Callaghan, ed. Kenneth Scott and Kenn Stryker-Rodda (Baltimore: Genealogical Publishing Company, 1978), 9.

19. *Records of New Amsterdam,* vol. 1, 298.

20. Baptisms from 1639 to 1730 in the Reformed Dutch Church, New York, 29.

21. Edmund B. O'Callaghan, ed., *Calendar of Historical Manuscripts in the Office of the Secretary of State, Dutch Mss.* (Albany: Weed, Parsons and Company, Printers, 1865–66), 256.

22. *The Register of Salomon Lachaire, Notary Public of New Amsterdam 1661–1662,* 22–23.

23. "Two letters written by Domine Henricus Selijns during his ministry in Breuckelen, 1660–1664," in *New York Historical Manuscripts: Dutch. Old First Dutch Reformed Church of Brooklyn, New York. First Book of Records, 1660–1752,* trans. and ed. A. P. G. Jos van der Linde (Baltimore: Genealogical Publishing Company, 1983), First letter, October 4, 1660, 229; and Second letter, June 9, 1664, 231.

24. Ibid.

25. "Vice Director Beck to Pieter Stuyvesant. Curacao, in Fort Amsterdam the 15 November . . . 1664," in E. B. O'Callaghan, Voyages of the Slavers St. John and Arms of Amsterdam, 1659, 1663; Together with Additional Papers Illustrative of the Slave Trade under the Dutch (Albany: J. Munsell, 1867), 226–27.

Chapter Three

Matters of "Trifling Moment"

New Netherland and the New York Tradition of Arbitration

Troy A. McKenzie and Wilson C. Freeman

When legal scholars look to the past, they evaluate what they learn in the light of present-day practice and dispute resolution. The Dutch in New Netherland had a robust arbitration tradition that may be compared to our present arbitration system. Troy McKenzie and Wilson Freeman examine the practice of arbitration, explaining how it worked in New Netherland, and the lessons it gives us. The chapter traces the utility of arbitration as an adjunct of the judicial system, comparing today's use of arbitration with that in New Netherland.

INTRODUCTION

The legal system of New Netherland would probably baffle a resident of contemporary America who happened to be transported to that seventeenth-century Dutch colonial outpost. Yet, the Dutch employed at least one commonplace of our twenty-first-century system of dispute resolution—arbitration. Are there lessons to be learned from a comparison between our approach to arbitration and the arbitral system known to the settlers of New Netherland?

Our inquiry matters because the appropriate use of arbitration remains an unsettled question in contemporary American law. To be sure, the use of arbitration as a mechanism for resolving disputes outside of the courts has grown dramatically in the last twenty-five years.[1] Once treated with hostility and suspicion by the judiciary,[2] arbitration has now found more favor as a means of diverting litigation from overburdened dockets while providing speedy and cost-effective decision making for litigants. Indeed, a close reading of a typical credit card agreement, the "terms of use" of many Web sites, and even many employment agreements will reveal embedded arbitration clauses that would have been unheard of a generation ago.

The rapid growth of the reach of arbitration has not been without controversy, however. Although some jurists and commentators have hailed arbitration as an indispensible device that cuts through the morass of court-centered procedures, arbitration faces sustained criticism. Because arbitrators often produce minimal written explanations for their decisions, and those decisions are typically subject to strictly limited pre-arbitration court oversight with only the most deferential postarbitration judicial review, some commentators object in principle to the expansion of dispute resolution by arbitration. They contend the high wall of separation between arbitrators and courts deprives the judiciary of the important power of declaring law in the course of determining legal rights.[3] A different, although closely related, objection to the expansion of the use of arbitration in everyday disputes is less absolute. This school of thought holds that arbitration may make sense among sophisticated business entities engaged in complicated commercial transactions.[4] Outside those limited cases, the argument goes, arbitration risks being unduly oppressive, in a systematic way, to one set of litigants due to the costs of the arbitral forum that the parties must bear (such as arbitrators' fees) or due to the risk of favoritism by arbitrators toward repeat-player parties (such as large businesses). If so, consumers will find themselves routinely disadvantaged in arbitral proceedings brought by credit card companies, and individual employees will be the losers when required to arbitrate a dispute with a large employer. This second objection to arbitration, when viewed more abstractly, springs from a similar motivating source as the first objection: the fear that the continued declaration and enforcement of important rights will be hobbled in the long run by the widespread acceptance of arbitration for dispute resolution over court-centered litigation.

It is not surprising, then, that the most hotly contested debates about the enforcement of arbitration provisions raise in conjoined form precisely these twin questions: What is the proper role of courts in a regime of routine arbitration? And what is the proper scope of the disputes that should be subject to arbitration?

The most controversial cases in the field turn on these two questions. For example, judges wrestling with whether to enforce arbitration clauses in routine employment agreements have had to decide both the proper place of courts in enforcing an arbitral scheme and the domain of disputes susceptible to arbitration.[5] Similarly, courts have taken confused approaches to the question whether to permit the aggregation of claims in arbitration (that is, class arbitration), a technique some plaintiffs have sought to employ in an attempt to counter the perceived imbalance of power in the arbitral forum. Some courts have struck down contractual limitations on class arbitration by reasoning that they improperly interfere with the enforcement of important substantive federal law rights.[6] But the Supreme Court's most recent rulings in the area have reversed lower courts' decisions that struck down, on state law grounds, arbitration agreements that forbid aggregate proceedings.[7] The debate in the courts has also generated increased scrutiny by political actors, who have pressed for limitations on the new wave of arbitration clauses.[8] In short, we need to develop an understanding of how courts should view their role in an arbitral regime and of what categories of disputes are best resolved in such a regime.

These legal-policy debates frequently lack a sense of historical grounding, and the experience of the New Netherland colonists might serve to help fill that gap. History can have a strong explanatory power in the law, because the law is peculiarly path dependant. It is difficult to understand the current state of the law—its rhyme, reason, and possible reform—without understanding what came before it. As Oliver Wendell Holmes Jr., famously declared, "The life of the law has not been logic: it has been experience."[9] Understanding our past experiences with arbitral regimes can shed some light on the desirability of limiting, expanding, or otherwise reforming the use of arbitration. It makes sense, then, to step back from the current debates about arbitration in early twenty-first-century America and trace the thread connecting arbitration today to earlier regimes.

The thread begins with the Federal Arbitration Act (FAA).[10] The expansive interpretation given to the FAA by the Supreme Court of the United States has served as the driving force behind the broadening reach of arbitration. The Court has held the FAA to be binding in state court as well as federal court,[11] meaning that it now more easily reaches disputes of all sizes and shapes. The Court has also steadily pushed the boundaries of the FAA's domain beyond maritime cases and complex commercial disputes to consumer cases,[12] disputes between individual investors and large financial services companies,[13] and disputes arising out of routine employment contracts.[14] It is not an exaggeration to say that the FAA forms the most important building block of the modern edifice of arbitration.[15]

But the thread goes back even farther. Congress did not create the FAA out of whole cloth. When drafting the statute in the 1920s, lawmakers looked to existing arbitral regimes and were greatly influenced by New York's laws governing the enforcement of arbitration clauses. New York, in fact, had the first statute that made arbitration clauses in contracts binding.[16] It was no accident that New York's arbitration regime was so well established as to serve as an easy model, for arbitration as a means of dispute resolution had been firmly planted by the Dutch when they settled in New Netherland in the seventeenth century. Tracing this thread all the way to the New Netherland colony reveals the existence of a thriving and frequent practice of arbitration in those early days.

Because our modern practice of arbitration departs in marked ways from the Dutch colonial practice, it is too much to say that arbitration in New Netherland served as the model for our understanding of arbitration. But the *differences* between the understanding of the uses of arbitration in New Netherland and contemporary America are highly instructive.

FIGURE 3.1. "New Amsterdam, now New York, on Manhattan Island," by Johannes Vingboons, watercolor, c. 1665. It is based on a 1648 drawing. Collection Nationaal Archief (National Archives of the Netherlands) 4.VELH 619-014.

FIGURE 3.2. Statue of Hugo Grotius at the concert hall of the National Philharmonic Orchestra in Amsterdam. Photo by Julia Rosenblatt.

As we consider the twin policy questions raised by modern-day disputes over the role of arbitration, the Dutch colonial experience reveals two potential lessons. First, it is possible to maintain a robust arbitral regime and also a robust role for the courts in framing and enforcing rights as part and parcel of that regime. Unlike our contemporary cleavage between courts and arbitrators, there was a close connection between courts and the arbitral regime of New Netherland. Second, arbitration can benefit courts and the parties in small and large disputes alike. The Dutch settlers made use of arbitration for a wide variety of disputes—from disagreements between neighbors to matters of great value between merchants of stature.

We must qualify the lessons we draw from history, of course. First, the success of the arbitration system in New Netherland may well have rested in large part on the close social, political, and economic connections tying the relatively small population of the colony together. Second, the practice of binding pre-dispute arbitration, which has generated much of the controversy in contemporary debates, was quite different from the typically court-annexed arbitration used by the Dutch. We might therefore take a word of encouragement and a word of caution from the history of New Netherland as we consider the place of alternative dispute resolution devices in contemporary America.

A BRIEF HISTORY OF ARBITRATION IN NEW NETHERLAND

Like any settlers forming a new society, the New Netherland colonists quickly found a need for some system to adjudicate disputes and dispense justice—a task at first highly centralized in the hands of the colony's director general.[17] But dissatisfaction with the sometimes autocratic rule of various directors general began to mount. After Petrus Stuyvesant was appointed director general of the colony, arriving in New Amsterdam in May 1647, the citizenry finally prevailed on him to allow a somewhat more participatory system of government.[18] With Stuyvesant's approval, the Board of Nine Men—the body that began what would become a New York tradition of arbitration—came into being in September 1647, sitting at the town of New Amsterdam.[19]

The board operated in a straightforward manner. Stuyvesant allowed the colonists to select eighteen men, from among whom he chose nine as a body to assist in public affairs.[20] They had an advisory role and some legislative authority, but primarily served as a dispute resolution body.[21] The board was thus a hybrid entity—both formal and informal in its structure and operation. The ordinance establishing the board noted its necessity due to the increase in lawsuits and disputes in the territory, including matters of "trifling moment," which the board was called upon to resolve through arbitration.[22] Three of the nine would sit as a panel of arbitrators in these civil cases.[23] Their decisions were binding, but appeal to the governor was possible with the payment of one pound Flemish.[24] Reliance upon arbitration through the board to resolve matters large and small was used to handle civil conflicts in the New Amsterdam court for seven years.[25] Eventually one of the nine, Adriaen van der Donck, sailed to Holland and prevailed upon the government there to establish a traditional burgemeester system in the colony.[26] While this would bring an end to the board, it would not end the pervasive use of arbitration that would characterize civil dispute resolution in New Amsterdam.

The new government continued to use arbitration as an important method of resolving cases. Established in February 1653, somewhat according to the custom of "old Amsterdam," the new court system in New Amsterdam consisted of a *schout,* two *burgemeesters,* and five *schepenen* appointed by Stuyvesant.[27] Like the Board of Nine Men, this group had some legislative function, but primarily they sat as a court of justice. They met every Monday morning to attend to "all disputes between parties, as far as practicable."[28] The minutes of this court are intact.[29]

In civil cases, the court frequently called upon arbitrators for assistance in cases that the court felt itself unable, or perhaps unwilling, to tackle on its own.[30] Other Dutch settlements in the colony relied upon this mixed system of courts and arbitration.[31] After the takeover of the colony by the English in 1664, the Dutch practice of relying upon arbitration continued.[32] Of course, arbitration was not altogether foreign to the English, who, despite the historical suspicion of arbitration in the English courts, had a familiarity with arbitral regimes dating back to the fourteenth century.[33] It was no surprise, therefore, that arbitration continued throughout the later English colonial period, and ultimately that the Court of Burgemeesters and Schepenen would evolve into the Mayor's Court of New York and continue the use of arbitration.[34]

A YEAR IN THE LIFE OF THE COURT OF BURGEMEESTERS AND SCHEPENEN

Many types of cases came before the Court of Burgemeesters and Schepenen, and usually the court's procedures were quite simple. The court's messenger would summon the adverse party, and the plaintiff would state his case orally before the court.[35] If necessary, additional witnesses would be called and the parties would be asked to swear to facts the court deemed material. In a majority of cases, no additional fact gathering was needed for the court to decide the case.[36] No member of the court except the *schout* was typically trained in the legal profession.[37] Some members were farmers, traders, or pursued other professions.[38] Nonetheless, Charles Daly, the former chief justice of the New York Court of Common Pleas, in his history of that court, rated them as having a "comprehensive knowledge" and praised their directness.[39]

The court's practice of referring matters to arbitration bore certain hallmarks. Although complex cases, often among merchants, tended to be referred for decision by arbitrators, smaller disputes were not exempted from arbitration.[40] In turn, arbitrators acted as quasi-mediators as well. The court always instructed arbitrators to try to bring about a reconciliation between the parties if possible.[41] Upon review of the records of the court, no set rule—in terms of the type of dispute that would be prone to arbitration—is clear.[42] The court submitted to arbitration cases of all shapes and sizes, of all types of disputes, and of varying complexity. If any pattern could be argued, it would appear to be the need to supplement the court's expertise or fact finding because, unlike English courts of the same period, the Dutch colonial court could not rely on the jury system to resolve factual disputes.[43] In a review of the records for the year 1656, for example, approximately 20 percent of the cases before the court were referred to arbitrators.[44] Some illustrative cases drawn from the records of the court that year will demonstrate the wide variety of cases and fact patterns that were sent to arbitration.

On January 10, 1656, one Luycas Eldertsen sued Carsten Jansen for nonpayment of rent, which the defendant claimed he did not owe.[45] The court gave very little explanation of the facts but appointed "two impartial persons" who were "authorized to decide the matter" and specified they ought to try to "reconcile [the] parties," and if not, decide the case "consist[ent] with equity."[46] Despite the apparently low stakes involved, the court elected to seek resolution by arbitrators. The emphasis on reconciliation shown in the treatment of the dispute between Eldertsen and Jansen forms a frequent theme in the record of cases sent by the court to arbitration.[47]

Two weeks later, on January 24, Roeloff Jansen, reported to be a mason, sued Egbert van Borsum and his wife for unpaid wages on account of work performed in the previous year.

The defendants claimed that the plaintiff did not finish his work, and that they would pay him when he completed the task.[48] The court used arbitrators as supplementary fact finders: "[T]he Court refer[s] [the] parties to two arbitrators, to wit; Jan Gerritsen, [a] [m]ason, and Cristian Barentsen to inspect the work done, how near [plaintiff's] contract is finished and how much over he has done; also if possible to make them agree."[49] The emphasis on encouraging the parties' mutual agreement to resolve the dispute once again appears as a prominent part of the arbitral regime. In addition, the court appointed an arbitrator with particular expertise by choosing a mason. Presumably, he would be in a superior position to inspect Jansen's work appropriately and judge whether it had been substantially performed.

In March 1656, Andrew Kilvert sued Jan Geraerdy to demand an explanation as to why Kilvert had been arrested and his galiot (a Dutch trading vessel) seized.[50] This dispute, unlike the previous ones, involved large stakes between merchants. This was a typical complaint in the court; rather than awaiting his creditor's commencing suit, a debtor would often demand explanation or release of his property, and the case would proceed from that starting point.[51] In this case, Geraerdy claimed that Kilvert and his galiot had been arrested in order to obtain promised payment in the form of 12,000 lbs of tobacco that they had agreed upon as the sale price of the galiot.[52] Kilvert however, had receipts of payment. On the other hand, Geraerdy claimed to have a paper signed by Kilvert asserting the payment was not made.[53] In deciding to send the case to arbitrators, the court ordered as follows: "The court . . . finds the case somewhat obscure . . . [and] no sufficient proofs or documents have been produced. In order then not to be troubled with a long and weary lawsuit at the expense of a stranger, the Court order[s] . . . that the matter shall be disposed of by four arbitrators."[54] The reference of the matter to arbitration gives some insight into the concerns of the court—notably, a concern about expensive, complex, and lengthy litigation that would tie up the court. More pressingly, the court also expressed an inability to determine the merits of the case given the lack of sufficient documentation. Resort to arbitration then, removed a complicated case from the court's hands and allowed for the resolution of vexing factual disputes. (The complexity of the matter apparently caused the court to appoint four arbitrators to act in the case—a greater number than the records typically show.)

In October of that year, another dispute arose of seemingly minor import compared to the previous example. The plaintiff, Jan Hendricksen, alleged that he had performed woodwork for the defendant, Jacob Cohun, for which Hendricksen demanded payment of three "beavers."[55] The defendant appeared to dispute the amount due and owing. The court declared that "the payment shall be made in beavers,"[56] which suggests that the dispute turned in part on the type of currency in which payment was to be made (not an uncommon dispute in New Netherland, where payment was often made in commodities rather than in specie).[57] The court appointed two arbitrators, Christiaen Barentsen and Gerrit Jansen Roos, to inspect the work and determine the value to be paid.[58] The value of this dispute could not have been great, and yet two arbitrators were appointed to resolve it.

In November, Jacob van Couwenhoven sued Tomas Lambertsen for nonpayment of 487 pounds Flemish on the accounts of Lambertsen's wife.[59] Lambertsen claimed that the amount sought did not match what his wife owed Van Couwenhoven.[60] Van Couwenhoven offered to settle the case by arbitration, and Lambertsen accepted. At that point, the court appointed a pair of arbitrators to reconcile the parties if possible.[61] This method of resolving a dispute—with one of the parties suggesting arbitration rather than the court's doing so on its own

Figure 3.3. L. F. Tantillo, *Fort Amsterdam, Manhattan, c. 1658.* The Dutch bark of Arent van Curler approaches the tip of Manhattan from the Hudson River. Two of the most distinct features of the city's skyline in the seventeenth century were its windmill and old stone fort. Reproduction courtesy of the artist.

motion—appears regularly in the court records.[62] Occasionally, the parties would select their own arbitrators, and the court retained a "backstop" role as decision maker only in the event that the parties' attempt at out-of-court resolution failed.[63]

FROM NEW NETHERLAND TO NEW YORK

The historical record indicates a "general use and acceptance of arbitration" in the colony in the Dutch era.[64] The widespread acceptance of resolution of disputes by arbitration carried through when in 1664 the English took possession of New Netherland. Newspapers from the later English colonial period evidence the accepted nature of resort to dispute resolution by arbitration. Newspaper advertisements, in particular, show the importance of arbitration in the day-to-day life of the colonists in the English era due to the very common and casual tone of their references to arbitration. For example, the colonial newspapers contain frequent advertisements for arbitration bond-forms (the necessary papers for filing a request for arbitration) listed among other legal documents from local stationers and printers.[65] On a similar note, there is an advertisement in a different colonial newspaper from a bookseller listing a text on arbitration, among other legal texts.[66] More pointedly, newspapers from the English colonial era contain advertisements announcing the dates and locations of important arbitrations.[67] One merchant even paid to place an advertisement seeking to contradict rumors allegedly spread by others that he was not willing to arbitrate a particular high-profile dispute. He vehemently protested to the world that he was willing "to have all Things in Dispute to the final Determination of any Merchant or Merchants in this City."[68] Arbitration appears to have been more than an occasional method of dispute resolution in colonial New York. In fact, it appears to have been entirely commonplace and even expected of respectable individuals.

The practice initiated by the Dutch, however, became more formalized in the English colonial period. In 1766, a statute concerning arbitration was enacted in the colony.[69] The statute provided that, on motion of either party, cases involving allegedly overdue accounts could be referred for decision by arbitrators.[70] This statutory framework did not represent some unfamiliar innovation. It merely reflected the practice firmly established in the colony.[71] Shortly thereafter, with the founding of the New York Chamber of Commerce in 1768, the arbitral system became further embedded in New York. The Chamber would take on a dual role, acting not only as a source of arbitrators for disputes among merchants and other businessmen in the colony, but also as a promoter of the practice of arbitration during and after the colonial period (indeed, continuing to the twentieth century).[72] Thanks in no small part to the Chamber, and to favorable laws embracing arbitration, New York continued to see the use of arbitration as a means of dispute resolution throughout the 1800s, even as the population of the city and state grew rapidly. Despite the fact that New York of the 1800s had grown beyond the small Dutch colony of the 1600s, there was never a time when arbitration was not used by significant numbers of litigants in New York.[73]

THE NEW YORK ARBITRATION ACT OF 1920 AND THE FEDERAL ARBITRATION ACT OF 1925

Given the long historical practice of arbitration in New York, it is no surprise that the law reform movement that saw its zenith with the passage of the Federal Arbitration Act of 1925 had New York origins. The saga of the FAA began in 1915 when the United States District Court for the Southern District of New York decided *Asphalt Refining Co. v. Trinidad Lake Petroleum Co.*[74] The parties in the case had entered into a contract stipulating that English law would govern their agreement. The contract also contained an arbitration clause. English law would have forbidden the prosecution of the matter in court in light of the arbitration clause in the parties' contract. The district court nonetheless refused to stay the suit and refer the parties to arbitration on the ground that, because the question was one of remedy and not of substantive right, the law of the forum governed, rather than English law.[75]

The perceived hostility to arbitration shown by the district court's decision spurred the New York Chamber of Commerce and the New York State Bar Association to action.[76] A national campaign to promote arbitration would follow, but New York was the first step on the road. By 1920 the Chamber and the New York State Bar Association drafted what would become the New York Arbitration Act of 1920.[77] The law's primary purpose, like the federal law that would come after it, was to ensure that courts would respect as binding pre-dispute arbitration clauses in contracts.[78] Before the act, New York had for a long time had a comprehensive arbitration statute in its Code of Civil Procedure.[79] The code had already modified the common law rule to the extent that revocation of an arbitration agreement could not occur after the proofs of the parties had been closed and submitted to the arbitrators.[80] The new law would not allow revocation of an agreement to arbitrate except on grounds normally invoked to void any contract at law or in equity.[81] The law also added a new right to petition the courts for an order directing arbitration to proceed and granted the court authority to appoint an arbitrator when a party failed to do so.[82] Other than those limited roles, however, the law contemplated a strict separation between courts and the arbitral forum before, during, and after the commencement of arbitration. These changes were essential in spurring reform forward at the national level.[83]

The federal law that followed in 1925 emerged directly from the New York Arbitration Act. Indeed, the first draft of the FAA was patterned on the New York law and was actually authored by New York Chamber of Commerce General Counsel Julius Henry Cohen.[84] The version of the bill that Congress ultimately enacted did not change the substantive purpose of the draft bill, but simply made it more complete.[85] Together with Charles L. Bernheimer, the chairman of the New York Chamber of Commerce's Committee on Arbitration, Cohen played a decisive role in the creation of the FAA.[86] Both Cohen and Bernheimer testified in favor of the bill.[87]

Cohen and Bernheimer explicitly invoked the historical pedigree of arbitration in the course of their campaign to enact the 1920 New York law and the 1925 federal statute. Cohen published an influential book in 1918 on commercial arbitration that marshaled historical and policy arguments for more favorable treatment of arbitration clauses by the courts.[88] His book

Rare Wood Engraving of First Market Place in New Amsterdam
Now Broad street in the Heart of the Financial District of the Western Continent

Figure 3.4. Wood engraving of the first market place in New Amsterdam. PR 020 Geographic File, box 2, harbor views—17th century; negative no. 83099d. Collection of The New-York Historical Society.

FIGURE 3.5. "The Dutch Surrender New Amsterdam, Sept. 8, 1664." Illustration in *The People's Standard History of the United States* (1895). Collection of the New York State Library call number: 973 qE47. Photograph by Lisa Bohanan.

recognized the long history of arbitration in New York, discussing specifically both the Board of Nine Men and the Court of Burgemeesters and Schepenen.[89] Historians recognize this book as an ambitious and important text in the reform movement pushing for the expansion of the use of arbitration and the enforceability of pre-dispute arbitration clauses in contracts.[90] Similarly, Bernheimer, in his testimony to the Senate Judiciary Committee during the consideration of the FAA, would make several references to the historical pedigree of arbitration (even going so far as to note that George Washington's will contained an arbitration clause).[91] In other words, the drafters of the FAA used the strong historical pedigree of arbitration as an argument for their reform movement.

SOME LESSONS FROM HISTORY

Although the modern arbitration schemes inaugurated by the New York Arbitration Act of 1920 and the FAA cannot be said to be modeled on the practice of arbitration in New Netherland, the tradition of arbitration in New York that dates back to the Dutch colonial period ties them together. It is therefore worthwhile to compare and contrast the modern arbitral regimes with the understanding of arbitration in New Netherland practices. In particular, three close parallels exist between the Dutch colonial use of arbitration and the arguments made by the early-twentieth-century law reformers in support of the modern arbitral regimes they inaugurated with the adoption of the New York Arbitration Act and the FAA.

First, the reformers, like the Dutch, sought to use non-court dispute resolution as a means of more than straightforward adjudication. They also sought to encourage amicable settlement and reconciliation among litigants. Julius Henry Cohen's 1918 book trumpeting the benefits of arbitration emphasized its importance as a means of bringing litigants together to settle conflicts without friction and with "complete understanding."[92] Similarly, Bernheimer emphasized arbitration's superior power to resolve disputes amicably through settlement, and listed that goal as one of the main purposes of the federal law.[93] The Dutch courts evidently recognized this dynamic as one of the benefits of arbitration as well, for they typically advised in the cases in which the parties were referred to arbitration that the arbitrators should "if possible . . . make them agree."[94]

Second, the twentieth century law reformers and the Dutch colonial settlers both perceived arbitration as having a superior power over court-centered litigation in fact finding, particularly in cases that turn on the specialized knowledge or insight of an expert. Cohen argued forcefully that, even if a court were to resolve such cases, the court would be better off relying on some source of outside expertise to elucidate the material facts.[95] The need for fact finding was perhaps the most important reason for the New Netherland courts' repeated resort to arbitration. Lacking the fact-finder powers of a jury, the tribunal turned to arbitrators to fill in important gaps in the record to resolve a dispute.[96]

Third, the law reformers who shepherded the modern regime of arbitration invoked the specter of the courts' being overwhelmed with complex cases in support of their efforts. Secretary of Commerce Herbert Hoover, in a letter to the Senate encouraging them to pass the FAA, noted the "clogging of our courts."[97] That concern had been voiced by the Dutch courts when resorting to arbitration.[98] Recall *Kilvert v. Geraerdy,* in which the court explicitly mentioned a concern of burdening its docket with a complex and bewildering case as the motivation for referring the matter to arbitration.[99]

These concerns have as much weight today as they did in 1920 or 1656. Indeed, they form what might be called universal constants in civil litigation. People will always become embroiled in disputes. Many—perhaps most—of those disputes are best handled amicably and without unnecessary contentiousness. Some of those disputes will unduly tax the expertise of the courts. And courts will undoubtedly find their limited resources overwhelmed by expanding dockets without some means of diverting particular cases for out-of-court resolution. It seems hard to reject the continued relevance of these lessons.

But can we call upon the Dutch colonial example to shed light on the proper relationship between courts and arbitrators, or the proper scope of the reach of arbitration in particular categories of disputes?

One clear theme in the historical record is that the Dutch colonists did not see a sharp and hostile boundary between matters resolved in court and matters resolved outside court. Courts had a meaningful say in framing and testing a case before referring the matter to arbitration. The fluid line between court and arbitrator preserved the important role of courts in declaring and enforcing rights and obligations without unduly diminishing the obvious practical benefits of arbitration.

Our understanding of arbitral regimes, on the other hand, assumes something in the nature of antagonism between courts and arbitrators. Perhaps because a hostile court opinion sparked the law reform movement leading to the creation of the contemporary laws governing pre-dispute arbitration clauses, a basic tenet of our alternative dispute resolution practice holds that courts and arbitrators should be kept as far apart as possible. Of course, courts have a role to play in our understanding of arbitral regimes, but it is usually a well-defined and strictly limited role. The Supreme Court has admonished courts that they should play only the most limited gatekeeping function at the commencement of cases in which the parties are bound by an arbitration clause.[100] At the other end of the litigation process, we have imposed extraordinarily cramped limits on judicial review of arbitral awards in such cases—essentially requiring a showing of fraud before a court may disturb an arbitral award.[101] We have enforced such a stark divide between courts and arbitrators that even private ordering by contract cannot easily overcome it. The Supreme Court quashed an attempt by parties to an arbitration agreement under the FAA to contract for expanded judicial review of the arbitral decision.[102]

We seem to assume that any softness in the line between courts and arbitrators will fatally undermine the attractiveness of an arbitral regime, but the Dutch colonial practice tests that assumption. Perhaps we should be more receptive to greater flexibility in the role of courts at both ends of our arbitration regime—before the commencement of arbitration and after an arbitral award has been rendered. The use of court-annexed arbitration—that is, arbitration invoked after a dispute has landed in court—might better serve to soften that line.

At the same time, the Dutch colonial experience serves as an interesting counterpoint to the heated debates about the categories of disputes that should be diverted to arbitration. Should arbitration remain limited to commercial disputes among sophisticated businesses and merchants, or would all disputes benefit from arbitration? The records of New Netherland suggest that an arbitral regime could successfully accommodate a variety of disputes, so that complex controversies as well as matters of "trifling moment" would benefit from arbitration.

The lessons we draw from the historical record must be calibrated by the different circumstances of our era and the past, however. Despite the universal constants of civil litigation, the colonial society of New Netherland was a very different one from our society in terms of size and complexity. According to a survey of the town at that time there were only "120 houses and 1000 inhabitants in the city" of New Amsterdam as of 1656.[103] Although New Netherland included people of diverse origins, its relatively small size necessarily meant that many disputes were among people who knew each other as neighbors, friends, and colleagues. The troubling scenario invoked by modern skeptics of arbitration—an individual consumer bound by a contract of adhesion to arbitrate a dispute against a large business headquartered far away—would have been unrecognizable to the Dutch colonists. Does a large corporate defendant have as much interest in reconciliation with an individual consumer as two neighbors might have in resolving their disagreement amicably? One might reasonably conclude, in other words, that the flexible arbitral regime of the Dutch colonists fit the society of the town of New Amsterdam more than that of the present-day City of New York.

CONCLUSION

Although little remains of the legal system erected in New Netherland more than three hundred years ago, the Dutch settlers began what would become an enduring tradition of arbitration in New York. That tradition, firmly established even after the end of Dutch rule, later served as a foundation for the law reform movement in the twentieth century that brought us our modern regime of arbitration. Like the settlers of the seventeenth century, we have found a need for an out-of-court dispute resolution system that encourages amicable settlement, brings to bear experienced, expert fact finding, and removes cases from burgeoning court dockets.

Yet the differences between our practice of arbitration and the Dutch practice are just as—if not more—telling. Keeping in mind the important caveat that we live in a society that would bewilder the Dutch colonial settlers in its size and complexity, the New Netherland arbitral regime can still shed light on current debates about arbitration. The system of arbitration in New Netherland suggests that it is not unthinkable to maintain a more flexible line between the role of courts and the role of arbitrators. It similarly suggests that disputes of all sizes and shapes could benefit from an arbitral forum. As we consider the proper place of arbitration in contemporary American practice, we would do well to keep these lessons in mind.

NOTES

1. Jean R. Sternlight, "Creeping Mandatory Arbitration: Is It Just?" *Stanford Law Review* 57 (2005): 1631.

2. Joseph T. McLaughlin, "Arbitrability: Current Trends in the United States," *Albany Law Review* 59 (1996): 906n4.

3. Sternlight, "Creeping Mandatory Arbitration": 1633.

4. Keith N. Hylton, "Agreements to Waive or to Arbitrate Legal Claims: An Economic Analysis," *The Supreme Court Economic Review* 8 (2000): 209–69.

5. *Circuit City Stores v. Adams,* 532 U.S. 105, 109 (2001).

6. *In re* American Express Merchants' Litigation, 667 F.3d 204, 218–19 (2d Cir. 2012); *Kristian v. Comcast Corp.*, 446 F.3d 25 (1st Cir. 2006). For a description of pre-dispute arbitration clauses in consumer credit agreements as "nothing but a shield against legal accountability," see Samuel Issacharoff and Erin F. Delaney, "Credit Card Accountability," *University of Chicago Law Review* 75 (2006): 173.

7. *AT&T Mobility LLC v. Concepcion*, 131 S.Ct. 1740 (2011); *Stolt-Nielsen S.A. v. AnimalFeeds Int'l Corp.*, 130 S.Ct. 1758 (2010). A handful of state courts had barred the enforcement of arbitration clauses

that prohibit class arbitration. See Alan S. Kaplinsky and Mark J. Levin, "Consensus or Conflict? Most (But Not All) Courts Enforce Class Action Waivers in Consumer Arbitration Agreements," *Business Lawyer* 60 (2005): 777n9.

8. For an example of a bill proposing to make invalid pre-dispute arbitration agreements in certain areas, see Arbitration Fairness Act of 2009, H.R. 1020, 111th Cong. (2009).

9. Oliver Wendell Holmes Jr., *The Common Law* (Boston: Little, Brown, 1881), 1.

10. 9 U.S.C. §§ 1–16 (2006).

11. *Southland Corp. v. Keating*, 465 U.S. 1, 10–16 (1984).

12. *Allied-Bruce Terminix Cos. v. Dobson*, 513 U.S. 265, 280 (1995).

13. *Rodriguez de Quijas v. Shearson/American Express, Inc.*, 490 U.S. 477, 480–82 (1989).

14. *Circuit City Stores v. Adams*, 532 U.S. 105, 109 (2001).

15. Sternlight, "Creeping Mandatory Arbitration": 1636.

16. Ian R. MacNeil, *American Arbitration Law* (New York: Oxford University Press, 1992), 36.

17. William E. Nelson, "Dutch Law in New Netherland," to be published by Oxford University Press, 4–5.

18. Jaap Jacobs, *New Netherland: A Dutch Colony in Seventeenth-Century America* (Ithaca: Cornell University Press, 2005), 142–43.

19. Ibid.

20. Ibid., 144.

21. Frances Murray, "A Legal History of New Netherland," 14, accessed July 13, 2011. http://www.courts.state.ny.us/history/essay/Illustrated%20Essay%20with%20edits%20and%20endnotes.pdf.

22. Sabra A. Jones, "Historical Development of Commercial Arbitration in the United States," *Minnesota Law Review* 12 (1927): 246–47.

23. Jacobs, *New Netherland*, 144.

24. Charles P. Daly, *Historical Sketch of the Judicial Tribunals of New York, from 1623 to 1846* (New York: John W. Amerman, printer, 1855), 8.

25. Murray, "Legal History," 14–15.

26. Ibid., 15. A "burgher" denoted a class of citizen qualified to hold, among other benefits, certain administrative offices or commissions. *Laws & Writs of Appeal, 1647–1663*, ed. Charles T. Gehring (Syracuse: Syracuse University Press, 1991), xxiii.

27. Jacobs, *New Netherland*, 151. The office of *schout* combined law enforcement and prosecutorial duties. The *schepen* held a quasi-judicial and administrative role. *Laws & Writs of Appeal*, xxvi. A burgemeester was an "executive urban magistrate." Jacobs, *New Netherland*, xv. Although these officials had distinct powers and roles in the legal system of the Netherlands, in New Amsterdam these distinctions tended to blur. Nelson, "Dutch Law," 15.

28. Daly, *Historical Sketch*, 10.

29. *The Records of New Amsterdam*, ed. Berthold Fernow, 7 vols. (New York: 1897, repr. Baltimore: Genealogical Publishing Company, 1976) (hereafter cited as *RNA*).

30. Ibid.

31. William Catron Jones, "Three Centuries of Commercial Arbitration in New York: A Brief Survey," *Washington University Law Quarterly* (1956): 196.

32. Ibid., 198.

33. Ibid.

34. Eben Moglen, "Commercial Arbitration in the Eighteenth Century: Searching for the Transformation of American Law," *Yale Law Journal* 93 (1983): 137–38.

35. See *RNA* at note 29 above.

36. Ibid.

37. See note 27 above.

38. Murray, "Legal History," 17.

39. Daly, *Historical Sketch,* 15.

40. See *RNA* at note 29 above.

41. Ibid.

42. Ibid.

43. Nelson, "Dutch Law," 12.

44. For a counting of civil cases, excluding default judgments, that were referred to arbitration, see *RNA,* vol. 2, 1–254.

45. *Eldertsen v. Jansen* (New Amsterdam Mun. Ct. 1656), in *RNA,* vol. 2, 5.

46. Ibid.

47. Daly, *Historical Sketch,* 15.

48. *Jansen v. van Borsum* (New Amsterdam Mun. Ct. 1656), in *RNA,* vol. 2, 20.

49. Ibid.

50. *Kilvert v. Geraerdy* (New Amsterdam Mun. Ct. 1656), in *RNA,* vol. 2, 69.

51. *Mischel v. Willemsen* (New Amsterdam Mun. Ct. 1656), in *RNA,* vol. 2, 111; *Linthout v. La Chair's Wife* (New Amsterdam Mun. Ct. 1656), in *RNA,* vol. 2, 159.

52. *Kilvert v. Geraerdy* (New Amsterdam Mun. Ct. 1656), in *RNA,* vol. 2, 69.

53. Ibid.

54. Ibid., 70.

55. *Hendricksen v. Cohun* (New Amsterdam Mun. Ct. 1656), in *RNA,* vol. 2, 201. Due to a lack of hard currency, the use of commodities as money became commonplace in New Netherland. For a discussion of beaver pelts, their use as commodity money, and their relative value, see Dennis J. Maika, "Commerce and Community: Manhattan Merchants in the Seventeenth Century" (unpublished PhD dissertation, New York University, 1995), 271–72, 272n44. "The most consistent commodity was beaver, usually listed as worth 8 guilders per pelt throughout the 1650's to the 1670's." Ibid.

56. *Hendricksen v. Cohun* (New Amsterdam Mun. Ct. 1656), in *RNA,* vol. 2, 201.

57. *Vinje v. Pietersen* (New Amsterdam Mun. Ct. 1656), in *RNA,* vol. 2, 156; *Van der Veen v. Couwenhoven* (New Amsterdam Mun. Ct. 1656), in *RNA,* vol. 2, 195.

58. *Hendricksen v. Cohun* (New Amsterdam Mun. Ct. 1656), in *RNA,* vol. 2, 201.

59. *Couwenhoven v. Lambertsen* (New Amsterdam Mun. Ct. 1656), in *RNA,* vol. 2, 222.

60. Ibid.

61. Ibid.

62. *Hendrix v. Greveraer* (New Amsterdam Mun. Ct. 1656), in *RNA,* vol. 2, 155; *Anthony v. Van der Veen* (New Amsterdam Mun. Ct. 1656), in *RNA,* vol. 2, 158.

63. Moglen, "Commercial Arbitration in the Eighteenth Century": 136.

64. Jones, "Three Centuries of Commercial Arbitration," 201.

65. *N.Y. Weekly Post-Boy,* Oct. 31, 1743.

66. *N.Y. Gazette or Weekly Post-Boy,* June 23, 1755.

67. *N.Y. Weekly Post-Boy,* Jan. 21, 1745.

68. *N.Y. Gazette,* March 15, 1731.

69. Charles Z. Lincoln, William H. Johnson, and A. Judd Northrup, *The Colonial Laws of New York from the Year 1664 to the Revolution* (Albany: J. B. Lyon, state printer, 1894), 4:1040–42.

70. Jones, "Three Centuries of Commercial Arbitration," 200.

71. Ibid.

72. Ibid., 207.

73. Ibid., 212.

74. 222 Fed. 1006 (S.D.N.Y. 1915).

75. *Id.* at 1012.

76. MacNeil, *American Arbitration Law,* 31.

77. 1920 N.Y. Laws, ch. 275 § 2.

78. "Settlements of disputes by arbitration are no longer deemed contrary to our public policy. Indeed, our statute encourages them." *Gilbert v. Burnstine,* 255 N.Y. 348, 353. For further information, see MacNeil, *American Arbitration Law,* 35.

79. MacNeil, *American Arbitration Law,* 34.

80. Ibid.

81. Ibid.

82. Ibid., 36.

83. "[O]ne cannot overstate the significance of a single salutary reform which made possible the extension of arbitration beyond the trade associations . . ." Ibid.

84. Ibid., 85.

85. Ibid., 87.

86. Ibid., 28.

87. Ibid., 93–94.

88. Julius Henry Cohen, *Commercial Arbitration and the Law* (New York: D. Appleton, 1918).

89. Ibid., 5–6.

90. MacNeil, *American Arbitration Law,* 31, 38.

91. *Sales and Contracts to Sell in Interstate and Foreign Commerce, and Federal Commercial Arbitration: Hearing on S. 4213 and 4214 Before the S. Comm. on the Judiciary,* 67th Cong. 3 (1923) (statement of Mr. Charles L. Bernheimer, Chairman, Arbitration Committee, New York Chamber of Commerce) (hereafter cited as Statement of Charles L. Bernheimer).

92. Cohen, *Commercial Arbitration and the Law,* 280.

93. Statement of Charles L. Bernheimer, 3–5.

94. *Jansen v. Borsum* (New Amsterdam Mun. Ct. 1656), in *RNA,* vol. 2, 20.

95. Cohen, *Commercial Arbitration and the Law,* 26.

96. Nelson, "Dutch Law," 12.

97. *Sales and Contracts to Sell in Interstate and Foreign Commerce, and Federal Commercial Arbitration: Hearing on S. 4213 and 4214 Before the S. Comm. on the Judiciary,* 67th Cong 14 (1923) (letter from Herbert Hoover, Secretary of Commerce).

98. MacNeil, *American Arbitration Law,* 29.

99. *Kilvert v. Geraerdy* (New Amsterdam Mun. Ct. 1656), in *RNA,* 69.

100. *Howsam v. Dean Witter Reynolds, Inc.,* 537 U.S. 79, 83–86 (2002). See also *Green Tree Financial Corp. v. Bazzle,* 539 U.S. 444, 452–53 (2003) (plurality opinion).

101. For an example of a court rejecting "manifest disregard" of law as a basis for overturning an arbitral award, see *Citigroup Global Markets, Inc. v. Bacon,* 562 F.3d 349, 358 (5th Cir. 2009).

102. *Hall Street Associates, LLC v. Mattel, Inc.,* 128 S.Ct. 1396, 1403–04 (2008).

103. I. N. Phelps Stokes, *The Iconography of Manhattan Island* (New York: R. H. Dodd, 1915), 1:57–59.

Chapter Four

The Declaration of Independence and the Dutch Legacy

Wijnand W. Mijnhardt

In the seventeenth century, the first steps toward political and religious freedom were just that: early strides on a labored road. Using words echoed two centuries later by Thomas Jefferson in the Declaration of Independence of 1776, the founding document of the Netherlands—the Dutch Act (Plakkaat) of Abjuration of 1581 (Plakkaat van Verlatinge) declaring independence from Spain—is often presented as a groundbreaking statement of rights. The Plakkaat speaks of "the law of nature" and the "defense of liberty," phrases that resonate in the Declaration of Independence. Although they are in some respects strikingly similar, the two declarations differ in one crucial respect: Our Declaration of Independence and Constitution contemplate power not in any prince, but in the people. The Dutch Plakkaat, nevertheless, is more than a milestone. It crossed a bright line.

More than one hundred years ago, in the fall of 1903, Edward Bok (1863–1930), founder of *Cosmopolitan* and editor of the *Ladies Home Journal*—then as well as now among the top ten best-selling magazines in this country—announced to his multimillion readership, "that Holland, not England, was the mother of America."[1] Citing evidence of Dutch influence in American politics, cultural institutions, social customs, and language, he came to the conclusion that the true American identity had its origins in the Dutch Republic of the sixteenth and seventeenth centuries, and that the Founding Fathers had focused on the political ideals of the Dutch to make their nation. According to Bok, four institutions that were vital to the young American Republic had their origins in Holland: free public education, freedom of religion, freedom of the press, and the secret ballot. It would, therefore, only be a question of time before the Dutchness of the American character and political institutions would become clear and England would be repudiated as the cradle of American civilization.[2]

Bok was not a naive journalist, and his praise of the Dutch no isolated incident. His article stood at the apex of a movement that between 1890 and 1920 sought to reassess the importance of the Dutch heritage for an understanding of American culture and identity.[3] It was supported by a massive visual crusade organized by no fewer than six different American artist colonies on Dutch soil and by an advertising industry that had begun to market a stunning variety of so-called Holland goods. Together with a series of successful children's books, led by Mary Elizabeth Mapes Dodge's (1831–1905) *Hans Brinker or the Silver Skates,* they succeeded in creating an image of the Dutch as an essentially rural, brave, righteous, god-fearing nation that still lived according to the morals and customs of the sixteenth and seventeenth-century freedom-loving Protestant Republic and one that should serve as a continuous source of inspiration to Americans.

One element of this Holland mania was a serious effort to rewrite and interpret American history. At its origins stood the work of John Lothrop Motley (1814–1877), especially his *Rise of the Dutch Republic* (1855), which offered an interpretation of the freedom wars against Spain, and his subsequent *History of the United Netherlands* (1868) that sought an explanation for the seventeenth-century ascendancy.[4] Motley's writings, immensely popular for their color and drama, contained a double message. First of all, he provided a vivid picture of the liberty-loving Dutch and of their ingenuity, moral rectitude, and bravery in their struggle for independence against Habsburg tyranny. Secondly, he tried to convince his readers that the Americans, by adopting the Dutch freedom struggle and the ensuing policies of tolerance, freedom, and equality as its revolutionary model, had embarked on a course to world power similar to that of the Dutch in the seventeenth century.[5]

Figure 4.1. Sextette learning Dutch folk dances as taught by the 1938 Recreational Agencies Program in New York City. Album File, PR 002-209, Photograph Record of WPA for the City of New York; negative no. 81606d. Collection of The New-York Historical Society.

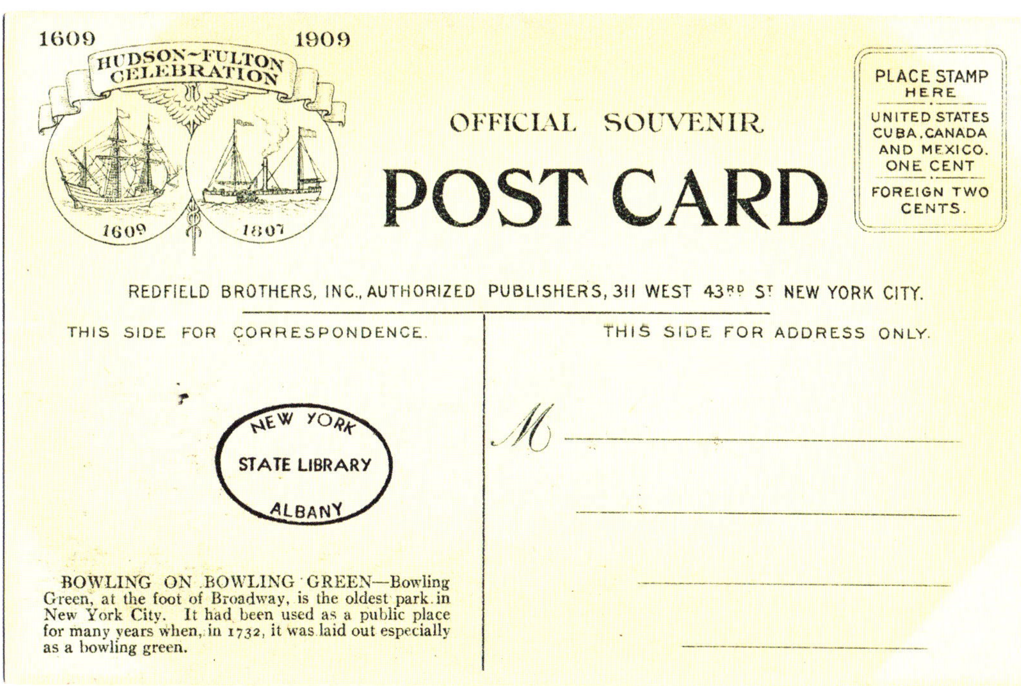

FIGURE 4.2. Float—"Bowling on the Bowling Green." Hudson-Fulton Celebration Commission Official Post Card no. 20. New York: Redfield Bothers, c.1909. New York State Library Postcard Collection call number: QC16510.

A pivotal figure of this revisionist movement was William Elliott Griffis (1843–1928), a famous Japanologist who in 1874 published the *Mikado's Empire,* the first American analysis of Japanese history and culture.[6] Griffis took an anthropological perspective on history, which he also applied to European-American cultural and intellectual relations. In order to reduce the significance attributed to the English heritage, Griffis wrote a series of books and pamphlets in which he tried to establish the importance of Dutch religious and political influences for American freedoms.[7] He published condensed versions of Motley's work and edited his collected writings.

A central theme for these revisionist historians was the parallel development of Dutch and American histories. Both countries had gone through similar phases of foreign suppression culminating in revolution. The crucial moment for both nations was when they had to declare their independence.[8] This vision inspired the first American translation of the Dutch Act of Abjuration of 1581—the document that declared Philip II forfeited of his sovereignty over the Low Countries.[9] Characteristically, the Act of Abjuration was rebaptized as the Dutch Declaration of Independence, a name the document has kept in the American-speaking world since.[10]

In the 1920s, the fascination for everything Dutch lost its edge. Holland as a subject had fallen out of favor with American artists, and the Roaring Twenties had led the advertising industry to less rural and more exciting horizons. The small group of historians advocating the reinterpretation of the English settlement and the American Revolution had failed to make any lasting impact on received British-oriented historiography. The publication of Carl Becker's *Declaration of Independence* in 1922, which did not even acknowledge the Dutch perspective, seems to have sealed the fate of the revisionist movement. Its scholarly harvest was limited. Though many claims had been made, hardly any of them had been substantiated by new research.[11]

However, it is questionable whether the almost complete silence on the significance of the Dutch legacy for the Declaration is justified. Let us review the available facts and interpretations. Admittedly, there was much ambivalence toward the Dutch Republic among American elites in the Age of Revolution.[12] Tom Paine, for instance, in his *Common Sense,* admired the Republic as "Holland without a king hath enjoyed more peace in the last century than any of the monarchical governments in Europe." But even Paine had doubts about the political system of the Republic.[13] Other Americans were much more critical and their views can be fairly summarized in the judgment of the reverend pamphleteer from Salem, Samuel Williams: "Holland has got the forms if she has lost the spirit of a free country."[14]

The quickly fading appeal of the contemporary Dutch political model can be easily shown from the constitutional debates. The Articles of Confederation, the first American Constitution of 1781, show a very strong resemblance to the founding document of the Dutch Republic, the Union of Utrecht of 1579 that served as its constitution for more than two centuries. To well-established eighteenth-century Dutch legal scholars such as Pieter Paulus (1754–1796) and Gerhard Dumbar (1743–1802) who had made an extensive study of all relevant documents, the parallels were obvious. In their view, the Americans had simply espoused the arrangements from the Union of Utrecht.[15] However, it is difficult to find American witnesses who unequivocally acknowledge such an adoption, nor is it easy to establish precisely what Dutch sources were available to them.[16]

Nevertheless, there can be no doubt that the participants in the debates leading up to the American Constitution of 1787 and its ratification quickly grew disenchanted with the Dutch example. They appreciated the Dutch defense of local liberties, they could concur in the Dutch abhorrence of the strong centralized state, but they also saw freemen abandoning the basic principles of a free republic by resigning their privileges of election and committing their liberties to a rich aristocracy.[17] Most of all, they saw endless internal dissension and the inability to reform itself. James Madison summarized these opinions. In the *Federalist* No. 20 of December 11, 1787, after a careful assessment of the political system of the Republic and informed by its most recent failure to reform itself, he wrote: "This unhappy people seem to be now suffering from popular convulsions, from dissensions among the States, and from the actual invasion of foreign arms, the crisis of their destiny."[18]

These harsh judgments on contemporary Dutch politics stood in sharp contrast to the appreciation of the Dutch Revolt of the sixteenth century. At the end of the eighteenth century, such admiration was widespread on both sides of the Atlantic. In Europe, Goethe's drama *Egmont* and Schiller's famous *Abfall der Vereinigten Niederlande* bear testimony to that sentiment, and Americans made no exception. According to Noah Webster (1758–1843), no other people since Leonidas's Spartans had fought with more bravery and perseverance to preserve their rights.[19] Benjamin Franklin was very fond of drawing parallels between the Dutch and American Revolutions; Holland, he often said, "and its love of liberty and bravery in defense of it" had been the great example.[20] John Adams, the first American Ambassador to the United Provinces, claimed "that the originals of the two Republics are so much alike that the history of the one seems but a transcript of the other."[21] In his *Autobiography,* Jefferson had remarked that the example of the Dutch Revolt convinced the Second Continental Congress that a revolution in the American Colonies could likewise succeed.[22] The central documents underpinning the parallel, according to Adams, were the Declarations of Independence of both countries: "[T]he analogy between the means by which the two republics arrived at independency . . . will infallibly draw them together."

The Dutch Act of Abjuration of 1581 is often presented as the first statement of the rights of man as drawn up by an early modern representative assembly and as such the basis of modern republican and constitutional government.[23] The Abjuration Act, though of eminent political importance, was a sober document. Unlike Jefferson's eloquent Declaration, it was not produced in the splendid isolation of a scholar's study but emerged from the complicated negotiating process in the meeting rooms of a great many representative bodies. It claimed that the Dutch political order was designed to preserve liberty by means of a constitutional framework the fundamental components of which were the privileges and the states as representatives of the people. The office of the prince was ordained for the sake of his subjects, to govern them according to right and reason. His sovereignty derived from the constitutional contract to which each prince had to swear an oath on the day of his inauguration. The states, as the guardians of liberty, had the duty to uphold the privileges. If the prince violated the privileges, he broke his contract and legally forfeited his sovereignty.

The series of pamphlets and treatises accompanying the Abjuration Act show that the political thought of the Dutch Revolt was firmly embedded in contemporary European intellectual debates. The extremely high degree of urbanization and continuous war obliged Dutch commentators to find a middle road between two extremes in Europe: the absolute sovereignty found among French theorists and the rigid constitutionalism of German stock. Because of its emphasis on liberty, constitutional charters, representative institutions, and popular sovereignty, the Dutch conception of politics might be located in the language of jurisprudence, the tradition that extolled freedom from authority as a principle. By their advocacy of concord, civic virtues, and citizenship as essential prerequisites of urban life and by their efforts to interpret their system as a mixed constitution, Dutch politicians and philosophers saw themselves also as heirs to the Italian republican city-state tradition and its conceptualization of politics as a civic philosophy that had the good life as its aim.[24]

At first sight, the resemblances between the two documents are striking.[25] Both declarations are characterized by sweeping preambles claiming that kings and princes can lawfully demand obedience as long as they protect the rights and privileges of their subjects. Both documents

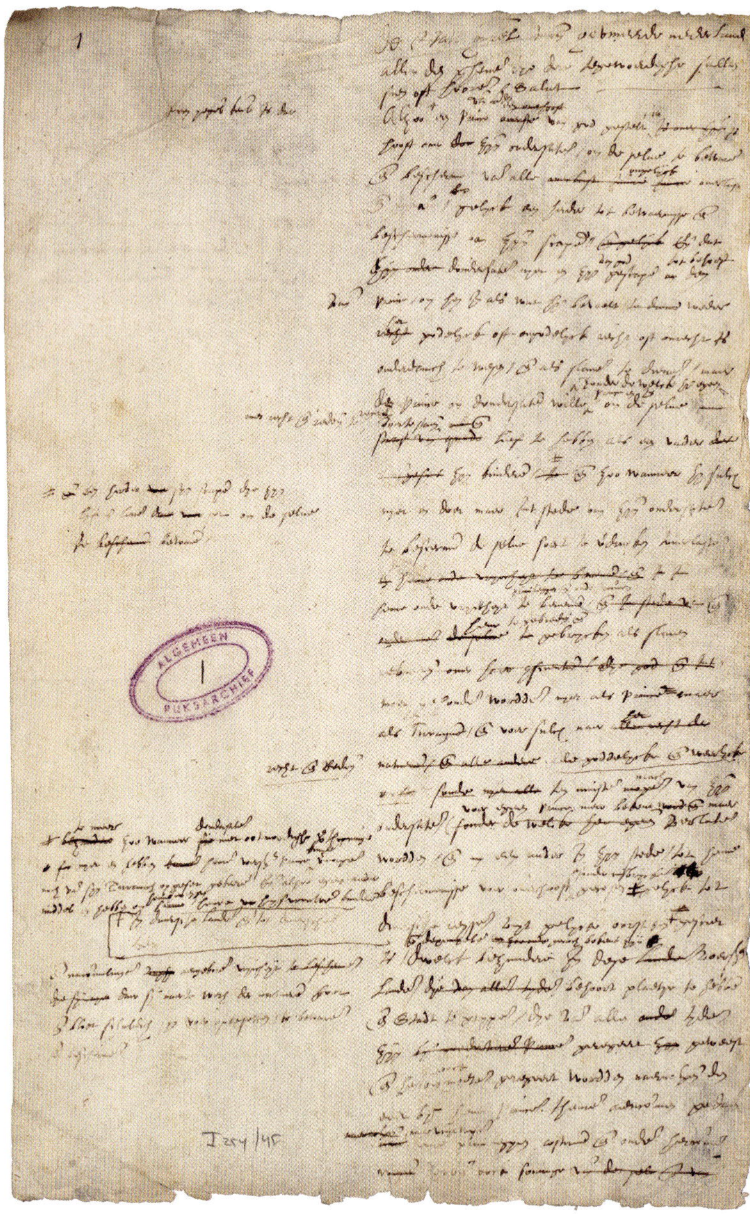

FIGURE 4.3. Dutch "Declaration of Independence" from Spain, 1581.

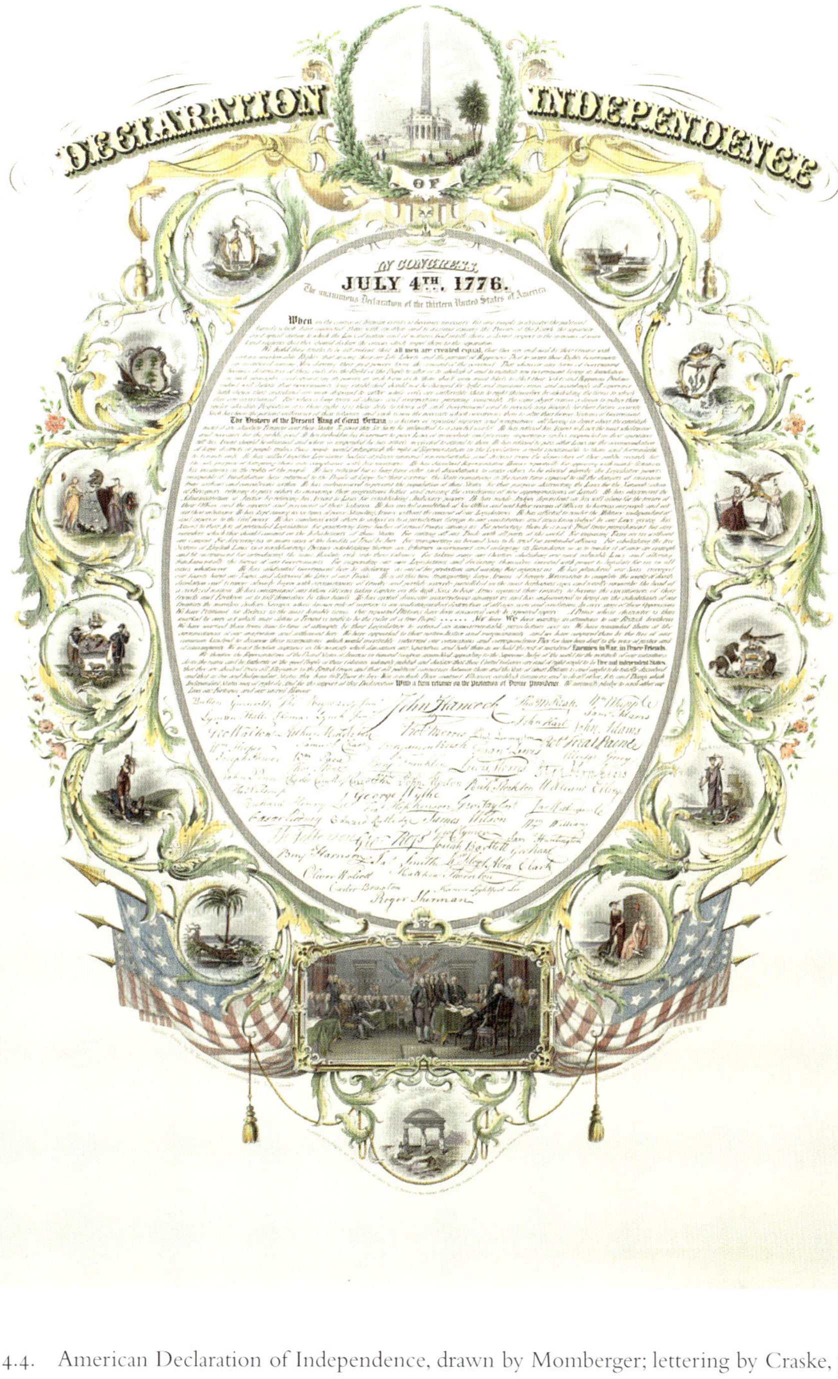

FIGURE 4.4. American Declaration of Independence, drawn by Momberger; lettering by Craske, published by J. C. Buttre, 48 Franklin St. New York City. PR 068 Subject File, flat file, documents (C-E); negative no. 83136. Collection of The New-York Historical Society.

contain similarly structured catalogues of almost identical grievances against the tyrant kings Philip II and George III, which in both cases take up about two-thirds of the text. The parallels between the two documents are indeed so remarkable that at least one historian has defended the thesis that the Act of Abjuration functioned as an archetype for the declaration that Jefferson and his Committee of Five had been requested to prepare. In a fascinating article, the American historian Stephen Lucas has recently analyzed the abounding rhetorical parallels between the two documents. Moreover, he demonstrated convincingly that this type of emulation had nothing to do with plagiarism and was not at all unusual in late-eighteenth-century practices of rhetoric.[26]

Just as in the case of the Articles of Confederation, no explicit confirmation of the use of the Dutch models can be documented. Members of both draft committees maintain a complete silence on the subject, although, as we have seen, they were well acquainted with the history of the Dutch Revolt. Though the texts of the Union of Utrecht and of the Act of Abjuration were available in the Colonies, no physical connection between the documents and the various committees and their members has yet been established. It might, however, be useful to rephrase the question. Is it conceivable in a period in which historical parallel and legal precedent played so dominant a role in daily life as well as in political practice, that these pertinent models would have been ignored? After all, when confronted with the task of drafting a constitution for such a rare and hardly respectable commodity as a republic, there were very few "living" examples available, among which the Dutch Republic was the most prominent. And when faced with the mission of legitimizing the almost unique and rather ominous political act of deposing a lawful king, isn't it highly improbable that Jefferson would have consulted the two available English examples and neglected the only continental example of early modern times?

But even if we concede that the Declaration of Independence belongs to a small and exclusive written tradition of king disposal of which the Dutch Act of Abjuration was the beginning, and even if we agree that Jefferson made extensive rhetorical use of the Dutch model while improving its literary qualities,[27] all that does not minimize in any sense the revolutionary novelty of the American Declaration. Though the political discourse surrounding the Dutch Abjuration Act was radically innovative in its time, Jefferson's Declaration included some fundamental breaks with that past. For instance, Jefferson abandoned the idea of a contract between prince and the representatives of the people, so central in the Act of Abjuration, and replaced it by the notion of the full sovereignty of the people. Secondly, Jefferson's concept of liberty is comprehensive in a sense the Dutch declaration never was. Characteristically, Jefferson's Declaration does not discuss freedom of conscience or freedom of religion as separate issues. The Dutch Act, on the contrary, tended to limit liberty to freedom of religion.[28] Most important, however, is the universal character of the Declaration. The concept of rights of the Act of Abjuration was particular and provincial: rights belonged to corporations rather than to individuals, to precisely circumscribed geographical regions rather than to large territories. Jefferson's Declaration was the first document that claimed—to cite Lynn Hunt—the fundamental equality, universality, and naturalness of rights.[29]

In the relevant literature—ranging from Becker through Bailyn and Wood to Pocock, Wills, Appleby, and Zuckert, to name only a few[30]—this fundamental transformation is by and large connected to English sources and English debates from the Civil War to the American Revolution. Claims of Dutch influence are almost nonexistent. Only Michael Zuckert, in his recent revision of the origins of American Republicanism, has reserved a pivotal place for

Grotius, who conceived of a fully functional human society, unaided by religion and based upon natural rights, the most important of which is self-preservation. But even Grotian philosophy only reached America mediated by Locke's *Two Treatises of Government*.[31]

Do we need therefore to conclude that, apart from their historical example and their rhetorical model, the Dutch had little to contribute? It is too early to say. There is another Dutch legacy that may help to explain the fundamental shift from the historical to the rational, from the corporate to the individual and from the particular to the universal: a legacy that we now call the Radical Enlightenment and that was grounded in the urban republicanism of the seventeenth-century Republic, exemplified by writers such as the brothers De la Court, Franciscus van den Enden, Balthasar Bekker, Spinoza, and their followers. Its outlines we have only recently begun to chart—thanks to the work of Margaret Jacob, Jonathan Israel, and a good number of Dutch scholars[32]—but much of it is yet unclear and its influence still largely awaits its historians. To these Dutch radicals, the "naturalness of rights" was commonplace, and the racial equality of mankind with its concomitant broad democracy and its revolutionary philosophy of education central, and its universal relevance self-evident.[33]

The radicals do not easily fit the political languages in which historians of political thought have been so fond of locating their authors.[34] But aren't we spending too much energy on including and excluding commentators from the various registers, and shouldn't we concentrate once again on the political and religious issues that confronted these writers? De la Court's emphasis on the passions and on self-interest—as has been recently argued—enabled him to arrive at a solution for the pressing problem of reconciling social mobility based on education and achievement with political stability and civic concord in a rapidly expanding commercial society. According to De la Court, subjection of a people made it impossible for a society to realize its full potential. Therefore, the only option in a state was the promotion of an active and prosperous population, since only then will the magistrates, out of their own interest be forced to care for the public interest. Also, for Spinoza, setting free the potential of the masses was the central principle of politics.[35] By accepting the natural economic character of society and by coining a new language of self-interest and individualism, if only hesitantly, weren't these commentators struggling to redefine virtue as a political concept in order to make it compatible with commerce?

What we need is an analysis of the international trajectories of these ideas, not as republican curiosities that are difficult to understand in terms of the received political languages, but as inspiring examples that make us aware that other options were available. Two possible transmission channels stand out. The first is the Dutch-British route through which Locke got much of his inspiration, if not some of his ideas. Other links between the closed world of the Dutch Radical Enlightenment (if only because of the language problem: much radical thought was available only in the Dutch vernacular) and England were radicals such as Toland, Collins, and especially Mandeville who, due to his Dutch background, was completely immersed in Dutch philosophical radicalism and continued to draw upon Dutch literature and examples, even after moving to London.

Even more fascinating, but almost completely unexplored, is the American connection. America not only was the place where Dutch enlightened radicals such as Van den Enden and Cornelis Plockhoy planned to establish a utopian society in which all of their ideals would be realized, it also might have functioned as a receptacle for Dutch ideas, especially for those of De la Court and Spinoza that advocated a dynamic set of political behavior congruent with the demands of the liberal marketplace.[36] Research in this field is close to nonexistent, but a first exploration was promising. It showed for instance that disputes over Balthasar Bekker's attack on witchcraft were well known in the Middle Colonies, that Cotton Mather knew his work well and, even more surprising, that the Mather family had a penchant for Dutch materialist and egalitarian pornography.[37]

Quite naturally, these few isolated examples do not at all justify the claim of Edward Bok I began this essay with, that Holland rather than England should be considered the cradle of America. They indicate, however, that for a fuller understanding of the genesis of the Declaration of Independence, a subtle reviving of the Holland Mania that had so successful a start in this country a hundred years ago might turn out to be an intellectually rewarding experience.

NOTES

This article was first presented as a part of the panel *Declarations of Independence and Rights* at the 11th Conference of the International Society for Eighteenth-Century Studies at UCLA, August 3–10, 2003.

1. Edward Bok, "The Mother of America," *Ladies Home Journal* 20 (October 1903), 16. For Bok cf: *The Americanization of Edward Bok, the Autobiography of a Dutch Boy Fifty Years After* (New York: Charles Scribner's Sons, 1920). Cf. Hans Krabbendam, *The Model Man: a Life of Edward William Bok* (Amsterdam: Rodopi, 2001), though Krabbendam has little attention for Bok's role in the revisionist process.

2. This type of praise for the Netherlands goes back to William Temple's *Observations upon the United Provinces* of 1673, the first serious analysis of Dutch sixteenth and seventeenth-century society and politics. Cf. William Temple, *Observations upon the United Provinces of the Netherlands*, ed. G. Clark (Oxford: Oxford University Press, 1972).

3. See Annette Stott, *Holland Mania, The Unknown Dutch Period in American Art and Culture* (Boston: Overlook Press, 1998), for a first analysis of this phenomenon.

4. A few years before his death Motley published the third episode of his trilogy: http://catalog.loc.gov/cgi-bin/Pwebrecon.cgi?SC=Author&SEQ=20030717073606&PID=25892&SA=Motley,+John+Lothrop,+1814-1877.The life and death of John of Barneveld, advocate of Holland; with a view of the primary causes and movements of the Thirty Years' War (London: J. Murray, 1874).

5. Stott, *Holland Mania*, 80–81.

6. Edward R. Beauchamp, *An American Teacher in Early Meiji Japan* (Honolulu: University Press of Hawaii, 1976).

7. William E. Griffis, *The Influence of the Netherlands in the Making of the English Commonwealth and the American Republic* (Boston: De Wolfe, Fisk, 1891); and *The Dutch of the Netherlands in the Making of America* (Boston: De Wolfe, Fisk, 1921); and *Brave Little Holland, and What She Taught Us* (Boston: De Wolfe, Fisk, 1894). Cf. William Elliot Griffis Collection in the Rutgers Special Collections and University Archives.

8. Tiemen de Vries, *Dutch History, Art and Literature for Americans* (Grand Rapids: W. B. Eerdmans, 1912).

9. *The Dutch Declaration of Independence. The Declaration of the States General of the United Provinces, Setting Forth that Philip the Second Had Forfeited his Right of Sovereignty over the Said Provinces. At The Hague, 26 July, 1581* (Boston: The Directors of the Old South Work, 1896). In the middle of the eighteenth century an English translation, originating in the circle of Lord Somers, a central figure in William III's English government, was published: *Somers' Tracts. A Collection of Scarce and Valuable Tracts on the Most Interesting and Entertaining Subjects,* 16 vols. (London, 1748–1751), vol. 14, 417–24; the most recent English translation is in E. H. Kosmann and A. F. Mellink, eds., *Texts Concerning the Revolt of the Netherlands* (Cambridge: Cambridge University Press, 1974), 425 ff.

10. The translation was included in Oliver J. Thatcher, ed., *The Library of Original Sources, Vol. V: 9th to 16th Centuries* (Milwaukee: University Research Extension, 1907), 189–97. Since Paul Halsall in 1998

made this text part of his *Internet Modern History Sourcebook*, the renaming of the original Dutch title has become almost universal practice.

11. It would seem that one of the few academic fruits was Friedrich Edler, *The Dutch Republic and the American Revolution* (Baltimore: Johns Hopkins University Press, 1911). Though Griffis assisted in the preparing of this PhD thesis and Edler in his introduction referred to the ongoing Dutch debate, Edler refrained from taking on the central question of to what extent the governmental system of the United States was derived from Dutch sources and limited himself to diplomatic history. Edler, *Dutch Republic*, vii–viii. The image of rural, frugal Holland continued to be kept alive in successful children's books such as Olive Beaupré Miller's *Tales Told in Holland* (Chicago/Toronto: Book House for Children, 1926), which was reprinted time and again until the 1950s.

12. Cf. J. W. Schulte Nordholt, "The Example of the Dutch Republic for American Federalism," *Bijdragen en Mededelingen betreffende de Geschiedenis der Nederlanden* 94 (1979): 437–49.

13. Daniel E. Wheeler, ed., *The Life and Writings of Tom Paine*, vol. II (New York: Vincent Parke, 1908) 13. For Chesterfield's 1745 memoir on the Republic, knowledge of which was widespread, see Philip Dormer Stanhope, Lord Chesterfield, "Some Account of the Government of the Republic of the Seven United Provinces," in B.Dobrée, *Letters*, vol. III (London: Eyre and Spottiswoode, 1932), 605–12.

14. Samuel Williams, "A Discourse on the Love of Our Country" (Salem, 1775), in Bernard Bailyn, ed., *Pamphlets of the American Revolution 1750–1776*, I (Cambridge: Belknap Press of Harvard University Press, 1965) 82.

15. Cf. Pieter Paulus in his *Verklaring der Unie van Utrecht*, 3 vols. (Utrecht: J. van Schoonhoven, 1775–1777), III, 242–53, remarked: "It is surprising and to the credit of our ancestors, that these inhabitants, after a lapse of some two centuries adopted practically the same measures and arrangements as they did when drafting the Union of Utrecht"; for the translation of Paulus, see Schulte Nordholt, "Dutch Republic as Example," 443. Cf. Gerhard Dumbar, *De oude en de nieuwe Constitutie der Vereenigde Staten van Amerika*, 3 vols. (Amsterdam: J. A. Crajenschot, 1793–1796). See also Herbert Rowen, "The Union of Utrecht and the Articles of Confederation, the Batavian Constitution and the American Constitution: A Double Parallel," in *Herrschaftsverträge, Wahlkapitulationen, Fundamentalgesetze*, ed. R.Vierhaus (Göttingen: Vandenhoeck and Ruprecht, 1977), 281–93. For an (incomplete) overview of American knowledge of Holland, cf. William H. Riker, "Dutch and American Federalism," *Journal of the History of Ideas* 18 (1957): 495–526.

16. See "Giles Hickory" in the *American Magazine*, in *The Debate on the Constitution*, vol. 2, ed. B. Bailyn (New York: Library of America, 1993) 309. Cf. Schulte Nordholt, "Dutch Republic as Example," 442.

17. *The Federalist*, ed. Jacob E. Cooke (Cleveland: World Publishing, 1965) nr. 20, 124–29, nr. 37, 238.

18. The *American Magazine*, February 1788, in Bailyn, ed., *Debate*, 309. Cf. Bernard Bailyn, *The Ideological Origins of the American Revolution* (Cambridge: Belknap Press of Harvard University Press, 1967), 66; and Pauline Maier, *From Resistance to Revolution* (New York: A. A. Knopf, 1972), 213.

19. Cf. Leonard Labaree, *The Papers of Benjamin Franklin* (New Haven: Yale University Press, 1959–), vol. 9, 90–91; vol. 15, 191; vol. 17, 269–70, 380. Cited by Stephen Lucas, "The Rhetorical Ancestry of the Declaration of Independence," *Rhetoric & Public Affairs* 1 (1998):166.

20. "Memorial to their High Mightinesses, the States-General of the United Provinces of the Low Countries (April 19, 1781)," in *Works of John Adams*, ed. Charles F. Adams ed., vol. 7 (Boston: Little, Brown, 1850–1857), 399–400.

21. In *Thomas Jefferson: Writings*, ed. Merrill D. Peterson (New York: Library of America, 1984). 16.

22. M. E. H. N. Mout, *Plakkaat van Verlatinge 1581, Facsimile, Inleiding Transcriptie en Vertaling* (The Hague: Staatshuitgeverij, 1979); J. P. A. Coopmans, "De herkomst van het Plakkaat van Verlatinge," in *Justicie ende Gerechticheyt. Handelingen van het zevende Belgisch-Nederlandse rechtshistorisch colloquium*, ed. G. van Dievoet (Antwerpen: Kluwer Rechtswetenschappen, 1983), 36–52.

23. For a modern analysis of this and other Dutch revolutionary texts, Martin van Gelderen, *The Political Thought of the Dutch Revolt 1555–1590* (Cambridge: Cambridge University Press, 1992); for a

translation of other relevant documents, see Van Gelderen, *The Dutch Revolt* (Cambridge: Cambridge University Press, 1993), especially "A Brief Discourse" (1579) and "Political Education" (1582), treatises that provide the philosophical background to the ideas presented in the *Act of Abjuration.*

24. Van Gelderen, *The Political Thought,* 260–87; E. O. G. Haitsma Mulier, *The Myth of Venice and Dutch Republican Thought in the Seventeenth Century* (Assen: Van Gorcum, 1980).

25. J. P. A. Coopmans, "Het Plakkaat van Verlatinghe (1581) en de Declaration of Independence," *Bijdragen en Mededelingen betreffende de Geschiedenis der Nederlanden* 98 (1983): 540–67.

26. Stephen Lucas, "The Rhetorical Ancestry of the Declaration of Independence"; and *Portents of Rebellion. Rhetoric and Revolution in Philadelphia, 1765–1776* (Philadelphia: Temple University Press, 1976).

27. Becker, *The Declaration of Independence,* ch. v.

28. Van Gelderen, *Political Thought of the Dutch Revolt.*

29. Lynn Hunt, "The Paradoxical Origins of Human Rights," in *Human Rights and Revolutions,* ed. Jeffrey Wasserstrom, Lynn Hunt, and Marilyn B. Young (Lanham, MD: Rowman and Littlefield, 2000), 7. Cf. Lynn Hunt, *The French Revolution and Human Rights* (Boston: Bedford Books of St. Martin's Press, 1996).

30. Bernard Bailyn, *The Ideological Origins of the American Revolution* (Cambridge: Harvard University Press, 1967); Gordon Wood, *The Creation of the American Republic* (Chapel Hill: University of North Caroina Press, 1969); John G. A. Pocock, *The Machiavellian Moment. Florentine Political Thought and the Atlantic Republican Tradition* (Princeton: Princeton University Press, 1975); Garry Wills, *Inventing America. Jefferson's Declaration of Independence* (Garden City, NY: Doubleday, 1978); Joyce Appleby, *Liberalism and Republicanism in the Historical Imagination* (Cambridge: Harvard University Press, 1992); Michael P. Zuckert, *Natural Rights and the New Republicanism* (Princeton: Princeton University Press, 1994).

31. Zuckert, *Natural Rights and the New Republicanism,* 216–46.

32. Margaret Jacob, *The Radical Enlightenment* (London: Allen and Unwin, 1981); Theo Verbeek, *Descartes and the Dutch* (Carbondale: Southern Illinois University Press, 1992); Wiep van Bunge, *From Stevin to Spinoza: An Essay on Philosophy in the Seventeenth Century Dutch Republic* (Leiden/Boston: Brill, 2001); Jonathan Israel, *Radical Enlightenment. Philosophy and the Making of Modernity, 1650–1750* (Oxford: Oxford University Press, 2001).

33. E. H. Kossmann, *Political Thought in the Dutch Republic* (Amsterdam: Koninklijke Nederlandse Akademie van Wetenschappen, 2000), 167–94.

34. Cf. Jonathan Scott, "Classical Republicanism: England, The Netherlands," in *Republicanism. Volume I: Republicanism and Constitutionalism in Early Modern Europe,* ed. Martin van Gelderen and Quentin Skinner (Cambridge: Cambridge University Press, 2002), 81–84. Cf. the contributions of Van Gelderen and Hans-Erich Bödeker to that volume.

35. Eco Haitsma Mulier, "The Language of Seventeenth-Century Republicanism in the United Provinces: Dutch or European," in Anthony Pagden, *The Languages of Political Theory in Early-Modern Europe* (Cambridge: Cambridge University Press, 1987), 179–96; Hans W. Blom, *Morality and Causality in Politics. The Rise of Naturalism in Dutch Seventeenth-Century Political Thought* (s.l., 1995), 178; G. O. van de Klashorst, H. W. Blom, and E. O. G. Haitsma Mulier, *A Bibliography of Dutch Seventeenth-Century Political Thought: An Annotated Inventory* (Amsterdam: APA-Holland University Press, 1986).

36. Joyce Appleby, "The Social Origins of American Revolutionary Ideology," *Journal of American History* 64 (1978): 937; and *Capitalism and a New Social Order: The Republican Vision of the 1790's* (New York: New York University Press, 1984).

37. John Dixon, "Desperately Seeking Spinoza: or Whatever Happened to the Radical Enlightenment in America," Unpublished graduate paper, UCLA, 2002. For Dutch philosophical pornography, Inger Leemans, *Het Woord is aan de Onderkant. Radicale Ideeën in Nederlandse pornografische romans, 1670–1700* (Nijmegen: Van Tilt, 2002).

Chapter Five

Real Estate or Political Sovereignty?

The Dutch, Munsees, and the Purchase of Manhattan Island

Paul Otto

One legacy of New Netherland is legend. A particularly persistent story is of Peter Minuit's "purchase" of Manhattan from the Native Americans for twenty-four dollars. In the essay that follows, Paul Otto describes relationships between the Dutch and Native Americans and debunks some of the popular myths about how the Dutch acquired Manhattan.

Relations between the Native Americans and Dutch in the New Netherland region began with trade. In 1625, the West India Company issued instructions to its employee Willem Verhulst as to how he and those in his charge should deal with Native Americans. The Company's directives were detailed and reflecting good intentions: Verhulst and his people were to treat the Native Americans with respect, deal with them honestly, refrain from attempting to convert them religiously, and keep from becoming embroiled in quarrels among competing tribes.

This trade partnership created not only mutual dependency but also entailed complicated adjustments, considering the cultural differences. Trade and its mutual advantages sustained the relationship, but social, political, and economic clashes were all but inevitable. Tensions sometimes led to violence.

In 1626, Pieter Schagen, representative of the States General in the West India Company, wrote of the arrival in the fatherland of a ship, the *Arms of Amsterdam,* from New Netherland. He reported news from the colony and listed the goods arriving in the Dutch Republic. He also nonchalantly reported that the Dutch in New Netherland "have purchased the Island Manhattes from the Indians for the value of 60 guilders; 'tis 11,000 morgens in size."[1] A seemingly innocuous statement of fact about a land transfer between Native Americans and the Dutch, the statement is nonetheless of profound significance. For New Yorkers, this letter, the primary documentation of the transfer of Manhattan Island to the hands of Europeans, serves as a kind of birth certificate for New York City.

This is the closest thing we have to a formal notice of this purchase, but it provides little of the information we might hope for from official documents, leaving us many questions. As a birth certificate, the document fails to provide an exact date of the "birth," and it does not identify where the event took place. As documentation for the most infamous land transfer in American history, it also falls short of the mark. Besides not identifying the place and date of this historic transfer, it does not itemize the goods in the exchange or the exact identity of the parties to the exchange. More importantly, it is not an official land deed (nor does one

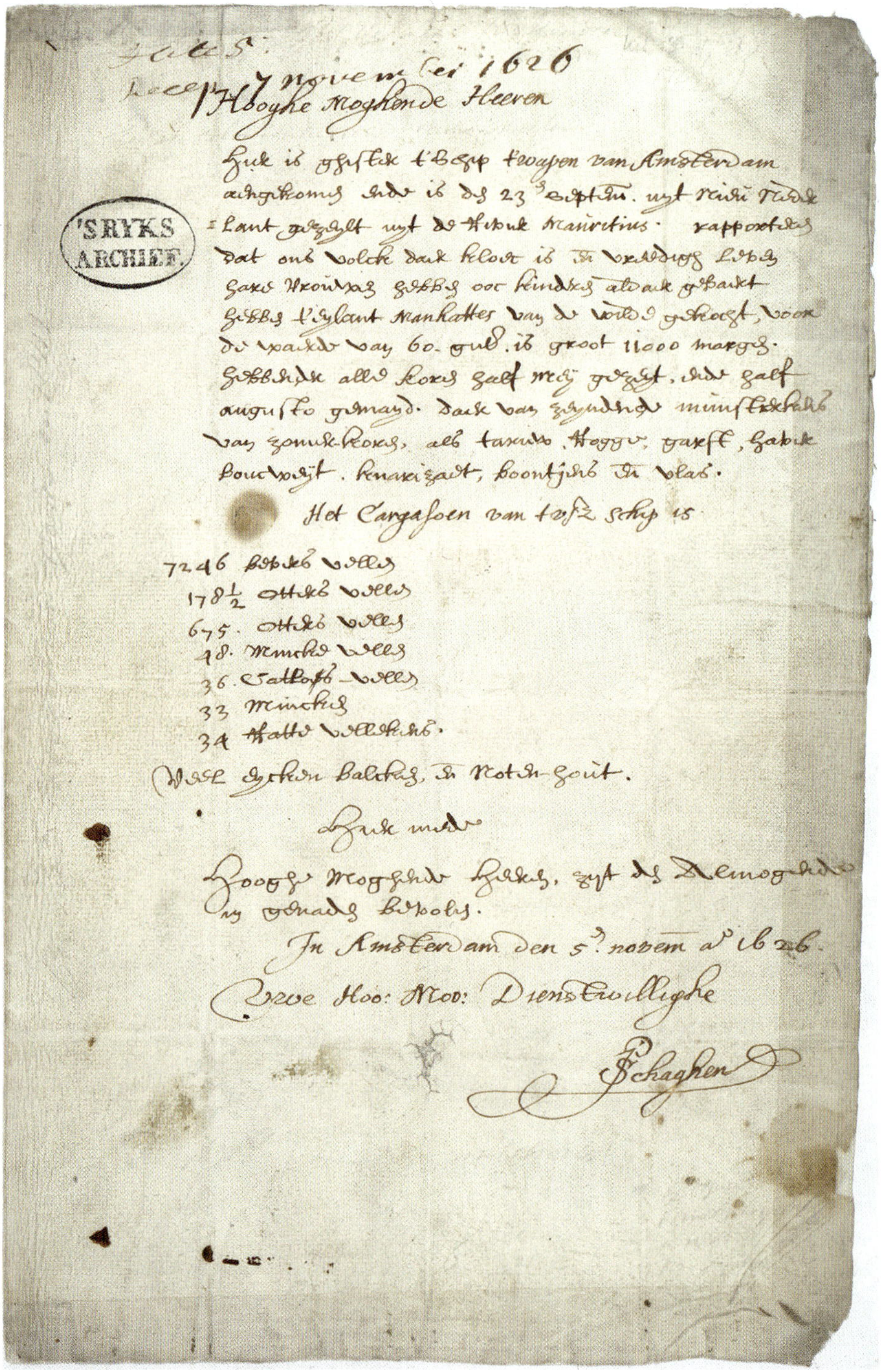

Rcept. 7 novembri 1626

Hooghe Moghende Heeren

Hier is gisteren 't schip 't Wapen van Amsterdam aengecomen ende is den 23en septemb. uyt Nieu Neder=lant gezeylt uyt de Riviere Mauritius. rapporteren dat ons volck daer kloec is en vredich leven, haere vrouwen hebben oock kinderen aldaer gebaert, hebben 't eylant Manhattes van de wilden gekocht, voor de waerde van 60. guld. is groot 11000 morgen. hebben alle koren half mey gezayt, ende half augusto gemaeyt. daer van zijnder monsterkens van zomerkoren, als tarwe, rogge, garst, haver, boeckweyt, knariezaet, boontjens en vlas.

Het Cargasoen van 'tselve schip is

7246 bevers vellen
178½ otters vellen
675. otters vellen
48. mincke vellen
36. catlosse vellen
33 mincken
34 ratte vellekens.

Veel eycken balcken en note-hout.

Hiermede

Hooghe Moghende Heeren, zijt den Almogende in genade bevolen.

In Amsterdam den 5en novem. ao 1626.

Uwe Hoo: Moo: Dienstwillighe

P. Schaghen

FIGURE 5.1. Letter from Pieter Schaghen in which the "purchase" of Manhattan is mentioned, paper, 1626. Collection Nationaal Archief (National Archives of the Netherlands) 1.01.04, inv.nr. 5751 II.

exist).[2] Despite all these imperfections, and in the absence of a true deed, New Yorkers must satisfy themselves with this document, which they have done since it was first uncovered in 1844.[3] But even if a deed did exist, New Yorkers would still be left with some important questions. First, deed or no deed, confusion surrounds the amount paid for Manhattan Island. The Schagen letter records the figure of sixty guilders while American tradition holds that it was twenty-four dollars. Second, it is not clear why Native Americans would sell or transfer the island for this or any amount of money. Third, and most important, what did the Indians mean by "selling" the land? The answer to the first question is one of translation and an anachronistic effort by nineteenth-century men to make sense of seventeenth-century sums. But translation is really also at the root of the other two issues. The actions, motives, and understandings of native people at the time of contact does not naturally translate into our own time even as it did not translate well into Dutch thinking of the same period. This chapter seeks to answer questions about the transfer of Manhattan Island from the Munsee Indians to the Dutch by considering these people in their historical, cultural settings. In particular, it demonstrates that the transfer of Manhattan Island from Indian to Dutch was both more and less than an exchange of real estate as understood in the European American tradition. As an agreement between two groups of people, it had more to do with a question of sovereignty than it did with who sold what land to whom.

In the heart of the territory where New York City and portions of New York and New Jersey would someday be located, lived the Munsee people. These Native Americans had lived in the region for at least hundreds of years. They have also been known as Lenapes and Delawares. No term adequately describes the group, in part because it is not fully accurate to describe them as a single Indian tribe. Instead, the Munsees represented a collection of villages, clans, and larger groupings sharing a common language and cultural practices. The Munsees were also linguistically linked to their southern and western neighbors, the Unami, who have also been known as the Delawares or Lenni Lenape.[4] In the seventeenth century, these people would find themselves the "hosts" of wave after wave of European "guests." In the earliest years, native people may have welcomed these visitors and the advantages a relationship with them brought in trade, but eventually they found control of their territory challenged and their sovereignty in the land threatened.

Dutch colonization of New Netherland did not begin with settlement or land acquisitions. It began, rather, with a series of trading voyages to the Hudson River valley and elsewhere along the Atlantic coast.[5] By 1611, Dutch captains plied American waters seeking to exchange European wares for North American furs. The Munsees mostly welcomed these voyages and for more than ten years a thriving fur trade existed in lands occupied by Munsee Indians and labeled on Dutch maps as "Nieu Nederlandt." Most of these trade expeditions consisted of ships traveling the marine and riparian coasts and making exchanges where they could. Certain locales became particularly important, such as the region where Albany now stands. There, in 1614, Dutch traders established an outpost, Fort Nassau, which was abandoned after 1616. But for the most part, in this era of trade, the Indians remained the masters of their lands. Dutch traders did not establish long-term outposts and apparently did not purchase land from the Indians. Certainly no settlers came to live there. As far as the scarce records indicate, this situation was mutually acceptable and beneficial to European and Indian alike. The Indians of the Hudson River valley happily exchanged the products of the forest for goods that they found both exotic and useful.

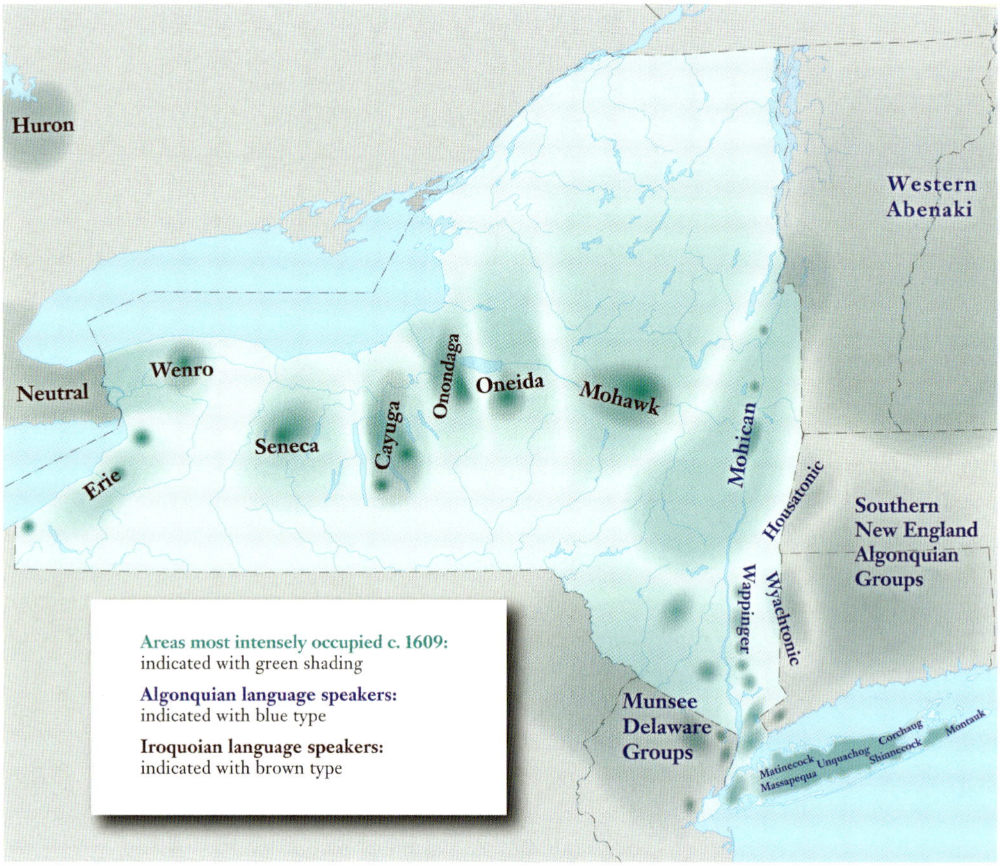

Figure 5.2. Map of Native populations and land use c. 1609. From New York State Museum.

After 1621, this situation began to change. In the Dutch Republic, the West India Company was created and given a monopoly of Dutch commercial activity throughout the Atlantic world. While the West India Company's earliest activities in New Netherland centered mostly upon trade, the WIC had considered the possibility of settlement almost from the beginning and soon took more concrete steps in that direction.[6] France and England began to challenge the Dutch Republic's claims in the New World based primarily on the right of first discovery. With the States General adding pressure to the West India Company to respond to this crisis, the Company decided to establish a permanent settlement in New Netherland. The availability of several Walloon families (Francophones from the southern Netherlands) willing to immigrate to New Netherland helped finalize their decision.[7]

The result was the establishment of a settlement colony in New Netherland. Thus, with the creation of the West India Company and the choice to establish European settlers in their North American territory, came a significantly different focus in Dutch attitudes toward a region that was also claimed, inhabited, and controlled by the Munsees. The West India Company was still committed to an emphasis on the fur trade and no plans were initially laid

Figure 5.3. L. F. Tantillo, *The Trading House: Fort Nassau on the Bank of the Hudson River on Castle Island* (present day Albany). This fort, built by the Dutch trader Hendrick Christiaensen, was the first nonnative structure to be built in New Netherland. Reproduction courtesy of the artist.

for large-scale settlement as was happening in Virginia and would later occur in Massachusetts Bay. But the presence of the Company nevertheless affected Dutch-Indian affairs in a number of ways. Because the West India Company needed to secure a solid legal claim to the territory and defend it against European competitors, it purchased land from the Indians and established settlements there. Furthermore, land exchanges signified presumed Dutch sovereignty over the region and its inhabitants.

In 1625, the Company instructed Director Willem Verhulst to acquire land from the Indians on which to establish a headquarters for the colony. Their instructions demonstrate the Company's approach to the native people—apparently respecting their indigenous rights on the one hand, but also to some degree presuming Dutch sovereignty over the region. In acquiring their land, the Indians were not to "be driven away by force or threats, but by good words be persuaded to leave, or be given something therefor to their satisfaction, or else be allowed to live among us, a contract being made thereof and signed by them in their manner, since such contracts upon other occasions may be very useful to the Company."[8] Thus, the Company was willing to accommodate Indian claims to the land, but not, in the final analysis, to bow to those claims. In later instructions, Verhulst was ordered to find a place to establish the Company headquarters that was "abandoned by the Indians or unoccupied," and if he could obtain "none but those that are occupied by the Indians, they shall see whether they cannot, either in return for trading-goods or by means of some amicable agreement, *induce* them to give up ownership and possession to us." Thus, the acquisition of some Indian land would have to be accomplished, but the means would be dictated by concerns of fairness and justice: "without however forcing them thereto in the least or taking possession by craft or fraud."[9]

Verhulst did not accomplish this task of purchasing a site for the administrative headquarters of the colony, but in the spring of 1626, his successor, Director Peter Minuit purchased Manhattan Island.[10] In addition to Pieter Schagen's reference to the purchase cited at the beginning of this chapter, other records also refer to it. West India Company director Johannes de Laet wrote in 1630 that there was an island at the mouth of the Hudson called "Manhattes or Manhatans Island, because this nation of Indians happened to possess the same, and by them it had been sold to the Company." In 1633 he also stated that "our people have bought from [the Manathans] the island separated from the rest of the land by the Hellgate, and have there laid the foundations of a fort, and of a town called New Amsterdam."[11]

Tradition holds that the island was purchased with "glittering beads and baubles," but the actual nature and content of the goods traded to the Indians for the island is unknown. It can be surmised that the Indians accepted the typical trade items. When the Dutch purchased Staten Island a few years later, they paid the Indians with "Duffels, Kittles, Axes, Hoes, Wampum, Drilling Awls, Jews harps, and diverse other small wares."[12] The value of the goods—sixty guilders—is documented, but here, too, tradition is misleading. Most Americans who have heard the price paid for Manhattan Island cite the figure of twenty-four dollars. This figure appeared in 1846 when E. B. O'Callaghan, who had access to the recently discovered Schagen letter, published his *History of New Netherland*. It was there that O'Callaghan introduced the figure of twenty-four dollars by using current rates of conversion. Since that time, the story of Manhattan Island being sold for twenty-four dollars in trade goods has been retold and republished many, many times, leaving the original Dutch amount of sixty guilders lost in translation, as it were.[13]

But the value of the guilder or dollar in the nineteenth century tells us little about the actual price the Dutch paid in 1626. Even to calculate the value in dollars today, given inflation, of sixty seventeenth-century guilders misses the point. Sixty guilders was not a large sum at the time, but neither was it minuscule. According to historian A. Th. van Deursen, it equaled three or four months' wages for an average artisan in the province of Holland. These wages did not represent a middle-class lifestyle, but they were adequate, if just barely, to support a small family.[14] Historian Jaap Jacobs claims it was also the value of a soldier's salary for about six months.[15] Sixty guilders was also the amount the Company paid a colonist (and presumably an Indian as well) for thirty beaver skins or twelve fathoms of wampum.[16]

To the Dutch, the land was certainly valuable at the time (it would be anachronistic to consider its value today as the commercial capital of the world). The fourteen thousand acre island became the Company's headquarters and the location of the Company's farms and agricultural endeavors. Domine Michaëlius reported that "this island is the key and principal stronghold of the country, and needs to be settled first, as is already done."[17] In fact, since controlling Manhattan Island meant controlling the Hudson River, which reached deep into fur country, the island's value can be understood in terms of the value of the fur trade. It is perhaps not without coincidence that Schagen's letter reporting the purchase of Manhattan

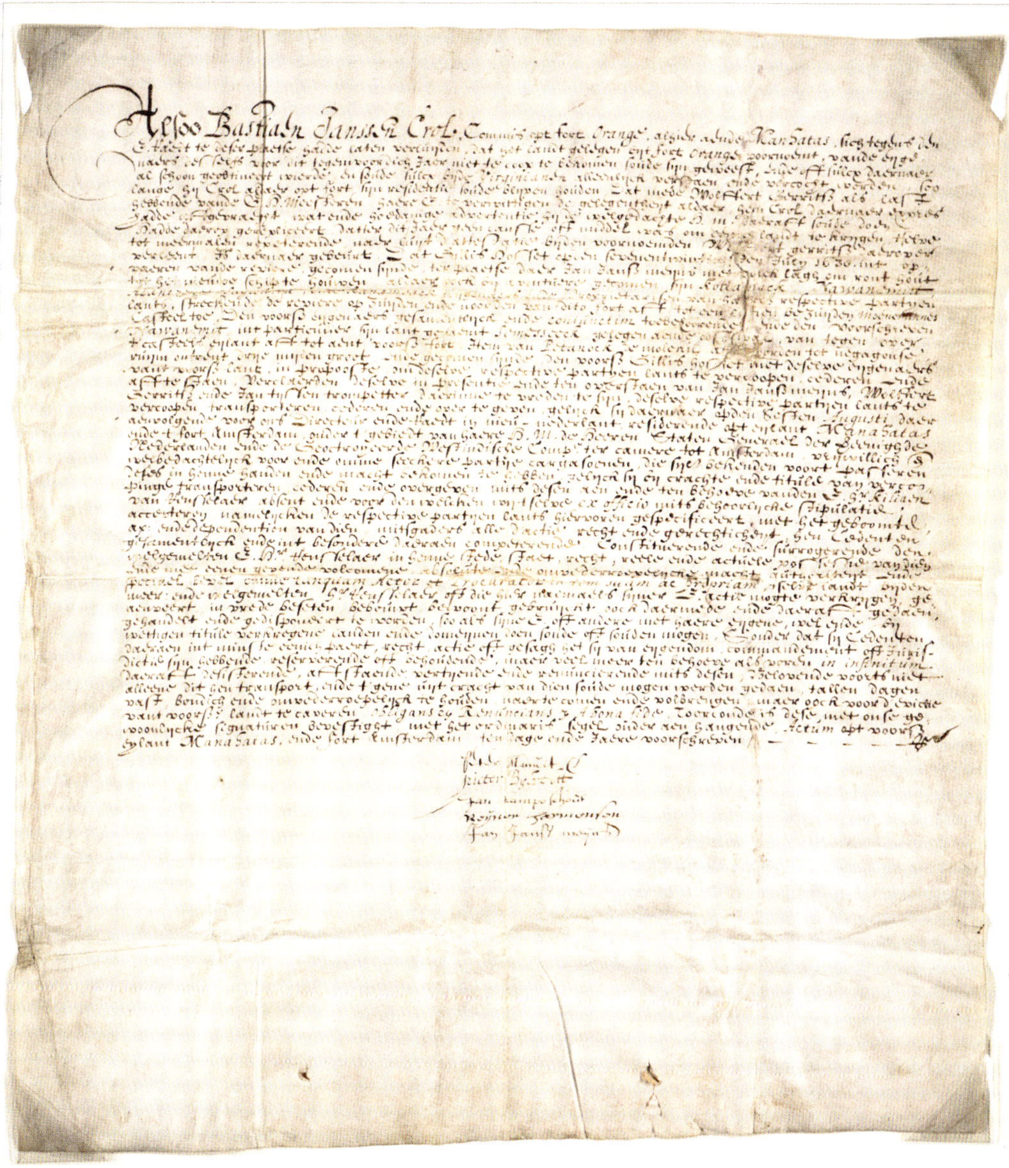

FIGURE 5.4. Contract of sale of land along the Hudson River from the Mohican Indians to Kiliaen van Rensselaer, August 6, 1630. New York State Library call number VSC7079 Item 1.

Island also reports the importation of 45,000 guilders worth of furs from New Netherland. It is possible that the Dutch attraction to Manhattan Island was also connected to the trade in wampum. The Dutch had early on discovered that wampum, or *sewant* as it was known among the Indians of Manhattan and vicinity, was highly valued by the Iroquoians and other inland tribes. These peoples exchanged various goods to coastal wampum makers for the beads. Although the heart of wampum production lay in eastern Long Island, it was manufactured throughout New York's coastal regions.[18] Whatever the case may have been regarding wampum, the Dutch certainly recognized at the time that they had purchased the Indians' land for a very low price, for Domine Michaëlius also noted, presumably referring to the purchase of Manhattan Island, that "for a small sum of money we can buy from them a large quantity of land," and elsewhere noted that there is land "which can be bought from the savages for a trifle."[19]

From the Indians' perspective, sixty guilders of trade goods was of enormous value to them. At the first, the Munsees may have valued European goods because they assigned spiritual or ceremonial power to items handled by those they animistically perceived as "other-than-human." But within a relatively short amount of time, this perception would have passed. While the exchange of goods still functioned in a socially cohesive way, the utilitarian function of the goods became important in native demand for certain products. Axes and hoes, for example, quickly became employed by Indians in place of native stone tools even though one oral tradition repeated by the Indians in the eighteenth century indicates that their forebears first wore axeheads received from Europeans around their necks as tokens of power.[20] For wampum producers, Indians who crafted the shell of the coastal whelk into strings of beads with significant social and religious power, the iron drills and awls they received greatly enhanced their manufacture of this vital artifact.[21] Duffels—a coarse cloth—had become an important item of trade in the 1620s. The Munsees began to substitute duffels for deerskins, using it for clothing during the day and for blankets at night. The native people preferred it in dark colors such as blue, grey, and black, possibly because they believed these would provide them better camouflage while hunting in the woods, but also likely because they attached dark colors to sources of power.[22] Demand for duffels also indicates the Indians' growing dependency upon European goods. As the Munsees increased the time they spent harvesting furs or producing wampum, they would have less time to produce basic necessities such as clothing, forcing them to acquire these items from the Dutch. De Rasière made clear the importance of duffels to the Indians when he suggested to the Company directors that if they could "supply me continually with duffels, I shall know how to get wampum and stock Fort Orange." De Rasière promised the directors ten thousand furs if they could provide him with sufficient duffels. The Munsees' northern neighbors, the Mohawks, prized it so highly that they announced they should not bother trading with the Dutch if they could not get it. It was so crucial, De Rasière pointed out, that without it they might lose the trade. "Why should we go hunting?" the Mohawks asked, "Half the time you have no cloth."[23] Thus, the goods offered by the Dutch for Manhattan Island satisfied important Munsee needs.

The transfer of Manhattan Island and other territories from the Munsees to the Dutch signified a great deal about the relationship between them. In the first place, they followed a formal protocol when conducting land transactions. Company regulations required Dutch officials to preside over agreements between Europeans and Indians and to create legal deeds. As historian Patricia Seed has shown, this reflected a long-standing Dutch tradition in which property conveyances took place before a district judge. Consequently, the native representatives were obligated to appear before the council at Fort Amsterdam for land sales. When circumstances prevented them from doing so, such as when the Unamis on Delaware Bay sold land, officials from the fort journeyed to the Indians' territory. The Indians were more than happy to oblige such formalities, since they too regarded these exchanges as significant affairs. Those who sold the land were usually tribal or village leaders or some other group representatives. For example, on July 12, 1630, Arromeauw, Tekwappo, and Sackwomeck, "co-owners of the land named Hobocanhackingh," according to one Dutch deed, appeared before the director and his council when they sold a tract of land to Michael Pauw. The next month, Waerhinnis Couwee (Wieromies), a minor Hackensack sachem, along with Krahorat, Tamekap, Tetemakwemama, Siearewach, Sackwewew, Wissipoock, and Saheinsios also presented themselves to Van Twiller and his council in order to seal the transfer of Staten Island to Michael Pauw. Similar transactions between Munsee leaders and Dutch officials occurred through the remainder of this period.[24]

Such formality in conducting land sales indicated that neither group saw the transaction as the ordinary exchange of land from one person or group of persons to another. Dutchmen could not simply move to New Netherland and purchase a tract of land from its indigenous owners. This was due, on the Dutch side, to West India Company recognition of Indian occupation of the land (remember Company dictates not to force "them thereto in the least or [take] possession by craft or fraud"), and the Dutch penchant for documenting such transactions. They insisted that colonial officials negotiate formal treaties ceding property rights to the Dutch. Therefore, individual Dutchmen could not purchase land directly from the Indians. The initial transfer of land was restricted to negotiated treaties between the West India Company and Indian representatives.

Munsees who signed documents ceding territory to the Dutch also viewed the transactions as carrying considerable consequence. Like Dutch officials, Indian leaders represented their people; any changes regarding their people's land had to be endorsed by them. However, the Indians' view of land ownership or sovereignty differed radically from that of the Dutch, and they initially understood these land transactions differently than did the Europeans. First, the Munsees did not recognize personal ownership of any particular tract of land. As a group, their band or village used different territories for hunting, fishing, agriculture, and habitation. When Indian leaders signed agreements "selling" their land, they were allowing for its joint use and occupancy by the Dutch and their own people. They did not envision a permanent transfer of land to the Dutch. For example, when Indians of Long Island sold a sizable portion of the island in 1639, they reserved the right to remain upon the land. While other deeds did not always specify such rights, it is clear from Munsee actions that they must have had similar intentions at other times. The Indians who sold Manhattan Island continued to live there, indicating that they assumed that they still retained possession of the land, not to mention sovereignty over it. Similarly, Munsee people also remained on Staten Island after selling it, and over the years, resold it several times.[25]

Furthermore, land transfers in the Munsees' perspective must be understood in terms of the Indians' emphasis upon social cohesion. In the perspective of the Munsees, as with so many other native people of the northeastern woodlands, maintaining social balance was of utmost importance. Establishing and continuing relationships held a greater priority than amassing wealth, but such relationship building usually included the exchange of goods. Colonial secretary Isaac de Rasière understood that the Indians always embellished trade with considerable ceremony and was careful to maintain it. "These people must . . . be kept on friendly terms by kindness and occasional small gifts," he wrote, and "one must be familiar with them and allow them to think that one trusts them fully." When a delegation of "thirty or forty" Indians presented De Rasière "with ten beavers," he responded by giving them "in return a fathom of duffel-cloth and a small quantity of beads, two hatchets, and a few other things." De Rasière noted that this "was done reciprocally in token of sworn friendship."[26] Transferring land, including the exchange of goods and attendant ceremonies, was a means to build and reinforce social relations. The Munsees saw the Dutch as more than just trading partners—they were allies and powerful neighbors with whom it was good to establish and maintain strong ties.

Moreover, land transfers served other purposes to the Munsees and did not reflect the natives' intentions to permanently alienate the land from themselves. As the Indians' population declined and their subsistence shifted from wide-ranging hunting to more intensive farming and wampum production, large hunting areas became less valuable. In the sachems' minds, the exchange of land for trade goods seemed reasonable. Such an exchange would also secure an alliance with the Dutch who would live among them and could help the Munsees defend themselves against their enemies. In fact, the same Indians on Long Island who reserved the right of occupancy in their deed of land in 1639, gained from the Dutch an agreement to protect them against their enemies. This pattern was not unusual for the Munsees or other Indian groups. As populations would increase or decrease for whatever reasons, native people would expand or contract their settlements and temporarily transfer unused land in the process. As population shifts again took place, land might be transferred back to the original occupants. In no case were the transfers considered permanent since Indian neighbors tended to recognize that possession or occupation of a territory was dependent upon the good graces of the group

Figure 5.5. L. F. Tantillo, *Visitors at Dusk*. A farmer and his family anticipate the arrival of Mohican fur traders in a dugout canoe. Reproduction courtesy of the artist.

who had earlier established sovereignty over the land. Also, with economic changes brought by the presence of the Dutch, the Munsees' growing dependency upon the Dutch may have compelled them to sell their lands, especially if they believed that doing so would ensure them continued access to European goods.[27]

But the exchange of land led to unpredictable changes in Native American relations with the Dutch. While the Munsees did not knowingly relinquish their permanent rights to the land when they sold it, they soon discovered that they had surrendered permanent control over the territory, along with their political sovereignty. Indeed, Dutch colonization brought some presumption that the Dutch were extending their sovereignty over all the lands claimed under the name of "New Netherland." The Company regulations for the colony that most clearly related to the Indians were ambiguous at times and did not clearly define the relationship of the Indians to the colony. On the whole, however, the regulations indicate that the West India Company claimed some political sovereignty over the indigenous inhabitants of the region, but also respected some degree of native autonomy for the sake of maintaining a successful trade relationship. These instructions included guidelines for Dutch interaction with their native hosts and required both settlers and colonial administrators to treat the Indians fairly and maintain peaceful interaction. The Amsterdam chamber commanded the Walloons in 1624 to "take especial care, whether in trading or in other matters, faithfully to fulfill their promises to the Indians or other neighbors and not to give them any offense without cause as regards their persons, wives, or property, on pain of being rigorously punished therefor."[28] The following year, Director Verhulst was similarly instructed to "see that no one do the Indians any harm or violence, deceive, mock, or contemn them in any way, but that in addition to good treatment they be shown honesty, faithfulness, and sincerity in all contracts, dealings, and intercourse, without being deceived by shortage of measure, weight, or number, and that throughout friendly relations with them be maintained."[29]

A second set of instructions to Verhulst a few months later provides a better indication of the relationship which the directors believed should exist between their colony and the Indians who lived within its boundaries. While on the one hand expecting justice accorded to their own people, the Company apparently respected tribal authority. In case any settler "suffer violence or be wronged by any Indian or native either in his person or with regard to the property entrusted to him, they shall notify the tribe to whom such Indian belongs of the wrong done and the person who committed it, demanding that he be punished therefor and that our people be notified of the punishment." Ultimately, though, the Dutch reserved final political authority for themselves. The Company ordered that Verhulst "advise" the Indians that if they did not carry out justice, then the administrators, "for [the colony's] protection" should "get hold of the delinquent and have him punished by the Council according to his deserts and as will be right and reasonable."[30]

It also appears that the Dutch believed their sovereignty extended over the natural resources of the region as well, thus challenging whatever natural rights to the resources the Munsees, as prior occupants of the land, could claim. Like the Virginia Company, the WIC directors dreamed of uncovering an abundance of wealth in the New World. They were well aware of the wealth that the Spaniards had found in Mexico and South America. Believing that the Indians could help them discover these natural riches, the Company instructed that Verhulst, "by small present," should "seek to draw the Indians to our service, in order to learn from them the secrets of that region and the condition of the interior." Apparently not looking for

DUTCH TRADERS AT MANHATTAN.

FIGURE 5.6. "Dutch Traders at Manhattan." PR 068 Subject fil, box 21, f. Colonial Period, Gen.; negative no. 71357. Collection of The New-York Historical Society.

trade opportunities but actually new resources to develop themselves, the directors ordered that Verhulst "shall cause diligent inquiry to be made among the Indians whether there are no sulphur or salt mines, or whether any of the Indians have anything that looks like metal, such as gold, silver, copper, iron, lead, etc., asking them where they got it." Furthermore, the company directors worried about European competitors encroaching on their territory, for they wanted to discover from the Indians "when our cattle arrive . . . whether they have ever seen or heard of any animals like them."[31]

In selling Manhattan Island and other properties, the Munsees did not intend to permanently transfer their land to the Dutch. Instead, they granted the Dutch the privilege of sharing the land with them. The Munsees could not foresee the future, however. What they did not anticipate was that the Dutch presence corresponded to a conflict of claims over control of the whole region. From the moment that the West India Company established Europeans settlements and sought to purchase land from the Indians, the Munsee people would struggle to maintain their own autonomy while increasingly being forced to recognize Dutch control. Ultimately, the importance of the selling of Manhattan had more to do with the Indians' loss of sovereignty in the long run than their loss of land in the short run. Neither was intended by the Munsee people. However, after decades of contact with Europeans, the Munsees experienced growing dependency upon European goods and suffered increasing population losses through disease and warfare. The effects wrought upon Munsee society as a result of Dutch colonization made the temporary transfer of Manhattan Island and other Munsee lands a permanent one. The Munsees could not have foreseen the permanent loss of their lands to the Dutch. And if the Dutch could have imagined the eventual loss of that same land to the English, none of them could have anticipated that Manhattan Island would become the metropolis that emerged in the nineteenth and twentieth centuries.

NOTES

Portions of this chapter first appeared as part of chapter 3, "Trade and Settlement, 1624–1638," in Paul Otto, *The Dutch Munsee Encounter in America: The Struggle for Sovereignty in the Hudson Valley* (New York: Berghahn Books, 2006) and are used here by permission of the author and the publisher.

1. Lias WIC, inventory no. 5751 II (ingekomen 1626), Nationaal Archief, den Haag.

2. A fraudulent treaty can be found in the New York State archives. See Charles T. Gehring, William A. Starna, and William N. Fenton, "The Tawagonshi Treaty of 1613: The Final Chapter," *New York History* 68, no. 4 (October 1987): 381.

3. Charles Gehring, "Dutch Colonial Manuscripts," *de Halve Maen* 54, no. 3 (Fall-Winter 1979): 5.

4. Otto, *The Dutch-Munsee Encounter,* 4, 20 n. 7.

5. See *The Dutch-Munsee Encounter,* chapter 2, for a full account of these trade voyages and encounters.

6. Resolution of the States of Holland and Westfriesland, 21 April 1622, in *Documents Relative to the Colonial History of New York: Procured in Holland, England, and France* (hereafter *DRCHNY*), ed. E. B. O'Callaghan, vol. 1, *Holland Documents: 1–8, 1603–1656* (Albany: Weed, Parsons and Company, 1856), vol. 1, 28.

7. Van Cleaf Bachman, *Peltries or Plantations: The Economic Policies of the Dutch West India Company in New Netherland, 1623–1639,* Johns Hopkins University Studies in Historical and Political Science, 87th ser., no. 2 (Baltimore: Johns Hopkins University Press, 1969), 57–58, 57 n. 39, 58 n. 40; Oliver Rink, *Holland on the Hudson: An Economic and Social History of Dutch New York* (Ithaca: Cornell University Press; and Cooperstown: New York State Historical Association, 1986), 69–76.

8. Instructions for Director Willem Verhulst, in *Documents Relating to New Netherland, 1624–1626, in the Henry E. Huntington Library* (hereafter *DRNN*), ed. and trans. A. J. F. van Laer (San Marino: Henry E. Huntington Library and Art Gallery, 1924), 51–55.

9. Further Instructions for Director Verhulst, in *DRNN,* 105–106; emphasis mine.

10. For debate over who actually purchased Manhattan Island from the Indians, see Charles A. Weslager, "Did Minuit Buy Manhattan Island from the Indians?," *de Halve Maen* 43, no. 3 (October 1968): 5–6; and Charles T. Gehring, "Peter Minuit's Purchase of Manhattan Island—New Evidence," *de Halve Maen* 55, no. 1 (Spring 1980): 6–7, 17.

11. Johannes de Laet, "New World," in *Narratives of New Netherland, 1609–1664* (hereafter *NNN*), ed. J. Franklin Jameson (New York: Charles Scribner's Sons, 1909), 45 and 53–54. Other evidence includes a remonstrance of the Ambassadors of the States General to King Charles I, dated 1633, which included the statement that the Dutch had "purchased from the native inhabitants and paid for a certain island called also Manathans." *DRCHNY,* vol. 1, 56. In a letter from the Assembly of the XIX to the States General, 25 October 1634, they noted that the "Company purchased from the Indians, who were the indubitable owners thereof, the Island of the Manhattes." *DRCHNY,* vol. 1, 94. Van Wassenaer implied that the island had been purchased when he reported that Minuit "took up his residence in the midst of a nation called Manates, building a fort there, to be called Amsterdam." "Historisch Verhael," October 1628, in *NNN,* 88.

12. Peter Francis Jr., "The Beads That Did *Not* Buy Manhattan Island," *New York History* 67, no. 1 (January 1986): 5–22; "Melyn Papers," in *Collections of the New-York Historical Society*, 1913, v.46, 124. During this early period, neither firearms nor alcohol seem to have been a part of the lower Hudson trade.

13. E. B. O'Callaghan, *History of New Netherland; or, New York under the Dutch* (New York: D. Appleton, 1846), vol 1, 103–104.

14. Special Instructions for the Engineer and Surveyor Cryn Fredericksz. and for the Director and Council regarding the building of the fort and the houses, April 22, 1625, in *DRNN,* 140; Van Deursen, *Plain Lives,* 4–5, 15, 23, 27, 28.

15. Jaap Jacobs, "Soldiers of the Company: The Military Personnel of the West India Company in New Netherland," in *Jacob Leisler's, Atlantic World in the Later Seventeenth Century. Essays on Religion, Militia Trade, and Networks by Jaap Jacobs, Claudia Schnurmann, David W. Voorhees, and Hermann Wellenreuther,* ed. Herman Wellenreuther (Münster: LIT Verlag, 2009), 20–25.

16. Isaack De Rasière noted having paid about two guilders for a beaver skin and five guilders per fathom of wampum. De Rasière to the Directors of the Amsterdam Chamber, 23 September 1626, in *DRNN,* 215–19, 251.

17. Michaëlius to Van Foreest, 8 August 1628, in A. Eekhof, *Jonas Michaëlius: Founder of the Church in New Netherland* (Leiden: A. W. Sijthoff's Publishing Company, 1926), 109.

18. Paul Otto, "Henry Hudson, the Munsees, and the Wampum Revolution," in *Henry Hudson, New Netherland, and Atlantic History*, ed. Jaap Jacobs and Lou Roper, forthcoming.

19. Michaëlius to Van Foreest, 8 August 1628, in Eekhof, *Jonas Michaëlius,* 110; Michaëlius to Smoutius, 11 August 1628, in Eekhof, *Jonas Michaëlius,* 136.

20. Otto, *The Dutch-Munsee Encounter,* 57.

21. Otto, "Henry Hudson, the Munsees, and the Wampum Revolution."

22. Adriaen van der Donck, *A Description of New Netherland,* ed. Charles T. Gehring and William A. Starna, trans. Diederik Willem Goedhuys (Lincoln: University of Nebraska Press, 2008), 79–80; De Rasière to the Directors of the Amsterdam Chamber, 23 September 1626, in *DRNN,* 192–95, 228–31; De Rasière to Blommaert, 1628(?), in *NNN,* 106; Alfred Cave, "The Pequot War," in *Native Americans of the Northeast: Culture, History, and the Contemporary,* ed. Colin G. Calloway and Barry O'Connell (Amherst: University of Massachusetts Press, 1996), 62–63; Margriet de Roever, "Merchandises for New Netherland: A Look at Dutch Articles for Barter with the Native American Population," in *One Man's Trash is Another Man's Treasure: The Metamorphosis of the European Utensil in the New World,* ed. Alexandra van Dongen (Rotterdam: Museum Boymans-Van Beunigen, 1995), 78–82.

23. De Rasière to the Directors of the Amsterdam Chamber, 23 September 1626, in *DRNN,* 224–31.

24. Patricia Seed, *Ceremonies of Possession in Europe's Conquest of the New World, 1492–1640* (New York: Cambridge University Press, 1995), 170; Charles T. Gehring, trans. and ed., *Land Papers, NYHM,* vols. GG, HH, and II (Baltimore: Genealogical Publishing Co., 1980), 1–7. As Robert Grumet has demonstrated, Wieromies's presence represented a typical pattern of Indian land sales in which those who signed the deeds were usually significant representatives or leaders of one level or another within native society. Robert Grumet, "'We Are Not So Great Fools': Changes in Upper Delawaran Socio-Political Life, 1630–1758" (PhD diss., Rutgers, The State University of New Jersey, 1979), 109, 200. Furthermore, these transactions were formally recorded in detailed written deeds, typical of Dutch practice, Seed, *Ceremonies of Possession,* 160–78.

25. *Land Papers,* ed. Gehring, 9. This corresponds with other interpretations of European-Indian affairs in other colonies. See, for example, William Cronon, *Changes in the Land: Indians, Colonists, and the Ecology of New England* (New York: Hill and Wang, 1983), 62–67. Other writers disagree. Robert Grumet, for example, argues that if a Munsee village or clan was decimated by disease and war, the Indians would sell their land and unite with another band until they restored their population. When strengthened, they would attempt to buy or win back their land. "Selling" their land represented a kind of peacetime

treaty in which they acknowledged the "rights" of the stronger power to the property and received some token goods in return. They could justifiably win back such land during war. Grumet, "'We Are Not So Great Fools,'" 264; Robert S. Grumet, "The Selling of Lenapehoking," *Bulletin, Archaeological Society of New Jersey* 44 (1989): 2–5.

26. De Rasière to the Directors of the Amsterdam Chamber, 23 September 1626, in *DRNN,* 212, 192–95; Otto, *The Dutch-Munsee Encounter,* 15–16.

27. Robert Grumet suggests that Munsee leaders "probably hoped that Lenape cooperation would buy European protection and forbearance." "Selling of Lenapehoking," 4; *Land Papers,* ed. Gehring, 9.

28. Provisional Regulations for the Colonists, in *DRNN,* 17.

29. Instructions for Willem Verhulst, in *DRNN,* 39.

30. Further Instructions for Director Willem Verhulst, in *DRNN,* 110–13.

31. Instructions for Willem Verhulst, in *DRNN,* 75–76.

Chapter Six

Crimen Laesae Maiestatis or Abuse of Power?

The 1647 Trial of Cornelis Melijn and Jochem Pietersz Kuijter

Jaap Jacobs

Petrus Stuyvesant comes down to us as a larger-than-life figure. Legend has him as a peg-legged tyrant. Although the peg leg is genuine, Jaap Jacobs explains that a full picture of Stuyvesant is considerably more complicated. From a single trial, Jacobs shows us how legal and governmental authority was understood and exercised in New Netherland. Jacobs notes the eighteenth-century shift in political philosophy from the top down (divine right, monarchical) authority to ascending governmental authority in which the power is lodged with the people.

When new Director General Petrus Stuyvesant arrived in New Netherland in May 1647, he declared that he would "be and govern like a father over his children, for the profit of the chartered West India Company, this citizenry and this land."[1] The metaphor of government or monarch as father and the subjects as children was a common trope in the early modern age, and its use by Stuyvesant, by extension an official of one of the very few republics of Europe, should not come as a surprise. The same metaphor was employed by Sir Robert Filmer in his *Patriarcha, or the Natural Power of Kings,* written at the time of the English Civil War, but published decades later. Filmer defended the royal claim to absolute power with a reference to the authority of a father over his family, by using biblical models, such as Noah who divided the three continents of the Old World among his sons, making the power of kings hereditary, absolute, and divine in a single stroke. The New Testament, closer to Stuyvesant's Calvinism, also provides examples, as do Seneca and Aristotle. For Stuyvesant, the metaphor did not only point to power and authority, but also to care. He was responsible for the welfare of the colonists, in the same way that a father had to take care of his children.[2]

Another metaphor regarding the relation between government and subjects can be found in the correspondence between the Amsterdam directors and director general and council of New Netherland. In April 1648, the directors wrote, "that the people have run very wild and are to be found without discipline." Stuyvesant and his council had to restore this, as "a tree grown too long and having run wild must be pruned in proper fashion and slowly bent and brought into a good form."[3] In this metaphor, the Amsterdam directors position themselves as owner of a garden, with their servants in the colony as the gardeners. But did the colonists see it the same way? In their writings the organic metaphor is neither confirmed nor denied.

Figure 6.1. Portrait of Petrus Stuyvesant, attributed to Hendrick Couturier. Oil on wood panel, 22½ x 17½ inches; accession no. 1909.2. Collection of The New-York Historical Society.

Their role was that of the obstinate tree, who pleads with the owner of the garden to replace the gardener.

Especially during the first five of his seventeen years as director general, Stuyvesant collided with some of the colonists. Several aspects played a role in these conflicts: unclear structures of government, personal antagonisms, disparate ideas on the forms of colonial government, and different opinions on the source of governmental authority. The most common idea in medieval times was that sovereign powers, including government and justice, emanated from God. Those powers were put into the hands of rulers, such as princes, kings, and monarchs, who were entitled to delegate part of their powers to lower governmental bodies. This way of thinking about the ultimate source of authority remained basically intact, if not unchallenged, in the early modern age. Even though the United Provinces formed a republic, with sovereignty having been transferred from an individual (the Spanish monarch) to collective bodies (the States General and provincial estates), the basic principle of descending authority, that is, the top-down model, was unchanged.[4]

Vestiges of the principle of descending authority can be discerned in New Netherland as well. The States General had through a charter transferred sovereign prerogatives to the West India Company, which in turn had empowered the Amsterdam Chamber, which appointed the highest official in the colony.[5] Even local officials derived part of their authority directly from the divine source. During his conflict with Everardus Bogardus, Director Willem Kieft found it necessary to inform the minister that his attitude toward "your magistrate, placed over you by God" was not acceptable. Of course, the conflict between Kieft and Bogardus was considerably more complex, but Kieft's remark shows the extent to which the ascending theory of government was adhered to, at least by magistrates.[6] Yet a counter theory also existed, both in the Dutch Republic and in New Netherland. Ever since the rediscovery of Aristotle in the second half of the thirteenth century, the theory of descending governmental authority had been challenged by the theory of ascending governmental authority, in which the source of sovereignty and authority is placed with the people. In practice, however, the balance between the two was always shifting to and fro, with variations over time and place, depending on the vagaries of political situations. The terminology employed depended upon the vehemence of the conflicts at the time, and both theories were not considered as incompatible as modern Western views on democracy would make us believe. The sphere of descending authority was often

Figure 6.2. "Fort Amsterdam, Now the Battery, in Kieft's Days" ([S. l.: P. Sander], c. 1909). Hudson River Steamboat and Navigation Ephemera Collection, 1866–1964, William S. Clark, collector. New York State Library call number SC23080.

confined to specific duties of the monarch, such as military defense against external enemies and defending the faith, whereas the sphere of ascending authority could be seen as limited to a local community's say over its own, local affairs. It was not until the eighteenth century that, under the influence of the political philosophy of the Enlightenment, the idea of popular sovereignty came to be extended to the level of nations, eventually becoming incompatible with the descending theory and culminating in the age of democratic revolutions.[7]

Yet in the sixteenth and seventeenth centuries, this theoretical incompatibility was often mitigated by hybrid structures and practices of government. The privileges granted to cities by monarchs over time became to be perceived as rights instead of favors. And with some justification, as they were only revoked in times of political crises, such as in the case of Charles V and the city of Ghent in 1540, when violence had driven away the use of arguments and made it into different kind of struggle. By that time it did not matter who was right, but who was stronger.

Few people in the Western world nowadays locate the source of sovereignty at the divine level, as the idea of popular sovereignty has become the most common. This is reflected in the historiography. Ever since Edmund B. O'Callaghan published the first scholarly history of New Netherland in 1846, Stuyvesant's conflict with the New Netherland population has been depicted as the tyrannical subjugation of freedom-loving colonists. The conflict is even seen as a precursor of the American Revolution.[8] But the modern, often implicit, rejection of the divine origin of governmental authority is inappropriate for the seventeenth century and leads to anachronistic and teleological interpretations. It offers little help when we try to assess Stuyvesant within the framework of his own age.

Considering how much importance historians have attached to the conflict between the colonists and the West India Company in the years of Stuyvesant, it is remarkable that few have

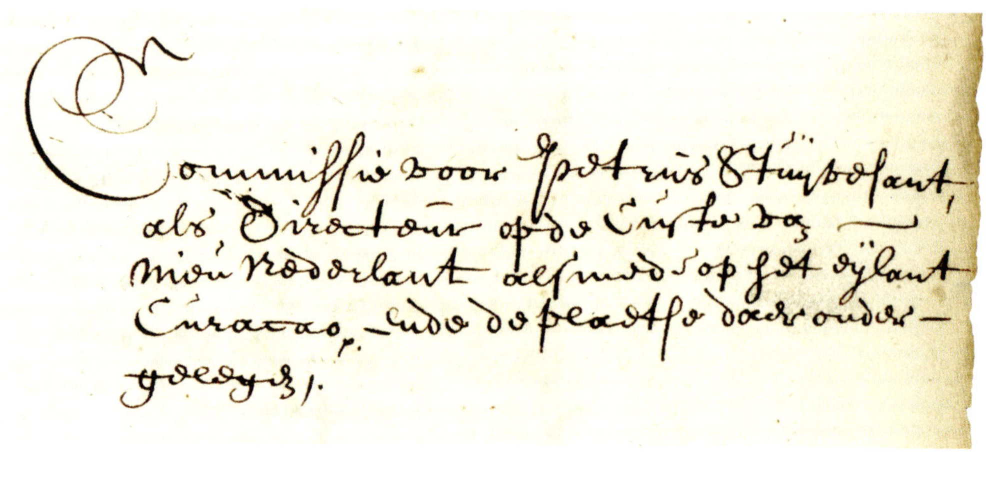

Commissie voor Petrus Stuyvesant, als Directeur op de Custe van Nieu Nederlant als mede op het eylant Curacao, ende de plaetse daer onder gehoorende.

Figure 6.3. Commission of Petrus Stuyvesant as Director General: Order Books of the States General, 1646. Nationaal Archief (National Archives of the Netherlands), 1.01.06, inv.nr. 12272, fol. 201.

analyzed how the newly arrived director general first became involved in the conflict. Edmund B. O'Callaghan, the first historian of New Netherland, introduces Stuyvesant as a haughty and authoritarian soldier, who on arrival immediately began to restore order and discipline. In the view of O'Callaghan, Stuyvesant thus clamped down on the first sign of colonists behaving badly and thereby set the tone for the years to come. But although O'Callaghan was the first to use primary sources to describe the trial of Cornelis Melijn and Jochem Pietersz Kuijter, his bias toward the colonists, his limited translation skills, and his insufficient understanding of Dutch judicial and administrative procedures, severely hampered his interpretation. On the whole, most historians have followed O'Callaghan, usually without looking at the Melijn-Kuijter trial in detail, but only focusing on the outcome. Hence, there is sufficient reason to take a new look at this trial and the way it progressed, and to include in the discussion the question whether any of the parties involved could have made different decisions at specific times.[9]

The new director general was of course aware that his predecessor, Director Willem Kieft, had been involved in serious problems with the colonists. Although the instruction to Stuyvesant did not specify it, it was very likely the intention of the directors in Amsterdam to improve relations by recalling Kieft. Restoring the authority of the West India Company was probably intended as well, and this implied that it was Stuyvesant's task not to involve himself in the quarrels of the past. Willem Kieft would have to answer for himself after returning to patria, and it did not befit his successor to judge him. That could also hamper building up good relations with the colonists.

After his arrival on May 11, 1647, a couple of weeks elapsed before Stuyvesant called a meeting of the council. The meeting of May 27 approved the promotion of some Company servants, while others were appointed to new positions. These were hardly controversial decisions. The first inkling of the new director general's being dragged into an existing conflict came on June 6. Willem Kieft, who would very likely not leave the colony until later that summer, put in a remarkable request. He asked director general and council to summon some of the colonists to the meeting in order to interrogate them. The council minutes do not specify the names of the colonists nor the topic of the examination, but the former director was clearly preparing his defense and was gathering material for that. The crucial question was who was to be held responsible for the decision in February 1643 to attack a group of Indians in Pavonia, the massacre that had sparked off the first war with the Munsees.[10]

Director general and council acceded to Kieft's request and unanimously decided that the witnesses would be summoned to appear before the full board, not just before a committee. That is an indication that the matter was considered important. Also interesting to note is that it was a unanimous decision. Unlike what is usually thought, director general Stuyvesant could not act on his own, but had to obtain the consent of the council in many matters. As the chief executive officer, he would then carry out the decisions, sign letters, et cetera. Neither were the councilors, as is often supposed, handpicked yes-men. They were appointed by the directors of the Amsterdam Chamber, and Stuyvesant could exert little influence on the choice of his superiors. Councilors had the right, even the duty, to have their dissenting opinions recorded in the council minutes, so as to give account of themselves to their superiors.[11] Differences of opinion are frequent in the council minutes, yet the decision to grant Kieft his request was unanimous, and, unfortunately, that means that the motivation for director general and council to act in this case remains unspecified. They must have been aware that Kieft's main reason to collect eyewitness accounts was that he obviously could not do so once he had left New

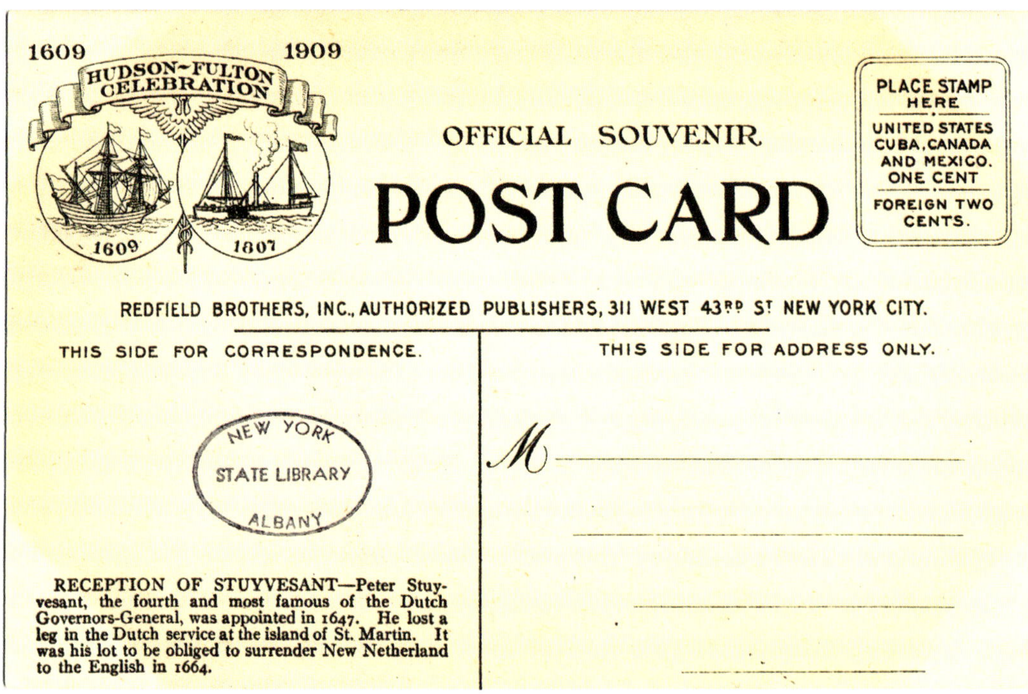

FIGURE 6.4. Float—"Reception of Peter Stuyvesant." Hudson-Fulton Celebration Commission Official Post Card no. 19. New York: Redfield Bothers, c. 1909. New York State Library Postcard Collection, call number: QC16510.

Netherland. But his request also indicated that the consent of the council was required to obtain these accounts, as the witnesses were unwilling. Thus, director general and council must have been aware that once Kieft had made his request, a decision either way would involve them, at least procedurally, in a conflict that was not theirs. But turning down Kieft, their West India Company colleague, in what seemed a reasonable request, was difficult. Not only would it further damage the reputation of the government of the Company in New Netherland, but also, who could object to having the truth put down in writing? That was, after all, the duty of any honorable man.

The first witness Kieft called was Jan Evertsz Bout, and to him, and other colonists, Kieft's resort to legal action must have appeared quite differently. It put new fuel on the fiery conflict, which had died down a bit in anticipation of the arrival of the new director general. Bout had earlier served on the Twelve Men and the Eight Men, advisory boards set up by Kieft and his council in 1641 and 1643 respectively. During the First Munsee War, his leased farm in Pavonia had been lost, and Bout subsequently relocated to Long Island, where he had become magistrate in the newly started village of Breuckelen. Yet he had shown himself obstinate and recalcitrant to authority in the past. Living up to his reputation, he refused to testify before director general and council. As his refusal was interpreted by director general and council as contempt of court, he was arrested, presumably meaning house arrest, not necessarily confinement in the dungeon of Fort Amsterdam. From the perspective of Bout and others, the decision to approve Kieft's request may have looked different. Bout had already, four years earlier, about a month after the attack on the Indians in Pavonia, made a declaration about a conversation he had had with Kieft. There was no need to do so again. Bout may have considered that Kieft was simply trying to trick him and others into making contradictory statements, in order to attack their credibility.[12]

Whether Bout gave in and agreed to testify or not is unclear. He is not mentioned in the council minutes in the following weeks, but he did stand as a baptismal witness, alongside Judith Stuyvesant, in August, and in September was chosen as one of the Nine Men.[13] This omission in the council minutes need not surprise us. In fact, the character of record keeping in the seventeenth century does not allow a complete reconstruction of the subsequent events involving Cornelis Melijn and Jochem Pietersz Kuijter, either. The minutes of director general and council for the most part contain resolutions and do not give a complete picture of what went on in the weekly Thursday meetings. Rather than present a smooth and persuasive narrative in which suppositions are presented as certainties, it is necessary to distinguish between what part of the historical record is unambiguous and where uncertainties and speculations begin.

A week after approving Kieft's request and arresting Bout, director general and council convened for their next meeting. Although other matters may have been discussed as well, only two decisions were made. First, to subject Michel Picquet to torture as he refused to confess, despite the fact that witnesses had sworn that he had slandered Kieft and threatened Stuyvesant. Torture was not cruel or unusual in such cases, but was a requirement before the case could be concluded. Picquet's remarks may be an indication that some enmity against former and current director had arisen among the colonists, possibly emanating from the decision the week before. The other decision was to punish two sailors who had stayed on shore without leave. At the close of the meeting, the councilors were presented a petition of Jochem Pietersz Kuijter and Cornelis Melijn. They requested permission to submit "all of the former councilors with the exception of the honorable director" to an interrogation, and they had attached copies of the interrogation as well.[14]

Cornelis Melijn and Jochem Pietersz Kuijter had been members of the Eight Men and had shown themselves intractable opponents of Kieft in the preceding years. They replied to Kieft's attempt to gather exonerating depositions by asking director general and council permission to interrogate former council members, as they too were gathering ammunition for the impending litigation in patria. The essential difference was one of status: Kieft was a former magistrate questioning subjects, but Melijn and Kuijter were subjects wishing to interrogate former magistrates.[15]

Melijn and Kuijter submitted their petition in multiple copies at the end of the meeting of the council on June 13, 1647, too late for discussion that day. The next morning, Stuyvesant wrote a letter to the council members, pointing out that each of them separately had received a copy and would thus have read and deliberated upon it. As the reply to the petition could have far-reaching consequences, he asked the council members to contemplate four questions and come to the next meeting prepared with answers. In doing so, the director general adhered to the usual procedure: the director general in his role as chair of the meetings decided which issues were on the agenda, and put these before the councilors, either orally during the meeting, or in writing beforehand. The latter was preferred when important matters were at stake. The councilors would then make up their minds and express their opinion, usually called *advies* or *advijs* [advice], again either orally or in writing. Depending on the outcome, decisions would be taken unanimously or by majority. This meant that the director general could be outvoted, as actually happened on a number of occasions. The rationale behind this procedure was to come to the best decision and to inform the WIC directors in the fatherland of individual opinions. Yet in formulating the questions, and thereby determining what would be discussed, the director general could steer the decision process. The questions Stuyvesant sent to his councilors this time clearly indicate what he thought the far-reaching consequences might be.[16]

Stuyvesant's first question was whether there was any precedent for subjects interrogating their magistrates. Second, whether this would not have evil consequences and worse would be to follow if "two malignant private subjects" would usurp this right. Third, would it not lead to a repetition against current magistrates and would these two thereby not arrogate superiority over director general and council? And fourthly Stuyvesant, taking a specific legal-institutional perspective, returned to the question of who was responsible for the murderous attack on the Native Americans in Pavonia. If the directors in Amsterdam had written to Kieft and his councilors about imposing a contribution on the Indians, could director general and council force the secretary, entrusted with such secrets, to answer questions relating to the decision?[17] It could lead to making public a secret decision by their superiors. The secretary was still Cornelis van Tienhoven, the same man it had been when Kieft was in charge. It is likely that he foresaw how an interrogation would endanger his position, regardless of what it might reveal. Considering the close relationship he developed with Stuyvesant later on, he may have indicated to the director general what dangers lay ahead, and he could thus have been responsible for the fourth question.[18]

Yet the first three questions already indicate what the bigger issue was: Stuyvesant considered the request of Melijn and Kuijter an attempt to undermine governmental authority in general and that of the West India Company and himself in particular. Whether Kieft was right or wrong was not an issue that concerned him as yet. But the fact that the men to be questioned were former council members elevated the request to a different level. It would necessitate breaking the confidentiality of the council chamber, which prevented dissenting opinions from becoming public.[19] It is more difficult to surmise what the opinion of Kuijter and Melijn might have been, as the petition is no longer extant. Yet two points require our attention. First, their request concerned interrogatories to be put to all the former councilors *with the exception of Kieft* (emphasis added). As Kieft was their target, he could not be expected to produce evidence against himself. As a consequence, the only men who could provide answers were the former councilors, former *fiscael* Cornelis van der Hoykens (about to leave for the fatherland), councilor Johannes La Montage (who was continued in his position), current *fiscael* Hendrick van Dijck (who had been military commander in 1643), and secretary Cornelis van Tienhoven (who did not actually have a vote in the council, but was *ex officio* present at all the meetings).

Second, drawing up petitions and interrogatories was usually done by notaries or lawyers, as it required being acquainted with the legal formulas. As neither Melijn nor Kuijter had any legal training, it seems likely that in this case, as is more obvious from later documents, they were assisted by Adriaen van der Donck. Van der Donck had spent a couple of years at university, but there is no indication that he had actually obtained a degree.[20] He had a few years of experience as *schout* of Rensselaerswyck, but lacked experience in government. Kuijter, Melijn, and Van der Donck may have regarded the interrogatories as actions in a civil suit and have been ignorant of the extent to which it impinged on governmental authority. The reaction of director general and council may therefore have caught them by surprise.

Stuyvesant reconvened the council on the afternoon of June 14 to discuss his questions. In accordance with the usual procedure, the secretary read the answers aloud: director general first, vice-director second, followed by the other councilors as ranked by seniority. Stuyvesant's answers were unequivocal: (1) no, it is unheard of; (2) it would be dangerous; (3) repetition is to be expected, although Stuyvesant added "that I have little fear on that score"; (4) absolutely not. Subsequently, the prepared answers of vice director Dinclagen, *fiscael* Van Dijck, lieutenant Newton, commander Looper, commander Jelmer Thomasz, *equipagemeester* (superintendent of equipments) Paulus Leendertsz van der Grift, and skipper Jan Claesz Bol were read aloud. While the phrasing varied, all turned out to agree with Stuyvesant. Three of the councilors even went farther than the director general and suggested charging Kuijter and Melijn with sedition.[21]

Yet no measure to that effect was decided upon as yet. Instead, director general and council tried to de-escalate. The anger and indignation of the new magistrates remained veiled behind a restrained legally phrased reaction. Although director general and council perceived hostility in the tone of the petition, as it voiced the suspicion of partiality, they decided in favor of interrogations. But Melijn and Kuijter would not obtain these until a number of conditions had been met. The most important of these were that Melijn and Kuijter proved in writing that: (1) they acted on behalf of the entire community, and (2) they had been authorized by the directors in Amsterdam to gather information pertaining to the cause of the war. Of course, director general and council were fully aware that Melijn and Kuijter would have a problem fulfilling the first condition and were unable to meet the second condition. In this way, director general and council may have hoped to achieve three aims: (1) to divert the request of Kuijter and Melijn to higher authorities, (2) to provide the directors with the required information, and (3) to show themselves impartial—at least in their own minds—in a conflict that was not theirs.[22]

If Stuyvesant and his councilors expected that this answer would smother the reigniting conflict, they were mistaken. But the impetus for continuation came from an unexpected side:

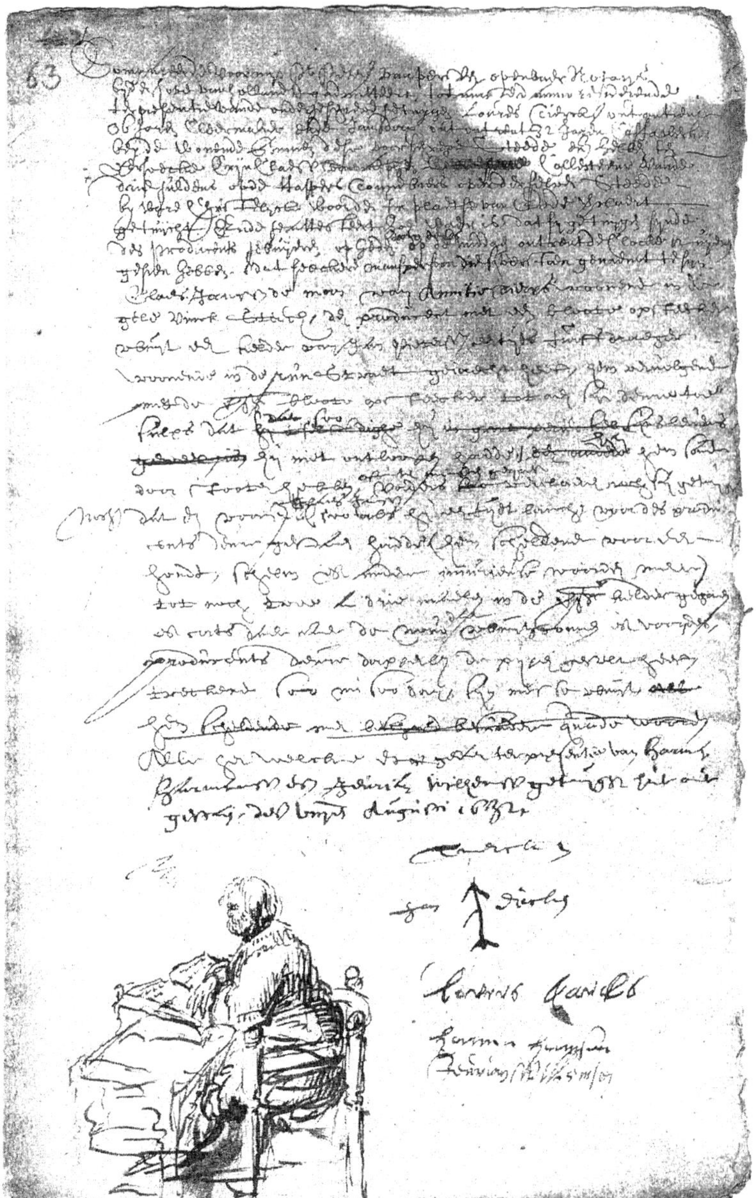

FIGURE 6.5. Sketch of Dutch notary. According to Charles Gehring, "It is rare to find expressions of artistic talent in the usually sober and dry administrative records of the seventeenth century. Imagine the surprise when the accompanying drawing appeared upon turning the page of Pieter Perssens protocol of notarial records. It shows the notary sitting at his desk reviewing his records. Not only does the drawing offer a rare glimpse into the world of this important position in the Dutch judicial system, but it also exhibits the artistic talent of his clerk. Although Notary Perssens records survive in the Municipal Archives of Amsterdam for everyone to read, further artistic expressions of his anonymous clerk are unknown." Courtesy of the New York State Library.

Figure 6.6. L. F. Tantillo, *The Ferry.* By the 1640s Dutch colonists had started to build homesteads outside of Fort Orange (now Albany, NY). They settled on both sides of the Hudson, farming the lands of the Patroon, Kiliaen van Rensselaer, the employer of Adriaen van der Donck. Reproduction courtesy of the artist.

the former director. Willem Kieft had been present at many of the meetings of the council, but not at those concerning the request of Melijn and Kuijter, doubtlessly because he was the subject of their investigation Yet four days after the decision of director general and council, he poured fuel on the smoldering embers by pointing out that Melijn and Kuijter had, together with others, back in 1644 sent a calumnious letter to the directors in Amsterdam, containing slanderous remarks.[23] Kieft now petitioned director general and council to order Melijn and Kuijter to prove these. Very likely, he was spurred on by the repetition of these allegations in the proposed interrogatories. It may have been his intention to obtain a conviction, or at least a charge, for slander, so as to weaken the position of his opponents in any subsequent procedures in the Dutch Republic.[24]

Considering their earlier restraint, it is surprising that director general and council acceded to Kieft's request, the more so because of the legal impossibility that now arose. In order to fully clear themselves of the charge of slandering the former director, Kuijter and Melijn had to gather evidence from the former councilors. Yet director general and council had prohibited this by making permission of the Amsterdam directors a prerequisite. Caught in this legal bind, Kuijter and Melijn must have become aware that their chances of a good outcome of procedures in New Netherland were not great. There is another remarkable point here as well. In reply to Kieft's petition, director general and council on June 18 ordered the *fiscael* to "institute an action for slander" against Kuijter and Melijn. In designating the *fiscael* to be plaintiff, instead of the injured party, namely, Kieft himself, the issue at stake was moved from civil to criminal law. That indicates how serious the director general and council took it.

On June 24, Kuijter appeared in the council meeting with a written reply, in which all of the points Kieft had raised were answered. These concerned details of events during the war in 1643 and 1644, on which Melijn and Kuijter did not yield an inch. The latter part of their reply contains references to some classical authors: Livy, Propertius, Ambrosius, Aristides, and Xenophon.[25] There is little in the background of Kuijter and Melijn that points to much education, and it is therefore assumed that Adriaen van der Donck, possibly in collaboration with minister Everardus Bogardus, played a part in drawing up the letter.[26] Melijn and Kuijter ended their reply by asking permission to return to the Dutch Republic not "*als pestel. ende schadel. menschen* [as pestilent and harmful men]," but as "*goede patrioten ende Liefhebbers van N: Neederlant* [good patriots and lovers of New Netherland]."[27]

Even at this juncture, Stuyvesant and his councilors could have made a different decision. As Kieft, as well as Melijn and Kuijter had indicated their intention to repatriate and the ship *Prinses* would leave within a couple of months, director general and council had the option to let the antagonists continue their fight in the Dutch Republic. They could have enforced an armistice in New Netherland by putting a stop to accusations flying to and fro. It is possible that Stuyvesant informally urged a halt to hostilities, as he did so on later occasions. But the book of resolutions shows no sign of that. On the other hand, it seems likely that Stuyvesant felt sympathy for Kieft, not so much for the man personally (there are no indications for that), but for the former official, the magistrate under attack. Social class affinity may also have played a role. In later situations, Stuyvesant's behavior displays a tendency to react vehemently when protests against his governmental authority showed what he considered disrespect.

Whatever the case may be, from this moment on the conflict escalated beyond the point of no return. *Fiscael* Hendrick van Dijck began preparations for a trial for slander. In anticipation, Melijn and Kuijter were subject to house arrest from July 4 onward, the day on which *fiscael* Van Dijck entered his *eis* (demand) with director general and council. In the opinion of director general and council—and Stuyvesant's influence is visible here—Van Dijck's demand was not elaborate enough, as it did not sufficiently distinguish between the joint and separate charges against Kuijter and Melijn.[28] Van Dijck was ordered to rectify his demand, but the problem was not allowed to prevent proceedings from moving forward. All points against Kuijter and Melijn concerned threats and slanderous remarks dating back to 1643 and 1644, which indicates the extent to which director general and council were now involved in the affairs of former director Kieft. On July 16, first Melijn and subsequently Kuijter appeared before the council to answer the charges. Melijn pleaded guilty on a minor point, but not guilty on the three other points. He also requested a copy of the charge, which was usual in any trial. Kuijter was less clear in his statement, denying outright only one of the four points, and supplying what appears to be exonerating information on the other three, without, however, clearly pleading not guilty. Director general and council decided to pass judgment on the next court day. Meanwhile, Kuijter and Melijn would remain under arrest.[29]

Yet Stuyvesant was not pleased. In his opinion, *fiscael* Van Dijck had not done his job in amending the complaint. Even the second bill of complaint did not suffice. So he again addressed his fellow council members, outlining in much more detail than Van Dijck what Kuijter and Melijn were exactly accused of, jointly and individually. He added a number of points to Van Dijck's list, partly drawn from Kieft's letter, and included new charges, for instance that Melijn and Kuijter were solely responsible for the letter that the Eight Men had sent to Amsterdam in October 1644. They had deliberately misled the other members of the advisory board. By including this charge, director general and council could justify not prosecuting the other six. Additionally, Kuijter and Melijn were charged that in their second petition, the one presumed to have been drawn up by Van der Donck, they appeared to suspect the director general and council of partiality. And finally, they were charged with attempting to withhold requested evidence, which they intended to use in the Dutch Republic, "thus repudiating the new council." By introducing these last two charges, Stuyvesant changed the character of the trial. Instead of being confined to the time that Kieft had been in charge, the trial now also concerned current affairs, related to the new magistrates. Interestingly, Stuyvesant did not criticize the conclusion of *fiscael* Van Dijck, who had first demanded the death penalty, only to change it a week later into banishment and a heavy fine.[30]

Stuyvesant sent the revised indictment to his councilors, who prepared their written advice in advance. The director general did likewise himself. These were read at a meeting on the afternoon of July 18. The four councilors considered Melijn and Kuijter both guilty, but were not very specific as to the charges. Slander, calumny, sedition, mutiny, opposition to justice, forgery are all mentioned in their opinions, but none of them made a distinction between old times and new. They were, however, unanimous on the sentence: banishment and a fine, with varying lengths and heights, with Melijn getting a slightly heavier punishment.[31]

The opinion of the four councilors combined take up about one page in the manuscript of the council minutes. Stuyvesant's runs to more than three full pages. This was not unusual for the director general, as becomes more evident in later years. But in 1647 his councilors may have been taken aback by his prolixity and attention to detail. Stuyvesant began with objecting to the lack of references to legal authorities in the charges. Van Dijck had failed to indicate why the death penalty, banishment, or a fine, three completely different punishments, were required. Both the charges and the penalties demanded were dubious and not consistent with legal form. Stuyvesant also considered the evidence produced by the *fiscael* on the whole insufficient, as it did not sufficiently distinguish between Melijn and Kuijter. In his opinion, the offenses could not be combined or punished in one single complaint, and he therefore concentrated on the components. While rejecting some of the charges, Stuyvesant considered it proven that Melijn had threatened Kieft, opposed the exercise of justice, defied the law, and had incited others to mutiny and sedition. Stuyvesant opined that, according to divine and human law, this was *crimen læsæ maiestatis,* an injury to the dignity of a state or a sovereign. To modern minds, this may appear as a bit of a stretch. But in the seventeenth-century mind, the highest official in New Netherland represented Dutch sovereignty through his appointment by the West India Company, which had been chartered by the sovereign States General.[32]

Stuyvesant corroborated his charge with several references to divine and human law, starting with the Bible: "*Den rechters sult ghy niet vloecken: ende de Overste in uwen volcke niet lasteren* [Thou shalt not revile the gods, nor curse the ruler of thy people]" (Exod. 22:28); "*Vloeckt den Coninck niet, selfs in uwe herte* [Curse not the king, no not in thy thought]" (Eccl. 10:20); "*Sijt uw voorneme macht onderdanich* [Let every soul be subject unto the higher powers]" (Rom. 13:1).[33] These biblical references are twinned with legal authorities. Stuyvesant first refers to the "*Prax.*

Crim." of Johannes Bernardinus Muscatellus, most likely his *Practica criminalis de cognitione seu probatione delictorum in genere,* published in Frankfurt in 1600, in which speaking evil of one's superiors is labeled one of the worst offenses. Stuyvesant's reference to "Lodovic in *Tractan. de Injuries*" is as yet unidentified. Stuyvesant used this treatise to indicate that censuring the government of supreme authorities amounted to *crimen læsæ maiestatis*. The third authority is the well-known Joost or Jodocus Damhouder, whose *Praxis Rerum Criminalium* (shortened by Stuyvesant into "*Criminalibus*") was printed several times in Latin and Dutch between 1554 and 1647. The director general used Damhouder and the *artikelbrief* (articles of war) of the West India Company to indicate that *crimen læsæ maiestatis* demanded the death penalty and confiscation of property. And that was what he thought Melijn was guilty of.[34]

In the case against Kuijter, Stuyvesant also considered some of the points insufficiently proven. But to him it was clear that Kuijter had insulted and threatened the former director and this was a serious offense. Again, Stuyvesant refers to the *artikelbrief* and to Muscatellus, but he also brings in Ambrosius Theodosius Macrobius and Albricus (probably Albricus Philosophus's *De Romanorum Magistratibus*)[35] to make a distinction between criticizing the person of the ruler and his administration. As the first, lesser, offense applied to Kuijter, Stuyvesant considered a fine of three hundred guilders and "reparation of injury, that is, to acknowledge before *God ende d' Justitie* [God and the court] that he spoke evil" sufficient.[36] In both cases, Stuyvesant's method of arguing is straightforward and syllogistic, bordering on dogmatic, without taking into account the background of the conflict between the parties involved.

The meeting of the council on July 18 was probably limited to the reading of the opinions of the councilors. There is no indication that a verdict was pronounced or a sentence was decided upon. Four days later, the council convened for a meeting full of other business. The only item relating to the Kuijter-Melijn case was their appearance to answer whether they wished to submit anything further relating to the matter of the letter to the directors in 1644. They did not. After this session, Stuyvesant changed his mind about the joint charge, which he now added to the case in the form of an additional opinion of two-and-one-half pages. He now considered Kuijter and Melijn equally guilty of writing the slanderous letter: they were the principal authors, had composed the letter behind Kieft's back and had misinformed the other signatories, who were for the most part illiterate. Again refering to Damhouder and to the Bible (Exod. 20:16, Deut. 5:26, 9:19–21), as well as to Godefridus *Tractatu rea tuum,* as yet unidentified, Stuyvesant proposed perpetual banishment and confiscation of all property. But this did not absolve Melijn from the earlier death penalty. Ending his advice Stuyvesant admitted that it was a little long, but he maintained that it was due to the negligence of the *fiscael*. And of course, "each of the honorable members of the council [remained] at liberty to use his own judgment and the right to decide as in his conscience he shall see fit."[37]

When the council met to finalize the case on July 25, it became clear that the councilors had exercised their own judgment. The death penalty, which had for some time seemed an option, went out of the window. Finding the defendants guilty of *crimen læsæ maiestatis,* Melijn was sentenced to seven years banishment and a fine of three hundred guilders, Kuijter to three years banishment and a fine of one hundred fifty guilders. Presumably, Kuijter and Melijn were present in the meeting while the verdict was read. About two weeks later, they received an official copy of the sentence.[38]

Although Kuijter and Melijn were not sentenced to death, banishment and a heavy fine were considerable punishments. Even so, we should take into account that in many cases in which banishment, the eviction of an individual from the local community, was pronounced, it was not actually executed. Often, pronouncing banishment was intended to be a warning. The convicted man or woman could seek to avoid having to leave by submitting a petition, often supported by others, to the court and beg for mercy from God, justice, and, if applicable, the injured party. Sometimes this act of submission was accompanied by symbolic gestures, like baring the head, bending the knees, and folding the hands.[39] Such rituals, which had to be initiated by the convicted party, implied recognition of the authority of the court, which in granting mercy could show itself gracious. It is not impossible that director general and council expected such an action from Melijn and Kuijter, as it would defuse the immediate conflict, while the underlying causes would still be subject to an investigation by authorities in the Dutch Republic.

Yet Kuijter and Melijn decided against asking the court for mercy and a commutation of the sentence. They had already decided to take their complaints against Kieft and the West India Company to higher authorities in the Dutch Republic, and to their mind the sentence could be used as additional proof of the perverted character of Company rule. So in August 1647, Kuijter, Melijn, Kieft, and several other people left New Netherland to return to patria. Perhaps Stuyvesant, for a fleeting moment, as the ship *Prinses* disappeared beyond the horizon with the troublemakers, thought that his problems were now over.

Figure 6.7. "Peter Stuyvesant's Country House." PR 086, Samuel Hollyer Print Collection, #49, box 1, folder 4; negative no. 83109d. Collection of The New-York Historical Society.

Figure 6.8. "Town house of Peter Stuyvesant." PR 086, Samuel Hollyer Print Collection, box 1, folder 4; negative no. 3228. Collection of The New-York Historical Society.

Temporarily, he was right. The relationship between the West India Company authorities in New Netherland and the colonists showed a clear improvement in the next sixteen months or so—until Melijn returned, and then the conflict resurfaced and entered a new phase, in which the leading role was taken by Adriaen van der Donck. But that is another story, which is too long to include here.[40]

This reconstruction of the trial of Kuijter and Melijn leads to conclusions on three levels about order and authority, and conflict and justice in New Netherland. On a general level, descending and ascending theories of authority collided in the council chamber in Fort Amsterdam, as they did in many other places throughout Europe and its colonies when assumptions from the local community about having a say in their local affairs were blocked by higher authorities. Yet what made the situation in New Netherland in 1647 exceptional was that trajectories of three distinct developments intersected. The transition of New Netherland from a string of trading forts to a settlement colony had only started a few years earlier after the abolition of the West India Company fur trade monopoly. This first development had, catalyzed by the war with the Native Americans in the early 1640s, created a community with its own perception of local identity. Yet a second development, the transformation of colonial government into an institutional framework that allowed for distinct, albeit partly overlapping, spheres of influence of central and local authorities, lagged behind the first. And so did the third development, the demographic growth of the colony, which only really took off when immigration increased rapidly in the 1650s. The conflict between WIC authorities and the colonists in the early 1640s was the first in a series that continued for about a decade. Only after about 1654 did the governmental framework in New Netherland became robust enough to absorb potential conflicts to such an extent as to avoid them getting out of hand.

FIGURE 6.9. "Totius Neobelgii nova et accuratissima tabula" A New and (Most) Accurate Map of (the Entirety of) New Netherland, by R. and J. Ottens. Amsterdam, 1720s. The copper plate of this map was produced by Hugo Allard c. 1656 as a facsimile plate of Nicolas Visscher's 1651 composite map of New Netherland and New Amsterdam. The baroque cartouche shows the wall erected by Stuyvesant in 1653 against a possible English attack. It also depicts Broad Street (then a canal) and Stuyvesant's mansion at the end of Whitehall Street facing the East River. Bert Twaalfhoven Collection, Fordham University Library, Bronx, New York, Map #14.

On a procedural level, the Kuijter-Melijn court case highlights some of the characteristics of the Dutch forms of government as employed overseas. The reconstruction shows that however strong the director general may have been as an individual, government and the administration of justice remained a collective responsibility, with specific delineated tasks for *fiscael,* secretary, councilors, and director general. What we from a modern perspective might perceive as improper behavior, such as changing the points of the indictment during the trial, or even as abuse of power, was in fact a standard operating procedure in an age in which separation of powers did not exist. Blaming director general and council for an inequitable verdict is unwarranted, but it remains to be seen whether they trumped up the charges into a spurious indictment for *crimen læsæ maiestatis*.[41]

On an individual level, it is clear that Stuyvesant and the councilors regarded the request of Kuijter and Melijn to submit former councilors to interrogation as a challenge to their governmental authority. Yet they issued a cautious reply at first. It was not until Kieft requested a trial for slander that director general and council embarked on a collision course. This was a crucial turn in the conflict, a moment when they could have decided differently. Stuyvesant was criticized by his superiors for his failure to do so, but by then the consequences had become more obvious and the Amsterdam directors had the benefit of hindsight.[42] Even so, as the directors pointed out, Stuyvesant should have steered clear of meddling in the affairs of his predecessors. Other options had been available, such as dismissing Kuijter and Melijn's petition "for pregnant reasons," the usual formula when authorities did not want to divulge their motivation. Alternatively, the petition could have been accepted with the promise to send it on to Amsterdam. In a similar way, director general and council could have turned down Kieft's request to start a trial for slander, again with the argument that such matters ought to be decided by their superiors in Amsterdam. Yet it also understandable that Stuyvesant and his councilors acted as they did. After their initial restraint, Kuijter and especially Melijn did not mend their ways, but continued to go after Kieft in a way that was bound to antagonize the newly arrived magistrates, as they showed scant respect for any authority. Thus escalation became unavoidable, and the trial for *crimen læsæ maiestatis* became the first act in a play that would continue for some years.

NOTES

This essay is an adaptation of parts of chapter 6 of my work-in-progress, a full biography of Petrus Stuyvesant.

1. National Archives (hereafter abbreviated as NA), Archives of the States General (hereafter abbreviated as SG), *loketkas* West India Company, inv. no. 12564.36 (6 September 1650; translated in E. B. O'Callaghan and B. Fernow, trans. and ed., *Documents Relative to the Colonial History of the State of New York,* 15 vols. [Albany: Weed, Parsons, 1853–1883] [hereafter abbreviated as *DRCHNY*], 1: 446). All translations from the seventeenth-century Dutch are mine.

2. H.G. Koenigsberger, *Monarchies, States Generals, and Parliaments. The Netherlands in the Fifteenth and Sixteenth Centuries* (Cambridge: Cambridge University Press, 2001), 37; David Hackett Fischer, *Albion's Seed. Four British Folkways in American History* (New York, London: Oxford University Press, 1989), 321.

3. New York State Archives (hereafter abbreviated as NYSA), New York Colonial Manuscripts (hereafter abbreviated as NYCM) 11: 12 (7 April 1648; Charles T. Gehring, trans. and ed., *Correspondence 1647–1653.* New Netherland Documents Series, vol. XI (Syracuse: Syracuse University Press, 2000) (hereafter abbreviated as *Corres. 1647–1653*), 54). Occasionally, the metaphors of father-child and gardener-tree

were combined: the child as a young tree that should be carefully raised. Roelof van Gelder, *Naporra's omweg. Het leven van een VOC-matroos (1731–1793)* (Amsterdam: Atlas, 2003), 48.

4. Walter Ullmann, *Medieval Political Thought* (Harmondsworth: Penguin, 1975, repr. 1979); Koenigsberger, *Monarchies, States Generals, and Parliaments*; Jonathan I. Israel, *The Dutch Republic. Its Rise, Greatness, and Fall, 1477–1806* (Oxford: Oxford University Press, 1995; 2nd ed. 1998), 760–66.

5. The hierarchy as outlined here should be sufficient to dispel the myth that New Netherland was a province of the Dutch Republic, on par with provinces such as Holland, Utrecht, or Gelderland, with its autonomous cities and regions sending delegates to provincial estates. While the word *province* is occasionally applied to New Netherland, an exclusively institutional interpretation, spurred on by the modern meaning of "province," is incorrect. In the context of the seventeenth century, "province" indicates "region" or "area." Willem Frijhoff and Jaap Jacobs, "The Dutch, New Netherland, and Thereafter (1609–1780s)," in *Four Centuries of Dutch-American Relations,* ed. Cornelis A. van Minnen, Hans Krabbendam, Giles Scott-Smith (Amsterdam: Boom Publishers, 2009), 31–48, esp. 48, n. 13.

6. NYSA, NYCM 4: 242 (2 January 1646; *NYHM* 4: 291). For an extensive analysis of the conflict between Kieft and Bogardus, see Willem Frijhoff, *Wegen van Evert Willemsz. Een Hollands weeskind op zoek naar zichzelf, 1607–1647* (Nijmegen: SUN, 1995).

7. Ullmann, *Medieval Political Thought,* 159; Koeningsberger, *Monarchies, States Generals, and Parliaments,* 4.

8. E. B. O'Callaghan, *History of New Netherland, or New York under the Dutch* (New York: D. Appleton, 2 vols., 1st ed. 1846–1848, 2nd ed., 1855), 2: 548–49.

9. Ibid., 2: 20–34. Without being comprehensive, the Melijn-Kuijter trial is mentioned in Henry H. Kessler and Eugene Rachlis, *Peter Stuyvesant and His New York. A Biography of a Man and a City* (New York: Random House, 1959), 68–76; Russell Shorto, *The Island at the Centre of the World: The Epic Story of Dutch Manhattan, The Forgotten Colony That Shaped America* (New York: Doubleday, 2005), 171–79; Willem Frijhoff, *Fullfilling God's Mission: The Two Worlds of Dominie Everardus Bogardus, 1607–1647* (Leiden: Brill, 2007), 549.

10. NSYA, NYCM 4: 288 (6 June 1647; *NYHM* 4: 364). Both Kessler and Rachlis and Shorto overlook Kieft's request, thus missing the start of the conflict.

11. Jaap Jacobs, "Incompetente autocraten? Bestuurlijke verhoudingen in de zeventiende-eeuwse Nederlandse Atlantische Wereld," *De zeventiende eeuw. Cultuur in de Nederlanden in interdisciplinair perspectief* 21 (2005): 64–78.

12. On Bout, see Jaap Jacobs, *New Netherland. A Dutch Colony in Seventeenth Century America* (Leiden: Brill, 2005), 75, 137, 146, 149, 145, 351, 391, 488; and Frijhoff, *Wegen,* 722, 726–27, 736. See also Jaap Jacobs, "Fortune in the New World: Jan Jansz Damen in America," in *Explorers, Fortunes, and Love Letters: A Window on New Netherland,* ed. Martha Dickinson Shattuck (Albany: Mount Ida Press, 2009), 50–58 For the arrest, see NSYA, NYCM 4: 288 (6 June 1647; *NYHM* 4: 364). For the earlier deposition, Nat. Arch. 1.01.07 inv. no. 12564.25 letter G (27 March 1643; *DRCHNY* 1: 194).

13. Th. G. Evans and T. A. Wright, eds., *Records of the Reformed Dutch Church in New Amsterdam and New York. Baptisms from 25 December 1639 to 29 December 1800.* Collections of the New York Genealogical and Biographical Society 2, 2 vols. (New York: 1901–1903, reprint Upper Saddle River, NJ: 1968), 269; NYSA, NYCM 4: 334–35 (25 September 1647; *NYHM* 4: 438–42).

14. NYSA, NYCM 4: 290–91 (13 June 1647; *NYHM* 4: 368–70), 291–92 (14 June 1647; *NYHM* 4: 370–71).

15. NSYA, NYCM 4: 291–92 (14 June 1647; *NYHM* 4: 370–71). The interrogatories for Van Dijck, Van der Hoykens, La Montagne, and Van Tienhoven are in Nat. Arch., SG, loketkas WIC, inv. no. 12564.25 "Stucken raeckende den staet van Nieu Nederlandt ende de proceduren tegen Cornelis Melijn ende den aencleve van dien," letter M (not dated, June 1647; *DRCHNY* 1: 195–201).

16. Jacobs, "Incompetente autocraten?"

17. This was not a tax, as has been supposed. It was usual in time of war to impose involuntary levies, called contributions, on the population of adjoining territories, as a form of protection against plunder. See Jacobs, *New Netherland,* 133–34.

18. NSYA, NYCM 4: 291–92 (14 June 1647; *NYHM* 4: 370–71).

19. Jacobs, "Incompetente autocraten?"

20. Van der Donck is sometimes called the first lawyer in New Netherland. This is a mistake, as Lubbert Dinclagen, who in 1621 obtained a doctorate in law from the Université d'Orléans, was already a *fiscael* in New Netherland in 1634. Willem Frijhoff, *Wegen van Evert Willemsz. Een Hollands weeskind op zoek naar zichzelf, 1607–1647* (Nijmegen: SUN, 1995), 672–75. After Van der Donck returned to the Dutch Republic in 1649, he received a doctorate from Leiden University and was admitted to the Court of Holland. Jaap Jacobs, "De frustatie van Adriaen van der Donck, kolonist in Nieuw-Nederland," *Historisch Tijdschrift Holland* 31 (1999): 74–85.

21. NYSA, NYCM 4: 293–94 (14 June 1647; *NYHM* 4: 372–74).

22. NYSA, NYCM 4: 294–95 (14 June 1647; *NYHM* 4: 374–75).

23. Nat. Arch., SG, loketkas WIC, inv. nr. 12564.25 "Stucken raeckende den staet van Nieu Nederlandt ende de proceduren tegen Cornelis Melijn ende den aencleve van dien," letter O (18 June 1647; *DRCHNY* 1: 203–204), letter Q (28 October 1644; *DRCHNY* 1: 209–13).

24. NSYA, NYCM 4: 296 (18 June 1647; *NYHM* 4: 377); Nat. Arch., SG, loketkas WIC, inv. no. 12564.25 "Stucken raeckende den staet van Nieu Nederlandt ende de proceduren tegen Cornelis Melijn ende den aencleve van dien," letter O (18 June 1647; *DRCHNY* 1: 203–204).

25. Roman historian Livy, Roman poet Sextus Propertius, theologian Ambrose of Alexandria, Athenian statesman Aristides, and Greek historian Xenophon. In view of Van der Donck's legal training, it is remarkable that none of the classicial authors he refers to are known to have written legal works. Cf. Shorto, *The Island of the Center of the World,* 178, who omits Livy.

26. Shorto, *The Island at the Center of the World,* 175–78.

27. NYSA, NYCM 4: 302 (24 June 1647; *NYHM* 4: 380); Nat. Arch., SG, loketkas WIC, inv. no. 12564.25 "Stucken raeckende den staet van Nieu Nederlandt ende de proceduren tegen Cornelis Melijn ende den aencleve van dien," letter P (22 June 1647; *DRCHNY* 1: 205–209). The translation by O'Callaghan ("pestilent and seditious persons" and "good patriots and proprietors") is faulty here.

28. NYSA, NYCM 4: 305 (4 July 1647; *NYHM* 4: 392).

29. NYSA, NYCM 4: 306–307 (16 July 1647; *NYHM* 4: 394–97).

30. NYSA, NYCM 4: 308–10 (18 July 1647; *NYHM* 4: 397–402).

31. NYSA, NYCM 4: 310–11 (18 July 1647; *NYHM* 4: 402–405).

32. Jacobs, "Dutch Proprietary Manors in America," 309–11.

33. NYSA, NYCM 4: 313 (18 July 1647; *NYHM* 4: 407). Translations into English are from the King James Version of 1611, which Van Laer used for his translation in *NYHM*. Yet by doing so, Van Laer hides the fact that Stuyvesant on p. 313 appears not to have used the *Statenvertaling* of 1637 but rather an older Bible translation, possibly a revised Deux-Aes version which was printed many times in the early seventeenth century. In the *Statenvertaling,* the exact quotes are: "De goden en sult ghy niet vloecken: ende de Overste in uwen volcke en sult ghy niet lasteren" (Exod. 22:28); "Vloeckt den Coninck niet, selfs in uwe gedachte" (Eccl. 10:20); "Alle ziele zy den Machten over [*haer*] gestelt onderworpen" (Rom. 13:1) (http://www.biblija.net/biblija.cgi?lang=nl, accessed 28 January 2010; and http://www.digitalebibliotheek.be/tekst/_deu001deux01_01/index_uitgebreid.htm#10/, accessed 31 January 2010).

34. NYSA, NYCM 4: 311–14 (18 July 1647; *NYHM* 4: 405–408).

35. Interestingly, some of the works of Macrobius and Albricus are combined with several other authors in a compilation by Jacobus Micyllus (Jacob Moltzer). Possibly Stuyvesant owned a copy of the 1608 edition.

36. NYSA, NYCM 4: 314–15 (18 July 1647; *NYHM* 4: 408–11).

37. NYSA, NYCM 4: 318–20 (22 July 1647; *NYHM* 4: 413–17).

38. NSYA, NYCM 4: 321–23 (25 July 1647; *NYHM* 4: 419–22); Nat. Arch., SG, loketkas WIC, inv. no. 12564.25 "Stucken raeckende den staet van Nieu Nederlandt ende de proceduren tegen Cornelis Melijn ende den aencleve van dien," letter R (25 July 1647; *DRCHNY* 1: 213–14); Nat. Arch., SG, loketkas WIC, inv. no. 12564.25, *memoriaal* Melijn, doc. 3 (25 July 1647; *DRCHNY* 1: 349–50).

39. For instance, Albany County Hall of Records, Court Minutes of Fort Orange 1652–1656, 227 (20 July 1655; Charles T. Gehring (trans. and ed.), *Fort Orange Court Minutes 1652–1660*. New Netherland Documents Series, volume XVI, part two (Syracuse: Syracuse University Press, 1990), 202.

40. See Jaap Jacobs, *The Colony of New Netherland: A Dutch Settlement in Seventeenth-Century America* (Ithaca: Cornell University Press, 2009), 81–87; Simon Middleton, "Order and Authority in New Netherland: The 1653 Remonstrance and Early Settlement Politics," *William and Mary Quarterly*, 3rd Series, 67 (2010): 31–68.

41. Frijhoff, *Wegen*, 799. It requires a comparison with trials with a similar charge in the early-modern Dutch Republic and its colonies. See for instance Pieter Wagenaar and Otto van der Meij, "Een schout in de fout?," *Tijdschrift voor Sociale en Economische geschiedenis* 2 (2005): 22–46; and Florike Egmond, "Recht en krom. Corruptie, ongelijkheid en rechtsbescherming in de vroegmoderne Nederlanden," *Bijdragen en Mededelingen betreffende de geschiedenis der Nederlanden* 116 (2001): 1–33.

42. NYSA, NYCM 11: 14, 5 (27 January 1649; *Corres. 1647–1653*, 65), 18, fol. 3 (16 February 1650; *Corres. 1647–1653*, 81). Both of these letters appear to be letters sent to Stuyvesant alone, rather than to the entire council. The correspondence between the Amsterdam directors and their servants in New Netherland is divided into two kinds of letters: *particuliere missiven* (private letters) to the director general and *gemeene missiven* (general letters) to director general and council. The private letters were read by just the director general and he was not supposed to divulge its contents to his councilors. Thus, the directors' displeasure with some of Stuyvesant's actions very likely remained secret. Jacobs, "Incompetente autocraten?"

Chapter Seven

Imagining the Stadt Huys

Diana diZerega Wall and Anne-Marie Cantwell

As settlers multiplied and saw themselves as part of a new polity, they wanted—and ultimately acquired—something closer to a miniature version of Old World Amsterdam, with magistrates, laws, political officials, and a building; an official place for public business.

And so, it came to pass during Petrus Stuyvesant's administration. This was the Stadt Huys, New Amsterdam's first municipal edifice, transformed in 1653 from the West India Company's tavern, the Stadt Herbergh, built in the early 1640s. We have no reliable depictions of the building, but from available data, Diana diZerega Wall and Anne-Marie Cantwell give us a good idea of what it was like.

When New Amsterdam was transformed from a frontier trading outpost to a municipality in the 1650s, the Dutch West India Company's tavern, the Stadt Herbergh, was transformed into the new municipality's first Stadt Huys, or city hall and courthouse. The history of this legendary building, one of the most important in New Amsterdam, is the focus of this chapter. The story starts three decades earlier, in 1624, with the first settlement of New Netherland when the Dutch West India Company established the colony of New Netherland to exploit the trade in North American furs. Although the colony extended from the Connecticut River to the Delaware, its heart was at Fort Orange on the Hudson River, the Company's center for the fur trade, which took place primarily with the Mohawks, an Iroquoian people who lived to the west. Two years later, they established the small settlement of New Amsterdam on the island of Manhattan, overlooking the great natural harbor at the river's mouth. This site, in Algonquian territory, was ideally suited to protect the Hudson (the route to the furs) from competing European powers such as the English and to establish an entrepôt where the Company could transfer cargo from river-plying watercraft to oceangoing vessels for the trip to the Netherlands. If Fort Orange was the heart of New Netherland, New Amsterdam, with its administrative center at Fort Amsterdam, was its head.[1]

For the first decade and a half of the colony's existence, the Company ran New Netherland and maintained a monopoly on the trade in furs. In many ways, the colony *was* the Company. But in 1639–1640, the Company, feeling threatened by the English who surrounded New Netherland, tried to attract a critical mass of settlers to counteract that threat by removing its monopoly and opening the trade. This step completely changed the colony's trajectory.[2] In New

Netherland, the Company was no longer a "joint-stock company. It had become a government."[3] Whereas in the past, Company employees had left the colony after fulfilling their term of service, now they stayed on as free colonists,[4] and they wanted a say in their governance. The colony, in other words, was transformed from an exploitative one with an ephemeral European population narrowly focused on trading for furs, to a settler colony that attracted European immigrants who wanted to make their lives and fortunes there. This transformation is expressed in the history of the building that the West India Company built on Pearl Street as its tavern but later gave to the newly founded municipality of New Amsterdam for its first city hall.

In 1642, the Company's director, Willem Kieft, built the tavern, the Stadt Herbergh or City Tavern, out at the fledgling city's edge, to accommodate English travelers who were sailing back and forth from the English colonies of New England and Virginia; he reportedly found their presence in the fort annoying.[5] Together, the Company's tavern and the Church in the Fort, built at around the same time, dominated the skyline of the little settlement, anchoring each of its ends along Pearl Street.

These buildings are long gone, and there are of course no photographs of Pearl Street in the seventeenth century, so we must rely on contemporary maps, views, documents, and archaeological studies in trying to imagine the tavern and its environs, and its transformation into a city hall at that time. These may or may not be accurate representations, since early image makers freely borrowed from each other, changed early views, and sometimes painted either a glossier version of reality in order to attract further exploration or intrigue European readers,[6] or a shabbier version to underline to those in the metropole the need for further investment in the colony.[7] Documents may also reflect the biases and hopes of the time. So, although our imagining may not be photo-perfect, nonetheless it does reflect a twenty-first-century assessment of the admittedly biased documents and images we have from that time.

Figure 7.1. "De Stadt Nieuw Amsterdam gelegen op het Eylandt Manhattans in Nieuw Nederlandt," showing the Company town from the East River, 1648. The large building to the right is the Stadt Herbergh. Courtesy of the Austrian National Library, Vienna.

With that caveat, we might reasonably imagine that anyone approaching the tavern in the 1640s would see a large, free-standing building placed with its broad side facing the waterfront and with two stories plus a cellar and an attic. Because the ground sloped up toward the east, that part of the cellar was below grade, while its western end was aboveground.[8] Contemporary sources suggest that the structure was probably made of brick, with a red tiled, steeply pitched roof supported by stepped gables in the Dutch manner.[9] The tiles and the bricks had probably been imported from the Netherlands as ballast, as was the custom in many of the Dutch colonies.

A closer look might reveal the tavern's Pearl Street façade with its central, round-arched doorway and a stoop flanked by two windows on the first floor and three windows on the second. On its western façade was another central, round-arched doorway at ground level that led to the cellar,[10] two small windows above it on the first story, and a pair of larger windows on the second story, all surmounted by a small, single window that gave light to the attic.[11]

Patrons entered the tavern through a central hall. Turning left, they likely climbed a few steps into the tap room. The floor here was probably raised to allow height for the cellar kitchen below. Next to the tap room was likely a small side room with a fireplace that served as the private quarters of the innkeeper and his wife.[12] Turning right from the central hall was likely the "large hall," the principal room where food and drink were served. The floor above provided sleeping quarters for travelers, and was probably divided into smaller rooms. A wooden spiral staircase connected the different stories. In the western side of the cellar, which was partially above ground and was both airier and brighter than the eastern side, were the kitchen and its hearth. That bleaker space may have been used for storing the Company's wines and brandy along with kegs of beer. The fireplaces were typical Dutch jambless ones, built without side walls (or jambs) but with a hood above to catch the smoke. The wall of the building served as the back wall of the fireplaces. They probably each featured an iron fireback that prevented damage to the back wall from the heat and flames, and were flanked by Dutch tiles, as they were in the Netherlands. The walls were likely plastered, with ceilings of exposed timber, made up of beams and the wooden boards of the floor above.[13] The plaster may well have been made locally by the Company's enslaved Africans who, at one time, were reported to be employed burning oyster shells to produce lime for making plaster.[14]

The Stadt Herbergh, then, was probably built as a typical Dutch colonial tavern, albeit company owned. Taverns and tap houses in those days served an important function in the colony. They were places where people could meet and socialize and, ultimately, form a community.[15]

Around the time the tavern was built—the early 1640s—some colonists were already petitioning the West India Company headquarters in Amsterdam and the States General (the Dutch government) to have more representation in the town's governing and to have Kieft recalled. He had made life unsafe for all by provoking the Native Americans, provocations that had led to the bloody Kieft's War (1640–45), which had ravaged the colony. Finally, at war's end, Kieft was recalled, and in 1647, Petrus Stuyvesant became the new director general. By then, the colonists were increasingly determined to have more input into the running of the city. Later, in 1652, after a great deal of pressure from both the colonists and the States General, the West India Company allowed New Amsterdam to become a municipality on the Amsterdam model, with a court no longer completely under the jurisdiction of the Company. The directors sent a letter to Stuyvesant approving the establishment of "a bench of justice formed as much as possible after the laws of this city [Amsterdam]."[16] The Company made this concession particularly in order to encourage unity among the colonists in case of English attack—the

First Anglo-Dutch War had just begun.[17] The new government was made up of a *schout,* who combined the duties of sheriff and prosecutor, two *burgemeesters,* who had administrative and legislative duties, and five *schepenen,* who shared judicial duties with the *burgemeesters.*[18] This new governing body, whose jurisdiction included ships anchored in the harbor, also employed functionaries such as a dog catcher, a harbormaster, a town crier, a secretary, a court messenger, etc.[19] The members of the court took their duties seriously and prayed that they "may distinguish right from wrong, truth from lies, and give clean and just decision as judges."[20]

The new city government then moved quickly to establish itself as an independent entity and asked the Company for the use of its tavern for their meetings and for holding court—it was the only building designed for secular purposes that was large enough to house such meetings. The Company agreed, and the city government announced "that they shall hold their regular meeting in the house hitherto called the City tavern, henceforth the City Hall on Monday mornings . . . to hear there all questions of difference between litigants and decide them as best as they can."[21] This was a fundamental change for New Amsterdam. It meant that its status as a city was recognized and, over time, "its powers and prerogatives were gradually enlarged, following the model of the development of city rights in Holland."[22] The court was no longer completely under the jurisdiction of the Company, and the city government had made its first important step in wresting administrative and judicial power from Company control. Although their judicial duties changed over time, initially the *burgemeesters* and the *schepenen* served as a lower bench of justice, hearing cases limited to those involving fines of less than one hundred guilders, such as those concerning debts, slander, wounding, threats, and fighting. Anyone convicted by this court had the right of appeal to the director general and the council. Other, more serious cases, with more severe punishments, such as adultery, blasphemy, manslaughter, or theft, were tried before the director general and the council at Fort Amsterdam. But by 1656, the court successfully argued for more judicial powers and could now hear all criminal cases brought before them by the *schout,* with the exception of capital offenses which were reserved for the director general and council. The latter also advised the municipal government on fines and other forms of punishment.[23] Henceforth, New Amsterdam was no longer simply a Company trading outpost. It was a municipality and its inhabitants were now "citizens of a modern republic entitled to protection under its laws."[24]

By the end of the year, the municipality's officers asked the Company's directors for the ownership of the building to house the city government. The city's officials used their request, made on Christmas Eve, 1653, as an occasion to remind the Company of the importance of civil government in the difficult times in which they were living, under the English threat. They requested the Company to take measures to protect the country "for without that and *a well regulated civil government,* it is impossible for this country ever to grow to a permanent and prosperous state" (emphasis ours).[25] The Company complied with their request,[26] and the building, now the Stadt Huys, continued to serve as a city hall for New Amsterdam, and when New Amsterdam became New York, it continued to serve as the seat of government until 1697.[27]

But the transition of the tavern to a city hall and courthouse was not an easy one. The building had to be emptied of lodgers as well as of a merchant's stores of salt. Well over a year later, the new city government still worried "that the City Hall be not wholly spoilt by salt, nor occupied by others."[28]

And the interior of the building changed after the tavern became the City Hall. The cellar was now the jail (occupied by prisoners of the municipality; the Company's prisoners were kept in the fort). It was divided into two parts—a detention room for those under civil arrest, who enjoyed the amenities of fire and candlelight, probably located in what had been the tavern's kitchen, and cells for those accused of criminal offenses, who had neither fire nor candlelight and were likely confined to the old, dark storage area.[29] By an odd quirk of chance, in 1670–71 (under British rule), the jail, most likely the section that had once hosted the tavern's storage, was where Hans Dyckman was confined on suspicion of trying to set fire to the City Hall, which now imprisoned him. He was subsequently banished from the province.[30]

On the first floor, the old innkeeper's room was probably still occupied, although not by an innkeeper but by the jailer or occasionally by people who needed a place to stay in an emergency. The large hall on the other side of the building, where travelers once ate and drank, may have served as a schoolroom, and the night watch probably used the old tap room as its headquarters. Finally, the central hall continued as a hall, and may have been the place where the *burgemeesters* stored the city's fifty leather fire buckets.[31]

The entire second floor, where travelers used to sleep, became the new courtroom, where trials were held and the newly formed municipal government met. In addition to its judicial functions, the government also had administrative tasks to perform in the new City Hall, including those related to defense, education, public works, and economic matters.[32] Court officials probably sat at the front of the room in high-backed chairs with cushions, near the fireplace, separated from the rest of the room by a railing. In the year 1659, and perhaps in other years as well, the cushions that the court officials sat on were shared with the church in Fort Amsterdam. The records state that an annual salary of fifty florins was paid to one Jan Gillis Koeck for transporting the cushions back and forth between the Stadt Huys and the church and for ringing the municipality's bell.[33] The public, made up, at various times, of Europeans, Africans, Natives, and interpreters, may have sat on plain wooden benches facing the court officials. There were likely also *kasse*,[34] or cupboards, in the room, used for holding papers, books, etc., for the court's use, as well as a hand bell to call meetings to order and an hourglass to time the arrival of the officials, so they could be fined for being late.[35] New Amsterdam's citizenry were involved in the renovations. For example, in the 1650s, wainscoting was added to the courtroom through the generosity of a wealthy and influential office holder, Cornelis Steenwyck, who was both the last named *burgemeester* of New Amsterdam and the third mayor of New York.[36]

Above the court, the single attic that had served the inn appears to have been carved into two stories. The lower one, with new dormer windows, may have been where supporting services for the court took place—where robes were kept and the appurtenances of the court were stored (sometimes under lock and key), where offices for the secretary and space for the court messenger and doorkeeper were located, and a place where meetings were held. The attic's uppermost level was probably used for storage; for example, the property of those who died intestate may have been stored there until their estates were settled.[37]

The tavern's exterior also underwent several changes after it became the City Hall (Figure 7.2). In 1659, its windows were embellished with the Arms of New Amsterdam,[38] and by 1660 the building appears to have been topped by a central belfry. But the most striking change came in 1670, after the British takeover, when the provincial secretary informed the mayor's court that Governor Francis Lovelace, the second English governor of the province, "intended to build a howse uppon the lott, adjoining next unto the State-house, and to make the sd. House to be an Inn or Ordinary." He asked permission for "his honn'r to build the upperpart

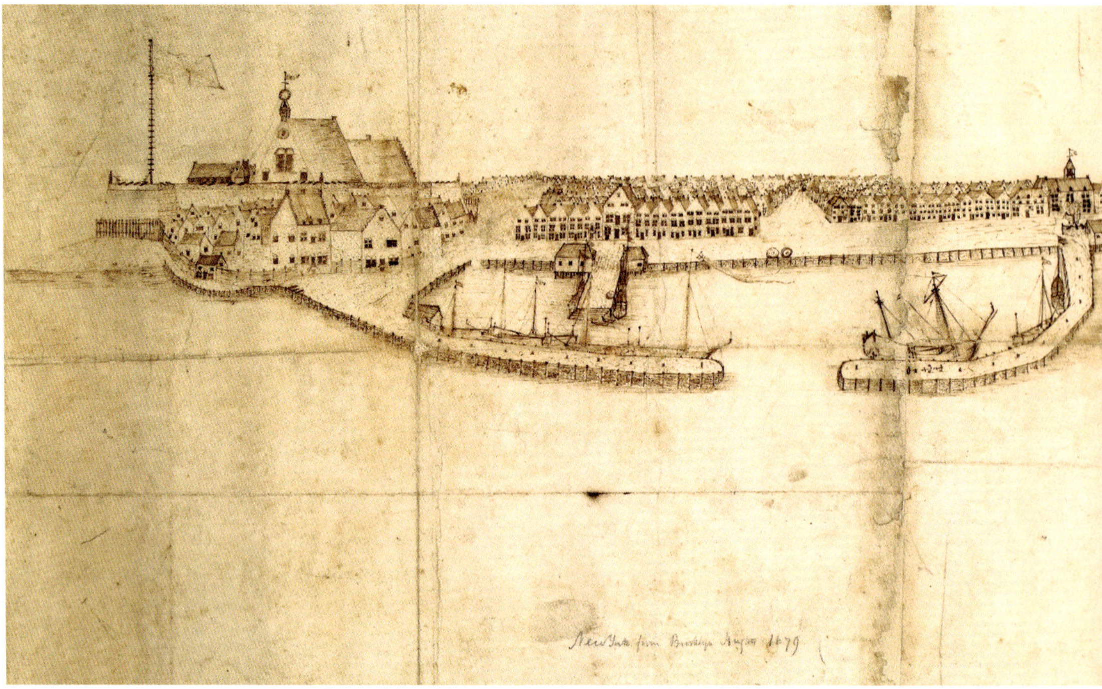

of the house somthing ouer the passage of the Towne wch. Lyeth betweene the Statehouse & the sd. Lott as also that he might make a doore to go from the upperpart of the howse into the Court's chamber."[39] The governor's request was granted, and the State House, which had been a freestanding building for almost thirty years, became part of a row: the eastern second story wall of the new tavern and the western second story wall of the State House became a shared party wall, although the first floors were separated by the lane that provided access to the jail in the cellar of the State House. Dormer windows were probably placed in the attic at around the same time, to make up for the attic window that was lost when the new tavern was built next door. And so the Stadt Huys, which had begun life as a tavern before becoming a city hall, was now a city hall physically joined to another tavern.[40]

In the late 1690s, the building had become dilapidated and there were concerns about its safety. The City Council held its last meeting there in 1697, and in 1698 declared it to be unsafe for use. The following year, it was sold to a John Rodman, who soon demolished the building and built two smaller buildings on its site.[41] A new City Hall was built at the corner of Nassau and Wall Streets, where today's Federal Hall now stands. But the story of the Stadt Huys does not end there.

Several times over the intervening centuries, tantalizing references were made to the fate of the remains of New Amsterdam's and New York's first City Hall and courthouse, before the site became the focus of two separate archaeological excavations. In the nineteenth century, several writers mentioned that the original foundation walls of the Company's tavern and City Hall had been incorporated into the buildings that were later built on the Rodman parcel of

Figure 7.2. Detail of the Labadist General View, by Jasper Dankaerts, showing the East River shoreline c. 1679. The large building at the head of the right dock is the Stadt Huys; the King's House Tavern is to its right.

land. When those buildings, too, had been demolished, parts of the Stadt Huys's foundation walls were also said to have survived that cycle of destruction, and were still to be seen in the basements of the new standing structures that took their place. One of these accounts, an 1831 book of views of New York City, mentioned that "[i]n the vaults and cellars of the buildings of the Brinkerhoffs, its [the first city hall's] ruins may yet be easily traced."[42] Two years later, a book on the history of the city noted that the original jail and courthouse of New York "was the house of A. Brinkerhoff, corner of Dock [Pearl] and Coenties streets, the dungeons [of which] are still to be seen in the cellar."[43] Next, I. N. Phelps Stokes, the city's great biographer, observed that when he visited the cellar in 1909, "some of the masonry, especially in the walls on the south side, appeared to date from the period of its [the City Hall's] erection."[44]

Subsequently, more than half a century later, on the eve of the property's next redevelopment, there were two separate archaeological investigations of the site to explore whether or not the Stadt Huys's stone foundation walls had in fact survived and been incorporated into the later buildings.[45] The archaeological projects, like so much related to major real estate deals in Manhattan, had a complex history. In 1966, the Landmarks Preservation Commission designated as a city landmark one of the buildings where the Stadt Huys had been because it was the only known late federal commercial building graced by double stories of arched windows left in the city. Two years later, Lehman Brothers, the brokerage house, bought the landmark along with several adjacent properties and began plans to build an office tower. Because the newly amassed parcel of land included a landmarked building, they needed to have the commission rescind the building's landmark status so that they could tear it down. The commission agreed to de-designate the building on two conditions: the developers would have to rebuild its façade at a new location and support limited archaeological work in the area where the Stadt Huys had once stood. The developers agreed and the building was torn down and its façade put into storage.

Regina Kellerman conducted limited archaeological testing in 1970–71 as part of the agreement between Lehman Brothers and the commission and used the results in her doctoral dissertation.[46] She worked at the site with Joseph Shelley, another architectural historian. Her goal was to determine whether or not the foundation walls of 71 Pearl Street, the late federal commercial building, did in fact incorporate parts of the City Hall walls, and if so, to document the dimensions of the seventeenth-century building. First, they explored the south wall of the building and, second, the north wall.[47] She contended that their finds confirmed that parts of both the front and the rear walls of the federal building were in fact from the original Stadt Herbergh and Stadt Huys.[48] Soon thereafter, Lehman Brothers, responding to changes in the economy, changed its plans and decided not to build. The property was paved over and leased out as a parking lot, a common holding pattern for real estate in the city.

A decade later, in 1979, the Dollar Savings Bank had acquired the parcel and was negotiating with a developer who was interested in building on it. Since the developer did not want to buy a property with strings attached, the bank had to fulfill the decade-old agreement with the Landmarks Preservation Commission: it had to reconstruct the façade from the long-demolished building. But that, as it turned out, could not be done, because parts of the façade had disappeared. So both the bank and the commission were in a bind: something had to be done to satisfy the demands of preservation.

By this time, the National Historic Preservation Act had made protecting archaeological sites an integral part of the preservation process and the commission's staff wanted to find out what role archaeology might play in protecting New York City's heritage. Some staff members were intrigued by the fact that earlier archaeological testing had suggested that an archaeological site from Dutch New Amsterdam might be buried under the parking lot and thought that excavations there could provide a test case for the potential of archaeology in New York.[49] So they proposed that the bank substitute a full-fledged archaeological investigation of the block that was to be developed, for the reconstruction of the lost façade and thereby satisfy the de-designation requirements for the landmark property. The bank agreed. Thus, New York City's first large-scale archaeological project got underway with archaeologists Nan Rothschild and Diana diZerega Wall as co-directors and Bert Salwen as senior advisor.

In 1979–1980, Rothschild and Wall and their team excavated throughout most of the Stadt Huys block, including in the remaining undisturbed deposits around the walls purported to be from the Stadt Huys. Although they found parts of the 1670 tavern that had abutted the Stadt Huys, they found no traces of the city's first municipal building itself. When they dug the undisturbed deposits remaining around the south wall, which was purported to be from the Stadt Huys, they found no seventeenth-century deposits associated with it. Furthermore, the analysis of the mortar from that wall showed that its composition was similar to that of mortar made in the eighteenth and nineteenth centuries.[50] So they concluded that the wall was not from the Stadt Huys but had been built later.[51] Since the area around the north wall had been removed in conjunction with the Kellerman excavation, they could not confirm Kellerman's contention that that wall was from the seventeenth century Stadt Huys. There is only a brief summary of that earlier testing available today and no detailed archaeological field report describing the details of the stratigraphy and the context of the artifacts that Kellerman found in her excavations.[52] Therefore, it is impossible to ascertain whether her finds associated with the north wall were in their original contexts of unmixed seventeenth-century soils, indicating the wall had been built in the seventeenth century, or whether they had been mixed with later materials, indicating that the wall (like the south wall) had been built later, in the eighteenth century. Unfortunately, then, there is no conclusive archaeological evidence that confirms the rumors that the Stadt Huys walls had survived.

So the physical traces of the building that began as a tavern owned by one of the world's first great international corporations—the Dutch West India Company—and that later became New York's (and New Amsterdam's) first city hall and courthouse may well have disappeared at the turn of the eighteenth century. Ironically, however, its site today went back to its corporate roots. It first became the corporate headquarters of Goldman Sachs, one of the great global investment banking and securities firms of the twenty-first century, and now houses Oppenheimer and Company, a leading investment firm (Figure 7.3). International corporations

Figure 7.3. The former Goldman Sachs building at the corner of Broad and Pearl Streets stands on the site of the original Stadt Huys.

again dominate the skyline of the city, as well as the city itself. But if you look closely at the plaza in front of this modern building, you will see paving stones outlining the footprint of the Stadt Huys, the city's first municipal building, as it was imagined in the twentieth century.

ACKNOWLEDGMENTS

We are indebted to the late Regina Kellerman, who worked tirelessly to protect New York City's past. In particular, her research breathed life into seventeenth-century New Amsterdam and New York by making the Stadt Huys come alive. We are honored to follow in her footsteps. We would also like to thank Charles Gehring for his help in interpreting the fabric of the building, as well as Nan A. Rothschild, Albert Rosenblatt, and Julia Rosenblatt for their comments on an earlier version of this essay.

NOTES

1. Anne-Marie Cantwell and Diana diZerega Wall, "Landscapes and Other Objects: Creating Dutch New Netherland," *New York History, Quarterly Journal of the New York State Historical Association* 89, no. 4 (2006): 315–45; "New Amsterdam: The Subordination of Native Space," in *Soldiers, Cities, and Landscapes: Papers in Honor of Charles L. Fisher,* ed. P. B. Drooker and John Hart (Albany: The New York State Museum, 2010); Jaap Jacobs, *New Netherland: A Dutch Colony in Seventeenth-Century America* (Leiden: Brill, 2005).

2. See Jacobs, *New Netherland,* 132–33, and Oliver A. Rink, *Holland on the Hudson: An Economic and Social History of Dutch New York* (Ithaca: Cornell University Press, 1986), for discussions of Articles and Conditions and Freedom and Exemptions and their effect on the reorganization of the colony.

3. Rink, *Holland on the Hudson,* 136.

4. Jacobs, *New Netherland,* 133.

5. David DeVries, in *Narratives of New Netherland, 1609–1664,* ed. J. Franklin Jameson (New York: Charles Scribner's Sons, 1909), 212. Kieft also agreed to dig a well and either to build a brew house nearby or to grant the use of the Company's brew house to the innkeeper (A. J. F. van Laer, trans. and ed., *New York State Historical Manuscripts,* 4 vols. [Baltimore: Genealogical Publishing Company, 1974], II: 103).

6. Annette Stott, "Inventing Memory: Picturing New Netherland in the Nineteenth Century," in *Revisiting New Netherland: Perspectives on Early Dutch America,* ed. Joyce Goodfriend (Leiden: Brill, 2005), 20–21.

7. See Stott "Inventing Memory" for an analysis of some of the problems involved in using early views. For example, our Figure 7.1 is a watercolor thought to have been made on-site to support the colonists' Remonstrance to the Staats General to gain more control of the governing of the colony. Perhaps to support its case, it presents a view of a shabby New Amsterdam (Museum of the City of New York, "New York Begins: A Rare Drawing of New Amsterdam. ca. 1650," brochure prepared for an exhibit of the same name [New York, n.d.]). As such, it may or may not reflect the actual landscape of the time.

8. Regina Kellerman, "The Stadhuis of New Amsterdam: New York's First City Hall" (PhD diss., Pennsylvania State University 1983), 68–69. Kellerman conducted extensive research for her dissertation. She was the director of historical and architectural research at the NYC Landmarks Preservation Commission in the 1960s. Her documentation of the physical aspects of the Stadt Huys—its ground plan, its construction materials, its appearance both inside and out, and how it changed through time—has proved invaluable to the present authors. Her work was based on the use of seventeenth-century views and narratives of New Amsterdam and the United Provinces, as well as on the examination of seventeenth-century structures that are still standing in the Netherlands today. As such, by necessity, her reconstruction (and therefore ours), no matter how meticulous, is based upon analogy and probability, and not necessarily on fact. However, although it may err in the details, the reconstruction is probably correct in its overall

conception, and was invaluable to us in writing this essay. Stott ("Inventing Memory," 20–21, 16–17) discusses the difficulties in interpreting the various views of the Stadt Huys. Such limitations, inevitable in such reconstructions, must be taken into account in reading the description that follows in this chapter.

9. The fabric of the Stadt Huys is something of a problem. Although David de Vries noted in 1642 that Kieft told him that it was "of stone" (DeVries in *Narratives of New Netherland,* 212), Van Laer (*New York Historical Manuscripts, Dutch,* II: 124, n.15) points out that the phrase *"steenen huys,"* or "stone house," may be used for houses made of either brick or stone and in fact in Holland it usually referred to brick houses because there is so little stone there. However, he suggests that in New Netherland houses might most likely have been made of stone because of the abundance of that material (*New York Historical Manuscripts,: Dutch,* I: 131, n. 1). Kellerman, "The Stadhuis of New Amsterdam," 28, citing Van Laer's translation but not following his interpretation, suggests that the inn was made of brick, based in part on the fact that when repairs were made to the structure, bricklayers (and not masons) were hired. The building is shown as yellow in color on the only contemporary, on-site, in-color drawing that we have of it, shown as Figure 7.1 here, suggesting that it was made of yellow brick. However, the use of yellow could be due to artistic license. Charles Gehring of the New Netherland Institute suggests that it was probably of brick, but whether the brick was red or yellow is not clear; in any case, any brick would have to have been imported as ballast at the point in the colony's history when the tavern was built, because the Dutch only began to make bricks successfully there in the 1650s, a decade after the tavern's completion (personal communication 2009). We tend to support the latter's interpretation.

10. The western façade is the only other side of the building depicted in contemporary images, which by convention showed the city viewed from the shore.

11. Kellerman, "The Stadhuis of New Amsterdam," 44–45. See Stott, "Inventing Memory," 26–27, on the difficulties in reconstructing the façade.

12. The tavern's keepers included Haarlem native Phillip Gerritsen, who rented the tavern from the Company with the stipulation that he serve Company wines to his customers (I. N. Phelps Stokes, *Iconography of Manhattan Island, 1498–1909,* 6 vols. [New York: Robert H. Dodd, 1915–1928], IV 98: 2/17/1643), and, after Gerritsen's death, Adriaen Dircksen, who had married Gerritsen's widow. Then in 1652, Abram de la Noy was given the lease to the tavern (Stokes, *Iconography of Manhattan Island,* IV:125 1/24/1652).

13. Kellerman, "The Stadhuis of New Amsterdam," 76–77, 75, 83, 88, 71, 89–90.

14. Ibid., 90; Van Laer, *New York Historical Manuscripts: Dutch,* I:112.

15. Jacobs, *New Netherland,* 240; Russell Shorto, *The Island at the Center of the World* (New York: Doubleday, 2004), 257.

16. Charles T. Gehring, ed. and trans., *Correspondence, 1647–1653* (Syracuse: Syracuse University Press, 2000), 149.

17. Jacobs, *New Netherland,* 150–52.

18. Jaap Jacobs, "'To Favor This New and Growing City of New Amsterdam with a Court of Justice': Relations between Rulers and Ruled in New Amsterdam," *De Halve Maen* 76 (Winter 2003), 65–72; *New Netherland,* 168.

19. Jacobs, *New Netherland,* 169, 172.

20. Berthold Fernow, ed., *The Records of New Amsterdam from 1653–1674 anno domini.* 7 vols. (New York: The City of New York/Knickerbocker Press, 1897), I: 48.

21. Ibid., I: 49.

22. Jacobs, "To Favor This New and Growing City," 72.

23. Ibid., 57, 67–68, 70; *New Netherland,* 168–70.

24. Shorto, *The Island at the Center of the World,* 258.

25. Fernow, *Records of New Amsterdam,* I: 146.

26. Ibid., I: 219, 291.

27. Stokes, Iconography of Manhattan Island, IV: 402.

28. Fernow, *Records of New Amsterdam,* I: 292.

29. Kellerman, "The Stadhuis of New Amsterdam," 7, 72.

30. Fernow, *Records of New Amsterdam,* VI: 287.

31. Kellerman, "The Stadhuis of New Amsterdam," 79–82.

32. Jacobs, *New Netherland,* 170.

33. Fernow, *Records of New Amsterdam,* VII: 218.

34. This use of *kas* for the singular and *kasse* for the plural is derived from J. P. Volk, "The Dutch Kast and the American Kas: A Structural/Historical Analysis," in *New World Dutch Studies: Dutch Arts and Culture in Colonial America, 1609–1776,* ed. R. H. Blackburn and N. A. Kelley (Albany: Albany Institute of History and Arts, 1987), 107, who states that these were the terms common in the seventeenth century.

35. Fernow, *Records of New Amsterdam,* I: 306.

36. Kellerman, "The Stadhuis of New Amsterdam," 84–85, 91–93; Philip White, "Municipal Government Comes to Manhattan," *New-York Historical Society Quarterly* 37, no. 2 (1953): 157.

37. Kellerman, "The Stadhuis of New Amsterdam," 86–87.

38. Fernow, *Records of New Amsterdam,* VII: 208.

39. Ibid., VI: 215.

40. Kellerman, "The Stadhuis of New Amsterdam," 20, 47.

41. Stokes, *The Iconography of Manhattan Island,* VI: 532.

42. Ibid., IV: 423.

43. Ibid.

44. Ibid.

45. See Anne-Marie Cantwell and Diana diZerega Wall, *Unearthing Gotham: The Archaeology of New York City* (New Haven: Yale University Press, 2002), 16–30; Kellerman, "The Stadhuis of New Amsterdam"; Nan A. Rothschild, Diana diZerega Wall, and Eugene Boesch, "The Archaeological Investigations of the Stadt Huys Block: A Final Report" (on file with the New York City Landmarks Preservation Commission, 1987).

46. Kellerman, "The Stadhuis of New Amsterdam."

47. Ibid., 109–12.

48. Ibid, 112.

49. The commission staff members who were active in bringing archaeology to the city included then executive director Lenore Norman, preservationist Kathryn Misch, and counsel Dorothy Miner; the commission's chairman at that time was Kent Barwick.

50. Mary B. Dierickx, "Stadt Huys Block: Architectural Analysis. Appendix A," in Rothschild, Wall, and Boesch, "The Archaeological Investigation of the Stadt Huys Block."

51. Rothschild, Wall, and Boesch, "The Archaeological Investigation of the Stadt Huys Block," 220–21.

52. Kellerman, "The Stadhuis of New Amsterdam," 110–12.

Chapter Eight

Prosecution or Persecution?

The 1657 Flushing Incident

Charles Gehring

As soon as the Dutch began to settle in New Netherland in 1624, the West India Company insisted that everyone be granted "freedom of conscience." This did not necessarily include freedom to worship. The Stuyvesant administration passed an ordinance in 1656 prohibiting the practice of any religion other than the Reformed. Enforcement gave rise to friction with Quakers, resulting in the Flushing Remonstrance. Charles Gehring gives the historical background and a nuanced account of the events.

In 1657, Petrus Stuyvesant, Director General of New Netherland, jailed several officials of the mostly English village of Vlissingen [Flushing] on Long Island. Their crime was insubordination and contravention of their oaths by allowing Quakers to meet in their homes.[1] On the surface it appears to be a clear-cut case of intolerance by an authoritarian figure and a heroic act of resistance by intrepid citizens, striking a blow for religious freedom. The remonstrance or grievance was in protest of an ordinance prohibiting the harboring of Quakers.[2] It was written by Tobias Feake, village *schout,* and read aloud by Edward Hart, village clerk, for which they were jailed. The protest is based primarily on the principle of "Freedom of Conscience."[3] It all seems so cut and dried, as Stuyvesant had a history in these matters. Several years earlier he had recommended to the West India Company directors in Amsterdam that a group of Jews fleeing Brazil not be allowed to settle in New Netherland;[4] while several petitions by the large Lutheran community to call a minister were denied out of hand.[5]

In contrast, the English settlers in Vlissingen had fled religious persecution in New England hoping to enjoy the fabled religious tolerance of the Dutch. It couldn't be more black and white. However, when put into its cultural context it may prove to be many shades of gray. You be the judge.

When Stuyvesant became director general of New Netherland in 1647, the Dutch eighty years' revolt against the Hapsburg Empire was just drawing to a close. The Dutch of the newly independent United Provinces of the Netherlands were, in 1648, the first in history to win their freedom from a world-class empire; the next people to do so, a century and a half later, should be familiar to every American.

The Dutch revolt against the Hapsburg Empire was caused by a complex set of social, religious, political, and economic issues. In simple terms, the revolt was in reaction to two

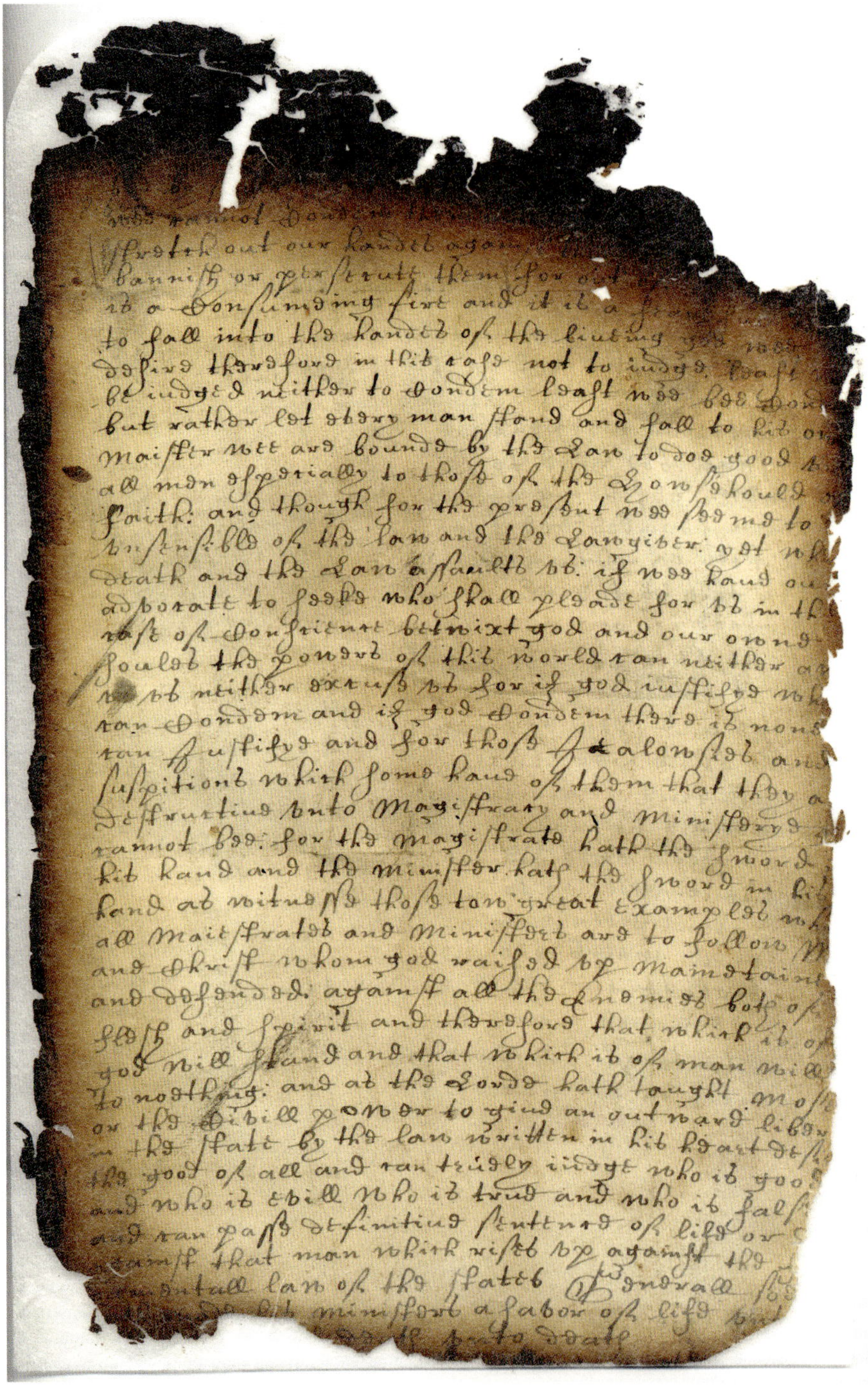

wee cannot condem th
stretch out our handes again
bannish or persecute them for out
is a consuming fire and it is a fe
to fall into the handes of the liveing god wee
desire therefore in this case not to iudge least
we iudged neither to condem least wee bee con
but rather let every man stand and fall to his o
maister wee are bounde by the law to doe good
all men especially to those of the household
faith: and though for the present wee seeme to
unsensible of the law and the lawgiver: yet wh
death and the law assaults us: if wee have ou
advocate to seeke who shall pleade for us in th
case of conscience betwixt god and our owne
soules the powers of this world can neither a
us neither excuse us for if god iustifye wh
can condem and if god condem there is none
can iustifye and for those iealousies and
suspitions which some have of them that they a
destructive unto magistracy and ministerye
cannot bee: for the magistrate hath the sword
his hand and the minister hath the sword in hi
hand as witnesse those two great examples wh
all magistrates and ministers are to follow M
and Christ whom god raised up maintaine
and defended against all the enemies both of
flesh and spirit and therefore that which is of
god will stand and that which is of man will
come to nothing: and as the Lorde hath taught Mo
or the civill power to give an outward liber
in the state by the law written in his heart des
the good of all and can truely iudge who is good
and who is evill who is true and who is fals
and can passe definitive sentence of life or
against that man which rises up against the
fundamentall law of the states generall so
his ministers a savor of life
death unto death

FIGURE 8.1. The Flushing Remonstrance—A petition from the freeholders of Flushing and Jamaica, Long Island, to Governor Petrus Stuyvesant protesting his ban on Quaker religious meetings, 1657. New York State Archives. Dutch colonial council minutes, 1638–1665. Series A1809-78.

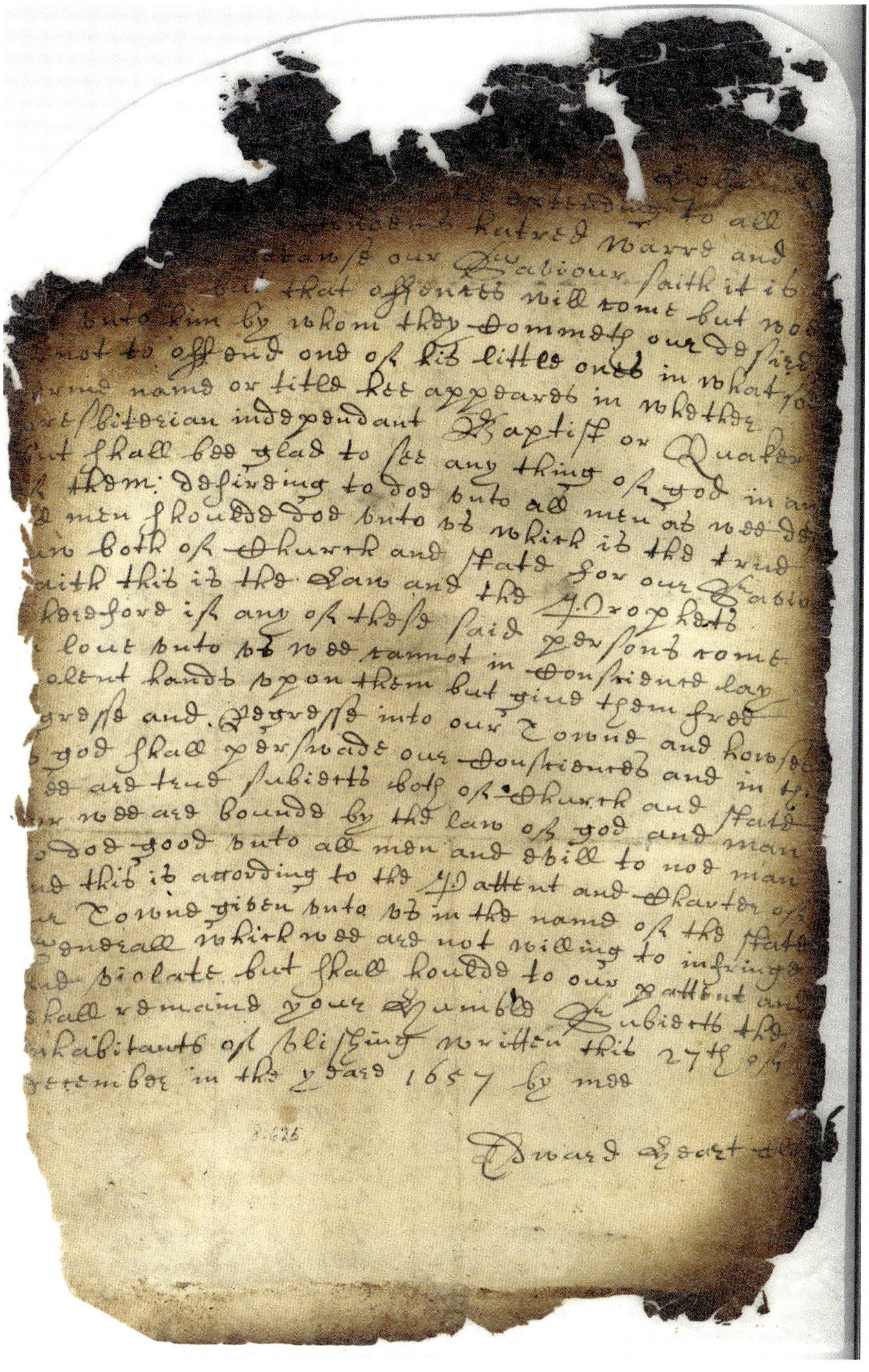
...attending to all
...woords ... hatred warre and
...because our Saviour saith it is
...but that offences will come but woe
unto him by whom they commeth our desire
not to offend one of his little ones in what
...forme name or title hee appeares in whether
...presbiterian independant Baptist or Quaker
but shall bee glad to see any thing of god in any
of them: desiring to doe unto all men as wee desire
all men shoulde doe unto us which is the true
law both of Church and State for our Saviour
saith this is the Law and the Prophets
Therefore if any of these said persons come
in love unto us wee cannot in conscience lay
violent hands upon them but give them free
egresse and regresse into our Towne and howses
as god shall perswade our consciences and in this
wee are true subjects both of Church and State
for wee are bounde by the law of god and man
to doe good unto all men and evill to noe man
and this is according to the Pattent and Charter of
our Towne given unto us in the name of the States
Generall which wee are not willing to infringe
and violate but shall houlde to our Pattent and
shall remaine your humble subjects the
inhabitants of Vlishing written this 27th of
december in the yeare 1657 by mee

Edward Hart Cl...

FIGURE 8.1. *Continued.*

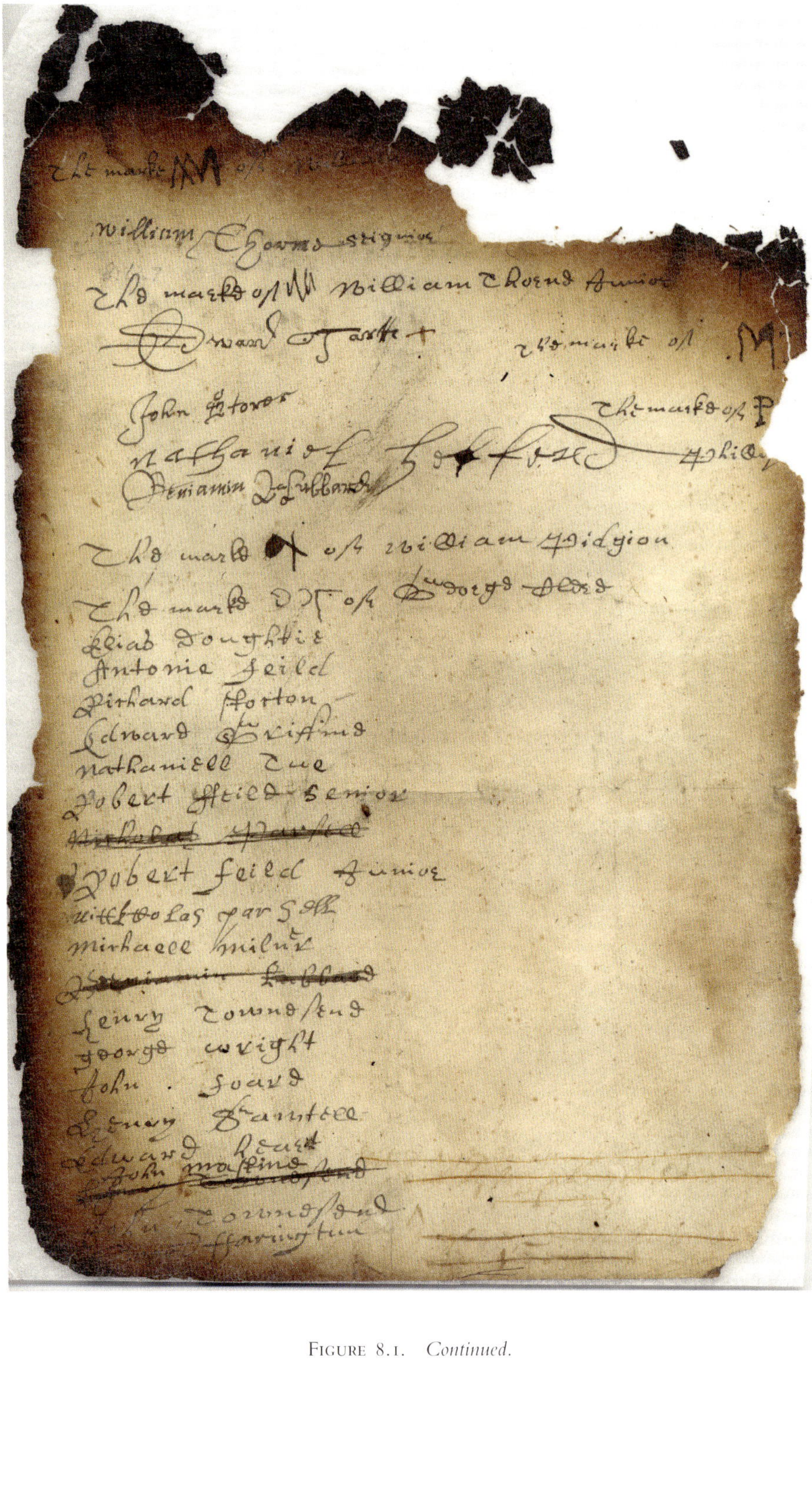

FIGURE 8.1. *Continued.*

Hapsburg initiatives: an attempt to establish a central control and authority in the Netherlands—to the detriment of local privileges, and the establishment of the Inquisition to suppress the Protestant heresy.

The cerebral issue was perceived as an attack on the ancient rights and privileges of every political entity in the Netherlands. The emotional issue was seen as an attempt to suppress the religious threat to the Roman church by the Reformed religion of John Calvin. Both issues were ideal for Spain's Philip II to pursue. Unlike his father Charles V, he had no affection for the Netherlands. He viewed these Northern provinces merely as fatted cows to be exploited. A centrally controlled Netherlands was to provide economic and human resources for Philip's political agenda. As a devout Catholic he viewed the Reformed movement in the North as a disease that had to be stamped out before it spread. Philip's inability to deal compassionately with these forces in the Netherlands and his inability to view the Dutch as anything but hostile heretics, led to the establishment of a new country, the United Provinces of the Netherlands.

Because of the brutality of the Spanish Inquisition's attempt to suppress the inexorable spread of the Reformed religion, the principle of tolerance was written into the 1579 Union of Utrecht—a defensive treaty among the northern provinces, which would serve as the constitution of the new nation. Article 13 stated that although the only public religion was the Reformed each person was to remain free, especially in his religion, and that no one shall be persecuted or investigated because of his religion.[6] This is the tenet of "Freedom of Conscience"; everyone is free to believe whatever he or she wishes without fear of persecution. No longer would so-called heretics be hanged or burned at the stake. The Dutch felt strongly about this as more Protestants were executed in the Low Countries than any other place in Europe during the Reformation.[7] Although "Freedom of Conscience" was central to the new country's tenets, more important was the principle of *pax et concordia*—peace and concord.[8] Or, what price tolerance amid chaos?

In order to survive in that congested corner of Europe, the Dutch needed order and stability in their communities. Although people could believe what they wished, it was a basic belief that unity of religion was the goal. However, as rapid as was the spread of Calvinism throughout the Netherlands, it never became a majority religion, let alone a national religion. How was it possible to maintain *pax et concordia* in communities where "Freedom of Conscience" was a basic tenet, where Lutherans, Mennonites, and other Christian sects were tolerated and allowed to worship surreptitiously? It was done by a very human reaction to possible conflict called connivance, or *oogluijckinge* in Dutch, literally to wink at something. The Dutch sensed that a strict prohibition of worship would cause an even greater threat to *pax et concordia*. Thus, a narrow path had to be navigated between "Freedom of Conscience" and the preference for religious unity in a community in order to maintain stability.

For New Netherland, the matter was less complicated. The revised West India Company "Charter of Freedoms and Exemptions" of 1640 clearly states that no other religion shall be publicly admitted in New Netherland except for the Reformed, as it is presently preached and practiced by public authority in the United Provinces. The charter also clearly states that care be taken to maintain "Freedom of Conscience" for everyone, provided that forbidden assemblies and conventicles are avoided.[9] To Stuyvesant and his council, and the Reformed *predicanten*, there was no room for debate. In an apparent attempt to discourage "connivance" of any kind, an ordinance was passed in February of 1656 prohibiting the practice of any religion other than the Reformed.[10] This ordinance, which, by the way, all *schouts* were obligated by oath to uphold, was soon put to the test.

During the summer of 1657 a Lutheran minister by the name of Johannes Ernestus Gutwasser arrived at New Amsterdam. The Lutherans apparently hoped that, although their petitions had failed to receive permission to call a minister, if one happened to appear, the authorities would look the other way or just wink. This wasn't to be the case. Gutwasser preached surreptitiously but eventually was ordered back to Europe in 1659.[11]

Shortly after Gutwasser's appearance, another arrival contributed to the religious tension on Manhattan. In August 1657, a ship approached the fort at the tip of Manhattan flying no flag and without firing a salute. The ship's master showed neither the *fiscaal* any respect when he came on board, nor Stuyvesant when he came before him, but stood still "with his hat firm on his head, as if a goat." The ship had left London eight weeks before with Quakers on board. When the ship left Manhattan for its destination of Rhode Island, one of the Dutch ministers commented that is where all the cranks of New England retire. Before the ship sailed through the Hell Gate, two women were left behind: Mary Weatherhead and Dorothy Waugh, strong, young women, who, as the ship sailed out of sight, "began to quake and fly into a frenzy, crying

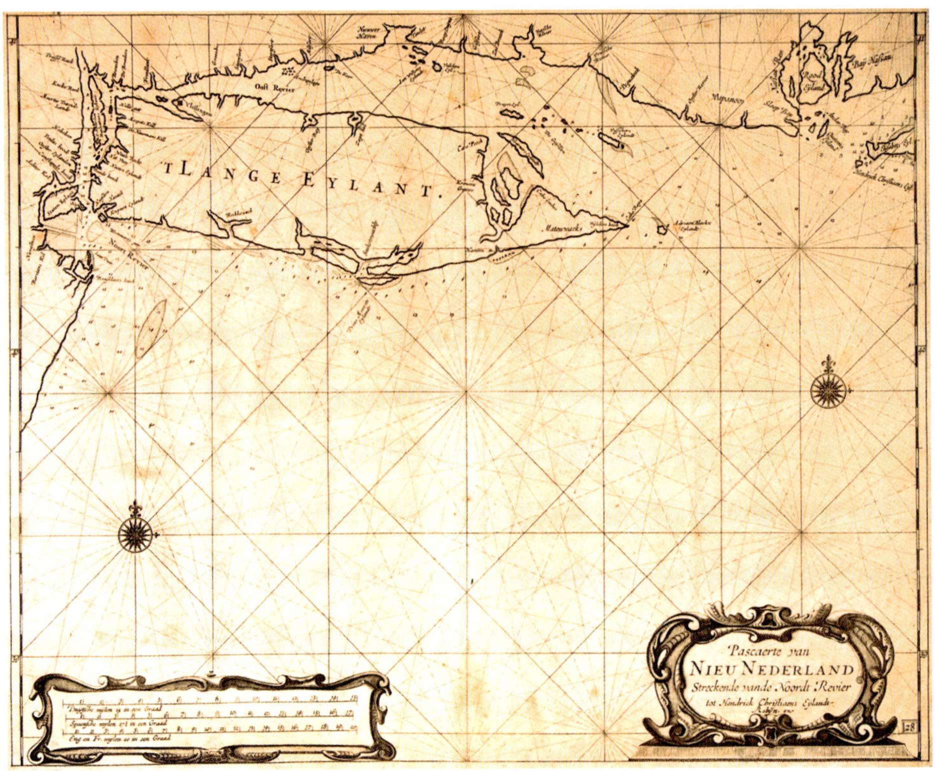

FIGURE 8.2. "Pascaerte van Nieu Nederland Streckende vande Noordt Revier tot Hendrick Christiaens Eÿlandt," by Jacob Robijn, 1685. Long Island Sound served as a funnel between Rhode Island and Manhattan: In August 1657, the reverends Megapolensis and Drisius surmised that the departure of an English ship with Quakers had sailed for Rhode Island, because "all the cranks of New England retire thither." From the collection of Joep de Koning.

FIGURE 8.3. Postage stamp commemorating the Flushing Remonstrance Tercentenary (1957). Photo by Teodors Ermansons.

out loudly in the middle of the street that men should repent, for the Day of Judgment was at hand." The inhabitants, "not knowing what was the matter, ran to and fro, while one cried 'Fire' and another something else." The two women were seized by the *fiscaal* and an assistant, who led them to the prison as they "continued to cry out and pray in their manner."[12] Not the *pax et concordia* Stuyvesant was trying to maintain in the community.

Unfortunately, we don't know what happened to the two women—whether they remained in prison or were released. It is possible that they eventually made their way to Vlissingen and were sheltered by Tobias Feake, the *schout*. In any case, Feake was accused of harboring a Quakeress, which was interpreted as allowing a conventicle or illegal meeting in contravention of his oath. It is no secret that Stuyvesant considered the Quakers an abominable sect who "vilify both the political authorities and the ministers of the Gospel and undermine the state and God's service." For Stuyvesant it all probably was a matter of authority, which for the Quakers was a private spiritual experience or the "inner light" devoid of training, and examination of ministerial candidates, and without structure as in other religions, such as the Reformed. Quakers were viewed by civil authorities as seditious anarchists, and by ecclesiastical authorities as "machinations of Satan."[13] However, Feake had broken his oath to enforce the ordinances of New Netherland, for which Stuyvesant had him prosecuted. During this entire episode Quakers were still being hanged in Massachusetts; the last one was Mary Dyer in 1660.[14] No Quakers were ever hanged in New Netherland.

To Stuyvesant the issue was insubordination; he didn't need to consider the ideas in the remonstrance because it was an expression of "Freedom of Conscience." Stuyvesant's fault was that he refused to connive with or wink at the Quakers.

Several years later the issue of the Quakers was returned to the Netherlands in the form of John Bowne. His banishment from New Netherland for holding Quaker meetings brought about a rebuke from the West India Company regarding Stuyvesant's handling of the problem. In 1663 the WIC directors wrote that they would rather that such dissidents went elsewhere but doubted whether "we can proceed against them rigorously without diminishing the population and stopping immigration, which must be favored at a so tender stage of the country's existence." They ordered Stuyvesant to shut his eyes, at least not force people's consciences, but allow everyone to have his own belief, as long as he behaves quietly and legally, gives no offense to his neighbors and does not oppose the government.[15] Stuyvesant was back on the narrow path between "Freedom of Conscience" and *pax et concordia*. In the end Stuyvesant was forced to wink.

POSTSCRIPT

If you compare the ideas expressed in the 1657 Flushing Remonstrance with Article XIII of the 1579 Union of Utrecht, they are essentially the same.

NOTES

1. *Documents Relating to the Colonial History of the State of New York*, ed. Bertold Fernow (Albany: 1865–1883), 14: 403ff. (Hereafter cited as *NYCD*).

2. Text of the Flushing Remonstrance is published in *NYCD*, 14: 402–403.

3. See the Union of Utrecht, Article 13, published in *Texts Concerning the Revolt of the Netherlands*, ed. E. H. Kossman and A. F. Mellink (Cambridge: Cambridge University Press, 1974), 169–70.

4. See Stuyvesant's September 22, 1654, letter to the West India Company directors in Amsterdam, published in Samuel Oppenheim's *The Early History of the Jews in New York, 1654–1664,* American Jewish Historical Society, No. 18 (1909), 4–5. For the directors' response see *New Netherland Documents, Correspondence 1654–1658,* trans. and ed. Charles Gehring (Syracuse: Syracuse University Press, 2003), 49.

5. See *Ecclesiastical Records. State of New York,* ed. Hugh Hastings (Albany: State of New York, 1901), vol. 1, 317. (Hereafter cited as *ER*).

6. See Union of Utrecht, op cit.

7. See Jonathan Israel, *The Dutch Republic* (Oxford: Oxford University Press, 1995), 100.

8. For an article on the idea of tolerance in the Dutch Republic see Jaap Jacobs, "Between Repression and Approval: Connivance and Tolerance in the Dutch Republic and in New Netherland," *de Halve Maen* LXXI, no. 3 (Fall 1998): 51–58.

9. See *Documents Relative to the Colonial History of the State of New York,* ed. E. B. O'Callaghan (Albany: 1856), vol. 1. 123.

10. For this ordinance see *New Netherland Documents, Laws and Writs of Appeal,* in the series, ed. and trans. Charles Gehring (Syracuse: 1991), 55.

11. See "Dutch Colonial Manuscripts, Council Minutes," vol. 8, 845, 1026 for orders on the disposition of Gutwasser.

12. See *ER*, vol. 1, 399 for the letter of Domines Megapolensis and Drisius dated August 14, 1657.

13. Ibid., 400.

14. See Edward Burrough, "A Declaration of the Sad and Great Persecution and Martyrdom of the People of God, Called Quakers, in New-England for Worshipping of God" (1661), *Electronic Texts in American Studies,* University of Nebraska, 2007.

15. See *NYCD*, 15: 526, for a letter from the WIC directors to Stuyvesant, dated April 16, 1663.

Chapter Nine

Lutherans and the Law in New Netherland

The Politics of Religion

Peter R. Christoph

Peter Christoph describes the religious conflicts during the 16th century that led eventually to the ability of Lutherans to worship publicly in Amsterdam. They were not, however, allowed to do so in New Netherland. Peter Christoph recounts the attempts by New Netherland's Lutherans to establish congregations.

We cannot well leave; yet, without the exercise of religion can still less live.

—Petition of Lutherans in New Netherland to the
Directors of the West India Company, May 20, 1659

INTRODUCTION

The government of New Netherland has long been denounced in both scholarly and popular history as intolerant of religions other than the Reformed. Yet the laws of the colony were modeled after those of the parent Netherlands, which was probably the most liberal country in all of Europe, granting freedom of conscience to everyone. That is, it allowed for private worship within households. Public worship was another matter entirely, granted only to the Reformed Church. Nonetheless, that was an extremely generous position, in an age of inquisitions and wars of religion. But of course the nonestablished churches wanted more.

THE 1500s

To understand denominational relations in New Netherland, it is helpful to review, albeit briefly, some of the events in Europe during the previous century.

The Protestant Reformation had begun exactly a century before the founding of the West India Company, and there were rival understandings from the beginning. From 1525 to 1528 Martin Luther and the early leader of the Reformed movement, Huldrych Zwingli, engaged in a pamphlet war with such terms as *heretic* and *fanatic* being tossed about. A conference of Protestant leaders in 1529 failed to resolve the one principal difference, as to whether Holy Communion was a memorial meal (Zwingli), or a sacrament in which Christ was physically present in the bread and wine (Luther). They would also split over *adiaphora,* matters neither required nor forbidden by scripture, such as liturgy and images of saints, which Luther thought were a matter of local choice, but Zwingli insisted had to be eliminated.

THE NETHERLANDS

The Reformed religion, particularly in its Calvinist form,[1] dominated Protestantism in both the Belgian and Dutch Netherlands from the beginning. It was also politically active, a leading force in the opposition to both Spanish rule and Catholicism.

In August 1566, Calvinist rioters swept through Catholic churches in several cities, smashing statues of saints and destroying church property in general. At the bequest of William the Silent, Prince of Orange, Lutherans joined with Catholics and others to restore order in Antwerp. Calvinists throughout the Netherlands long remembered the Lutherans' opposition to the iconoclasts, charging them with treachery to the Protestant cause.

In Amsterdam that same year, immigrant Germans, Frisians, and Scandinavians sought permission from the civil authorities to organize a Lutheran congregation. Calvinists feared a divided Protestantism in the face of Spanish aggression, and proposed a plan of union. This was rejected by the Lutherans, which the Reformed took as further evidence that Lutherans were inimical to the cause of winning the country over completely to Protestantism.[2]

When Antwerp fell to a Spanish army in 1585, many Flemish Lutherans fled northward to the Dutch Republic. Those that found refuge in Amsterdam joined with the resident Lutherans in organizing a congregation in 1588. They worshiped in each others' homes until 1600, when the States General (national parliament) granted tolerance to Roman Catholics and Lutherans.

However, in that same year the Reformed synods of South and North Holland appealed to the magistrates of all the towns to prohibit Lutheran public worship. For a time, tolerance even in Amsterdam was rescinded. However, the Netherlands was in its Golden Age; Amsterdam had a large number of foreign merchants and workers; and whether these refugees had come to improve their economic, political, or religious situation, they wanted to hold public services. In 1604 the city government restored toleration to the Lutherans. Elsewhere, the States General allowed Lutheran services to be held in large towns, but forbade them in all but two villages.[3]

Eventually, tolerated denominations were permitted to build houses of worship, provided they did not look like churches. The Lutherans in Amsterdam obtained the use of a warehouse, which they converted into a church, dedicated in 1633. Written signs were not permitted outside but logos were allowed, and Lutheran churches throughout the Netherlands used the image of a swan (which has appeared in the seal of First Lutheran Church in Albany since the eighteenth century).[4]

A synod of six congregations in the Amsterdam area was formed in 1614. However, the real authority was held by the consistory (congregational government) of the Amsterdam church, which was the agency to which Lutherans in New Netherland would look for help.

NEW NETHERLAND

The operation of overseas colonies was expensive, as was the Dutch Republic's decades-old war of independence against Spain. Citizens were suffering from an ever-increasing financial burden and this did not help the government's popularity. The States General decided to charter two commercial enterprises, the East India Company, to own and operate the colonies on the Pacific Ocean, and the West India Company those on the Atlantic. The companies were required to wage war overseas against the enemies of the nation, with any prizes taken on the high seas to be theirs and theirs alone, together with whatever profits they could realize from the colonies. With a few strokes of the pen some of the country's largest expenses had been turned over to private companies.

Naturally, the chief concern of the West India Company's director in New Netherland was to develop the profitability of local operations. Principal among these was the fur trade, which required only traders, a business manager (*fiscaal*), and soldiers for their protection. Any permanent settlers were an expensive nuisance and the company in 1629 granted its principal stockholders the right to establish their own private colonies within the now-designated *province* of New Netherland and recruit settlers to operate farms and mills. These private investors were granted the elegant title of *patroon* (patron); ten such colonies were started but only Rensselaerswyck surrounding Fort Orange survived, largely due to the personal wealth of Kiliaen van Rensselaer: his colony never turned a profit until the 1690s.

In short, the West India Company, like the Dutch generally, looked for pragmatic solutions to problems. Religion was one such problem, and the company tried to find ways to balance the desires of the Reformed church against the wishes of the colonists, of whom nearly half were originally immigrants from someplace else into the Netherlands.[5]

Figure 9.1. View of New York from the North, 1679. PR 020 Geographic File, flat file, 19th century reproductions of 17th century views; negative no. 75087. Collection of The New-York Historical Society.

Figure 9.2. The beaver trade was so important that the animal was part of the seal of New Netherland. This image was prepared for The Huguenot-Walloon New Netherland Commission, instituted by the Federal Council of the Churches of Christ in America, for the celebration of the 300th anniversary of the settling in New Netherland of Walloons (French and Belgian Huguenots) by the Dutch West India Company, in 1624. State Library call number N,284.573,H89.

THE WEST INDIA COMPANY'S GOVERNING OF NEW NETHERLAND

Unlike settlers in some of the English colonies, immigrants to New Netherland came generally to improve their economic, not religious, situations. The first Reformed minister at Fort Orange[6] reported in 1642 that many people chose not to attend services, and an order was issued requiring their attendance, on pain of fine.[7] Regulations forbidding the serving of alcohol during the hours of divine service were regularly renewed but, to judge by court records, frequently ignored.

The West India Company was under pressure in the Netherlands from the politically powerful Reformed Church not to grant toleration in the colonies.[8] There was nothing about religion in the documents of 1621, 1622, or 1623.[9] The 1624 "Provisional Regulations for the Colonists" had a proviso against religious presecution.[10] The "Freedoms and Exemptions" granted by the West India Company in 1629 to the *patroons* said nothing on the subject of religion.[11] However, the 1640 "Freedoms and Exemptions" limited public services to the Reformed Church.[12]

When the province's first director general,[13] Petrus Stuyvesant, arrived at New Amsterdam on May 11, 1647, it was with the firm resolve to carry out his sworn duties in full. He would prove particularly conscientious in repressing "conventicles." He told the Reformed clergy that he would rather resign his office than violate his commission and his oath by permitting "any other than the Reformed doctrine."[14]

Company directors in Amsterdam,[15] however, were happy to have any kind of workers in the colony and at various times asked Stuyvesant to ease restrictions on Lutherans, Quakers, and Jews.[16] Stuyvesant was agreeable to allowing worship according to their own traditions in their own homes, but the Lutherans naturally pressed for the rights they had enjoyed in Amsterdam, where they had been allowed a church and ministers (or, more accurately, where the congregation tried to draw no attention, and the city government pretended to be unaware of them).[17]

On September 22, 1647, Stuyvesant appointed an advisory council, the Nine Men, to represent the inhabitants. His instructions to them made clear his priorities: "to promote the honor of God and the welfare of our dear fatherland, the greatest advantage of the Company and the prosperity of the worthy commonalty here, and the advancement of the pure Reformed religion."[18]

THE CONGREGATION IN AMERICA

The earliest known Lutheran to become a permanent resident of New Netherland was Albert Andriessen Bratt.[19] Originally from Frederickstad, Norway, he had lived in Amsterdam and worked at various trades before emigrating once again. He arrived at Fort Orange with his family on Easter Sunday 1637.[20]

FIGURE 9.3. L. F. Tantillo, *Fort Orange, 1635*. Reproduction courtesy of the artist.

The first permanent Lutheran settler at Manhattan was Jonas Bronck, a sea captain turned landowner, from whose name comes the Bronx. He apparently died in 1643 before any known Lutheran activities began. His nationality is uncertain; his birthplace is given variously as Komstad, Sweden, and Copenhagen, Denmark, and he may have been raised on the Danish Faroe Islands. His personal library contained several books in Danish and none in Swedish.

It is unknown how early it was that Lutherans in the colony began meeting together to worship. The first evidence of their existence appeared in the minutes of the Lutheran consistory in Amsterdam for October 12, 1649: "There was opened and read the letter from some members in New Netherland, who declared themselves to be adherents of our religion of the Unaltered Augsburg Confession,[21] requesting that they may be supplied there with a pastor."[22]

The consistory meditated on the proposal for a week before deciding on more delay, "as it is a matter of far-reaching consequence and the most serious consideration to engage therein, in view of the state of the country and the situation of our churches at this juncture of time."[23] Apparently the consistory was worried that stirring up trouble in New Netherland could produce retaliation at home.

The Lutherans in New Netherland had written collectively as one "community," including therein Lutherans at any location in the province. In 1653 they claimed to have about 150 families "on Manhattan,[24] at Fort Orange, as well as on Long Island," and in 1659 wrote, "At Ft. Orange there are from 70 to 80 families; here at Manhattan and on Long Island also fully that many."[25]

Although the two congregations seem to have been about equal in numbers, we know the names of many more at Manhattan. As a congregation they frequently petitioned the director general, the West India Company, and the Lutheran consistory at Amsterdam. These petitions provide us with some eighty-two names,[26] apparently every male they could muster. But we know little else about them collectively for they kept a very low profile, no doubt because of the proximity of Director General Stuyvesant.

While we know far fewer names at Fort Orange than at Manhattan—about thirty-two men from the seventy or eighty families there—many of the members we do know were active, particularly in challenging local prejudices. They were a scrappy bunch and appear often in court, as members of the congregation, especially after 1664.[27] The Lutherans in the Fort Orange area represented a significant part of the total population there: in a 1653 estimate, the region had about 230 men capable of bearing arms.[28] Seventy or eighty Lutheran families must have comprised fully one-third of that population.

Just as immigrants arrived in the Netherlands from all over Europe, so this was reflected in the membership of the Lutheran Church in New Netherland. Harry J. Kreider has identified seven nationalities of Lutherans in New Amsterdam: German, Danish, Frisian, Norwegian, Dutch, Polish, and Swedish; and five at Fort Orange: Frisian, Danish, Norwegian, German, and French. In 1704, the Rev. Justus Falckner, Lutheran minister for New York and New Jersey, reported that his members were "mostly Germans, also Swedes, Danes, Norwegians, Poles, Lithuanians, Transylvanians, and other nationalities."[29]

The Lutherans in 1653 still wanted a minister: nothing had happened since their petition four years earlier. Paulus Schrick, a Lutheran merchant based in Hartford, Connecticut, but with an office on Manhattan, was contemplating an extended trip to Europe, and was appointed to act as the congregation's representative while there. Prior to his leaving New Amsterdam, the Lutherans drew up two petitions, one to the directors of the West India Company and the

FIGURE 9.4. Stained glass depiction of Petrus Stuyvesant at St. Mark's Church in-the-Bowery. It was donated by Daughters of the Holland Dames in 1903. Photo by Teodors Ermansons.

Figure 9.5. L. F. Tantillo, *Castle Island, 1645,* depicting one of two farms located in the vicinity of the present day Port of Albany. Reproduction courtesy of the artist.

other to the States General. Both were presented to Stuyvesant for transmission to Holland. A third was addressed to the Amsterdam consistory, urging them to induce the home authorities to approve the petitions. The writers included an agreement promising to pay eight hundred guilders annually with free lodging and firewood (a commitment they had failed to make in 1649). They added in a postscript that Stuyvesant promised "not to obstruct us if we ourselves could obtain permission from the supreme authorities."

Stuyvesant apparently alerted the local Reformed clergy, Johannes Megapolensis and Samuel Drisius, who wrote to the Reformed classis of Amsterdam, asking that it use its influence with the directors of the West India Company, "that the project of our Lutheran friends may be rejected, and thus the welfare, prosperity and edification of the church in this place, may be promoted." The letter further warned that giving in to the Lutherans "would also pave the way for other sects, so that in time our place would become a receptacle for all sorts of heretics and fanatics." Deputies of the classis acted promptly, saw the directors, and were assured that the petition would be refused. The directors thereafter instructed Stuyvesant not to receive any similar petitions.[30]

Paulus Schrick arrived in Amsterdam in January 1654 and appeared before the Lutheran consistory on the twentieth. He was told that "in view of the dangerous consequences thereof," not to contact either the States General, or the directors of the West India Company. Rather,

"He should quietly seek to contract with someone" to go to New Netherland as minister, and the consistory promised a helping hand.[31] But no candidate for a ministry in New Netherland could be found.

The consistory wrote to the Lutherans at Manhattan that when it came to Lutheran public worship in Amsterdam, the authorities both high and low "are willing to connive to some extent and to overlook," but not to give their written consent. They went on to say that they had "free and unmolested practice and exercise of our [Lutheran] religion, this has likewise come about in no other way than in length of time, by connivance, and we advise you to follow this example."[32]

Although Paulus Schrick returned to America in 1655 without success at finding a minister, he was determined that the Lutherans should begin worshiping together. They met with all the secrecy they could muster, but the city's two Reformed ministers were soon aware of Schrick's activities.[33] So was Stuyvesant, who had two of the group's leaders jailed (their names were not recorded). Nothing is found in the city court records about this affair, so Stuyvesant must have dealt directly with the situation.[34]

The congregation at Fort Orange also decided to worship together. On January 30, 1656, sixteen Fort Orange–area Lutherans tested the resolve of the Reformed Church and the Beverwyck town magistrates by an act of civil disobedience: they held a public service. In fact, they were rather obvious about it: they met in the house of Willem Juriaensz, across the street from the Reformed Church, on a Sunday morning.

Members of the two congregations encountered each other immediately after the services. The Lutheran layreader, Tjerck Claessen de Witt, was soon engaged in a fistfight with Calvinist Willem Teller, and during the fracas Sander Glen's goat was killed. At the next session of town court, De Witt was fined six guilders for performing divine service without a license, and another twenty guilders for the goat.

The meeting had been organized by Albert Bratt, who was later fined 115 guilders: six guilders for each of the other people at the meeting, and twenty-five guilders for himself for organizing it. Presumably, he was free to seek reimbursement from the others at the meeting; however, the court would not be involved in that. Bratt would hold the title of elder in 1670, but whether he was serving in any sort of titled office in 1656 is not known.[35]

We cannot know for sure which congregation began meeting first, although most writers assume that the movement began with Schrick at Manhattan.[36] The actions of the Lutherans either at New Amsterdam or Fort Orange, or both, produced serious consequences. Acting quickly, Stuyvesant and the council issued an ordinance on February 1, 1656. After railing about unqualified persons expounding the holy word of God without being appointed by ecclesiastical or civil authority, they warned that "many dangerous heresies and schisms are to be expected." Therefore, the director general and council forbade all such conventicles, whether public or private, and the leaders, "whether preacher, reader, or singer," would be fined one hundred pounds Flemish, while anyone merely attending such a meeting, public or private, "whether man or woman, married or unmarried," would be fined twenty-five pounds.[37]

Some of the members of the Lutheran consistory at Amsterdam were outraged by all that was going on, and visited friends among the company directors. The directors, on November 1, 1656, did send a rebuke to Stuyvesant:

> We would also have been better pleased, if you had not posted the placard against the Lutherans—a copy of which you sent us—and committed them to prison, for

> it has always been our intention, to deal with them quietly and peacefully. Hereafter you will therefore not post such or similar placards without our knowledge, but you must pass it over quietly and let them have free religious exercises in their houses.[38]

Written on the same day as the company directors' rebuke to Stuyvesant, the Amsterdam Lutheran consistory sent a letter to the New Netherland Lutherans with the startling news that the company directors had decided "in the West Indies and New Netherland our religion of the pure doctrine according to the Unaltered Augsburg Confession shall be tolerated by connivance, in the same way it is at present time tolerated here in this country." The consistory encouraged the New Netherlanders "to look around for a capable person and to call him as regular preacher and spiritual leader."[39]

At least that is what the members of the consistory had learned from their friends at the West India Company, that permission had been granted for congregational worship. The Manhattan Lutherans were overjoyed at this seemingly good news and acted quickly, sending a petition to Stuyvesant and the council on October 24. After stating that since the order against conventicles was issued in February they had "not gathered anywhere to hold divine services," they went on to report that their friends in Amsterdam had obtained from the West India Company directors "a resolution and decree that the doctrines of the Unaltered Augsburg Confession should be tolerated in the West Indies and New Netherland . . . in the same manner as in the Fatherland." They then asked "to be unhindered in our services until a qualified person shall come next spring to be our minister and teacher."[40]

Stuyvesant replied that their petition would be sent to the directors "and the truth thereof ascertained." In the meantime, they were expected to abide by the restrictions of the existing ordinance.[41]

Back in the Netherlands, the Reformed classis' Deputies for Indian Matters had heard the same thing: that the New Netherland Lutherans had been granted the privilege of the public exercise of their religion. There was then a flurry of activity by members of the classis in contacting some of their own friends among the directors, who "said that they knew not of any such complete toleration of the Lutherans there, but neither did they know what more there might be of such designs." Apparently, different directors had different impressions as to what was going on.[42]

The peripatetic Paulus Schrick then headed back to the Netherlands, carrying a letter from the congregation, which detailed the latest denial by Stuyvesant of the right of public worship. He arrived in January 1657, to find the Lutheran consistory was less positive than they had been—there appeared to be no chance of a formal order from the directors—but as late as April 2, 1657, they were reporting that "by one person and another it had been suggested in private" that if the consistory "sent a pastor thither, public worship would doubtless be tolerated by connivance and closing of the eye."[43]

However, five days later the company directors instructed Stuyvesant, "We have by no means the intention to grant the Lutherans any more liberty regarding the exercise of their religion."[44]

The confusion may have been caused in part by a statement in the rebuke to Stuyvesant, which said to "let them have free religious exercises in their houses."[45] The Lutherans could have taken that to mean that they could hold their "conventicles" in private homes, in the manner of a house-church, such as had existed at Woerden in Utrecht for decades until its official recognition in 1580, but to the Reformed it meant only that the Lutherans could continue to worship privately, each in his own household.

A MINISTER IS CALLED

On April 2, 1657, the Amsterdam consistory told Schrick that they would "try to secure a capable and pious person and in their name extend a call to him. That the council had someone in mind seems obvious, for the next day the consistory met and recorded that "Magister Johannes Ernestus Goetwasser, with the approval and after communication with Mr. Paulus Schrick, was offered and tendered the service and call of New Netherland."[46]

The candidate was a German; his name was actually Gutwasser. The Dutch equivalent is Goedwater (good water) and various combinations and spellings appear in the records. His home was in Schoenberg, near Masan in Saxony. He held the degree of Master of Theology, although the consistory minutes do not indicate from which university. He had been visiting his brother Andreas, who was living in Amsterdam and presumably attended the Lutheran church there, and so must have come to the attention of local clergy.[47]

Since Gutwasser held the degree of Master of Theology, he was not examined for his knowledge, but instead for the soundness of his faith and his capability, after which he preached a trial sermon. That he was not Dutch was beside the point: all the Lutheran pastors in the Netherlands were German.

Gutwasser was quickly approved and then on April 10 ordained in the Lutheran church.[48] Three days later, he was ready to depart, after receiving credentials to present to his congregation.

While Schrick had been seeking a pastor in Europe, the Reformed classis of Amsterdam was taking countermeasures, "in order to counteract this approaching evil."[49] By April 10, the Deputies for Indian Matters had learned from the company directors that the decision had once again been reversed, "that a resolution has already been adopted pretending to permit free worship of the sects, by connivance." However, after many arguments, the directors were finally convinced "never to consent to the permission by connivance, or in any other way."[50] Gutwasser was unaware of this development: he was aboard the *Draetvat,* which had set sail from Amsterdam on April 2.

Again and again, we find the directors being pulled by the interested factions, trying to satisfy both the Reformed clergy and Stuyvesant, as against the company's need to have an attractive opportunity in its province so that people might want to immigrate there, especially the numerous refugees from other countries. That the directors thought that Stuyvesant would connive on this issue makes one wonder how well they knew their man.

AN ASIDE—LUTHERANS ON THE DELAWARE

As if religious matters were not already complicated enough, political matters in America had added new fuel to the fire. Two colonies, New Netherland and New Sweden, had overlapping claims to territory along the Delaware River. New Sweden occupied land from Delaware Bay to the present site of Philadelphia, and in 1654 seized a Dutch fort at present-day New Castle, Delaware. Stuyvesant responded in 1655, taking a small flotilla south and defeating Swedish forces at that fort and at the Swedish headquarters, Fort Christina (Wilmington, Delaware). The

Swedish governor surrendered the colony, which Stuyvesant made subject to New Netherland. As part of the terms of surrender, freedom of religion was granted to the resident Swedes and Finns, who were overwhelmingly Lutheran, in part because no Calvinist minister was available who spoke their languages. Stuyvesant nonetheless managed to expel two of the three Lutheran ministers before other affairs intervened. In Stuyvesant's absence from Manhattan, and perhaps in retaliation for his attack on New Sweden, a series of attacks by hundreds of warriors from several Indian tribes destroyed settlements all around the area of what is today New York harbor, including New Jersey and Long Island. Stuyvesant was forced to abandon his cleansing of New Sweden and sailed back to Manhattan with most of his troops, leaving the Rev. Lars Lukenius, a Finnish minister, in place.

Thus, the Deputies for Indian Matters in Amsterdam were doubly distressed, having learned that the treaty made with the Swedes provided for a Lutheran minister among them, and that a Lutheran minister had been sent from Amsterdam to New Netherland. The deputies feared that if the Swedes on the Delaware could have a Lutheran minister, the congregation on Hudson River could hardly be denied the same.[51]

Figure 9.6. Map of the South River (now Delaware River) in New Netherland, by Johannes Vingboons, watercolor, c. 1639. Geography and Map Division, Library of Congress, Washington, DC. G3291.S12 coll. H3 Vault: Harr vol. 3, map 14.

To make matters even worse, on April 12, 1657, title to the former colony of New Sweden was transferred to the city of Amsterdam, and thus was no longer under West India Company control. Unlike the malleable company directors, the Amsterdam city government was able to resist the inducements of the Reformed Church, continuing the Lutheran freedom of worship in what was now called New Amstel, and even granting permission to a group of Mennonites to start a community there.

Megapolensis and Drisius were distraught at this turn of events. They wrote to the Reformed classis of their distress, that Gutwasser was a "snake in our bosom," and went on to repeat wild rumors about Lukenius, whom they had never met, "a man of impious and scandalous habits, a wild, drunken, unmannerly clown," and more of the same.[52] There is nothing in the provincial records to bear any of this out.

Of course, the Lutherans could indulge in the same sort of thing. They wrote to the Lutheran consistory that they needed a minister who was well-learned, "since among the Reformed here there is a preacher who formerly was a Jesuit and who on that account is very politic and disputatious." Nothing raised Protestant hackles more than mention of the Jesuits. The reference is probably to Megapolensis, who was raised Roman Catholic, but I find nothing to indicate any serious religious education prior to his conversion.

GUTWASSER'S ADVENTURES IN AMERICA

Magister Gutwasser arrived in New Amsterdam on July 6, 1657,[53] unaware of all the changes that had taken place since his departure from the Netherlands. He quickly learned.

Not long after he had set sail, the company directors examined the list of passengers, and saw his name. The Reformed classis had a good idea what that was about, writing of him to the Reformed consistory of New Netherland on May 25, "This is indeed a matter of great importance, which might most signally hinder the progress of the truth. . . . Deputies of the Classis, have been occupied since last year, in seeking to stop the growth of this evil."[54]

The very day of Gutwasser's arrival, the ever-vigilant *domines* Megapolensis and Drisius warned New Amsterdam city officials of the arrival of a Lutheran minister. "We feel sure that great contention and discord will develop therefrom, not only among the inhabitants and citizens in general, but also in families . . . some husbands have forced their wives to leave their own church, and attend their conventicles."[55]

Gutwasser was ordered to appear before the director general and council. When he did not show up on the assigned date, the court messenger was sent to his lodgings and learned that he had sailed on the flute-ship *Het Draetvat*.[56] The messenger was then ordered on the fourteenth to serve notice on Gutwasser "that he is not to hold any conventicles within this province," nor "to perform any manner of religious services, whether by preaching or by administering the sacraments."[57]

Around August 5, Gutwasser was taken before Stuyvesant and then before the city magistrates. He told them that he had been sent as a preacher and he "trusted that a letter of permit would come by the ship *Waegh*, giving them freedom of religion as in the Fatherland." Since he could not show any commission of appointment to preach, except from the Lutheran consistory of Amsterdam, "He was forbidden to preach and ordered to regulate himself according to the Placards of the land, and to depart at the first opportunity."[58]

From Gutwasser's standpoint, "The authorities here begin to use all diligence to prevent us from exercising the authentic, true and pure religion. Of the passing of ordinances and the imposing of heavy fines against holding private and public meetings, to throw a scare among the congregation, there is no lack." Stuyvesant and the council "listened very little to reason." Finally, on September 4, no "proof from political or ecclesiastical authorities in our fatherland" of Gutwasser's qualifications having arrived, Stuyvesant and the council issued a resolution in which he was both requested and ordered to depart to the Netherlands by the first ship.[59]

Gutwasser wrote to the Lutheran consistory four days later, reporting all this, and noting that because of the costly fines in the published ordinance, "we thus far neither hold nor intend to hold any meeting or religious services." There was a "lack of unity" among the Lutheran at Manhattan, and "if some of Fort Orange did not help bear the expense I could hardly be supported."[60] This last statement is especially noteworthy because it is a clear indication that the Lutherans at Fort Orange were aware of his existence and were supporting him. The Reformed ministers at Manhattan also wrote that "the Lutherans . . . at Fort Orange, had collected one hundred beaver skins, valued at eight hundred guilders, for the support of their minister."[61]

On October 19, orders were issued again for Gutwasser to leave New Netherland, this time expressly "by the ship *De Waegh,* now lying ready to sail." A petition was written to the director general and council that same day and signed by twenty-four Lutherans seeking further delay "until we shall have received further and more definite orders" from the States General and the company directors. They signed as "joint members adhering to the Unaltered Augsburg Confession in New Netherland."[62]

The response to their petition stated "the Director General and Council do not recognize the Unaltered Augsburg Confession, much less any members thereof." It was noted that since the first order to Gutwasser to depart, two ships had sailed, and he had neglected to leave "in contempt and disregard of the government of this province." He was ordered once again "to depart on one of the ships lying ready to sail."[63]

Figure 9.7. Section of the 1673 view of New Amsterdam, by Hugo Allard. This section of the Restitutio map, celebrating the Dutch recapture of New Netherland in 1673, shows the location of the Lutheran Church in New Orange (formerly New Amsterdam). From the collection of Joep de Koning.

It was now obvious to the local Lutherans that it was only a matter of time until the government tired of sending letters and orders and would proceed to having Gutwasser physically placed on board ship. On October 20, 1657, they sent him to live with a farmer outside the city.[64] It was indeed a close thing: his bedding and books followed on the twenty-third, and so the authorities were foiled when they came to arrest him on that day and again on the twenty-fifth.[65]

Gutwasser, in a letter to the Amsterdam Lutheran consistory dated October 23 from Mitspatskill (Maspeth Kill), wrote, "In order to save myself from violence, I have, with the consent of the congregation, been obliged to flee from the island of the Manhates to a colony, where I now reside. . . . For this absence the Hon. Secretary has [threatened] me with imprisonment and the loss of all I possess, but I fear neither of them."[66]

Gutwasser's hideout, then, was with a farmer at Maspeth Kill, now Newtown Creek in what is today Queens. We do not know why he referred to this as a colony, since he was still in New Netherland. The always well-informed Megapolensis and Drisius eventually learned that Gutwasser stayed with the farmer "during the whole winter, where [the Lutherans] supported him at the rate of six guilders per week."[67]

Megapolensis and Drisius also said that they had heard that Laurens Andriessen Noorman (the Norwegian) hid the minister.[68] That the farm may have belonged to Laurens is possible, but he was not himself a farmer. He was a tradesman and merchant in New Amsterdam, and in any case was on his way to deliver information to the Lutheran consistory in Amsterdam. The letter Laurens carried from the Manhattan congregation said the he could give "verbally better information," apparently information best not committed to writing.[69]

The congregation originally thought that if Gutwasser was not safe with the farmer and was "further prosecuted by the Director General and Council we shall send him outside the jurisdiction, being about 6 or 8 miles away, under the jurisdiction of the English." That apparently proved unnecessary. Such a location, at a distance of six or eight miles (probably the Dutch geographical mile of about 4.6 English miles), could mean the congregation was thinking of sending him to Connecticut.[70]

BAPTISMAL RITES

With Magister Gutwasser in hiding, attention now shifted to Lutheran complaints about the formula for baptism in the Reformed Church, which was the only authorized agency to perform that rite. The issue was summed up by the company directors in a letter to Stuyvesant. When Lutheran parents and witnesses presented a child for baptism at the Reformed Church in New Amsterdam, they were required to "acknowledge the dogma taught in the Christian Church there according to the Synod of Dort,[71] as the true one," and they could not avoid it: "they were compelled to be present at the baptizing of their children." The directors advised that "the Church here [in the Netherlands] does not lay such great stress upon the presence of the parents and witnesses; we think, also that the old formulary of baptism is still used in many churches here, as being less offensive and more moderate, than the new." A follow-up letter urged not only that "the old Formulary of baptism be used, but also the words 'present here in the Church' be entirely omitted, because we believe that thereby these and other dissenters will be satisfied and kept in the Reformed Church."[72]

Domines Megapolensis and Drisius expressed their absolute outrage that such charges could be brought against them: "We wish that the Lutherans in their complaint had simply stated the truth, and not encompassed us with untruth." The council members had been present at baptisms and "could justify us from these false charges. . . . As far as our knowledge goes, there never has been any agitation, or even appearance of such, among them, in relation to such a question."[73] One supposes the Lutherans would not "agitate" with the Reformed ministers if they knew there was no point in appealing to them.

"To our knowledge, there is hardly one among them here who has any proper acquaintance with the teachings of Dr. Luther. . . . They are Lutherans, and will remain such, because their parents and ancestors were Lutherans."[74] Having thus dismissed any knowledge or credibility in the benighted Lutherans, the irate clergymen continued:

> It is false that we, in the Formula of Baptism, ask the parents or sponsors, whether the doctrines taught "here" in this church, according to the Synod of Dort, are the true doctrines. . . . [W]e do not use such a Formula, but that which is found in the printed liturgy. . . . The Lutherans have done us wrong in their statement . . . that we strictly compelled parents and sponsors to be present at the baptism of their children. This is untrue. . . . There are instances in which neither of the parents are present at the baptism of their child. . . . [N]o undue strictness has been used towards the Lutherans in the baptism of their children, but that their own perverseness has led them to make false representations.[75]

One is left wondering whom to believe. Did the Lutherans invent these "offenses"? Or were they at least sometimes forced into them? A final thought in the screed from Megapolensis and Drisius may suggest an answer: "As the Form now used has been so long employed, the alteration or omission of it in behalf of the Lutherans, may perhaps give offence to our own people."[76] If the ministers were using a form of the baptismal service that should give no offense to the Lutherans, why do they write that changing the service would upset Reformed parishioners? The only reason for changing the service would be if it were in fact offensive to the Lutherans. Megapolensis and Drisius are arguing against themselves.

Eventually, a copy of the letter reached the company directors, who responded to Stuyvesant, "Our intentions are still the same, as we see no other reason, why the preachers there should raise difficulties about it; for it is an order practiced in most of the Reformed Churches here."[77]

The Deputies for Indian Matters also received a copy, and thought that Megapolensis and Drisius "must be earnestly admonished not to depart from the customary formulae." The West India Company directors "are poorly informed" and should not "attempt to make any alterations in the customary forms."[78]

Drisius wrote to the Reformed classis again on Oct 4, 1660, that they were omitting the word "here," as requested by the directors, but the classis was telling them to keep it in.[79] In time the two *domines* would plead with the classis and company directors to come to an agreement and stop sending contrary orders.

WITHOUT A PASTOR AGAIN

Gutwasser had been holding meetings and preaching, according to the *domines*. It was not easy to do that secretly with many curious eyes watching. He himself would write that "all possible means were exerted . . . to start religious worship, services being held under the blue sky of heaven, but even this was prevented by many arrests." [80]

That was only part of Gutwasser's problems. He also had financial woes: he had been heavily fined by Stuyvesant, had not been paid his promised salary of eight hundred guilders a year, and was surviving only through the generosity of some members.

And then he was taken sick, and lay ill at the farmer's place. The Lutherans went to Stuyvesant and asked that he could be brought to New Amsterdam for treatment, which was granted. The *fiscaal* was then empowered to watch over him, and when he was well again to send him to Holland. To make certain that he did not slip away again, he was incarcerated until a ship was ready to sail. Gutwasser spoke of "my confinement and custody by court messengers and soldiers, and finally by my being sent away and deported."[81]

Megapolensis and Drisius recorded that he was sent back to Holland on *De Bruynvisch,* but he wrote that he was on *De Washleecker.* The *domines* noted with obvious satisfaction, "There is now again quietness among the people, and the Lutherans again go to church, as they were formerly accustomed to do."[82]

Gutwasser's adventures were not quite over. He was shipwrecked off Barbados, losing necessary personal items and most of his books. Having set out on this enforced voyage with little money, he was indebted for his passage to Skipper Cornelis Maertsen.[83]

After his return to the Netherlands, Gutwasser told the Amsterdam consistory that he intended to enter his name with a consistory at Dresden, in hopes of receiving a call somewhere in his home state of Saxony. He asked for a testimonial, and the consistory in Amsterdam gladly supplied that, saying that "in matters of doctrine as well as in daily life, [he] has conducted and comported himself . . . as behooves a true and faithful pastor and teacher in Christ, all according to the testimony and reports thereof sent to us from time to time." The reason for his having left his call was that "by the severe persecutions of the Hon. Director Stuyvesant and Council of New Netherland, [he] was forced to depart again from there."[84]

The Lutheran congregation in New Netherland struggled on. They petitioned the directors, again:

> [A]s long as our pastor has been in this country many people, thinking that here freedom [of worship] had been obtained for us, have come and still continue to come. . . . [W]e have, in a petition to our magistrates and the Hon. Director General, requested to grant us a wild, uninhabited place . . . to practice our religion in all quietness and reverence, and this in order that we might not be in their way and that thereby a wild place might be brought under cultivation, but this also has been refused us.[85]

There was still the occasional rumbling at Fort Orange. Domine Gideon Schaets wrote from there to the Reformed classis on Sept 22, 1660, that "the Lutherans are now again, as before, making up subscriptions for the salary of a Lutheran preacher. They say, or pretend, that this has been allowed to them by the gentlemen of the West India Company." After celebrating that several have joined the Reformed Church, and others "are being gradually led to us," he was sorry to report, "There are some unstable Lutherans, who do not seem to like any other form of baptism than that according to Luther, and his religion. They have not the least comprehension of the difference." Still, even these "unstable" folks "are satisfied, as long as the hope of obtaining a Lutheran preacher is deferred. They were indeed somewhat restless about it, when they first heard of it, but having quieted down a little they come again to church."[86]

The Reformed classis checked with the company directors and responded to Schaets that permission for a Lutheran minister was nothing but an idle rumor. Not only would the company not allow such a thing, but "General Stuyvesant . . . would not endure the existence of the Lutherans, if they should grow too bold."[87]

For the next three years the Amsterdam consistory heard not a word from the Lutherans in New Netherland, until the consistory received a letter from one Hendrick Bosch, dated August 19, 1663. He explained that "he had come over here a little over two years ago. . . . I found here a large congregation adhering to our Christian Unaltered Augsburg Confession." He then explained to the consistory why they had heard nothing for so long. "They dare not come together here to offer any sign of devotion, much less trust themselves jointly to sign a petition to your honors, for fear of being betrayed."[88]

Memories of those times long survived. In a letter of 1725 to members of the Amsterdam consistory, Albert and Jan van Loon of the consistory at Albany wrote of a story they had doubtless heard from old-timers in New York:

> When Governor Stuyvesant ruled here, we were not allowed to have any pastor or the liberty of hearing one; the pastor left and the congregation scattered. When they held a meeting for prayer and were found, they had to give a certain sum of money; when they thought they were hidden in the woods, there was always one who could find them, namely, Klaes van Elslant, so that it grieved them and they wished that God would punish him, as did happen to him, for he went about stooping, as he had done in creeping up on them, until his death. [89]

UNDER THE ENGLISH

In September 1664 the province of New Netherland fell to a British naval force, and became the colony of New York. Among the terms offered and accepted among the articles of capitulation was one concerning religion: "The Dutch here shall enjoy the liberty of their Consciences, in Divine Worship, and church discipline."[90]

These freedoms were another kind of religious politics. The proprietor of the colony, the Duke of York, was a Roman Catholic. He had known religious prejudice, had often had to go into exile despite being the brother of the king. He wanted to give religious equality a chance, to demonstrate to his countrymen that it could work. He was, after all, heir-apparent to the throne, motive enough to want to convince his future subjects that they need not revolt over his religion.

So it was that the Duke of York had ordered his deputy governor, Richard Nicolls, to practice tolerance of non-Anglicans, which of course included almost everyone in the colony. Nicolls on December 6,[91] 1664, granted freedom of public worship to the Lutherans:

> Whereas several Persons under my Government who professe the Lutheran Religion . . . having requested mee for Liberty to send for one Minister or more of their Religion, and that they may freely and publiquely exercise Divine worship, according to their Consciences, I do hereby give my Consent there unto.[92]

Two days later the Manhattan Lutherans wrote a letter to the Amsterdam consistory, reporting the good news and noting that after the years of struggle and disappointment, they still had in New York City "about 100 persons, and perhaps more, who are not yet known."[93]

This was not the end of the Lutherans' troubles, particularly at Albany, where the Reformed Church remained the established church. Lutherans had to pay the Reformed gravedigger, who had the city monopoly, even when they buried their own parishioners in their own churchyard. They had to be married before the magistrates prior to a church wedding, which was not required of the Reformed. They could not have the church bell rung at different times than the Reformed rang it. But the magistrates were evenhanded in reconciling parties in dispute over religion, and in fining serious troublemakers on both sides.

The intention of this chapter on the political application of religious laws was not to make the Dutch or the Reformed Church into evildoers, although the Lutherans of New Netherland may have seen them that way. But Lutherans were no more generous in territories where theirs was the established church, and usually less so, and the same could be said of virtually any other church of that era. In the Holy Roman Empire of the German Nation, each independent or semi-independent kingdom, duchy, and city set its own rules for religious practice, usually establishing one church and banning the others. One of the odder situations occurred in the free city of Frankfort-am-Main, where Lutheranism was established; Catholics were also granted freedom of public worship, but the Reformed Church was not.

The Lutherans of New Netherland never tried to have the law changed, only asked that it be overlooked. This was the practical sort of solution to a problem that the Dutch understood and sometimes opted to practice. It occurs in governments everywhere, and as an official practice is never committed to writing.

Certainly, the Reformed ministers would eventually be proved right when they prophesied that if the Lutherans were given freedom of worship, the land would soon be filled with every sort of "heretic and fanatic" (or at least a multitude of sects and religions). The issue is: Between tolerance and intolerance, which is the bad choice and which is the good one? In many nations even today, tolerance is not viewed as a virtue; the American experience has dictated otherwise, although the limits are still being tested, these many years later.

NOTES

1. Zwingli died in 1531 and within a decade John Calvin was his leading successor. While the terms *Reformed* and *Calvinist* are not always synonymous, for our purposes they will be used as such, just to avoid wearing out either word.

2. The history of Lutheranism in the Netherlands is discussed in many places, including *The Encyclopedia of the Lutheran Church,* ed. Julius Bodensieck (Minneapolis: Augsburg, 1965), 1719–24; *Lutheran Cyclopedia,* ed. Erwin L. Lueker (St. Louis: Concordia, 1975), 571–72; and E. Theodore Bachman and Marcia Brenne Bachman, *Lutheran Churches in the World: A Handbook* (Minneapolis: Augsburg, 1989), 435–37.

3. Harry Julius Kreider, *Lutheranism in Colonial New York* (dissertation, Columbia University, New York, 1942), 3–4.

4. When Johannes Hus was martyred in 1415, he supposedly said before the fire consumed him, "It is thus that you silence the goose [Hus, in Czech], but a hundred years hence there will arise a swan whose singing you shall not be able to silence." Martin Luther proclaimed himself that swan.

5. David Steven Cohen has identified the place of origin of 904 heads of families who immigrated to New Netherland, 49 percent of them non-Dutch. Two-thirds of those were from the Lutheran

strongholds of Scandinavia and Germany. Cohen, *The Dutch-American Farm* (New York: New York University Press, 1992), 16–18.

6. I use the name of the fort generically, as did most persons in the seventeenth century, to include the adjacent town of Beverwyck (established 1652) and private colony of Rensselaerswyck.

7. A. J. F. van Laer, trans., *Van Rensselaer Bowier Manuscripts* (Albany: University of the State of New York, 1908), 694.

8. *Ecclesiastical Records, State of New York,* (Albany: New York State, 1901–1916), 320–21; hereafter cited as *Ecclesiastical Records.*

9. There was nothing in the Charter of the West India Company granted by the States General in 1621 relating to religion, nor in the Amplifications of 1622 and 1623, and not in the 1623 "Agreement between the directors and the chief participants of the West India Company." The texts of these documents in both Dutch and English can be found in *Van Rensselaer Bowier Manuscripts,* 86–135.

10. However, the "Provisional Regulations for the Colonists," adopted by the West India Company in 1624, stated, "They shall within their territory practice no other form of divine worship than that of the Reformed religion as at present practiced here in this country." There was a proviso that religious persecution was forbidden, "leaving to every one the freedom of his conscience." A. J. F. van Laer, trans., *Documents Relating to New Netherland 1624–1626 in the Henry E. Huntington Library* (San Marino, CA: Henry E. Huntington Library and Art Gallery, 1924), 1.

11. Text in *Van Rensselaer Bowier Manuscripts,* 137–53.

12. *Documents Relative to the Colonial History of the State of New York* (Albany: Weed, Parsons, 1856–1861), 1:123.

13. *Ecclesiastical Records,* 318. Although governor in fact, his title indicates his position in the West India Company as a regional manager whose responsibilities extended to the Caribbean islands of Aruba, Bonaire, and Curaçao.

14. Stuyvesant's avowed motivation was his strong sense of professional duty in fulfilling his oath and his company's charter, but it is worth noting that both his father and father-in-law were Calvinist ministers.

15. To save space and avoid boredom I will use the term *company directors* throughout to refer to the directors of the Amsterdam Chamber of the West India Company. Chambers in other cities controlled other colonies of the company.

16. Harry J. Kreider, *The Beginnings of Lutheranism in New York* (New York: United Lutheran Synod of New York, 1949), 5–6, 27; E. B. O'Callaghan, *History of New Netherland,* 2: 457; *Ecclesiastical Records,* 338.

17. A. J. F. van Laer, trans., *The Lutheran Church in New York, 1649–1772: Records in the Lutheran Church Archives at Amsterdam, Holland* (New York: New York Public Library, 1946), 19; hereafter cited as *Lutheran Church in New York.*

18. Van Laer, *New York Historical Manuscripts: Dutch, Volume IV, Council Minutes, 1638–1649* (Baltimore: Genealogical Publishing, 1974), 440.

19. Useful histories include Kreider, *The Beginnings of Lutheranism in New York,* which expands upon the first portion of his dissertation, *Lutheranism in Colonial New York*; and Frederick J. Zwierlein's dissertation, *Religion in New Netherland,* (Rochester: J. P. Smith, 1910).

20. *Van Rensselaer Bowier Manuscripts,* 809–10.

21. The Augsburg Confession, written in 1530, is the primary statement of Lutheran doctrine. Efforts to "improve" on it led to the emphasis on the original, "unaltered" version.

22. *Lutheran Church in New York,* 13.

23. Ibid.

24. The terms *Manhattan* and *New Amsterdam* were used interchangeably, whether referring to the area generally or to the city specifically.

25. *Lutheran Church in New York,* 14, 39.

26. Actually, there were eighty-three names, but one signer was Vockert Douw from Fort Orange.

27. I have previously discussed this congregation in "Lutherans at Albany: The First Two Centuries," in *Historic Albany, Its Churches and Synagogues,* ed. Anne Roberts and Marcia Cockrell (Albany: Library Communications Services, 1986), and in "Albany's Colonial Lutherans: Ecumenism and Conflict among the Churches," *de Halve Maen* (Spring 2000). The standard history is by Henry H. Heins, *Swan of Albany* (Albany: First Lutheran Church, 1976).

28. Charles T. Gehring, "An Undiscovered Van Rensselaer Letter," *De Halve Maen* 14, no. 3 (Fall-Winter 1979): 28.

29. Kreider, *Lutheranism in Colonial New York,* 53–55.

30. The letter to the classis is in *Ecclesiastical Records,* 317–18; the sequence of events is discussed in Kreider, *The Beginnings of Lutheranism in New York,* 20–22.

31. *Lutheran Church in New York,* 18.

32. Ibid. 19.

33. *Ecclesiastical Records,* 429.

34. The Lutheran consistory speaks of civil confinement (*Lutheran Church in New York,* 254), the West India Company directors of a commitment to prison in, Gehring, trans., *Correspondence, 1654–1658* (Syracuse: Syracuse University Press, 2003), 93. One searches in vain for any reference to Lutherans in the New Amsterdam city records: they were Stuyvesant's problem.

35. I discuss Bratt's career at length in Christoph, *A Norwegian Family in Colonial America* (Salem, MA: Higginson, 1994).

36. There are no records for the New Netherland period at either of the original congregations, First Lutheran Church in Albany or the Evangelical Lutheran Church of St. Matthew in New York City.

37. Gehring, trans., *Laws and Writs of Appeal, 1647–1663* (Syracuse: Syracuse University Press, 1991), 55–56; Gehring, *Council Minutes, 1655–1656* (Syracuse: Syracuse University Press, 1995), 209–10.

38. Gehring, *Correspondence, 1654–1658,* 93.

39. *Lutheran Church in New York,* 254; Kreider, *The Beginnings of Lutheranism in New York,* 25.

40. *Lutheran Church in New York,* 20.

41. Ibid., 20; *Ecclesiastical Records,* 358–59.

42. *Ecclesiastical Records,* 354–55.

43. *Lutheran Church in New York,* 22.

44. *Ecclesiastical Records,* 373.

45. Ibid., 352.

46. *Lutheran Church in New York,* 22.

47. Kreider, *The Beginnings of Lutheranism in New York,* 29–30. Kreider's source was an unpublished manuscript prepared for the United Lutheran Synod of New York in 1948 by the late Simon Hart, archivist of both the city of Amsterdam and the Lutheran Church there.

48. Kreider includes the text of the service, which had recently been discovered by Simon Hart, in *The Beginnings of Lutheranism in New York,* 32–37.

49. *Ecclesiastical Records,* 372.

50. Ibid., 374–75.

51. Ibid., 377.

52. Ibid., 394–96.

53. *Magister* is Latin for "master," the usual title for a Dutch Lutheran minister; the title for a Reformed minister was *domine* (lord).

54. *Ecclesiastical Records,* 380.

55. Ibid., 386–88.

56. This was the ship that brought him to New Amsterdam. Why he would now go aboard we cannot imagine, since he certainly was not going anyplace.

57. *Lutheran Church in New York,* 24.

58. *Ecclesiastical Records,* 389, 425–26.

59. *Lutheran Church in New York,* 24–27.

60. Ibid., 27–28.

61. *Ecclesiastical Records,* 409.

62. *Lutheran Church in New York,* 30.

63. Ibid., 31.

64. Ibid., 32.

65. *Ecclesiastical Records,* 412.

66. *Lutheran Church in New York,* 34.

67. *Ecclesiastical Records,* 433.

68. Ibid., 430.

69. *Lutheran Church in New York,* 32.

70. Ibid.

71. A reference to an essential Reformed Church document, *The Decision of the Synod of Dordt on the Five Main Points of Doctrine in Dispute in the Netherlands.*

72. *Ecclesiastical Records,* 423, 425.

73. Ibid., 428.

74. Ibid., 429.

75. Ibid., 429–30.

76. Ibid., 431.

77. Ibid., 441.

78. Ibid., 440.

79. Ibid., 485–86.

80. Ibid., 449; *Lutheran Church in New York,* 43.

81. *Ecclesiastical Records,* 433, 444, 449, 454; *Lutheran Church in New York,* 44.

82. *Ecclesiastical Records,* 449.

83. *Lutheran Church in New York,* 44. Megapolensis and Drisius seem to have been right about the name of the ship: Maertsen sailed *De Bruynvisch* from Amsterdam to New Amsterdam in 1658.

84. Ibid., 46–47.

85. Ibid., 39.

86. *Ecclesiastical Records,* 483.

87. Ibid., 515–16.

88. *Lutheran Church in New York,* 48.

89. Ibid., 125.

90. Peter R. and Florence A. Christoph, eds., *Books of General Entries of the Colony of New York, 1664–1673* (Baltimore: Genealogical Pub., 1982), 36; also in *Ecclesiastical Records,* 558.

91. According to the Julian calendar still in use in England. For the Dutch it was the sixteenth.

92. *Books of General Entries of the Colony of New York, 1664–1673,* 67.

93. *Lutheran Church in New York,* 50.

Chapter Ten

A Flourishing City

Jews in New Amsterdam, 1654

Leo Hershkowitz

All non–Dutch Reformed practitioners experienced barriers. When a group of Jewish refugees arrived in New Netherland in 1654, they experienced objections to their very presence. Leo Hershkowitz describes the experiences of the Jewish minority in New Netherland, under the adminstration of Petrus Stuyvesant.

The first attempt to establish a Jewish presence in North America began in 1654. Who were the first arrivals; what led them to the Dutch settlement of New Amsterdam; what was their experience in the community; and what role did religion play in their story?

The scarcity of records makes it difficult to find answers. These early visitors left no personal accounts of their experiences. We do know that in late summer 1654, two ships anchored in New Amsterdam harbor. One, the *Peereboom* (*Peartree*) arrived from Amsterdam on or about August 22. The other, also a Dutch vessel, the *St. [Sint] Catrina,* (often wrongly referred to as a French ship, the *St. Charles,* or *Ste. Catherine*) entered a few days before September 7 from the West Indies.

The *Peereboom,* with skipper Jan Pietersz Ketel, left Amsterdam July 8 for London, soon after peace negotiations in April concluded the first Anglo-Dutch War (1652–54). Among the several Jews aboard, one, Jacob Aboaf possibly the first identified Jew to be in England since 1290, departed the ship in London. Following a short stay, the ship sailed for New Amsterdam, where passengers and cargo were ferried ashore because there were no suitable docks or wharves. Among those who disembarked were Jacob Barsimson, probably together with Asser Levy and Solomon Pieterson, the first known Jews to set foot in the Dutch settlement. With them begins the history of that community in New York.[1]

A number of vessels arrived and departed New Amsterdam during 1654 to early 1655. Given the extensive use of the *Peereboom* it seems likely they would have been on that ship. As Dutch-Jewish merchants they were part of the prosperous and tolerant Dutch Republic.

The second arrival, the Dutch *St. Catrina,* Jaques de la Motthe (probably a Walloon or Huguenot) in command, carried, as reported by Pietersen, twenty-three Jews. Here, the story becomes somewhat confusing. The vessel came from St. Anthony, a place Berthold Fernow, the editor of the *Records of New Amsterdam,* believes was in Brazil (there also was one in Jamaica and one in Cuba), just as he insists in his first mention that the vessel was the *St. Charles,*

Figure 10.1. Painting by Gordon Miller, depicting the *St. Catrina* and *Peereboom* in Nieuw Amsterdam harbor, 1654. From the collection of Leo and Marcia Hershkowitz. Reproduction with permission of the artist.

although later correctly writing *St. Catrina.* Strangely, he does not correct his first impression, and leaves unquestioned his Brazil conjecture. Historians such as Samuel Oppenheim and Jacob Marcus repeat Fernow's original error.[2]

We can infer that Solomon Pietersen (possibly originally from Italy) arrived on the *Peereboom* because he was already in New Amsterdam, having witnessed and noted the arrival of twenty-three Jews "big and little' (elders and children) on the *St. Catrina.* Furthermore, he is not listed in Brazilian congregational records. He says nothing as to who the twenty-three were. Was his count correct? The number cannot be verified, but it is commonly used in referring to the St. Catrina arrivals.

Asser Levy also probably arrived on the *Peereboom.* He did not come from Brazil and was not on the *St. Catrina,* but was also in New Amsterdam when the twenty-three arrived. Originally from Vilna, then in Poland, one of the few Jews whose place of origin is known, Levy like the other two was Ashkenazic, Eastern European. Although they were Jews, Petrus Stuyvesant did not object to them, probably because all three had passports issued by the West India Company. Barsimson's passport is certain. Probably the other two had them as well. Historians such as Samuel Oppenheim, Arnold Wiznitzer, and numerous others have placed Levy in Brazil, but they appear to be mistaken.[3]

Levy and others who departed from Eastern Europe probably left because of the Chmelnitzki pogroms begun in 1648. After that year, the Jewish population, particularly in Amsterdam, grew steadily to six thousand, or 3 percent of the population by 1700. This expansion mirrored The Netherlands' economic growth and a flourishing overseas trade.[4]

New Amsterdam's resident minister Domine Johannes Megapolensis noted their arrival. On March 18, 1655, he sent a letter to the Classis at Amsterdam: "Last summer some Jews came here from Holland in order to trade." His reference to "some Jews" supports the view that there were at least three Jews on the *Peereboom*. He continued, "Afterwards, some Jews, poor and healthy, also came here on the same ship with D[omine] Polhemius." This was certainly a reference to the arrival of the *St. Catrina*. The clergyman further wrote, "God has led Domine Joannes [Johannes] Polhemius from Brazil over the Caribbean Islands to this place," probably meaning Jamaica and Cuba. He then voiced his resentment at having to spend several hundred guilders to support the new, indigent, arrivals. Megapolensis continued, "They came several times to my house, weeping and bemoaning their misery. If I directed them to the Jewish merchants, they said they would not even lend them a few stivers." Were the Jewish merchants Barsimson, Levy, and Pietersen? Why refuse help? Was the *St. Catrina*'s passengers' poverty a result of having

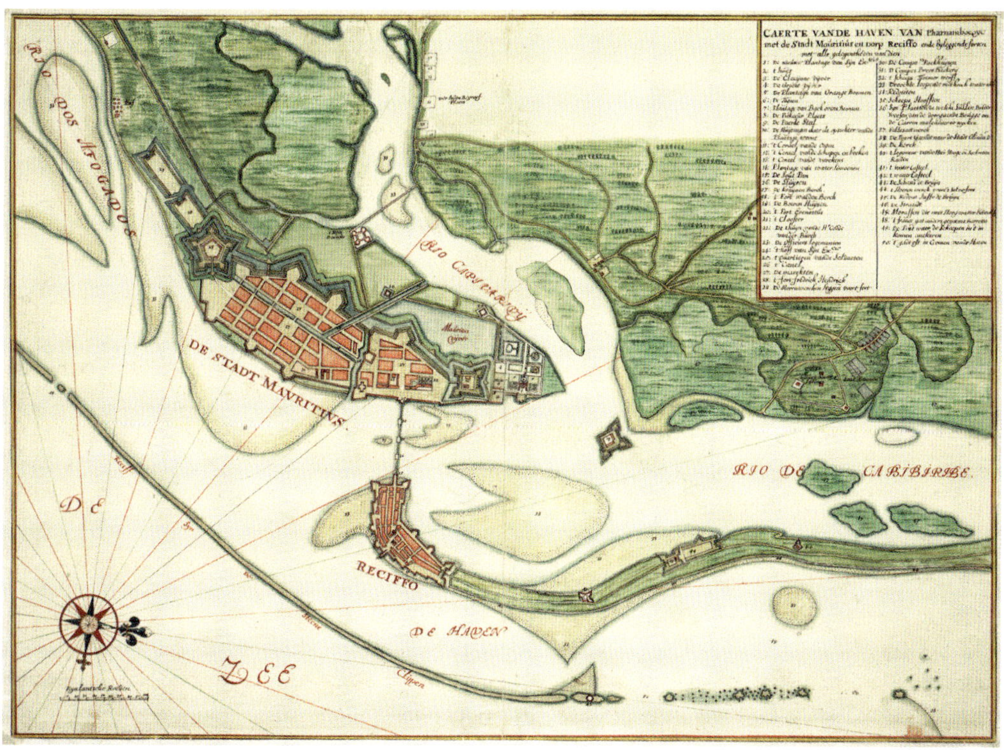

Figure 10.2. "Pernambuco," by Johannes Vingboons, watercolor, c. 1665. After the Portuguese recaptured Brazil from the Dutch in 1654, an estimated 23 Jewish refugees arrived in New Amsterdam. Collection Nationaal Archief (National Archives of the Netherlands) 4.VELH 619-074.156

their goods and money taken or lost during their voyage from Brazil "over the Caribbean Islands?" Surely, a good deal of their property had to remain in Brazil after the Portuguese seizure. Megapolensis further argued that the followers of the "unrighteous Mammon" aimed to get possession of Christian property, and to outdo all other merchants by drawing all trade toward themselves. These "godless rascals, who are of no benefit to the country, but look at everything for their own profit, may be sent away from here."

While Stuyvesant, like the Domine, seems not to have objected to passengers on the *Peereboom,* nor to those coming later directly from Amsterdam, he did raise questions about the twenty-three, who were poor and without documentation. He had written letters on September 22 and 25, 1654, to the directors of the West India Company asking, if not insisting, that "these new territories not be invaded" by people of the "Jewish race." Another letter dated October 27, 1654, arrived in Amsterdam via England. Ships carrying such letters were the *Schaal* and the *Beer.* Stuyvesant's writing came after the *Peereboom* arrival and seems to have been a reaction to the *St. Catrina*'s passengers. Stuyvesant used the same objections raised by Domine Megapolensis. The directors replied on April 26, 1655 stating that, although they recognized these objections,

> [w]e observe that it would be unreasonable and unfair, especially because of the considerable loss, sustained by the Jews in the taking of Brazil and also because of the large amount of capital, which they invested in shares of this Company. After many consultations we have decided and resolved upon a certain petition made by said Portuguese Jews, that they shall have permission to sail and trade in New Netherland and to live and remain there provided the poor among them shall not become a burden to the Company, or the community, but be supported by their own nation. You will govern yourself accordingly.[5]

For the Domine, trade and profit were basic motives for those "godless rascals." These "obstinate and immovable Jews," who "come to settle here," he continued, caused greater confusion in the troubled colony, which already included dissident Catholics (Papists), Congregationalists, Quakers, Mennonites, and Lutherans. This notion of the supposed acquisitiveness of Jews was often offered to restrict immigration. In 1641, resident merchants in Dutch Brazil told Governor General Johan Maurits that the colony was being overrun by Jews and "every contract with a Jew ends in bankruptcy of a Christian." Maurits in his reply, however, stated Christians should be more careful, avoiding their own "lust for speculation," and besides Jews deserved and earned more liberties than others as they have always been "reliable political allies."[6]

Who were these "godless rascals"? On January 26, 1654, some twenty-five years after the Dutch had taken Brazil from Portugal, the colony once again fell to Portuguese control. The Portuguese commander, Francisco Barreto, approved the apparently generous terms of surrender. Movable property could be retained, and ships were provided for those who chose to leave. No reprisals would be taken; this included Jews who were largely at Recife and Mauricia (principal ports of the colony). Further, three months stay was granted and all, including Jews, would be treated with "great respect and courtesy." What Jews could carry with them is not clear. Were gold, silver, jewels taken by the Portuguese? Certainly real property remained.

At the time of the Portuguese takeover, there were about 150 Jewish families in Brazil and most left for the Dutch Republic.[7] Barreto provided at least sixteen ships as transport. Some were Dutch, some Portuguese.[8] One of the vessels, the Dutch *Valck* (*Falcon*), skipper Jon

Craeck, left Brazil on February 24, but was driven by adverse winds to Spanish-held Jamaica. Its passsengers apparently remained on the island until the end of April when they might have sailed to Cuba, perhaps on the *Valck*. Possibly Pietersen's twenty-three Jews and Domine Polhemius were also there, taken on board the *St. Catrina* and then to New Amsterdam.

In a letter dated November 14, 1654, at the request of the Amsterdam Sephardic community, a Dutch official wrote to the King of Spain to protest the detaining of persons of the "Portuguese Jewish Nation" in Jamaica, in contravention of a treaty between The Netherlands and Spain. This treaty may account for the presence of the Dutch *St. Catrina* in Spanish territory. The letter explained that Jewish passengers had left Recife for Martinique, but winds carried them to Jamaica. Their immediate release was requested.[9] Whether the *St. Catrina* came via Cuba or Jamaica, it was not the first ship to bring Jews to New Netherland. The *Peereboom* had arrived earlier from The Netherlands by choice. It was the second choice for those twenty-three who sailed from Brazil. If so, why did they select New Amsterdam? Answers are found in the story of the Dutch Republic, New Amsterdam, and the largely Sephardic Jewish community in Amsterdam.

For those on the *Peereboom* and *St. Catrina*, New Amsterdam could fulfill a variety of dreams and aspirations. This small outpost managed by the West India Company was settled in order to profit from trade in furs and agricultural products, especially grain. Interest in New Netherland was also related to the remarkable rise of the Dutch Republic during the days of glory in its "Golden Age," the time of Rembrandt, Grotius, Huygens, masters of art, law, and science. It was also the age of Dutch naval supremacy, when admirals such as Michiel de Ruyter, Cornelis Tromp, and Maarten Tromp could defeat their English adversaries. Chartered in 1621 following an armistice with Spain, the West India Company—which had a member of the States General (Parliament) on its governing Assembly of XIX—exemplified the aggressive spirit of the Republic. Willem Usselincx, a militant Calvinist, and one of the leading advocates for establishing the Company, was a zealous anti-Catholic refugee from Antwerp who sought revenge against an invading Spain.

The Dutch may also have had an interest in New Netherland as a base for possible seizure of Spanish treasure carried from Mexico and Peru. In 1628, Piet Heyn captured the Mexican silver fleet, a spectacular victory that helped stimulate the Dutch economy and fund Company operations. Certainly, a Protestant colony questioned the authority of Spanish Catholic claim to the New World. Usselincx also reasoned that immigrants and foreigners were a prime asset for the Republic. "It is," he wrote, "because of foreigners [like himself] that the country will be peopled as its might is derived most from those who come from abroad, settled here, marry and multiply." New colonies would strengthen the economy. Interestingly, he wanted to prohibit slavery.[10]

The views of Usselincx on the need for immigration and colonization to strengthen a free nation perhaps influenced these first Jewish travelers to New Amsterdam. In addition, the writings of Adriaen van der Donck particularly his *Description of New Netherland,* first published in 1655, after his 1649 *Vertoogh,* or *Remonstrance,* published in 1650, would have stimulated interest. This was known by 1655, when the thirty-five-year-old author died. Van der Donck, a Doctor of Laws, graduate of the University of Leiden, became a member of Stuyvesant's advisory Council of Nine. He was a severe critic of the Director General and the Company because of their failure to promote good government and permanent, substantial settlement.[11] The *Beschrijvinge van Nieuw Nederlant* (*Description*) Van der Donck's "little book," contained a detailed and positive account of the natural abundance found in the province. "It is a very beautiful, pleasant, healthy and delightful land, where all manner of men can more easily earn a good living and make their way in the world than in the Netherlands or any other part of the globe that I know."[12] This reference to health is quite interesting. In the seventeenth century a number of severe epidemics could have persuaded many to seek a more beneficial climate. In 1636, more than 17,000 out of a population of 120,000 died in Amsterdam. In 1654, almost 11,000 of some 60,000 died in Leiden, and in 1664 over 24,000, of about 200,000 died in Amsterdam. Surely seeking a "healthy" land was an added inducement to travel.[13]

Central to the rapid growth of the Republic was the Dutch attachment to freedom and liberty, exemplified by the Utrecht Union of 1579, which placed the seven provinces under an elected parliament, the States General, and the leadership of its elected Stadtholder, Willem of Orange, and after 1584 that of his son Maurice. Emphasized were concepts of free trade and the lifting of medieval economic restrictions. This freedom to trade, it was argued, also promoted freedom of ideas, toleration, and encouraged the first Jews to settle and flourish in the Republic. The rise of this community parallels the rise of the Republic. The histories of the Dutch nation and that of Jewish society are remarkably similar. The Netherlands, a small country geographically, achieved greatness through its initiatives and efforts, while the Jewish community, small in number, also was productive and in a free society prospered and contributed significantly to the general prosperity and growth of the country. In 1654, the arrival of the *Peereboom* and the *St. Catrina* reflected the accomplishments and ambitions of the "Golden Age."

The largely Protestant Dutch nation liberated itself from Spanish Catholic domination by the early seventeenth century after an eighty-year war of independence. The Utrecht declaration of toleration and religious freedom attracted Jews to the Republic. They began arriving some time before 1597 when the first Amsterdam congregation, Beth Ya'acob (House of Jacob) was established. Its synagogue opened in 1614, joining two others formed in 1604 and 1609.

Although the authorities and the people of The Netherlands did not openly welcome these largely Spanish-Portuguese (Sephardic) people—particularly after the 1648 influx of East European Jews—Usselincx and others like him recognized that members of this community took part in the vital business activity of the East and West India Companies ventures and were among the earliest seventeenth-century contributors to the prosperity of The Netherlands in general and Amsterdam in particular. Officials in Amsterdam made certain that competing cities such as Haarlem or Leiden did not lure away such important citizens.

The Dutch found that Jews were valuable assets in promoting the wealth of the Republic. This view was not lost on other European leaders. Beginning early in the seventeenth century, after seeing a vibrant Amsterdam aided by its Jewish population, King Christian IV invited members of the Sephardic Amsterdam community to settle in Denmark, and extended this offer to Ashkenazic Jews in 1640. Similarly, Oliver Cromwell by 1652 invited Jews to England. The celebrated Menasseh ben Israel together with his son and three rabbis arrived there in 1655, just after Jacob Aboaf.[14]

The philosopher Baruch Spinoza, one of the founders of seventeenth-century liberalism, noted this relationship of religious freedom to Dutch national progress. In his *Tracticus Theologico-Politicus,* published in 1670, he observed that his native city Amsterdam, center of a flourishing state, "reaps the fruit of this freedom in its own great prosperity and in the administration of all other people."[15] Religious difference was of secondary importance. Freedom, toleration, and individual liberty were ideas ingrained in Dutch settlement and were the foundation of a future New York.

Jews had further reasons for traveling to New Amsterdam. With the end of the First Anglo-Dutch War on April 5, 1654, the Dutch had to pay huge damages to the victorious English including loss of trade in the Orient. In Amsterdam, during the war, building of the Stadt Huys (City Hall) halted, grass grew in the streets, begging, almost unknown earlier, became very common. This economic downturn surely had an effect on decision making. Perhaps poor economic conditions were also a consideration in the minds of the Amsterdam *parnassim* (Jewish religious leaders) in support of colonization. In January 1655, they recognized that the Company had offered land free to immigrants under their 1650 Freedoms and Exemptions Act, and that these loyal people and citizens such as Jews would help pay taxes, and increase trade and population. The French and English had reluctantly admitted Jews in their colonies, why not the West India Company?[16] Such arguments were not lost in the streets of New Amsterdam. The Act of 1650 also stipulated that freemen obtaining land would have a year to put it under cultivation. This condition might have discouraged Jewish settlement. Jews seldom became farmers, but the attraction of property ownership was an inducement.[17]

The West India Company's interest in its colonial possessions was primarily one of trade and profit. Settlement came second. Still, as Usselincx suggested, increasing population could be turned into assets. New Netherland was a problematic colony from the start, despite its possibilities. Few people, including Jews, wanted to make the Atlantic voyage.

Even with its various problems, Amsterdam was still Europe's chief financial center. Its open economy produced a vast commercial market, supplying an endless quantity of French wines, colonial sugar, and Swedish coffee. Investment capital was readily available. Loans in England could be had at 6 percent, secured by adequate bonds while in The Netherlands loans were at 3.5 percent without "Pawn or Pledge." Surely, low interest rates stimulated possibilities of western Atlantic settlement. In 1656, Jews were about 4 percent of the chief investors in the Company and 6.5 percent by 1658. Portuguese-Jewish merchants were of vital importance to the Dutch economy, especially in centering the profitable sugar trade in Amsterdam.[18] Pictures of the wealth of The Netherlands were found in maps, such as those of Lucas Wagenaar, Nicolas Visscher, and other contemporary cartographers. These maps were often decorated with views depicting the abundant richness of the colony in vivid, complimentary detail. New Netherland was shown as a thriving, flourishing province full of promise. For the Dutch in the mid-seventeenth century, in their "Golden Age" all was well, and for their Jewish compatriots all was attainable.

In early 1655, or possibly late 1654, a third group of Jews arrived in New Amsterdam, all from the Dutch Republic. They all probably had passports, and Stuyvesant made no objection. Many had been in Brazil. These incoming Jews, the post-*Peereboom* and *St. Catrina* arrivals, had been asked by the Amsterdam Jewish *parnassim* to travel to New Amsterdam in order to provide financial aid to the poor twenty-three Jews, although as a group they were primarily interested in possibilities of commercial enterprise.[19] One, Jacob Cohen Henriquez, was the son of a principal investor Abraham Cohen, alias Francisco Vaez de Leon. He was accused of theft and smuggling, and like Isaac Israel became active in trade on the Delaware River, as did David Ferera and Joseph da Costa, a major shareholder in the Company. They dealt in furs, cattle, butter, cheese, tobacco, furs, cloth, and lumber. Ferera sold and bought tobacco in Maryland. In March 1655, da Costa was agent for a newly formed Gilles Verbrugge and Co.,

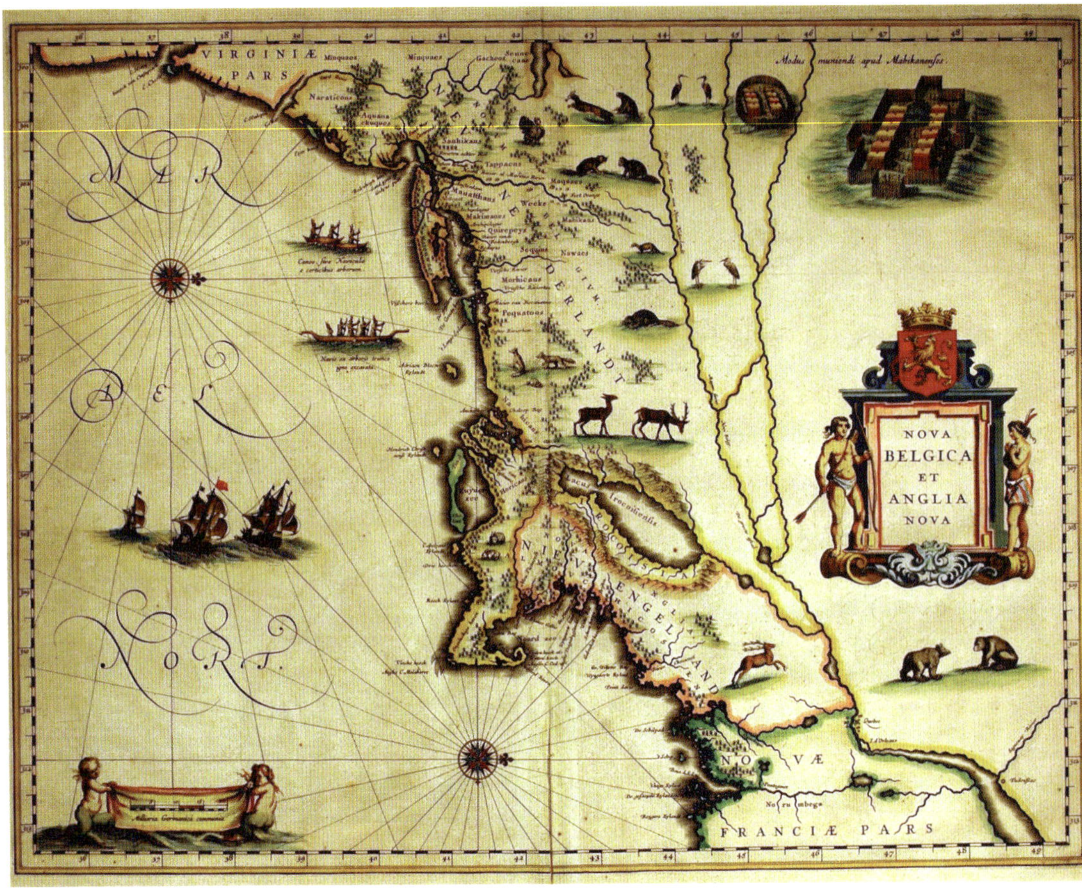

Figure 10.3. Nova Belgica et Anglia Nova (New Netherland and New England), by Willem Blaeu, Amsterdam, 1635. This is the engraved version of Adriaen Block's 1614 manuscript map. It is the first map to illustrate North American animals, particularly the fur-bearing kind that lured many traders. North is to the right. From the Bert Twaalfhoven Collection. Fordham University Library, Bronx, New York, Map #2.

engaged in trade between New Netherland and Amsterdam.[20] The directors of the Company, on June 14, 1656, instructed Stuyvesant not to interfere with trade engaged in by those of the "Jewish or Portuguese nation" on the Delaware River or in Fort Orange (Albany), but continued restrictions on Jews in public service or in having retail shops,[21] obstacles that could be overcome. Asser Levy and Jacob Barsimson, on petition, were permitted to become militia members. Jews were granted burgemeester rights on April 20 or 21, 1657. Abraham de Lucena and Levy carried on retail trade. Levy also became a property owner, purchasing property in 1663 at what is now known as 59 Stone Street in New York City.[22] Though Jews asked for permission to erect a synagogue, Stuyvesant did not grant it, and this issue was never pursued. Though early in February 1656, three members of the community asked for and were granted permission to purchase a burial ground "outside of this city," there is no record of any Jewish death in New Amsterdam, nor where the proposed cemetery was located. There appears to be no congregation established and these early arrivals do not appear to be the "Founding Fathers of Congregation Shearith Israel," which was formed in 1728. Abraham de Lucena, a leader of the last group had a *Sefer Torah* (Holy Scroll) given to him by the Amsterdam community, but there was little need for it. De Lucena left New Amsterdam soon after arrival and returned the scroll to its donors.[23]

Stuyvesant's dislike of these new immigrants might have also stemmed in part from some Jewish involvement in Curaçao. In 1651, the Company directors wrote to Stuyvesant, when he was Governor General of the island, that he should be aware of one Jan de Illan who was Jewish, as were his associates. They were under contract to bring a "considerable number of people" to settle on the island, but instead (the directors wrote) de Illan meant only to trade to the West Indies and the mainland. De Illan turned to exporting horses and timber instead of importing people. The contract appeared to have been a subterfuge. Perhaps Stuyvesant's suspicions and dislike were reinforced by the incident.[24]

Despite the possibilities and wonders described by van der Donck, the dream of success was quickly dispelled for all of the passengers on the *Peereboom* except for Asser Levy, as well as for all of those on the *St. Catrina,* and for the Abraham de Lucena, Salvador d'Andrada, and Joseph da Costa travelers, who may have arrived on the ship *Gevelekt Koe* (*Spotted Cow*), Pieter Jansen skipper, but more likely were on the ship *Groot Christofel* (*Great Christopher*), Willem Tomassen skipper, which was in port by spring 1655.[25] The de Lucena voyagers first appear in records on March 1, 1655 when *Fiscaal* [Sheriff] Cornelis van Tienhoven brought "Abram de La Sina, a Jew into court claiming the merchant had kept his store open during the sermon (Sunday) and sold by retail," the last as privilege reserved for burghers. Van Tienhoven asked for a fine of six hundred guilders, deprivation of trade and that Jews arriving last year from the West Indies (those on the *St. Catrina*) and "now from the Fatherland must depart forthwith." The Court of Burgemeesters and Schepenen decided to let the resolution "take its course." Eventually, the Jews, with the exception of Asser Levy, left quietly. David Ferera and Salvador d'Andrada were sued on May 5, 1655, for payment of freight shipped on the vessel arriving in 1655 from Amsterdam.[26] Ferera was accused of having improperly seized contested goods from the Bailiff and of using "many hasty words" in the process, for which he was sentenced by the City Court to pay a very large fine, as well as imprisonment, whipping, and banishment. His interpreter and spokesman was Joseph da Costa, who knew both Hebrew and Dutch. He appealed to Petrus Stuyvesant and his council and managed to have Ferera released from prison and only to pay a fine of 120 guilders.[27]

Later, on October 11, 1655, a "voluntary" tax was imposed by Director General Stuyvesant and his council to strengthen the outer wall on the site now known as Wall Street against "unexpected rencontre with the native Indians." Some 250 individuals were so taxed. Stuyvesant provided 150 guilders and some eleven other non-Jews paid 100 to 150 guilders, although on average the tax paid was between ten and twenty-five guilders. Interestingly, five Jews—Abraham DeLucena, Joseph da Costa, David Ferera, Salvador d'Andrade, and Jacob Cohen—paid one hundred guilders. All are listed together on the tax list. Jacob Barsimson and Asser Levy, however, each paid a smaller sum of six guilders.[28] Did they not have the wealth of the others? Was the tax another consideration for not remaining in New Amsterdam? Another cause for leaving may have been the reason the tax was imposed, fear of Indian attack, which was particularly present, especially after September 1655 when a large band of Indian warriors roamed the streets of New Amsterdam and surrounded settlements for some three days. An estimated one hundred inhabitants were killed. Conflict had also occurred in the Hudson Valley during the Esopus Wars.[29] Possibly, a sense that the colony would fall to mounting English pressure also hastened their departure. Whatever the cause, with the exception of Levy all left after a short, somewhat troubled stay.

Was anti-Semitism, as seen in the statements of Stuyvesant and Domine Megapolensis objecting to the *St.Catrina*'s twenty-three Jews, another reason for Jews to leave? Or were these sentiments aimed at the undocumented and seemingly poor, not at Levy and the other documented arrivals? On October 15, 1660, Levy along with five other persons, appeared before the City Council *(burgemeesters* and *schepenen)* and asked to be sworn butchers. One of these five, Gerrit Roos, became a partner with Levy in this trade. Interestingly, their slaughterhouse was on Wall Street, where in the present day "bulls and bears" are found. Levy's request, as the well as that of the other five, was granted. Levy at his request was exempt from slaughtering hogs and allowed to take his oath in the manner "which Jews were accustomed to take,"[30] a clear indication of, at least, a degree of religious accommodation accorded Levy. Would not this have applied to others? Where Levy learned his trade is not known, but what is known is for whatever reason, Levy had found a home in New Amsterdam as a respected member of the community. He is honored, to this day, by New Yorkers, who have named a public school after him, as well as a recreation center, a park, and a street.

IN SUMMARY

None of the twenty-three and none of those with de Lucena stayed very long in the province. Only Asser Levy remained. He died in New York in 1682. By 1664, seemingly no one, except Levy, of the original 1654–55 arrivals were present to see and accept the surrender to the English. These were not settlers. They did not establish a community, but were drawn basically by possibilities of trade, the urging of the Amsterdam Jewish community, perhaps by fear of plague, and possibly by the rhetoric of Usselincx or van der Donck. These few chose first to voyage to New Amsterdam, but then to take their leave. The West India Company also chose to surrender and leave. However, as a community, the Dutch settlers remained together with their property, customs, language, religion, and a committed sense of toleration and liberty, foundations upon which a world city, a new city, New York was built. For the Company, dreams and hope were lost in the face of reality, but a vision remained. For these first Jews, this was also an adventure that failed, yet there remained hope for future settlement.

There are many questions about the arrival of these first few. Unfortunately, those involved left no extant letters or journals or any account of their experience. Answers to questions raised by historians were far from the minds of participants. With material still available some reasonable assumptions may shed light on a time long past. Perhaps more evidence in Dutch archives will be brought forward and some of these basic queries can be answered. The importance of archival research and the use of primary sources, where possible, is evident, instead of depending on secondary information. For example, such research revealed that the "twenty-three" were not the first Jews in New Amsterdam and that they came on the Dutch *St. Catrina,* not the French *St. Charles,* nor the *St. Catherine.*

Most importantly, although the stay of these early travelers was short-lived, their struggle to expand religious and civil liberties is a legacy to be treasured, remembered, and preserved. The four hundred-year anniversary of the Hudson voyage should celebrate the Dutch Republic's

FIGURE 10.4. Ordinance exempting Jews from military service, Aug. 28, 1655. Jews were exempted from militia duty in the Netherlands, upon payment of a fine, and a similar exemption was granted to Jews in New Netherland. The reason was not only the legal precedent in the Netherlands, but also "the aversion and disaffection of this militia to be fellow soldiers of the aforesaid nation [Jews]." New York State Archives, accession A1875-78 Dutch Colonial Ordinances, vol. 16 (pt. 1), p. 59. In Charles Gehring, trans. and ed., *Laws & Writs of Appeal* 1647–1663 (Syracuse University Press, 1991), 50–51.

contribution to the development of progress and freedom in New York and the United States at large—ideas that contributed to the building of a flourishing City.

NOTES

Earlier versions of this chapter appeared as "By Chance or by Choice," *American Jewish Archives Journal* LVII, nos. 1 and 2 (2005): 1–13, published by the Jacob Rader Marcus Center of the American Jewish Archives; and "By Chance or Choice: Jews in New Amsterdam 1654," *de Halve Maen* 77 (Summer 2004): 23–30, published by the Holland Society of New York. Permission has been granted by the respective publishers for the present revised and expanded essay. "Flourishing City" refers to a work by Spinoza in which he described the city of Amsterdam as "this flourishing state, and most splendid city, [where] men of every nation and religion live together" and reap the benefits of such freedom "in its own great prosperity and in the admiration of all other people." The title refers to such freedom in New Amsterdam, leading to the same as it remains even today.

1. Ketel was probably the skipper, since in April he had agreed to command the *Peereboom,* although Jacob Jansz Huys in December 1654 while in New Amsterdam agreed to sail the vessel to the West Indies. See Municipal Archives, Amsterdam Inv. fol. 145 (25 April, 1654); Berthold Fernow, *The Records of New Amsterdam 1653–1674* (New York: Knickerbocker Press, 1897), I, 274, 278 (hereinafter *R.N.A.*); Zvi Loker, *Jews in the Caribbean in Colonial Times* (Jerusalem: Misgar Yerushalayim Institute for Research on the Sephardi and Oriental Jewish Heritage, n.d.), 63; Teunis G. Bergen, "List of Early Immigrants to New Netherland," *The New York Genealogical and Biographical Record* XIV (July 1883): 181 (cites July 8, 1654 as the date of the arrival of *Peartree*); A. J. F. van Laer translations of New York Colonial Manuscripts, Reel III, 625–28, microfilm in the State Library, Albany, New York; Peter Padfield, *Tides of Empire* (London: Routledge and Kegan Paul, 1979), II, 187, 233; Berthold Fernow, *Documents Relating to the History of Early Colonial Settlement* (Albany: Weed, Parsons, 1883), 315, 341, 484, 486, passim (hereinafter *Colonial Settlement*). The first mention of the name of the ship *St. Catrina* is in the original manuscript of the Records of New Amsterdam in the Municipal Archives, 31 Chambers Street, New York, although Fernow first translates the name as *St. Charles, R.N.A.,* 240, 241, 244. Captain de la Motthe had written a petition in French. This does not confirm the ship was French. There were many French-speaking Protestants (Huguenots and Walloons) in The Netherlands. There is no record of a *Saint Catherine* in French archives (see Wiznitzer reference below).

2. *R.N.A.,* I, 240–44; Jacob R. Marcus, *The Colonial American Jew 1492–1776* (Detroit: Wayne State University Press, 1970), I, 215, 216, passim; Samuel Oppenheim, *The Early History of the Jews in New York 1654–1664* (New York: Publications of the American Jewish Historical Society, 1909), 37–43 (hereinafter *Early History*). Oppenheim believes there was a direct voyage of what he calls the *St. Charles* from Brazil. For a contrary view, see Arnold Wiznitzer, "The Exodus from Brazil to New Amsterdam of the Jewish Pilgrim Fathers 1654," *Publications of the American Jewish Historical Society* (Philadelphia: 1954), XLIV, 88, 90 (hereinafter "Exodus"), referring to the *St. Catherine* and a Caribbean voyage. Wiznitzer is very critical of Oppenheim. Egon and Frieda Wolff. "The Problem of the First Jewish Settlers in New Amsterdam 1654," *Studia Rosenthaliana* XV (August 1981): 176–77, strongly supports the idea of a voyage from Surinam to New Amsterdam for the twenty-three Jews.

3. Samuel Oppenheim, "More About Jacob Barsimson, the First Jewish Settler in New York," *Publications of the American Jewish Historical Society* XVIII (Philadelphia: 1910), 39, 44 (hereinafter Jacob Barsimson); Leo Hershkowitz, "New Amsterdam's Twenty-three Jews—Myth or Reality," in *Hebrew and the Bible in America,* ed. Shalom Goldman (Hanover: University Press of New England, 1993), 172–73. The author finds no evidence to support the twenty-three figure. Wiznitzer cites his own publication of Recife's Congregation Zur Israel to support his assertion, but Levy does not appear on any such list, "Exodus," 92–93; Arnold Wiznitzer, *The Records of the Earliest Jewish Community in the New World* (New York: American Jewish Historical Society, 1954), 50–52; for a list of immigrants into New Netherland, see

"A List of Early Immigrants to New Netherland," *New York Genealogical and Biographical Record* XIV (New York: 1883), 181–90. Aboaf and Barsimson are noted on pages 182–83. Peterson was possibly a part of the Pieters family in Italy. See a contract between "Jan Pietarz Italieen" with Benjamin Bueno deMesquita relating to a transaction dealing with tobacco from Bermuda dated July 5, 1650, N.A. 1094/319 in the Municipal Archives, Amsterdam.

4. Jonathan Israel, *The Dutch Republic* (Oxford: Oxford University Press, 1995), 658; S. M. Dubnow, *History of the Jews in Russia and Poland* (Philadelphia: Jewish Publication Society of America, 1916), I, 144–52. See E. B. O'Callaghan, *The Laws and Ordinances of New Netherland* (Albany: Weed, Parsons, 1868), 192 (note) for mention of Polish Jews in Amsterdam.

5. *Doc. Rel.*, XIV, 315; Bloom, 126; Marcus, I, 218, 219.

6. Hugh Hastings, ed., *Ecclesiastical Records of the State of New York* (Albany: State of New York, 1901–1916), I, 335–36; Oppenheim, *Early History*, 2; H. S. van Straaten, *Maurits de Brazillean* (Den Haag: Van Soeren, 1998), 51. Translation and reference are provided by Joep de Koning, as well as many helpful suggestions.

7. There is an early account by Saul Mortera of a French ship rescuing the twenty-three from the hands of Spanish pirates. Often accepted by historians, this odd tale involving the *St. Catherine* or *St. Charles* has little substance. Wiznitzer, "Exodus," 80–86, 89, 91.

8. Isaac da Costa, *Israel and Gentile* (London: James Nesbit, 1850), 449; Pierre M. Netscher, *Les Hollandais, au Brazil* (The Hague: Belinfantes Frères, 1853), 163.

9. Wiznitzer, "Exodus," 86. Under Dutch law, Jews were considered, at least in part, as a separate entity governed by their own laws. But as citizens they were protected by Dutch law. Jacob A. Schiltkamp, *De Geschiedens van Het Notariaat in Het Octrooigebied van De West-Indische Compagnie* (S'Gravenhage: N. V. De Ned. Boek. En Steendrukkeru V/H. M. L. Smits 1964), 175–81. I would like to thank Dr. Schiltkamp for his insight and helpful corrections in regards to this article.

10. C. Ligtenberg, *Willem Usselincx* (Utrecht: A. Oosthoek, 1914) (Bijlage), cxvi. My thanks to Joep de Koning for this insightful information and translation. Amandus Johnson, *The Swedes on the Delaware 1638–1664* (New York: International Printing, 1970), I, 52–56. Angry at the Company for not receiving proper recognition, Usselincx traveled to Sweden in 1624. There, he met King Gustavus Adolphus and convinced him to establish a trading company in the New World. This expansion would not only defy Spanish power, but also add to the glory of Sweden even if on New Netherland property. Established was a short-lived New Sweden on the Delaware River. Herbert I. Bloom, *The Economic Activities of Jews of Amsterdam in the Seventeenth and Eighteenth Centuries* (Port Washington, NY: Kennikat Press, 1970), 124, 125, 162.

11. Thomas F. O'Donnell, ed., *A Description of the New Netherland* (Syracuse: Syracuse University Press, 1968), xxxi–xxxxix.

12. Adriaen van der Donck. *A Description of New Netherland,* ed. Charles T. Gehring and William A. Stern, trans. Diederik Willem Goedhuys (Lincoln and London: University of Nebraska Press, 2008).

13. Jonathan Israel, *The Dutch Republic,* 621, 625.

14. F. L. Dubiez, *The Sephardi Community of Amsterdam,* trans. C. F. L. Los (Amsterdam: American Friends of the Portuguese Synagogue in Amsterdam, n.d.), 5. For a thorough discussion of this subject, see Miriam Bodian, *Hebrews of the Portuguese Nation* (Bloomington: Indiana University Press, 1996), 51–75; Henri and Barbara van der Zee, *A Sweet and Alien Land: The Story of Dutch New York* (New York, Viking Press, 1978), 246–50; Marcus, I, 228; Odette Vlessing, "The Portuguese-Jewish Merchant Community in Seventeenth Century Amsterdam," in *Entrepreneurs and Entrepreneurship in Early Modern Times,* ed. Cle Lesger and Leo Noordegraaf (Den Haag: Stichting Hollandse Historische Reeks, 1997), passim.

15. Lewis Samuel Feuer, *Spinoza and the Rise of Liberalism* (Boston: Beacon Press, 1958), 65.

16. Jonathan I. Israel, "The Jews of Dutch America," in *The Jews and the Expansion of Europe to the West, 1450 to 1800,* ed. Paolo Bemardini and Norman Fiering (New York: Berghahn Books, 1997), 341, 344; "Jacob Barsimson" passim; Abraham J. Karp, ed., *The Jewish Experience in America* (New York:

Ktav, 1969), I, 37–38; Solomon Grayzel, *A History of the Jews* (Philadelphia: Jewish Publication Society, 1953), 497.

17. E. B. O'Callaghan, *Documents Relative to the Colonial History of the State of New York* (Albany: Weed, Parson, 1858), I, 400–401 (hereinafter *Doc. Rel.*).

18. Bloom, 126; Vlessing, 224, 225, and 233.

19. "Jacob Barsimson," 39, 40.

20. Hershkowitz, "New Amsterdam's Twenty-Three Jews," 176; *N.A.*, 1119/79, 1113/22.

21. Esther Singleton, *Dutch New York* (New York: Dodd, Mead, 1909), 349; E. B. O'Callaghan, *The Laws and Ordinances of New Netherland, 1638–1674* (Albany: Library of America, 1868), 194.

22. Morris U. Schappes, *A Documentary History of the Jews of the United States, 1654–1875* (New York: Citadel, 1950), 6–7, 12–13; J. H. Innes, *New Amsterdam and Its People* (New York: Charles Scribner's Sons, 1902), 87; Leo Hershkowitz, "Asser Levy and Inventories of Early New York Jews," *PAJHS* LXXX: 31; Oppenheim, *Early History,* 36 gives the date as April 20 for the granting of burgemeester rights, while E. B. O'Callaghan, *Calendar of Historical Manuscripts (Dutch)* (Albany: Weed, Parsons, 1865), 184 gives the date as April 21,1657. Both were able to see the original document, which was damaged by the destruction of the date in the Albany Library fire of 1911.

23. David De Sola Pool argued that Shearith Israel was founded during the Dutch period and this view accepted by the present Shearith Israel appears to have no basis in fact. David and Tamar De Sola Pool, *An Old Faith in the New World* (New York: Columbia University Press, 1955), 3; David DeSola Pool, *Portraits Etched in Stone* (New York: Columbia University Press, 1952), 8–9; Isaac S. Emmanuel, "New Light on Early American Jewry," *American Jewish Archives* VII (January 1955): 17.

24. *Doc. Rel.,* XIV, 135.

25. *R.N.A.* I, 336, 337; the skipper of the *Spotted Cow* appeared in Court on August 9, 1655, brought there by Joseph da Costa seeking to recover claims on damaged goods "spoiled" in the vessel. Since the De Lucena group including da Costa arrived in New Amsterdam no later than March 1655, the *Spotted Cow* seems not to be the vessel they used. Another vessel, the *Balance* from Amsterdam, arrived in mid-August 1655. The ship *Black Eagle* (*Swarte Arent*) was also in port April in August 1655.

26. *R.N.A.* I 290–91, 313; II, 136, 140–47; *Doc.Rel.* XIV, 135.

27. *R.N.A.* II, 130, 136, 140–42, 145, 147. When da Costa translated for Ferera, was Ferera speaking Hebrew, or (what is more likely) Yiddish, which the court considered to be Hebrew?

28. *R.N.A.* I, 366—75.

29. Edward R. Ellis, *The Epic of New York City* (New York: Coward, McCann, 1966), 64–67.

30. Hershkowitz, "New Amsterdam's Twenty-Three Jews," 179–80; *R.N.A.* VII, 259.

Chapter Eleven

Governors Island and the Origins of Religious Tolerance

Joep de Koning

Joep de Koning explains that religious tolerance in the Netherlands grew, in part, from the country's reaction against the Spanish Inquisition when Spain controlled the Netherlands and persecuted Dutch Protestants. He asserts that the West India Company's 1624 instructions to the colonists represented the first declaration of toleration in the New World, as limited as that toleration may have been. He gives its introduction to the Americas a sense of place: Governors Island, a landmark in New York Harbor, where the 1624 edict requiring tolerance was received in North America.

Religious freedom lies at the foundation of the United States of America. By constitutional command, the Congress may make no law respecting an establishment of religion, nor may it prevent its free exercise. These rights are enshrined in the First and Fourteenth Amendments to the United States Constitution.[1]

The Dutch Republic introduced the jurisprudence of religious tolerance into the Western Hemisphere in 1624, mandating it for its settlers to New Netherland. This jurisprudence accompanied the first settlers who disembarked on Noten Eylant, now Governors Island, in New York Harbor in 1624 and 1625. It was the start of New Netherland as a provincial extension of the Dutch Republic situated between 38 and 42 degrees latitude. This followed New Netherland's use as a territory for private trade under patents issued by the Republic's States General (parliament) since 1614. The settlers were bound by an elaborate set of orders, including an edict that accorded colonists and natives complete freedom of conscience and prohibited religious persecution as in the Republic where many thousands of persecuted Europeans had found a safe haven. The right to toleration gave birth to the diversity and pluralism that the world has come to associate with New York. Tolerance is essential to liberty. Consequently, Governors Island has not only national historical significance,[2] but also contains symbolic value as the lifeblood of American Liberty.

This New World introduction of religious tolerance can be traced to sixteenth-century events that eventually resulted in the division of the Low Lands (Netherlands) into two states: An independent federal republic in the north and a Spanish-occupied state under Spain's royal authority in the south.

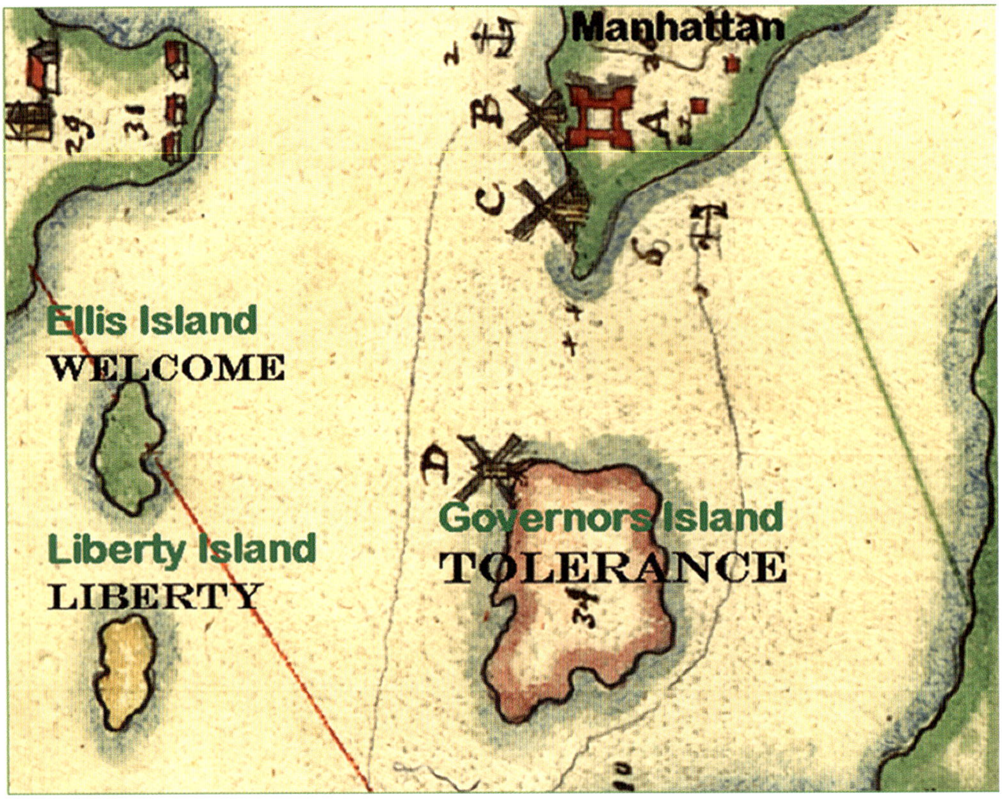

FIGURE 11.1. Adapted from a section of the Manatus map, by Johannes Vingboons, c. 1639, showing Governors Island in relation to Liberty Island and Ellis Island. Courtesy: Library of Congress, Geography & Map Division.

The Low Lands, comprising seventeen provinces of the Netherlands upon its first political integration in 1543,[3] came under the rule of Philip II, King of Spain, based on the "Pragmatic Sanction" of 1549.[4] He had proclaimed his right to rule by Divine Law, thereby dismissing privileges and liberties of the provinces, towns, and regional leaders.

Charles V, father of Philip II, had introduced the Spanish Inquisition to deal with Protestant heretics, thus superseding or diminishing the regional administration of justice. As a result, Spain persecuted the local elites' fellow townspeople for their religious beliefs, and through Spain's central authority, tortured, executed, or burned them at the stake in Brussels, the Netherlands' capital. The Spanish burned the first Lutherans in 1523 and the first Calvinist in Doornik in 1546. They put Anabaptists to death because of their "communist" ideas in various other cities, such as Amsterdam, which Anabaptists had tried to seize as their New Jerusalem in 1535, but took a particular heavy toll in Antwerp with ninety-six executions between 1555 and 1566.[5]

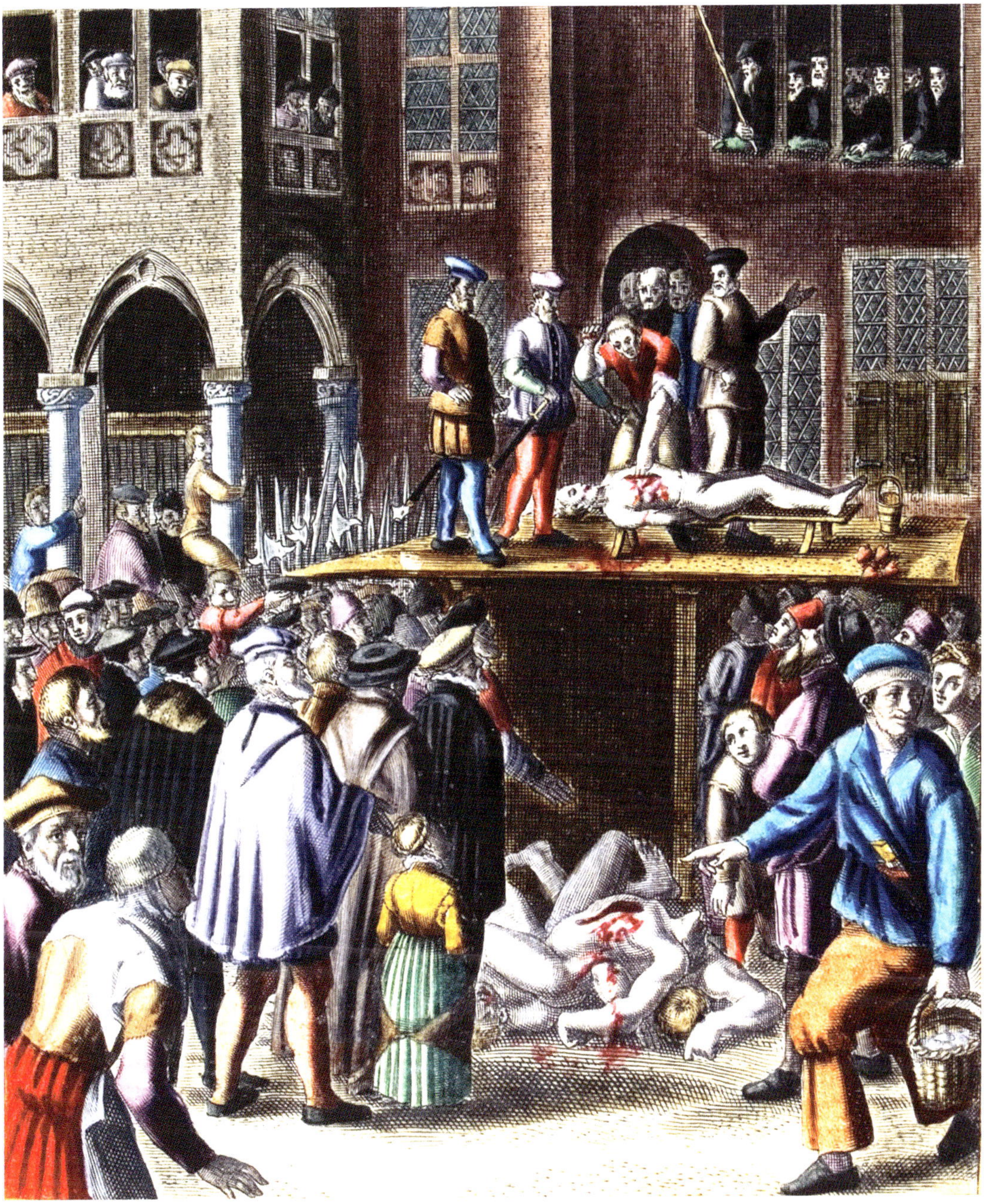

FIGURE 11.2. "Het boeck . . . van den oproer der weder-dooperen." Lambertus Hortensius, 1548: In their efforts to establish an ultra-theocracy, insurgent Anabaptists tried to seize various towns. They succeeded in taking Muenster in 1534 as their New Jerusalem, but not for long. In 1535, in Amsterdam, armed Anabaptists attempted to seize power but failed. The surviving offenders were executed. Courtesy: Library of the University of Amsterdam.

THE COMPROMISE OF NOBLES (EEDVERBOND DER EDELEN), 1566

The seminal incident, from which the introduction of toleration in New Netherland is traced, occurred in Brussels on April 5, 1566.[6] The economic underclass, represented by a group of dissatisfied lower nobles, had assembled in a league called the "Compromise." At least two hundred fully armed men walked in a procession to the Catholic Spanish Governor-General, Margaretha of Parma, and delivered a petition signed by more than four hundred lower nobles denouncing the Inquisition and protesting religious persecution. Though the petitioners styled it a lawful remonstrance, the rulers in Madrid viewed it for what it was—a popular uprising.[7]

In August that same year, the Iconoclastic Fury swept all over the Low Lands, as radicalized Protestants and disaffected segments of the population took to the streets and destroyed Catholic church interiors and statues of saints. This was not a spontaneous expression of popular anger but the work of determined and disciplined resistance groups organized in local consistories throughout the land.[8]

THE DUTCH WAR OF INDEPENDENCE, 1568

Religious clashes in Europe between Catholic and Protestant interests took particularly violent form in the Netherlands, then also known with its Latin appellation of Belgium. Religious dissatisfaction and economic distress exacerbated grassroots dissatisfaction and, ultimately, popular revolt against Spain's royal absolutism. It was instigated by some lower nobles with the help of their Protestant brethren. Events eventually led to what is known as the Dutch War of Independence from Spain. The war began in 1568 and lasted eighty years, producing its first victory in 1572 when Dutch Protestant rebels captured Brielle, a Spanish-occupied Dutch city.[9]

During heavy fighting between the years 1580 and 1621, approximately 150,000 persons left the southern provinces for the northern Netherlands.[10] It was a massive exodus, considering that Antwerp, upon its fall to the Spanish in 1585, was Europe's second-largest city north of the Alps with about 82,000 inhabitants of which 42,000 were Catholics, 27,000 Calvinists, and 13,000 Lutherans.[11] Moreover, militant Calvinists pushed for full freedom of worship by holding public services in the open, outside the town limits, often fully armed and sometimes attended by more than one thousand people. Spain saw this provocation as a political rather than a religious manifestation.[12]

This Protestant revolt, seeking unlimited freedom of conscience,[13] was supported by the majority of the Low Lands' people of diverse religious persuasions. They included regular Catholics and politically influential Catholics in the north, who also opposed the Inquisition and sought to mitigate its edicts, mostly for political, financial (i.e., taxation), and nationalistic reasons. In the southern Low Lands, where many cities were predominantly or entirely Calvinist, the rebellion drew on religious and political motives. From its beginning and during its early expansion throughout the mid-seventeenth century, Calvinism was a minority religion, mostly of the lower classes or "little people" ("kleyne luyden").[14] In their idle despair they stood ready to be hired in the service of merchants who held the bulk of the wealth of the Netherlands.

THE UNION OF UTRECHT, 1579

The members of the league of noblemen, known as the "Compromise," had viewed the "abominable tribunal of the Inquisition" as "diametrically opposed to all laws human and divine, and in cruelty far surpassing the barbarous institutions of heathenism—which raises the inquisitors above every other power, and debases man to a perpetual bondage, and by its snares exposes the honest citizen to a constant fear of death, inasmuch as anyone—priest, it may be, or a faithless friend, a Spaniard or a reprobate—has it in his power at any moment to cause whom he will to be dragged before the tribunal, and to be placed in confinement, condemned and executed, without the accused ever being allowed to face his accuser or to adduce proof of his innocence."

Members of the league went on to say, "We hereby pledge ourselves, and to this end bind ourselves as, and vow with a solemn oath to oppose to the best of our power the introduction of this tribunal into these countries, whether it be attempted openly or secretly, and under whatever name it may be disguised." They signed the common league and covenant in the "holy name of the living God, maker of heaven and earth and all that are therein, who searches the hearts, the consciences, and the thoughts, and knows the purity of ours."[15]

Just thirteen years after the formation of the "Compromise" League in 1566, their demands became codified, in the Union of Utrecht. This document was composed to foster economic and military cooperation among seven rebellious provinces.[16] Considered the basic law of the Dutch Republic, the Union of Utrecht of 1579 declared that "everyone shall remain free in religion and no one may be persecuted or investigated because of religion."

Hence, we begin with that juridical reference to toleration in the founding document of the Dutch Republic. Four years earlier, however, the public exercise of Catholic worship had been prohibited in the provinces of Holland and Zeeland notwithstanding the small number of Calvinist devotees relative to the mostly Catholic population.[17] Hence, the Union's decree was not an ironclad guarantee of religious freedom because the seven provinces retained their historically acquired rights, which included the power to decide in religious matters. These provinces, except Holland and Zeeland, had agreed in 1576 that Catholics were to be left in peace.[18] Now, in 1579, because their political and economic interests were larger than the principle of toleration, the Holland and Zeeland provinces maintained the status quo—i.e., no public Catholic worship but also no persecution of any religion. The Union's proclamation was an unusual pronouncement given the political and religious realities of the time, as most everywhere else in Europe it was unpopular or unlawful to respect the religious rights and opinions of others.

DUTCH INDEPENDENCE FROM SPAIN, 1581

It was thus that the three-pronged combination of political capital, financial capital, and grassroots capital, motivated by economic and religious considerations, had come together in a union of formidable power in combating Spain, the richest and most powerful nation on earth. It produced an eight decades–long war with Spain out of which New York was born while impoverishing Spain.

After the first thirteen years of warfare, seven provinces of the Netherlands were able to formally declare independence from Spain in 1581. This was known as the Act of Abjuration or Plakkaat van Verlatinge. The Act split the seventeen provinces that comprised the whole of the Netherlands into two states along a militarily determined dividing line, west to east, along religious-political axes. After sixty-seven more years of warfare, the final division, with greatly expanded borders for the united Netherlands provinces, became bilateral with the Treaty of Muenster of 1648.[19]

Under this treaty, the southern Netherlands, Belgium Regium, came into the hands of Spain, directly under its king's absolute authority. Only the Roman Catholic Church was permitted as a "state church," leaving no room in the southern region for civic or religious tolerance of any other faiths or sects. Even secular rights, such as the right to inheritance, were abrogated. This southern section, comprising the formerly important urbanized and industrialized Flanders, Brabant, and French-speaking Walloon provinces, had been the original cradle of Calvinism and religious militancy.

On the other hand, in the north, Belgium Foederatum took its place as a new European state. It was a multireligious republic wherein the Protestant Reformed religion, in a countervailing political act, was given various privileges from the start including the right as the only Christian religion permitted to be publicly visible and externally propagated in its main seafaring provinces of Holland and Zeeland. The other Christian faiths and sects received "freedom of conscience" without the ability to promote or promulgate their beliefs publicly.

Moreover, by confiscating Catholic churches and excluding Catholics—whose religion was the one of the Dutch Republic's archenemy—from governmental functions in the economically thriving Holland and Zeeland provinces, Calvinists would grow from about 10 percent of the Republic's population in the year 1600 to 25 percent by 1648, when Catholics still comprised half of the population.[20] Calvinism was not an officially established or state religion. However, Protestant political control was assured by a state law requiring all public officials to belong to the Calvinist Church. This law effectively reduced all other religions to second-class status and marginalized the Catholic majority through political domination by a minority religion. All religions were therefore not equal. Even though Calvinism thus became the public or privileged Church with its adherents envisaging an active and prominent role in the affairs of state, the state maintained its authority and responsibility independent from the Church. Conversely, the state had no authority or influence over Church theology or its internal workings.

This historic 1581 Edict—expressing a rights-of-man doctrine that enables oppressed peoples by their natural rights to throw off a tyrant and establish government by their own authority—stands central to the development of constitutional and republican government. This universal right provided an underpinning of the Dutch, American, and French republics, among others. John Adams recognized the linkage two centuries later when in 1781 he wrote:

> The originals of the two republics are so much alike that the history of one seems but a transcript from that of the other; . . . the great characters the Dutch Republic exhibits . . . have been particularly studied, admired, and imitated in every American state.[21]

WILLEM USSELINCX AND THE DUTCH WEST INDIA COMPANY (WEST-INDISCHE COMPAGNIE OR WIC)

To understand New Netherland's cultural implications we need to understand how the WIC had come into being. It was the brainchild of Willem Usselincx who with passionate dedication conceived and pursued vigorously his 1591 grand vision (*Groot Desseyn*) for a West India Company. Although almost forgotten, his vision coincides with the first European development of the New York region.

Born in Antwerp in 1567, and after having spent several years in Spain, Portugal, and the Azores as agent for trading companies, Usselincx settled in exile in Middelburg, Zeeland, at age twenty-four. He shared his religious conviction with most of the other orthodox exiles from the southern Netherlands' Walloon and Flemish provinces. He reserved his ire for those, including the enlightened branch of the Calvinist Church (Remonstrants), who advocated public exercise of religion—as if one could "get salvation in all religions without exclusion of the Jewish, Muslim or heathen religions." He saw Catholics and Jews as natural enemies of Calvinism and of his country's well-being. He named Mennonites "country-ruining misers."[22] In 1600, he presented the first written plans for his vision to the States General, various important town councils, and some influential persons.

Usselincx's vision, in contrast to his earlier religious prejudice, included the precept of tolerance as a reciprocal dynamic, from which notions of individual liberty and political freedom evolved. As the basis for New World settlement he envisaged a harmonious, three-way collaboration among aboriginals, patria, and colonists, based on barter where natives were treated with respect and engaged as equal partners in new economies. His views helped shape America's economic and cultural beginnings.

It was in Willem Usselincx, an indefatigable religious fundamentalist and by his own account "one of the richest in the land,"[23] that the concept of a WIC was born and, ultimately, established by charter in 1621. His efforts required collaboration with many branches of government and the cooperation of influential merchants. For the good of his religion and freedom, he wanted to establish America-based colonies without slaves. The success of the colonies would be based on peaceful barter of manufactured goods from the provinces for commodities from the colonies. His plan was designed "for the furtherance of God's honor through the propagation of the holy gospel; moreover to inflict [economic] loss on the enemy; thirdly to increase the country's revenues [through barter-trade] and discharge its overload population [because of a dearth of employment prospects]; finally for the general welfare of all residents of these united lands."[24]

Negotiations for peace with Spain in 1607 complicated Usselincx's vision. Those negotiations, he believed, could be morally justified only if the Protestant Reformed people under Spanish authority in the southern Netherlands would receive the same rights as in the Republic, including the right to hold government positions.

In his many efforts with respect to his WIC colonization—plans based on farming, cattle raising, and barter-trade as opposed to the extraction of gold and silver—he argued for the active involvement of the States General, its issuance of passports to colonists in order to assure that their actions would benefit the Republic.[25] He also advocated the separation of war and bounty from trade, and was against slavery and forced labor. He favored efficient, honest labor of both native and colonist; the latter through self-discipline and rearrangement of workdays according to climate and seasonal conditions in the colonies.[26]

Usselincx wanted the American Indian as a political ally of the Republic against Portuguese and Spanish interests because they had not only been disrespected and kept ignorant by the Portuguese in Brazil but also oppressed by the Spanish in Mexico and Peru and therefore couldn't be effective workers.[27] He envisaged that colonists would show natives the way, by attitude and example, and thus help "civilize" the aboriginals and make them equal partners in the success of the colonies' economies. Success, however, could not be had without assurances from the States General that the colonists would keep their privileges and freedoms and would live under the laws of patria.[28]

Ultimately, Usselincx's original colonizing design became reality in New Netherland where native men concerned themselves chiefly with war making and hunting. The indigenous women worked exclusively the land and collected the harvest. Providing the colonists with the fruits of their labor and soil (e.g., maize and potatoes) and the yields of meat from the hunt, satisfied the settlers' basic consumption needs while providing them with pelts as trade goods. Conversely, the natives' desire for European textiles, prestige goods, and metal products were acquired by bartering their own goods, services, and labor.

During the 1607–09 formal peace negotiations between Spain and the Dutch Republic, Spain had demanded an unfeasible requirement from the Republic, the defender of the free seas and free trade. Spain was seeking the exclusive right to trade with the East Indies and desired the cessation of all Dutch trade in the Far East. Such a peace treaty would have been the death knell for the East India Company. But even if only a truce would be signed, the Company's profits would dry up because of the loss of captured enemy prizes through privateering and the availability again of low-cost, low-profit spices and merchandise in the port of Lisbon.

As a solution to this predicament, the East India Company sought to expand its charter to include the North as well as all of the Americas. Such an outcome would have been fatal to Usselincx's vision and would have quashed any and all efforts for a WIC in whatever form.

One of the East India Company's founding directors, Petrus Plancius—who, as early as 1600, was interested in his friend Usselincx's vision for a WIC—was also a respected cartographer, astronomer, and minister of the Reformed Church. Because Plancius believed that there would be open sea at the North Pole, he was assured that a northern route to the East Indies over the Pole was possible. Previously, in 1594, he had produced a world map that revealed a northwest passage above North America to the Western sea following the Frobisher and Davis explorations in search of this passage in 1576–1587.

From an annotation on the East India Company's minutes of August 7, 1603, we find already evidence of an early desire to protect its interests and to exclude any competitors from making a voyage by the North. It noted, "If this navigation should be undertaken by any private person, it ought to be by all means prevented." Yet, competing Dutch private interests had been eager to challenge the Company's interests by trying to find a passage to the Indies that would fall outside its charter. The peace negotiations accelerated that process for all interested parties. In an effort to preempt the East India Company, they sought the backing of King Henry IV of France in order to achieve their objectives through a French East India Company. They met secretly with Henry Hudson in an effort to hire him. This became known to the East India Company, which rapidly sent him on his way without public announcement of his covert mission to the West.

Plancius had met with Henry Hudson in Holland in the winters of 1607–08 and 1608–09. Furthermore, Plancius was in the possession of the journals of Captain George Weymouth who, in 1602, had sailed fifty leagues into that Northwest Passage. Plancius had given these journals to Hudson upon his urging just before sailing to the Northeast or the West. Hence, they both understood that Weymouth's information would be used for the purpose of exploring a western route. Every geographer or experienced pilot, however, knew of the challenges that ice in the northeast and northwest routes to the Indies would present. Once Hudson decided

FIGURE 11.3. "Beschrijvinghe van Virginia, Nieuw Nederlandt/Nieuw Engelandt" and "Orbis habitabilis oppida et vestitus." Joost Hartgers 1651. (1) Early Mohawk native, c. 1628, with war-club in front of a stronghold and castle. The latter would often contain 20–30 houses, each a dwelling for 100-plus persons. The 1624 and 1625 Instructions stated that if the colonists' living quarters or forts had to be on a place already inhabited by Indians, they had to be persuaded with friendly words or be given remuneration to let the settlers live among them in peace and to the natives' satisfaction while making a contract which would be signed in their manner (i.e., the legend of the purchase of Manhattan). (2) Carolus Allard, c. 1695: Portrayal of the economic alliance between Indians in the foreground with colonial settlement in the background where manufactured goods (woolen duffel/textiles) are bartered with native men for peltries and with native women for produce. From the collection of Joep de Koning.

to abandon the northeast route, he sailed to the great river at 40 $^{2}/_{3}$ degrees using the course made eighty-five years earlier by Giovanni da Verrazzano who, in his 1524 letter to King Francis I of France, had indicated the existence of an estuary at precisely that latitude.[29]

In the spring of 1609, after a four months' residence in Holland, Hudson sailed in the yacht *Halve Maen* (*Half Moon*) out of Den Helder, Holland, officially for the Amsterdam Chamber of the East India Company, to find a North and Northwest Passage to the East Indies on April 6, 1609.[30] Three weeks later, a twelve-year truce with Spain, permitting free trade, was signed. This was a victory for the promoters of a West India Company. The States General denied the expansion of the East India Company's charter, thus preventing further attempts at adding the Americas to its sphere of influence.

After the truce, the Republic resumed war with Spain. Now, the goal of a proposed West India Company included war making as its chief function. Twenty-one years had passed from the first written WIC concept in 1600 as a vehicle for peaceful agrarian settlements in the New World to mostly a war machine as created by charter on June 3, 1621. It was a testament to Usselincx's vision, however, that three years later the laws and ordinances of the Republic's

Figure 11.4. Watercolor by Gordon Miller. Native Americans trading with the crew of the *Half Moon* (*Halve Maen*) on the Mauritius (Hudson) River in 1609: Sixteenth and seventeenth-century ships fostered cross-cultural global communications and opened up remote societies, which until then had been inaccessible. From the collection of Joep de Koning. Reproduction with permission of the artist.

Holland and Zeeland provinces were implanted onto the New Netherland territory with the ship *New Netherland* that carried the first WIC settlers and farmers to Governors Island (Noten Eylant), just south of Manhattan Island.[31] These laws, going back to 1587, and incorporated by reference in the instructions to the settlers of 1624 and 1625, are New York's oldest laws in the same way that Dutch law followed Roman law from Emperor Justinian as introduced into the Netherlands during the Middle Ages.[32]

Against this background, we must view New York's beginnings to include the precepts of freedom of conscience, religious tolerance, individual liberty, and justice in New Netherland. By 1643, visiting Father Isaac Jogues, a Jesuit priest, reported that more than eighteen languages were spoken in New Amsterdam on Manhattan and that beside Calvinists there were "Catholics, English Puritans, Lutherans, Anabaptists, etc."[33] What accounts for this religious plurality and ethnic diversity? Was it indeed rooted in that sixteenth-century Netherlandic struggle for freedom of religion and political independence from tyranny?

In 1579, the prominent cartographer Ortelius published his historical atlas with the statement: "Geography is the eye of history."[34] Hence, a visual link may exist that depicts the

Figure 11.5. "Map of the seventeen new provinces of Lower Germany accurately drawn in the shape of a lion," by Hessel Gerritsz, 1608. According to Joep de Koning, *Leo Belgicus* delivered to Governors Island the message of toleration as New York State's lawful patrimony, New York City's identity, and the island's legacy as the lifeblood of American Liberty. From the collection of Joep de Koning.

significance of the relationship between American cultural history, early legal-cultural New York history, and legal-political history of the Dutch Republic. This connection can be found on a map illustrating the conceptual similarity of the United States of America and the United Provinces of the Netherlands.

In this historical light, Leo Belgicus (Netherlands Lion), engraved as a united Netherlands in 1608, is New York's birthfather. The Latin words in its legend demonstrate that the Lion is equally pertinent to the cultural history of two nations: "The lion speaks. Just as my huge body has muscular limbs, you can see in my body powerful states. How good would it be if, united in everlasting peace, each state assisted the others."

Facing the Spanish enemy in defense, Leo Belgicus signifies natural law as exemplified by the declaration that "when the ruler of the people [King Philip II] does not behave thus, but on the contrary oppresses them . . . they may not disallow his authority, but legally proceed to the choice of another ruler for their defense" (1581).[35] This proclamation preceded by 195 years America's Declaration of Independence, that "the United Colonies are, and of Right

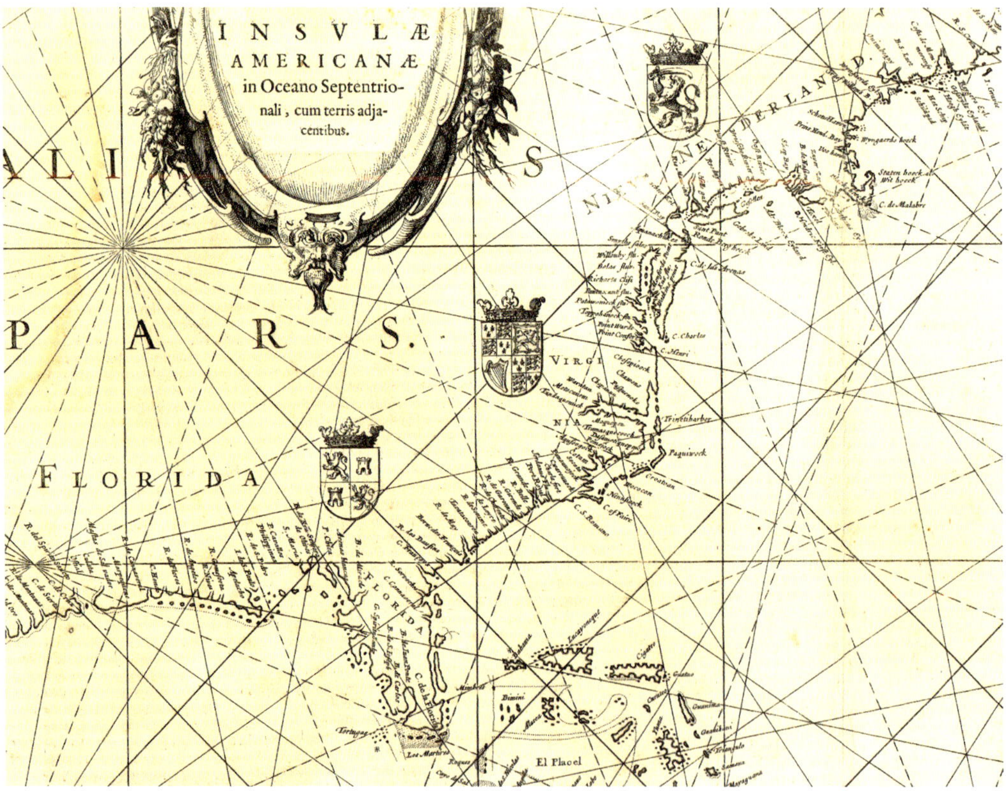

Figure 11.6. Section of a five-piece map called West Indische Paskaert, by Willem Blaeu, c. 1629. The West Indische Paskaert depicts the geographic reach of the June 1621 West India Company Charter to include all countries situated on the African west coast and in all of the Americas; this section published separately in 1630. From the collection of Joep de Koning.

ought to be Free and Independent States" because "whenever any Form of Government [the English Crown] becomes destructive to these ends, it is the Right of the People to Alter or to Abolish it and to Institute New Government."[36]

The provincial entity of New Netherland came into being in a unique way, giving New York its distinctive cultural history and identity. From having been a place for private trade through patents since 1610 and having been named New Netherland first on a map of 1614 in a patent application by the traders and explorers Adriaen Block and Hendrick Christiaensz, the region was transformed into a legal-cultural extension of the Dutch Republic in 1624 (see the North American segment on one of the map in five sections of c. 1629 made by Willem Blaeu and which, in its entirety, depicts the geographical area of the WIC's operation according to its 1621 charter).[37]

When leaving on the ship *New Netherland* on March 30, 1624, the WIC settlers had pledged their allegiance to both the States General and the WIC and were well acquainted with the provisional instructions given their commander, Willem Verhulst. This twenty-one-point Provisional Order spelled out the initial rules by which the settlers had to live. These rules contained the precept of religious tolerance as an active moral force as the colonists had to respect the consciences of others. Natives and nonbelievers would not have to submit to the settlers' religion. The policy was to try "to attract" them "through attitude and by example" only. On the other hand, natives and nonbelievers, when falling under the settlers' immediate authority, could be induced by the director and his council to respect the colonists' faith only when slandered. Most significantly for its time, nobody could be "persecuted for reason of his religion" and everybody had to be given "the freedom of his conscience."[38] This was made plain to the departing colonists on March 28, 1624, by their High Mightinesses of the States General and the WIC.

The WIC Charter of 1621, however, did not yet contain any wording referring specifically to government and justice. It merely mentioned that, in the name and authority of the States General, the WIC could . . . "make contracts, engagements and . . . appoint and discharge . . . officers of justice, and other public officers, for the preservation of the places, keeping good order, police (i.e., government) and justice . . . and the Company shall successively communicate and transmit to us (the States General) such contracts . . . as they shall have made with the aforesaid princes and nations."

Accordingly, the January 1625 Instructions and April 1625 "Further Instructions" from the WIC to director Willem Verhulst and the New Netherland council were expanded to include rules and regulations of government and justice by which all colonists had to live. Those injunctions were the colonists' sole legal guidance until October 13, 1629, and contained specifically a prohibition "to pass any new laws or ordinances or to sanction any new custom" and to "observe and obey" . . . "the ordinances and customs of [the provinces of] Holland and Zeeland and the common written law qualifying them." Settlers were to follow "the administration of justice, in matters concerning marriages, the settlement of estates and contracts" and "intestate estates, the placard issue by their great Mightinesses the States of Holland in the year 1587." In addition to these explicitly stated regulations, all such laws and ordinances had been incorporated by reference in the instructions, which were accompanied by some hard copies as noted in the statement that "some copies of which are sent to him herewith."[39]

Before transposing Dutch jurisdiction onto its North American colony in 1624 thus, the WIC directors had set into motion the codification of a WIC "Concept of Government" for

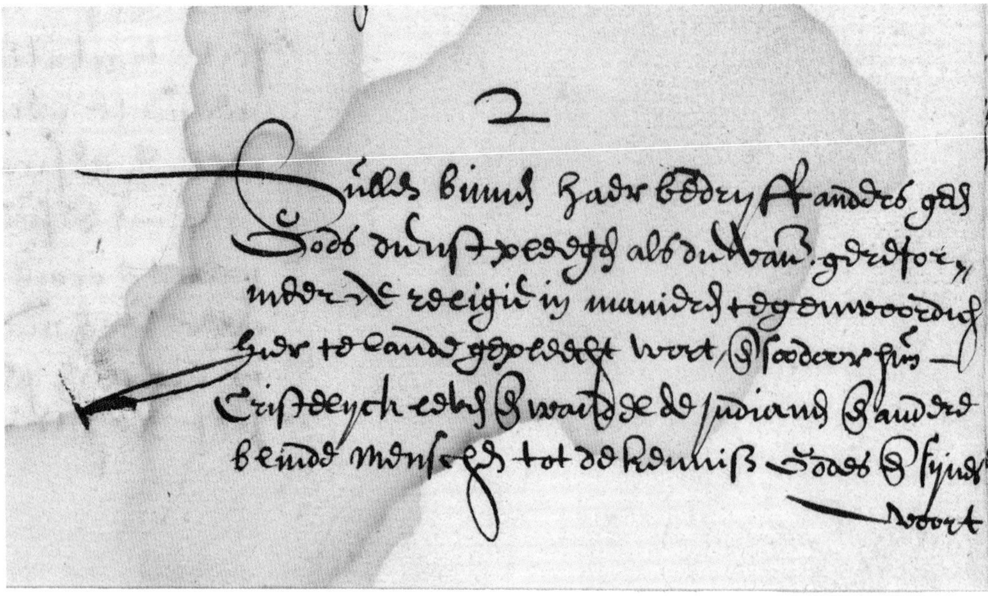

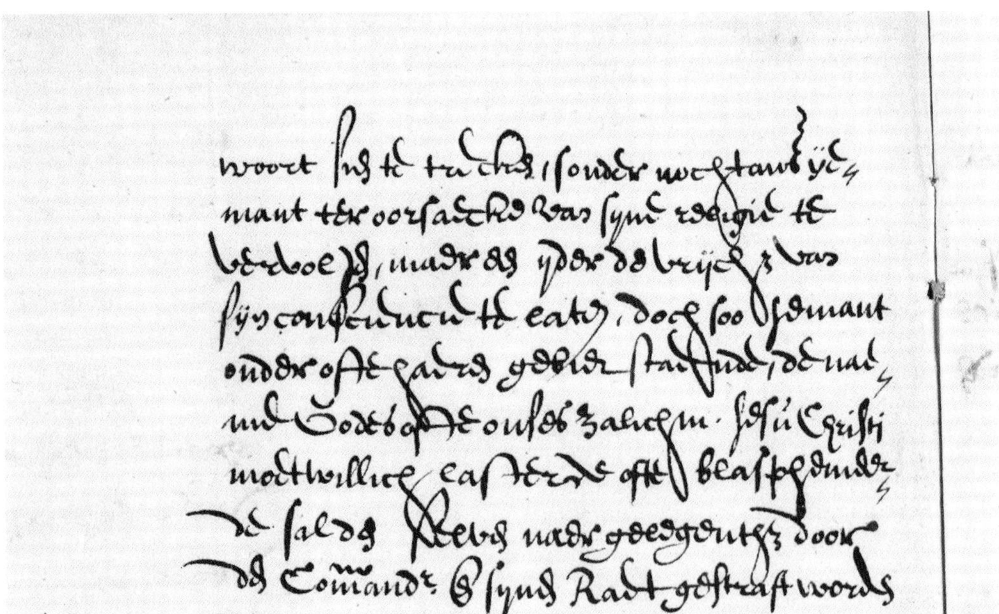

FIGURE 11.7. Article 2 of the Provisional Regulations for the Colonists. It specified freedom of conscience for the settlers and provided that no one should be persecuted for religion. This item is reproduced by permission of The Huntington Library, San Marino, CA, HM 548.

its prospective colonial empire in South America.[40] By November 1, 1624, the first rules and regulations for government and justice had been put in place for the takeover, in 1624, of Bahia de todos los Sanctos and the other places as yet to be conquered in [Dutch] Brazil. A year later, the Bahia capture was undone by the King's Spanish fleet with an army of 12,500 men. Not until 1630 was the WIC successful in capturing the northern part of Brazil (New Holland) with a fleet of sixty-seven ships and seven thousand men.[41]

On October 13, 1629, just before that conquest, the WIC had readied an expanded version in the "Order of Government, for Police (i.e., the complete exercise of the duties of government including government-administration and legislation) as well as justice in the places captured or still to be captured in the West Indies (i.e., an appellation for all of the Americas)." This 1629 Order of Government comprising sixty-nine articles provided uniformity of law among the colonies and with the United Netherlands. It contained nearly the entire Dutch system of government and jurisprudence, and was the vehicle through which Dutch laws and legal institutions were transferred to the Republic's possessions in the Americas including New Netherland. It is thus that we must see New York's development from its very beginnings not only in a local cultural context but also its global legal-political context with a direct connection to its Netherlandic birthfather. The October 13, 1629, Order's policy applicable to New Netherland provided specifically that "Catholics or Jews must be left free without interference or investigation in their consciences or homes."[42]

The general rule was that whenever the interests of state and church, or of commercial and ecclesiastical power, came into conflict, it was the secular authority that would prevail—and this certainly held true for both the West India and East India Companies. Therefore, if religious intolerance obstructed the Companies from achieving their stated goals, secular powers would prevail.

On March 15, 1608, the States of Holland had passed a secret resolution, followed by one from the States General, vowing never to give up the right of the free seas to any place in the world (hence the signing of a truce in April 1609 rather than a peace treaty). During the truce with Spain, intense domestic power struggles ensued over war or peace with Spain, advocated respectively by the adherents of two opposing Calvinist wings, each claiming to possess the theological truth. The Calvinist fundamentalists' war party won over the enlightened Remonstrants' peace party. It caused a substantial revision and expansion of Usselincx's benign vision. The Holland and Zeeland provinces, approved by the States General, had included military operations of strategic importance and economic gain as the Company's primary objective. As a result, the concept charter had made the WIC a vehicle for the defense of the free seas and trade on which the United Netherlands was dependent and for which a military offensive was warranted.

Yet, Usselincx's more idealistic vision of projecting the Republic's Protestant culture peacefully onto the Americas—in competition with what was viewed as the repressive Spanish/Portuguese Catholic approach—was still part of the final WIC charter of June 3, 1621. It was, however, rather obscured and of minor importance to the States General and the WIC. But the now two-pronged WIC's objective would focus its resources on inflicting economic loss on the enemy by attacking its fleets for bounty, seizing its possessions on the African coast for control over gold and slaves, and seizing territory from the Spanish/Portuguese enemy in the Americas. It hoped thus to divert the theater of war away from the Republic to where it counted most—the source of Spain's economic and political might.[43]

Within this context, it is easy to see why the massive military attack on Bahia in Brazil took place in 1624 and who and what caused the peaceful, modest introduction of agricultural settlers into New Netherland that same year, along with the subsequent introduction of a more effective agricultural system of patroonships. As pioneer colonists, the first WIC settlers, mostly Walloon families and of the Calvinist religion, taken to Governors Island in 1624 knew of Usselincx's leading role and profuse writings in persuading the States General to create a WIC. Doubtless, they were peaceful exponents of his original vision and deep love for the True Religion's gospel.

PETRUS STUYVESANT

In New Netherland, the seventh and last WIC appointee, Director General Petrus Stuyvesant, arrived in 1647. He was highly regarded because of his administrative and military capabilities. Intolerant by today's standards, he was a pillar of the orthodox wing of the Dutch Reformed Church and a loyal Company servant who, like Usselincx fifty years earlier, viewed religious

Figure 11.8. "Beschrijvinghe van Virginia, Nieuw Nederlandt/Nieuw Engelandt," by Joost Hartgers, 1651. This engraving shows the planned fort, superimposed on an authentic view of Manhattan with the (fudged) Raritan River in the background. The depiction follows the 1625 instructions to surveyor and fortification engineer Quirijn Fredericksz, wherein the streets were to be perpendicular to the fort's wall. Pearl, Bridge, and Stone streets are already clearly visible, adjusted for topography yet perpendicular to the fort's east wall, now Whitehall Street. The original place for securing cattle overnight became a parade ground, the Parade, and morphed into Bowling Green under English authority. From the collection of Joep de Koning.

heterodoxy as potentially divisive. Increased heterogeneity would undoubtedly compromise the organic unity of New Netherland and weaken Stuyvesant's control and his Reformed Church's quasi monopolistic power.

He and his like-minded council had hoped to forestall the possible destabilizing effects of ever-increasing diversity on political and cultural harmony or, perhaps, even political survival. He was answerable, however, to the WIC, and his ecclesiastical vision for New Netherland often clashed with the secular commercial interests of the Company's directors in Amsterdam as well as with patria's enlightened traditions.

Even though a sixteenth-century law that bestowed political privilege on a religion was no longer operative on the American side of the Atlantic, Stuyvesant and the Reformed Ministers tried, late in the game, to set back the clock of religious variety. They attempted to prohibit public expressions of religiosity other than the Privileged religion of Holland and Zeeland. Theirs was a desperate and vain attempt to reduce religious competition from non-Christian and non-Reformed Christian denominations such as Lutherans, Catholics, and Quakers.

In New Amsterdam, adherence to and even enforcement of the Privileged religion's rule that confined the exercise of one's religion to one's home—as in Amsterdam—served no other purpose than protecting an outwardly self-important but small, struggling congregation of the "True Religion," which was being outnumbered by ever-increasing immigration of persons of varied consciences. Stuyvesant and the Dominees thought that by insisting on the prohibitions against open worship and brick and mortar symbols (Lutherans, Jews),[44] street processions (Catholics), and public preaching (Quakers),[45] they could smother the outward signs of such faiths.

The petty fights conducted by the Reverends Megapolensis and Drisius and Director General Stuyvesant with these religious groups were essentially attempts at protecting their church. Its heartbeat (e.g., bells) and veins determined the rhythms of the community and influenced the civic rules by which the population of the nascent colony lived. By seeking religious subservience of New Amsterdam's population to Calvinist orthodoxy in the face of ever-increasing religious diversity, they hoped to create cultural harmony. Stifling religious diversity, however, was not the aim of the WIC leadership, as it didn't have an active conversion policy beyond requiring Stuyvesant to be supportive of the mission of Reformed Ministers.[46]

By 1653, the Lutherans had requested and petitioned for the right to practice their religion openly.[47] Stuyvesant dismissed their requests summarily. Their petitions to the WIC directors in patria and the States General fared no better, until after Director General Petrus Stuyvesant's rule ended in 1664. The underlying reason for the denial of public worship may best be summarized by the statement of the Amsterdam Reformed Church consistory that "imminent injury to this infant Church" had "been averted" by the "vigilance and discretion of the Dutch Ministers and Director-General."[48]

Patria drew the line at public worship, not wanting to set a precedent by permitting the open exercise of a non-Reformed Christian religion by recognizing a non-Reformed minister. Dominees Megapolensis and Drisius warned that "the Papist, Mennonites, and others, would soon make similar claims." Thus, they argued, the colony would soon become a Babel of confusion, instead of remaining united and peaceful. Indeed, it would prove "a plan of Satan to smother this infant, rising congregation, almost in its birth, or at least to obstruct the march of its truth in its progress."[49]

The WIC considered the freedom of conscience in religion to be a colonial building block that would appeal to many English settlers among the New Netherlanders, who had fled religious persecution in Massachusetts. This can be deduced from a WIC letter of April 21,

Figure 11.9. Johannes Blaeu, 1650: Adriaen van der Donck's 1649 petition to the States General seeking redress of grievance (now a First Amendment right) was accompanied by a 1648 pen and ink view of New Amsterdam. This 1650 engraved/etched version accompanied the printed version of his Remonstrance, published in 1650 as "Het Vertoogh." Careful perusal allows one to discern the bustle of 72 persons in this serene townscape. From the collection of Joep de Koning.

1664, to Stuyvesant. They wrote; "We are in hopes that as the English at the north (in New Netherland) have removed mostly from old England for the causes aforesaid, they will not give us henceforth so much trouble, but prefer to live free under us at peace with their consciences than to risk getting rid of our authority and then falling again under a government from which they had formerly fled."[50] The letter arrived in August 1664, just one month before the arrival of four English frigates in New Amsterdam's harbor in a planned takeover of New Netherland.

Shortly thereafter, the transfer of jurisdiction over "this Place and Province" (New Amsterdam and New Netherland) to the English became reality in the provisional Articles of Transfer of New Netherland on September 8, 1664. Stuyvesant's administration, however, ensured that, under Article VIII, New Netherlanders under English rule, "shall keep and enjoy the liberty of their consciences in religion."[51] After forty years since its inception in New Netherland, religious pluralism had become so well established that it was protected in the transfer of authority to England. It was thus no accident or historical anomaly that the Virginian William Byrd, commenting on his visit to New Amsterdam in 1682, remarked, "they have as many sects of religion there as at Amsterdam."[52]

This historic precept of toleration, unique for its time in 1624 and applicable to the New Netherland province, was enshrined in New York's first state constitution in 1777, in the following stirring language:

> XXXVIII. And whereas we are required, by the benevolent principles of rational liberty, not only to expel civil tyranny, but also to guard against that spiritual oppression and intolerance wherewith the bigotry and ambition of weak and wicked priests and princes have scourged mankind, this convention doth further, in the name and by the authority of the good people of this State, ordain, determine, and declare, that the free exercise and enjoyment of religious profession and worship, without discrimination or preference, shall forever hereafter be allowed, within this State, to all mankind: *Provided,* That the liberty of conscience, hereby granted, shall not be so construed

Figure 11.10. "Nieu Amsterdam or New York," by Carolus Allard, c. 1688. The provisional Articles of Transfer ceding New Netherland to the invading English forces in 1664 included freedom of the seas and trade to and from the Netherlands and the right to enjoy freedom of conscience in religion and church discipline. From the collection of Joep de Koning.

> as to excuse acts of licentiousness, or justify practices inconsistent with the peace or safety of this State.
>
> XXXIX. And whereas the ministers of the gospel are, by their profession, dedicated to the service of God and the care of souls, and ought not to be diverted from the great duties of their function; therefore, no minister of the gospel, or priest of any denomination whatsoever, shall, at any time hereafter, under any presence or description whatever, be eligible to, or capable of holding, any civil or military office or place within this State.

Twelve years later, as one of the first twelve proposed amendments to the United States Constitution, Congress introduced the juridical right to religious tolerance. Its proposal included the stipulations that Congress could make no law respecting an establishment of religion (i.e., that all religions were to be equal) and that it may not prevent its free exercise (i.e., that all religions were to be free.) The proposal was signed by the Speaker of the House of Representatives,

Frederick Augustus Muhlenberg, and the Vice-President of the United States and President of the Senate, John Adams.[53] Notably, John Adams had served from 1780–84 as congressional envoy and first plenipotentiary minister of the United States to the United Netherlands.

What was to become known as the right to religious freedom in the Bill of Rights, was ratified in the "State General" of New York by order of the New York State Assembly, Giulian Verplanck, Speaker, by order of the New York Senate, Isaac Roosevelt, President Pro Hac Vice and signed by the "well-beloved George Clinton, Esquire, Governor of our said State General" in February 1790.[54]

Religious tolerance as an individual liberty, optimized to make all religions equal and free under the Constitution, thus evolved from its earliest beginnings on the North American east coast in confirmation of New York State's polyglot culture since 1624, the date of its birth.[55] Its message of toleration is New York's birthright, and, in turn, the lifeblood of American Liberty.

NOTES

1. The First Amendment, adopted in 1791, prohibits the Congress from making any law respecting an establishment of religion. That amendment, however, initially did not apply to the individual states, many of which had official religions for the first half-century of the country's existence. One (Massachusetts) lasted until 1833. The United States Supreme Court has held that the Fourteenth Amendment, adopted in 1868, made the religion clauses of the First Amendment applicable to the states.

2. At the invitation of the NY State agency, Governors Island Preservation and Education Corporation (GIPEC), the Dutch government made Governors Island the locus of its 2009 quadricentennial parties, without noting the island's historical or historic significance. GIPEC's brochure stated merely, "New York Harbor's abundant waters and lands first attracted American Indian peoples like the Lenape [*sic*]. Dutch settlers in the 1620's took advantage of the diverse ecosystem and established maritime enterprises. The British noted the harbor's strategic potential and, by 1674, secured it for the Crown" (New York State's official Governors Island brochure).

3. Wim Klooster, *The Dutch in the Americas 1600–1800*, The John Carter Brown Library, Providence, RI, 1997, 4.

4. P. J. A. N. Rietbergen, *A Short History of the Netherlands* (Amersfoort: Bekking Publishers, 1998), 67.

5. L. Voet, "De Eerste Fase van Tachtigjarige Oorlog," in *Antwerpen en de Scheiding der Nederlanden, (17 augustus 1585)*, ed. Francine de Nave (Antwerp: Museum Plantin-Moretus en Stedelijk Prentenkabinet, 1986), 22.

6. Friedrich von Schiller, "Revolt of the Netherlands against Spain, Rise of the Gueux or Beggars," in *The Great Events by Famous Historians*, Volume X, The National Alumni (New York: The National Alumni, 1905), 81–99.

7. Rietbergen, *A Short History*, 70.

8. Voet, "De Erste Pase," 22.

9. Rietbergen, *A Short History*, 73.

10. J. G. C. A. Briels, "Zuidnederlanders in de Republiek in het begin van de 17de Eeuw," in *Antwerpen en de Scheiding der Nederlanden (17 augustus 1585)*, ed. Francine de Nave (Antwerp: Museum Plantin-Moretus en Stedelijk Prentenkabinet, 1986), 66.

11. Franchine de Nave, "Beschouwinge," in *Antwerpen en de Scheiding der Nederlanden (17 augustus 1585)* (Antwerp: Museum Plantin-Moretus en Stedelijk Prentenkabinet, 1986), 16.

12. Rietbergen, *A Short History*, 70.

13. Schiller, "Revolt of the Netherlands," 91.

14. J. Briels, *De Zuidnederlandse Immigratie 1572–1630* (Haarlem: Fibula-Van Dishoeck, 1978), 76.

15. Schiller, "Revolt of the Netherlands," 88–89.

16. Union of Utrecht, 1579, Article 13; A. Th. van Deursen, "Between Unity and Independence: The Application of the Union as a Fundamental Law," in *The Low Countries History Yearbook* 14 (1981): 50–65. The text of the Union of Utrecht is in E. H. Kossman and A. F. Mellink, eds., *Texts concerning the Revolt of the Netherlands* (Cambridge: Cambridge University Press, 1974), 165–73.

17. Briels, *De Zuidnederlandse Immigratie,* 26.

18. Rietbergen, *A Short History,* 74.

19. Oliver J. Thatcher, ed., *The Library of Original Sources, Vol. V: 9th to 16th Centuries* (Milwaukee: University Research Extension, 1907), 189–97.

20. Hugo de Schepper, in *Antwerpen en de Scheiding der Nederlanden (17 augustus 1585),* ed. Francine de Nave (Antwerp: Museum Plantin-Moretus en Stedelijk Prentenkabinet, 1986), 132.

21. John Adams, "Memorial to the States General," Leyden, April 9, 1781.

22. O. van Rees, *Geschiedenis der Staathuishoudkunde in Nederland tot het Einde der Achtiende Eeuw,* Volume 2, *Usselincx en de oprigting der Westindische Compagnie* (Kemink & Zoon over den Dom te Utrecht, 22 januarij 1868), 106–107.

23. Ibid., 72–142, 75.

24. Ibid., 74.

25. Ibid., 91, 94; Leo Hershkowitz, "The Arrival in New Netherland with Passports of the First-Known Jews, Ashkenazim, Happened in August 1654: By Chance or Choice: Jews in New Amsterdam 1654," *de Halve Maen* 77 (Summer 2004): 23–30.

26. Ibid., 93.

27. Ibid., 91. Benjamin Schmidt, "Exotic Allies: The Dutch-Chilean Encounter and the (Failed) Conquest of America," *Renaissance Quarterly* 52 (1999).

28. van Rees, *Geschiedenis der Staathuishoudkunde,* 93.

29. Henry C. Murphy, *Henry Hudson in Holland—An inquiry into the Origin and Objects of the Discovery of the Hudson River* (The Hague: The Brothers Giunta d'Albani, 1859), 16–46.

30. van Rees, *Geschiedenis der Staathuishoudkunde,* 42.

31. The Henry E. Huntington Library (San Marino, Cal.), Publications Americana: Folio Series. No. 1, *Documents Relating to New Netherland, 1624–1626,* Van Rappard Documents, ed. A. J. F. van Laer, 2, 255.

32. F. C. Wieder, "De Stichting van New York in Juli 1625" ('s-Gravenhage: Martinus Nijhoff, 1925), 17–35.

33. Franklin J. Jameson, *Narratives of New Netherland, 1609–1664*; Jogues, *Novum Belgium* (New York: Charles Scribner's Sons, 1967), 260.

34. Marcel van den Broecke, "Historical Maps and Their Texts in the First Modern Atlas by Abraham Ortelius," *Caert-Thresoor* 22 (2003): 2, 29–39. "The close connection he saw between history and geography is aptly expressed in the motto he provided for his Parergon, viz. 'Geography is the Eye of History,' Ortelius considered it impossible, impractical and unwise to study geography without considering its historical context . . . it is impossible to assess the significance of a map without studying the text that belongs to it."

35. English text of the Act of Abjuration is in E. H. Kossman and A. F. Mellink, eds., *Texts Concerning the Revolt of the Netherlands* (Cambridge: Cambridge University Press, 1974), 166–73, 216–28; Stephen E. Lucas, "The Plakkaat van Verlatinge," in *Connecting Cultures: The Netherlands in Five Centuries of Transatlantic Exchange,* ed. Rosemarijn Hoffte and Johanna C. Kardux (Amsterdam: VU University Press, 1994), 187–207, provides the most persuasive argument for Jefferson's use of the Plakkaat as a model in writing the Declaration of Independence. For the influence of these works on American constitutional development see James R. Tanis, The Dutch-American Connection: The Impact of the Dutch Example on American Constitutional Beginnings," in *New York and the Union: Contributions to the American Constitutional*

Experience, ed. Stephen L. Schechter and Richard B. Bernstein (Troy: Council for Citizenship Education, Russell Sage College, 1990), 22–28.

36. The Declaration of Independence, July 4, 1776.

37. The West India Company's geographic reach per charter of June 3, 1621: From "the coast and countries of Africa from the Tropic of Cancer to the Cape of Good Hope, the countries of America, the West-Indies, beginning at the fourth end of Terra Nova, by the streights of Magellan, La Maire, and any other streights and passages situated thereabouts to the straights of Anian, as well on the north sea as the south sea, and on any islands situated on the one side or the other, or between both; and in the western or southern countries reaching, lying, and between both the meridians, from the Cape of Good Hope, in the East, to the east end of New Guinea, in the West."

38. The Henry E. Huntington Library, *Documents Relating to New Netherland,* 2.

39. Ibid., 113, 20–21.

40. Jacob A. Schiltkamp, On Common Ground Legislation, Government, Jurisprudence, and Law in the Dutch West Indian Colonies: The Order of Government of 1629, *de Halve Maen* 70 (Winter 1997): 73–80.

41. Wim Klooster, *The Dutch in the Americas,* 31.

42. *Groot Placaet Boeck van Holland,* deel II, 1237, Article X (1664), "Ordre van Regieringe" (13 october 1629), 1235–47, National Archives, The Hague, Netherlands.

43. Charter West India Company, June 3, 1621; *The Federal and State Constitutions Colonial Charters, and Other Organic Laws of the States, Territories, and Colonies,* comp. and ed. Francis Newton Thorpe Under the Act of Congress, June 30, 1906.

44. Leo Hershkowitz, "By Chance or by Choice," *American Jewish Archives Journal* (2005): 1–13; George L. Smith, *Religion and Trade in New Netherland* (Ithaca: Cornell University Press, 1973), 212–16.

45. David Willem Voorhees, "The Flushing Remonstrance in Historical Perspective," *de Halve Maen* 81 (Spring 2008): 11–14; The text of the Flushing Remonstrance is found in Edmund B. O'Callaghan, ed., *Documents Relative to the Colonial History of the State of New York,* 15 vols. (Albany, 1853–1885), 14, 402–403. The original is in the New York State Archives, Albany. For details pertaining to the Flushing Remonstrance see Smith, *Religion and Trade in New Netherland,* 224–31.

46. Willem Frijhoff, "Jesuits, Calvinists, and Natives: Attitudes, Agency, and Encounters in the Early Christian Missions in the North," *de Halve Maen* 81, no. 3 (Fall 2008): 53.

47. Petition right: see Martha Dickinson Shattuck, *A Civil Society: Court and Community in Beverwijck, New Netherland, 1652–1664* (PhD diss., Boston University, 1993), 200–16; Joep de Koning, "From Van der Donck to Visscher—A 1648 View of New Amsterdam," *Mercator's World Magazine* 5, no. 4 (July–August 2000): 28–33. Pertinent section of the First Amendment of the Bill of Rights, 1791: "Congress shall make no law abridging the freedom of speech or of the press . . . or the right of the people to petition the Government for a redress of grievances."

48. *Ecclesiastical Records of the State of New York,* 7 vols. (Albany, 1901–1916), 1, 386–90.

49. Frijhoff, "Jesuits, Calvinists, and Natives," 48–49.

50. Jameson, *Narratives of New Netherland, 1609–1664,* 461.

51. See Article VIII of the original Dutch language version of the Provisional Articles of Transfer, August 27, 1664; *The New Netherlanders Here Shall Keep and Enjoy the Freedom of Conscience in Religion* (Den Haag: Koninklijke Bibliotheek).

52. William Byrd to Bro. Dan'l per Ruds, March 8, 1685/86, *Virginia Historical Register and Literary Companion* 2 (1849): 208 (misprinted 108).

53. Cato Institute, *The Declaration of Independence and the Constitution of the United States of America,* 1998, 41–42.

54. An Act from the State of New York Ratifying Certain Articles in Addition to and in Amendment of the Constitution, 03/27/1790;Series: *Enrolled Acts and Resolutions of Congress,* compiled 1789–2008,

Record Group 11: General Records of the United States Government, 1778–2006, National Archives Building, Washington, DC. Online version available through the Online Public Access (National Archives Identifier 1685236) at www.archives.gov; June 22, 2011.

55. The year of birth (1624) and the birthplace (Governors Island) of the State of New York were recognized in Senate Resolution No. 5476 and Assembly Resolution No. 2708 in May 2002. Joep de Koning, "The Mutually Exclusive Birth Years of the State of New York and the City of New York," *de Halve Maen* 81 (Winter 2008): 71–78.

CHAPTER TWELVE

Marital Litigations in New Netherland and Proprietary New York

Similarities and Differences in Application of Dutch and English Law

MICHAEL E. GHERKE

Michael Gherke observes in his essay that, although the Dutch attitude in the seventeenth century toward women was patriarchal, the European Dutch, and in turn New Netherlanders, had a more expansive view of women's place in commerce. They could engage in trade, appear in court, own land, inherit, and had somewhat more independence than did British women. Although the English brought with them a more restrictive attitude toward women's activities, Gherke compares marital litigation under the Dutch and the British and notes that divorce was not common under either legal system.

NEW AMSTERDAM MERCHANT-TRADER and burgemeester Nicolaas Boot was convinced he could neither reform nor continue to endure the behavior of his wife, Merritje Joris.[1] Consequently, on Monday February 18, 1658, he took the desperate step of appearing before the magistrates of the Court of Burgemeesters and Schepenen of New Amsterdam to present a formal complaint against her, and more. Prefacing his testimony with an expression of reluctance and an apology for bringing the matter before them, he accused Joris of, "drinking in all the groggeries and holes and being so drunk [I] cannot keep house with her." Then, revealing the depth of his frustration with Joris by indicating the legal measures he was prepared to pursue in seeking relief, he asked the court to, "reprimand her for her irregular life, and if she will not amend, that they separate one from the other."[2]

Owing to Joris's absence, the magistrates initially decided to postpone consideration of Boot's petition until the next court day, a common expedient in an age when the pace and length of a messenger's stride determined the speed of the court's communications. However, stating only, "the sooner t'was disposed of the better," they changed their minds about the delay and ordered the city messenger to summon Joris to appear, "forthwith."[3]

The magistrates may have been more circumspect in their effort to expedite a conclusion to the matter if they had known that the episode was the opening legal battle in a long and bitter war between the spouses. Not that caution would have altered the outcome or abridged the protracted process necessary to achieve it. Like other early modern European cultures that contributed to the colonial foundations of American civilization, the Dutch legally and socially supported marital indissolubility. Although Roman-Dutch law included grounds and procedures for effecting marital dissolutions, the process was slow and the outcome was unlikely to produce a level of closure satisfactory to aggrieved litigious individuals and couples.

This chapter examines application of seventeenth-century Dutch and English laws in marital litigations in New Netherland and proprietary New York (1664–1685).[4] Specifically, although there were significant differences between early modern Dutch and English laws governing marriage, both societies shared the pre-Reformation intransigence against marital dissolutions that influenced post-Reformation laws and legal decisions in New Netherland and proprietary New York. In 1930, historian Richard B. Morris published a treatise about the history of early American law asserting that the legal systems of American colonies began to diverge from their European foundations within a short time after initial settlement. In chapter 3 of that study, he explored departures from European laws governing marriage, marital dissolution, and capacities of married women in which he maintained colonial women emerged as distinct personalities and demanded greater political and social recognition and increased rights at law.[5] The legalities of marriage and specifically marital dissolution in colonial New York unambiguously support his thesis.

However, following Morris in 1955 was Matteo Spalletta's interpretation of New Netherland and proprietary New York divorces in which he emphasized differences in Dutch and English law. In doing so, he tacked on the label *liberal* to describe Roman-Dutch laws governing divorce.[6] However, the characterization was subjective. Spalletta's dismissal of New England divorce laws and the litigations they invited and Dutch judicial restraint in granting divorces and separations in New Netherland invite further analysis. More precisely, although Spalletta acknowledged Massachusetts, Connecticut, and Rhode Island laws permitting divorce, he dismissed their significance because there is no documentary evidence of approval by the Crown. Even without Crown approval, however, New England judges granted divorces and other forms of marital dissolution. Other scholars have maintained that these grants influenced legal and social behavior in those colonies.[7]

Before the Protestant Reformation, marriage and laws governing it were the prerogative of the Catholic Church. Those familiar with the unsuccessful efforts of Henry VIII, king of England, to achieve legal dissolution of his marriage to Catherine of Aragon through a Catholic ecclesiastical tribunal, are aware of the difficulties involved in seeking marital dissolutions in pre-Reformation Europe. The Protestant Reformation produced profound multifaceted legal and social changes in Western Europe that included jurisdictional and procedural regulation of marriage. Owing to different opinions about marriage among Protestant Reformers, cultural, social, and other distinctions, standardized regulation of marriage in Protestant Europe did not occur. Perhaps the most obvious dissimilarity in the development of post-Reformation Dutch and English laws governing marriage was that the Dutch Republic transferred jurisdiction to civil authority whereas in England the Anglican Church assumed that responsibility. Significantly, although post-Reformation reconfiguration of jurisdictional and procedural legalities differed in post-Reformation England and the Netherlands, both societies infused new laws governing marriage with pre-Reformation aversion to marital dissolution.[8]

As with other social constructs, legal systems mature in the ebb and flow of regionally distinct cultural and historical currents.[9] Currents affecting early modern Dutch society were particularly profound. Sweeping political, religious, intellectual, and economic events in the Netherlands that occurred from the latter sixteenth through the seventeenth century challenged traditional Dutch cultural paradigms and produced contradictions that resulted in what Simon Schama interpreted as a collective anxiety in the Dutch population.[10]

In addition to achievements in art, literature, science, jurisprudence, and other intellectual enterprises, the early modern Dutch experienced a protracted and eventually successful war for self-determination with Habsburg Spain, establishment of Calvinist Protestantism that resulted in official status for the Reformed Church, and unprecedented acceleration of commercial capitalism that became the envy of many of the Republic's European neighbors.[11]

Early modern Dutch artistic and intellectual achievements and historical events collectively affected what it meant to be Dutch in the latter sixteenth and seventeenth centuries. Metaphorically, the Dutch had one foot in psychologically comfortable traditions and the other in the challenges and opportunities presented by the golden age.[12] Contradictory social expectations of married women were indicative of Dutch efforts to reconcile conventions with innovations. Historically, Dutch wives experienced a dichotomy of domestic and nondomestic responsibilities that predated the golden age. As commerce began to accelerate in the latter sixteenth century, their nondomestic duties expanded, which made wives' promotion and defense of family financial interests in public forums such as court increasingly necessary. Some seventeenth-century native Dutch analysts of their home culture embraced wives' progressive participation in commerce and activities and responsibilities related thereto, while other Dutch analysts found it disconcerting.

Among the latter was Jacob Cats who, while he wrote thousands of verses and caution is necessary in interpreting his positions, emphasized traditional gender roles for wives and husbands to maintain relational and social constancy.[13] In advising affianced and recently married couples in the pamphlet, *Houwelijk* (matrimony), originally published in 1625, he took an uncompromising position concerning demarcation of gender-defined responsibilities. Specifically, he wrote,

> The husband must be on the street to practice his trade
> The wife must stay at home to be in the kitchen
> The diligent practice of street wisdom in man be praised
> But with the wife, there should be quiet and steady ways
> So you, industrious husband, go to earn your living
> While you, Oh young wife, attend to your household.[14]

However, compared with what was taking place for many married women, Cats's advice was anachronistic. Physician and holder of public offices Johan van Beverwijck more accurately reflected on the circumstances for married women.[15] Challenging Cats's prescription for a happy home based on tightly defined gender roles, Van Beverwijck wrote in 1643, "To those who say that women are fit for the household and no more, then I would answer that with us, many women, without forgetting their house, practice trade and commerce."[16]

More important was Van Beverwijck's recognition of the duality of wives' responsibilities and the effects of growing commercial (market) capitalism on women's public roles.[17] Although humanist thought and Protestant theology were catalysts for what one historian interpreted was "more generous treatment of women," Dutch society was institutionally as patriarchal as other early modern Western European societies. For example, seventeenth-century Dutch women could not hold public and church offices, and Dutch society frowned on higher

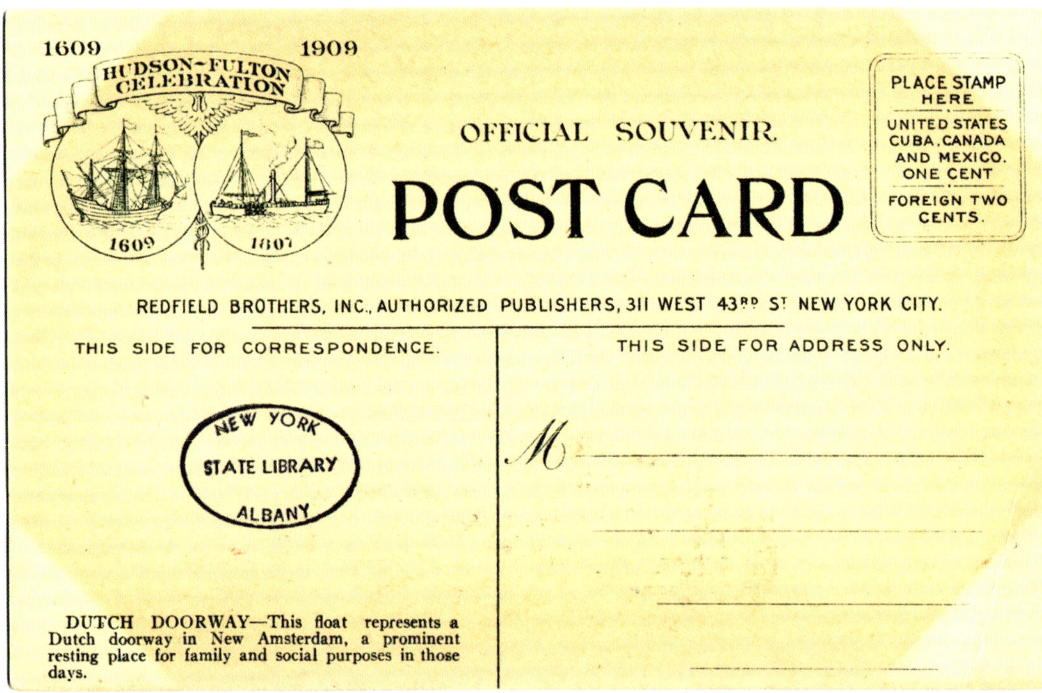

FIGURE 12.1. Float—"Dutch Doorway." Hudson-Fulton Celebration Commission Official Post Card no. 22. New York: Redfield Bothers, c. 1909. New York State Library Postcard Collection. New York State Library call number QC16510.

formal education for women.[18] By then, tolerance was already a fixture of Dutch culture, in areas such as religious pluralism, but did not extend to all cultural and social predispositions.[19] In her advocacy of more opportunities for higher education for women, perhaps the most highly educated women in the seventeenth-century Netherlands, Anna Maria van Schurman, connected learning with wives' domesticity. In a letter to theologian André Rivet arguing for women's education she included,

> [T]he goal of studies is presumed not to be vainglory and show or idle curiosity, but rather the general goal of the glory of God and the salvation of one's soul in order that she may also emerge the better and happier and may educate and guide her family.[20]

What has all this to do with dysfunctional marriages and marital litigations in New Netherland and proprietary New York? On the surface, there is little connection. However, wives' traditional participation in local and regional trade, increasing responsibilities for and growing acceptance of wives' participation in rapidly expanding commercial capitalism, contradictory views about appropriate roles for women, debate about women's education, and anxieties produced by the golden age affected individuals and society through institutions such as law. Given these circumstances and the legality of marital dissolutions under Roman-Dutch law, a corresponding increase in marital litigations might be expected. However, that did not happen in the Netherlands and New Netherland, or for that matter in other Western European cultures.[21] Several factors suggest why.

It is difficult to overestimate the importance of marriage, or more accurately family, as the foundational relationship upon which other social relationships were established. It was through family that culture, status, and wealth passed to future generations.[22] Consequently, throughout early modern Protestant Europe, reformers did not seek to liberalize the grounds for marital dissolution. In fact, their position was similar to that of the Catholic Church, minus its sacramental designation. Pre-Reformation canon law forbade divorce, but did permit separation from bed and board (*a mensa et thoro*). Areas of Protestant Europe that adopted civil law allowed divorce, but narrowly defined the grounds necessary to bring it about. Specifically, the only legal grounds for divorce were substantiated adultery and malicious desertion, which were illegal activities that undermined the purpose of marriage as a social construct for perpetuation of cultural paradigms.[23]

In addition, although secular civil law governed marriage in much of Protestant Europe, ecclesiastical authorities continued to exercise significant influence over marriage, particularly in England, where the Anglican Church regulated marriage. However, in many Protestant areas it was not as obvious.

Although Protestant reformers did not regard marriage as a sacrament, they continued to consider it a divinely based institution, which influenced the development of civil laws governing marriage.[24] Consequently, marital litigations and judicially approved dissolutions were anomalous. In Dutch society, only individuals or couples who persisted for years in pursuit of a marital dissolution had any chance of receiving one. Merritje Joris and Nicolaas Boot were among those who persisted.

Owing to sparse records that contain information intended for legal rather than historical purposes, we cannot determine what caused the discord in the troubled marriage of Joris and Boot. When they appeared before the magistrates in late February 1658, Joris's drinking was ostensibly the cause of their problems. However, the limited information in the records does not reveal if her drinking caused the dysfunction or was a consequence of it.

Perhaps more significant than Joris's apparent inability to control her drinking was the way she challenged seventeenth-century Dutch society and law with her answers to questions by the court. Even after more than 350 years, her intense indignation is evident. When the magistrates asked her about her husband's claims, she did not deny or apologize for her behavior. Indeed, she protested "[I] drink my own and not his substance . . . he himself goes drinking, rollicking and full."[25] Joris may have been unaware that the first duty of the magistrates in marital litigation was preservation of the unions. However, they made it clear to her when they ordered her to "live in peace with [your] husband so that no more complaints should be heard of [you]."[26]

Joris was able to stanch her anger. Although she refused to obey the order, she added an explanation for her differences with Boot. Specifically, she informed the magistrates that she and her husband

> always had wine and beer in the house, and that he does not put either wine or beer in the house for [me], which is why [I] go now and again for half a *Mutije* and a couple of pots of beer, and he does not pay the cost.[27]

The magistrates had authority to punish Joris for refusing to return to her husband and to reform her behavior, but she revealed something that suggests she had some knowledge of laws governing marriage. Specifically, she informed the magistrates that Boot, "frequently beat[s me] and divers times shut[s me] out [of the house]."[28]

Boot immediately denied the charge, but Joris's testimony was sufficient for the magistrates to order *Schout* Nicasius de Sille to investigate.[29] Spousal abuse was a crime under Roman-Dutch law, carrying "such punishment as the Magistrates shall judge proper as an example to others," including jail.[30] However, even though De Sille verified Joris's claim at the next court session, to which he added the charge of, "shutting her up in her house without order or authority [by] nailing the windows and doors," the magistrates did not allow prosecution of Boot for this instance of abuse or after Joris made a similar charge several years later.[31]

Before examining the implications of the court's failure to go forward with prosecuting Nicolaas Boot for spousal abuse, which will be discussed in the conclusion, more needs to be revealed about the legalities of and aversion to marital dissolution in New Netherland and the consequences on marital litigations of English expropriation of the colony. The Protestant Reformation removed some impediments to marital dissolution, but marital litigations in general and specifically judicial grants of dissolution were still exceptionally rare in Protestant countries and seventeenth-century America. Barring adultery or desertion, which could, but did not necessarily bring about divorces, the only legal option available to individuals and couples seeking marital dissolution in areas where Roman-Dutch law applied was separation from bed and board.[32] Separation from bed and board suggested judicial acknowledgment of irreconcilability, but only as a temporary condition. Separation meant couples could live in different domiciles, but the marriage remained intact, presumably to remove barriers to reconciliation.[33]

Nicolaas Boot made his first request for a separation from Merritje Joris in February 1658. As was their custom, the magistrates remained averse to martial dissolution under Roman-Dutch law in all litigations between Joris and Boot, despite the couple's desire to part company. Except for the last hearing, in which the court granted their petition for a separation, the magistrates repeatedly ordered the couple to reconcile their differences.[34]

The magistrates began to reconsider their position when the couple's differences literally spilled into the streets. In September 1663, *Schout* Pieter Tonneman asked the court to fine Joris, "one-hundred guilders . . . and two years banishment, because she created a noise both in the street and in the house, broke windows and made a riot." Joris initially denied the accusation, but recanted and admitted she had done so because "her husband shoved her out of doors, at which she was so vexed, that she acted so."[35]

At the same session, September 18, 1663, Nicolaas Boot demanded a separation from Joris. Nevertheless, the magistrates ordered the couple to live in peace with each other.[36] However, they may have been less resolute in the decision than in earlier hearings. Without another recorded instance of trouble between Joris and Boot, on Monday October 29, 1663, the magistrates granted the long-sought dissolution.[37] Their legal battles had lasted four years and ten months.[38]

The process might have taken less time if Boot had waited until 1664 to petition for dissolution of marriage. On August 27, 1664, New Netherland Governor General Petrus Stuyvesant surrendered the colony to English Colonel Richard Nicolls, commander of an expedition of four frigates sent from England to capture the colony on behalf of James, Duke of York, brother to King Charles II.[39]

Application of English law in marital dissolutions during New York's proprietary period, (1664–1685) offers interesting perspectives on use of English jurisprudence in colonial North America.[40] English law unambiguously opposed marital dissolution. Specifically, marital litigation was the prerogative of ecclesiastical (Anglican) courts, which generally prohibited marital dissolutions.[41] Although the prohibition was not absolute, the courts were so opposed to marital dissolution, some scholars regard early modern England as a "divorceless" society.[42]

Marital dissolution was easier in British North America, however, than in England. Owing to missing and limited information in extant records, it is difficult to count the number of marital dissolutions during the Dutch era. A sparse population stretching from the Delaware River Valley to the upper reaches of the Hudson River Valley, combined with changes in sovereignty from Dutch to English, English to Dutch, and finally permanently Dutch to English, mandate caution in use of court records. For example, sometimes litigations initiated during the sovereignty of one country concluded in the next, which necessitated innovative jurisprudence. More importantly, some spouses who initiated dissolution proceedings did not have sufficient resolve to overcome judicial reluctance to grant them. However, the records provide enough information to leave no doubt that Dutch authorities granted three divorces and at least one separation during their forty-year administration from 1624–1664.[43] During the proprietary period, governors Francis Lovelace (1668–1673) and Edmund Andros (1674–1681) granted five divorces, one annulment, and two separations.[44] Richard Morris, in *History of American Law* (1930), concluded the Lovelace and Andros dissolutions were innovations in an emerging distinctiveness in American law.[45]

Matteo Spalletta has maintained that the Lovelace and Andros decisions had no basis in English law. Specifically, that Lovelace and Andros wrongly assumed that dissolutions granted under Dutch authority established a common law precedent. Spalletta argued the basis for them was untenable because New York's colonial charter required conformity to, "the laws of the mother country."[46] However, that conclusion needs reconsideration.

FIGURE 12.2. "In 1664 the province of New Netherland passed from the Dutch to the English." Mural by Attilio Pusterla (1862–1941) in the ceremonial courtroom at New York County Courthouse, 60 Centre Street, New York, NY. Photographed by Teodors Ermansons. Artistic license: Stuyvesant never signed the Articles of Capitulation.

Several factors militated against application of English law in marital litigations in proprietary New York. Foremost among them was jurisdictional consideration, a point recognized but not examined by Spalletta. In England, marriage litigation was a matter for ecclesiastical courts, an institution that never existed in colonial British America. In addition, authority for granting marital dissolutions in England rested with Parliament, whereas the king and his council had jurisdiction over the American colonies.[47]

The conquest and subsequent administration of New York during the proprietorship of James Duke of York also presented special circumstances for English officials that affected marital litigations. They assumed authority over a population of between seven and eight thousand people who already lived under European institutions.[48] Owing to a pluralistic society that sometimes chaffed under West India Company regulations, Dutch institutions were never uniformly applied throughout New Netherland.[49]

The records of the Duke of York's instructions to Colonel Nicolls for the terms of surrender of New Netherland have not surfaced. However, generous conditions offered in the surrender agreement suggest official intent was a seamless transition to English authority, or to at least neutralize potential opposition. Initially it was not the polyglot population of the Hudson Valley and other mainland areas of New York, but the English villages on Long Island that gave Nicolls difficulty. Those colonists came from New England and owing to that region's de facto semiautonomy, were wary of the new English administration. More precisely, English Long Island was under the jurisdiction of Connecticut and, given their cultural and economic ties to Connecticut, the colonists preferred the status quo.[50]

Subsequent events justified the Long Islanders' caution. In devising a new law code for New York, which was later designated the Duke's Laws, Nicolls and his staff consulted the laws of New Netherland, Massachusetts Bay Colony, New Haven Colony, Maryland, and even Virginia, but not Connecticut. Moreover, in his effort to establish a boundary between New York and Connecticut, Nicolls placed Long Island within the jurisdiction of New York.[51] Significantly, New Netherland, Massachusetts Bay, and New Haven followed civil law legal systems.[52]

Regardless of whether proprietary New York officials faced a Dutch or English legal environment, civil law influenced the legalities of early colonial New York, including those relating to marriage. Proprietorship governors granted more marital dissolutions in a shorter period than did their predecessors, but the increase was negligible. Clearly, both Dutch and English authorities shared an aversion to marital dissolution.

As indicated, uniformity in legal regulation of marriage did not occur in Protestant Europe owing to cultural, historical, and other differences. For example, although most Protestant countries adopted civil law regulation of marriage, in England it was the responsibility of the Anglican Church, which took a conservative approach to marital dissolution. In 1543, Henry VIII convened a commission of theologians, lawyers, and other officials with related interests to devise the laws of the Anglican Church. The commission proposed legalizing divorce for adultery, desertion, and violence visited on wives by their husbands, but the Anglican Church rejected it and England did not break away from a policy of indissolubility until the nineteenth century.[53]

The dissolutions that governors Lovelace and Andros granted did not strictly conform to the common and ecclesiastical laws of England. Judicial acquiescence to marital dissolutions in proprietary New York not only reflects the distinctiveness of early colonial American legal systems, it also suggests a connection with legal ambiguities about marriage in seventeenth-century England. Although marriage and marriage litigations were the prerogative of ecclesiastical courts in England, owing to the Anglican Church's prohibition of divorce, the only way to end a marriage legally was through a private act by Parliament. However, it was not that simple. Early modern England followed three legal systems: common law, ecclesiastical law, and equity law, each with its own courts and procedural rules. Shared responsibility for marriage litigation by secular and ecclesiastical authorities and overlapping authority by the three legal systems sometimes produced uncertainties about jurisdiction. The only characteristic that remained consistent despite the ambiguities was a conservative position on marital dissolution.[54]

Conservatism of the law and its application in marriage litigation and substantial expense of pursuing a marital dissolution through a private act by Parliament caused extralegal innovations. Desertion was the cruelest form of extralegal dissolution in an age when marriage was a financial necessity for many women. Legal dissolutions required husbands to maintain their wives financially, but dissolutions occurring outside the law sometimes resulted in destitution for mothers and their children.[55] One extralegal method for avoiding destitution of women and children was a "wife sale," a ritualized means whereby the husband, "selling" his wife transferred authority over her, and presumably their children to another man who was "buying." Wife sales seem bizarre in the present day and may have been humiliating for some wives, and possibly some husbands, but they were a response to conservative laws that opposed marital dissolution and the expense of seeking dissolutions through Parliament.[56]

In addition, the decisions by Lovelace and Andros were part of emerging American regionalization of English law. As David Thomas Konig recently maintained, colonial American law developed through "reanimation and recombination of English legal practices in different ways in the new (regional) environments."[57] The Lovelace and Andros dissolutions were expressions of the growing distinctiveness of New York law despite the fact that they did not lead to permanent changes in application of conservative English laws governing marriage in the colony. That is, no other dissolutions occurred for the remainder of the colonial period.[58]

Nevertheless, Lovelace and Andros were not entirely innovative in granting divorces. They granted them owing to violations of marriage vows, that is, breach of marital contract by commission of an illegal act.[59] More precisely, in each case one of the spouses committed adultery, which gave the divorces a long established biblical basis.[60]

Moreover, we need to question whether Lovelace and Andros granted the divorces in the belief that earlier divorces granted under Roman-Dutch law established a common law precedent, as Matteo Spalletta believed. As indicated previously, officials who devised the Duke's Laws consulted the laws of colonial Massachusetts and New Haven, which included provisions for divorce and separation. For example, New Haven Colony's laws of 1638 expressly named adultery as grounds for divorce and permitted annulments if

> any man marrying a Woman fit to bear children, or needing and requiring conjugall duty, and due benevolence from her husband, it be found . . . and satisfyingly proved, that the husband, neither at the time of the Marriage, nor since . . . is like to be able to perform or afford the same . . . every such marriage shall by the court of Magistrates, be declared voyd, and a nullity.[61]

In Masschusetts Bay Colony, the Court of Assizes, a biannual court, had jurisdiction over divorce and granted the first divorce in America in 1639.[62]

Newijork october den 15 1697

weij ondergeschreven wilde Eygenaers van het Lande Genaemt Ramapoch Bekense ten vollen Verseckerdeert te zeijn met Blandina Baijard voor het geene hier ondergeschreven staet als volgt

x 5 wilde beers
x 5 combaersen
x 5 kleed duffels strowaters
10 kleedt duffels
x 50 pont kruijt
x 50 stave loot
100 vadem wit geregen sewant
10 wilde hemden
x 40 wilde messen
2 ketens
x 8 kindere rocktiës
x 30 kanne rom
x 20 kanne spaense weijn
x 1 barrel seyter
5 kleijne wilde keteltiës

hare namenen ondertekent aldus

Het merk van Zerickham
Het merk van Mettissiena
Het merk van Eghkenem
Het merk van Onarkommagh
Het merk van Kraghkon
Het merk van Saeuwapighkim
het merk van de wilde nanawaron

Volgen noch eenige van de parsepanten haer namen

sale wap
amekori
waykhagsanie
neanewight
oweswaghkie

Onderteekent bij mij Blandina Baijard

FIGURE 12.3. Blandina Bayard's agreement for purchase of Indian lands, October 15, 1697. New York State Library call number 17649. Agreement between Bayard and the following Indians: Zerickham, Mettissiena, Eghkenem, Onarkommagh, Kraghkon, Saeuwapigh Kim, and Nanawaron for the purchase of land at Ramapo, Rockland County, NY.

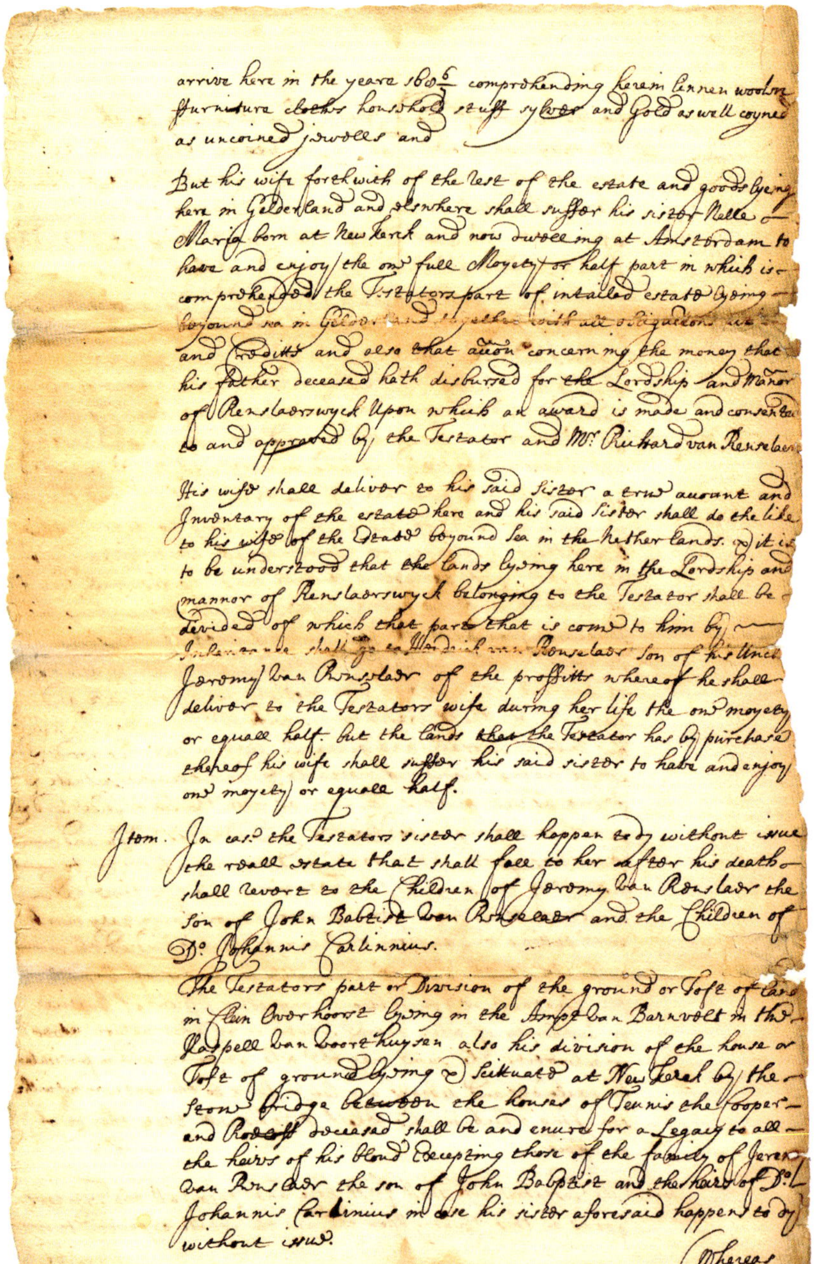

arrive here in the yeare 1606 comprehending herein linnen woolen ffurniture clothes houshold stuff sylver and Gold as well coyned as uncoined jewells and

But his wife forthwith of the rest of the estate and goods lying here in Gelderland and elswhere shall suffer his sister Nelle Maria born at New kerk and now dwelling at Amsterdam to have and enjoy the one full Moyety or half part in which is comprehended the Testators part of intailed estate lying beyound sea in Gelder[illegible] together with all obligations and Creditts and also that action concerning the money that his father deceased hath disbursed for the Lordship and Manor of Renslaerswyck Upon which an award is made and consented to and approved by the Testator and Mr. Richard van Renselaer

His wife shall deliver to his said sister a true account and Inventary of the estate here and his said sister shall do the like to his wife of the estate beyound sea in the Netherlands. & it is to be understood that the lands lying here in the Lordship and manor of Renslaerswyck belonging to the Testator shall be devided of which that part that is come to him by Inheritance shall go to Hendrick van Renslaer son of his Uncle Jeromy van Renslaer of the proffitts whereof he shall deliver to the Testators wife during her life the one moyety or equall half. but the lands that the Testator has by purchase thereof his wife shall suffer his said sister to have and enjoy one moyety or equall half.

Item. In case the Testators sister shall happen to dy without issue the reall estate that shall fall to her after his death shall revert to the Children of Jeromy van Renslaer the son of John Baptist van Renslaer and the Children of Do Johannis Carbinnius.

The Testators part or Division of the ground or Tofte of land in Clein Overhoorst lying in the Amst van Barnvelt in the Cappell van Voorthuysen also his division of the house or Tofte of ground lying & scituated at New kerk by the Stone bridge between the houses of Teunis the Cooper and Rodolff deceased shall be and enure for a Legacy to all the heirs of his blood Excepting those of the family of Jeremy van Renslaer the son of John Baptist and the heirs of Do Johannis Carbinius in case his sister aforesaid happen to dy without issue.

Whereas

FIGURE 12.4. Kiliaen van Rensselaer was Lord of the Manor of Rensselaerswyck, comprising most of present-day Albany and Rensselaer Counties. He left all his property to his wife Anna. Under Dutch inheritance law, which was continued in the colony of New York by the Articles of Capitulation of 1664, widows could inherit both personal and real property. In contrast, under English law, at least in theory, all real property passed to the eldest son and the widow received her dower share—one-third of the income of her husband's property for her lifetime. New York State Archives, accession J0038-82 Probated Wills, fileAV1.

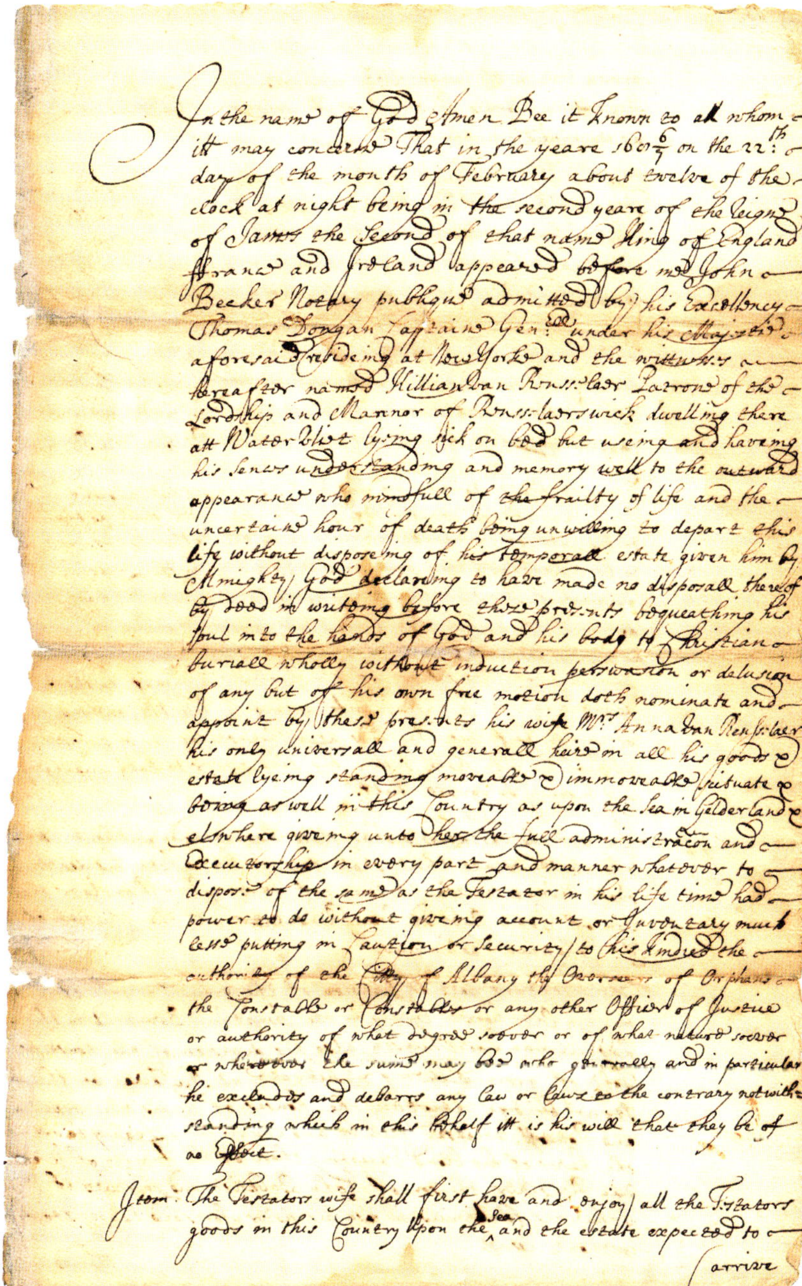

In the name of God Amen Bee it known to all whom
itt may concerne That in the yeare 168 6/7 on the 22th
day of the month of February about twelve of the
clock at night being in the second yeare of the reign
of James the Second of that name King of England
France and Ireland appeared before me John
Becker Notary publique admitted by his Excellency
Thomas Dongan Captaine Genll under his Majestie
aforesaid resideing at New York and the wittnesses
hereafter named William van Rensselaer Patroon of the
Lordship and Mannor of Rensselaerswick dwelling there
att Watervliet lying sick on bed but useing and haveing
his senses understanding and memory well to the outward
appearance who mindfull of the frailty of life and the
uncertaine hour of death being unwilling to depart this
life without disposeing of his temporall estate given him by
Allmighty God declaring to have made no disposall thereof
by deed in writeing before these presents bequeathing his
soul into the hands of God and his body to Christian
buriall wholly without induction perswasion or delusion
of any but of his own free motion doth nominate and
appoint by these presents his wife Mrs Anna van Rensselaer
his only universall and generall heire in all his goods &
estate lyeing standing moveable & immoveable situate &
being as well in this Country as upon the sea in Gelderland &
elsewhere giveing unto her the full administracon and
executorship in every part and manner whatever to
dispose of the same as the Testator in his life time had
power to do without giveing account or Inventary much
lesse putting in Caution or Security to his kindred the
authority of the City of Albany the Overseers of Orphans
the Constable or Constables or any other Officer of Justice
or authority of what degree soever or of what nature soever
or wheresoever the same may bee who generally and in particular
he excludes and debarrs any law or lawe to the contrary notwith-
standing which in this behalf itt is his will that they be of
no effect.

Item: The Testators wife shall first have and enjoy all the Testators
goods in this Country upon the sea and the estate expected to
arrive

FIGURE 12.4. *Continued.*

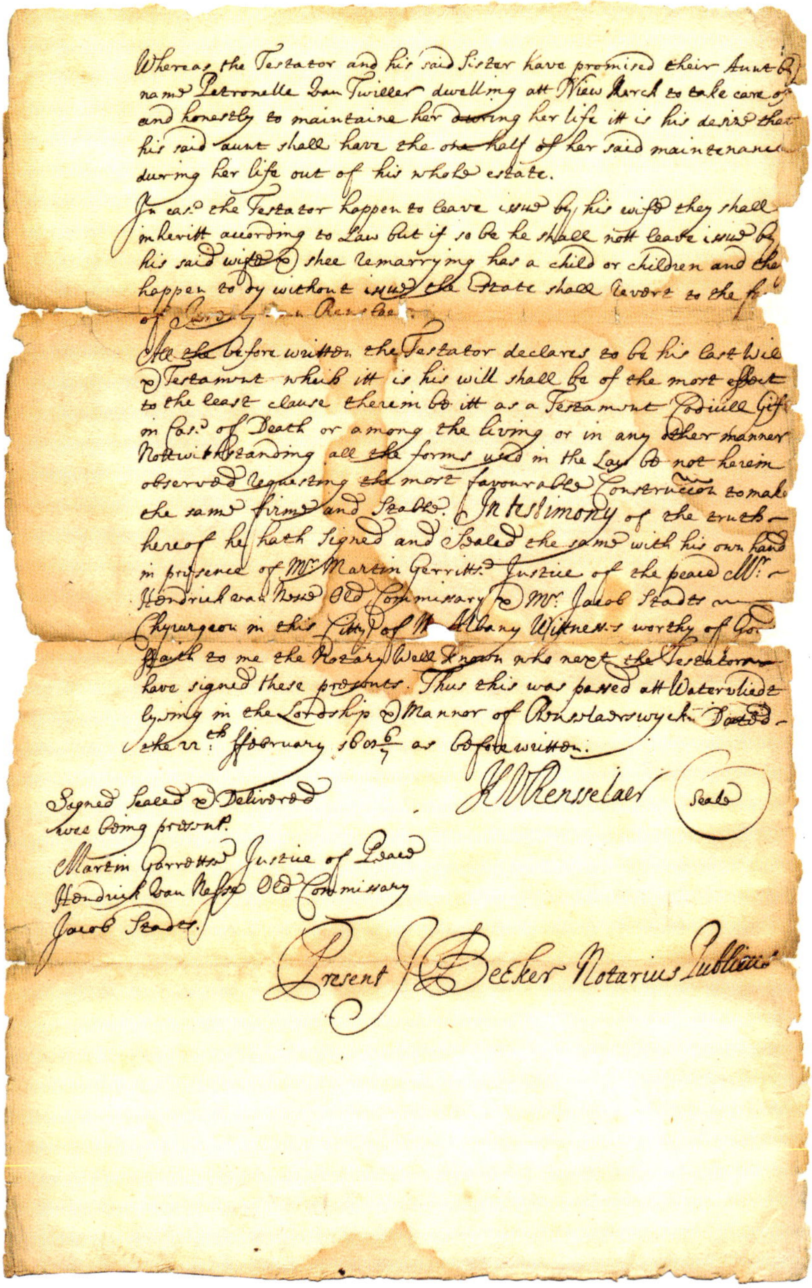

Whereas the Testator and his said Sister have promised their Aunt by name Petronelle Van Twiller dwelling att New Kerck to take care of and honestly to maintaine her during her life itt is his desire that his said aunt shall have the one half of her said maintenance during her life out of his whole estate.

In case the Testator happen to leave issue by his wife they shall inheritt according to Law but if so be he shall nott leave issue by his said wife & shee remarrying has a child or children and the happen to dy without issue the Estate shall revert to the f[illegible] of [illegible] Rensselaer.

All the before written the Testator declares to be his last Will & Testament which itt is his will shall be of the most effect to the least clause therein be itt as a Testament Codicill Gift in case of Death or among the living or in any other manner Notwithstanding all the forms used in the Law be not herein observed requesting the most favourable Construction to make the same firme and Stable. In testimony of the truth hereof he hath signed and sealed the same with his own hand in presence of Mr. Martin Gerritse Justice of the peace Mr. Hendrick van Ness Old Commissary & Mr. Jacob Staets Chyrurgeon in this Citty of Albany Wittnesses worthy of good faith to me the Notary well known who next the Testator have signed these presents. Thus this was passed att Watervliedt lying in the Lordship & Mannor of Rensselaerswyck Dated the 11th February 1706/7 as before written.

K V Rensselaer (Seale)

Signed Sealed & Delivered
wee being present.
Martin Gerritse Justice of Peace
Hendrick Van Ness Old Commissary
Jacob Staets

Present J Becker Notarius Publicus

FIGURE 12.4. *Continued.*

Another consideration for Lovelace and Andros was the Duke's Laws. Colonel Richard Nicolls invited only representatives of English Long Island and Westchester to the 1665 Heemstede (Hempstead) meeting at which he introduced the Duke's Laws. Representatives from Dutch Manhattan and mainland Dutch settlements were not invited.[63] Moreover, the government organized by Nicolls under the Duke's Laws applied to English areas of the proprietorship (1664–1685).[64] The Duke's Laws did not specifically address divorce and separation. Rather, they indicated, "In What Cases It Shall Not Bee Punishable to Re Marry."[65] Grounds for dissolution included adultery, under which bigamy and desertion were subcategories.[66] The Duke's Laws, with subsequent amendments, remained in place until 1691.[67]

It is easier to recognize the reasons why Lovelace and Andros took it upon themselves to approve dissolutions when viewed from the political, demographic, and legal circumstances that existed in New York at the time. In principle, Lovelace and Andros lacked authority to grant or deny marital dissolutions, but in assuming and applying that authority, they followed established legal custom in New Netherland, early proprietary New York, and Puritan New England. Moreover, granting the dissolutions was practical. In addition to the absence of ecclesiastical courts to try marital litigations, there were too many exigencies in governing non-Anglican and non-English populations that adhered to civil law to stray too far from accepted established practice.

While legalities governing marital dissolution were dissimilar in early modern Dutch and English societies, the small number of dissolutions granted under both New Netherland and proprietary New York authorities reflects a common aversion to marital dissolution. Moreover, that colonial officials granted any divorces, especially during the proprietorship, confirms Richard Morris's position that American law diverged from European law early in the colonial period and David Konig's assertion of regional distinctiveness in that process.

Finally, Nicolaas Boot's abuse of his wife—which violated Roman-Dutch law—and the court's failure to prosecute him despite confirmation by the *schout,* suggests that paternalism influenced officials in colonial Dutch America. The records of Boot's abuse are not extensive enough to arrive at definitive conclusions about it. Nevertheless, based on the information available, the court's failure to prosecute him implies that—despite Dutch women's increasing public responsibilities owing to commercial expansion—household dependents, including wives, were under the authority of husbands and fathers in ways not possible for women.

Consequently, New Netherland and proprietary New York marital dissolutions represent a historical anomaly rather than a portent for the future. Protestantism redefined marital dissolution in Western Europe, but variant legalities produced by regional cultural and historical distinctions met in seventeenth-century New York and temporarily produced innovations unlike those occurring elsewhere in colonial America.

NOTES

1. When the records reveal the names and doing so is appropriate for the context, this chapter identifies married women by their patronymics, a custom often applied in court minutes from seventeenth-century Roman-Dutch law jurisdictions. Merchant-trader designates individuals engaged in transoceanic commerce, as different from local retail merchants. For the meaning of Boot's status as a burgemeester see, Dennis J. Maika, "Securing the Burgher Right in New Amsterdam: The Struggle for Municipal Citizenship in the Seventeenth-Century Atlantic World," in *Revisiting New Netherland: Perspectives on Early Dutch America,* ed. Joyce D. Goodfriend (Leiden and Boston: Brill, 2005), 93–128.

2. Berthold Fernow, trans. and ed., *The Records of New Amsterdam, 1653–1674*, 7 vols. (1897; reprint, Baltimore, Genealogical Publishing, 1976), 2: 335, hereafter cited as *RNA*.

3. Ibid.

4. Robert C. Ritchie, *The Duke's Province: A Study of New York Politics and Society, 1664–1691* (Chapel Hill: University of North Carolina Press, 1977), 108, 178. The year 1685 is used as an ending date in this chapter for three reasons. First, King Charles II died in 1685 and the throne passed to the proprietor of the colony, his brother James, Duke of York. Second, in an effort to centralize administration of the northern British-American colonies, the Dominion of New England, which included New York, was established in 1685. Finally, although petitions were presented, from that year through the end of the colonial period no marital dissolutions were granted in New York.

5. Richard B. Morris, "Women's Rights in Early American Law," in *Studies in the History of Early American Law* (New York: Columbia University Press, 1930), 126–200, 133.

6. Matteo Spalletta, "Divorce in Colonial New York," *New York Historical Society Quarterly* 39 (October 1955): 422.

7. Paul A. Amato and Shelley Irving, "Historical Trends in Divorce in the United States," in *Handbook of Divorce and Relationship Dissolution*, ed. Mark A. Fine and John H. Harvey (Mahwah, NJ: Lawrence Erlbaum Assoc., 2006), 42–43; Peter Charles Hoffer, *Law and People in Colonial America* (Baltimore and London: Johns Hopkins University Press, 1992), 77; Glenda A. Riley, *Divorce: An American Tradition* (New York: Cambridge University Press, 1991): 11–23; see also, Nancy F. Cott, "Divorce and the Changing Status of Women in Eighteenth-Century Massachusetts," *William and Mary Quarterly* 3rd ser., no. 33 (October 1976): 586–614; Nancy F. Cott, "Eighteenth-Century Family and Social Life Revealed in Massachusetts Divorce Records," *Journal of Social History* 10 (Fall 1976): 20–43.

8. John Witte, "Church, State, and Marriage: Three Reformation Models," *Word and World* 23, no. 1 (Winter 2003): 42; Mia Karpiola, "Lutheran Marriage Norms in Action: The Example of Post-Reformation Sweden, 1520–1600," in *Lutheran Reformation and the Law*, ed. Virpi Mëkinen (Leiden: Brill, 2006), 132–33; R. H. Hemholz, "Western Canon Law," in *Christianity and the Law: An Introduction*, ed. John Witte and Frank S. Alexander (Cambridge and New York: Cambridge University Press, 2008), 82; Joel Francis Harrington, *Reordering Marriage and Society in Reformation Germany* (Cambridge and New York: Cambridge University Press, 195), 85.

9. Serena Zabin, "Women's Trading Networks and Dangerous Economies," *Early American Studies: An Interdisciplinary Journal* 4, no. 2 (Fall 2006): 291. Zabin applied this concept to capitalism, but it is appropriate to describe development of law as well. See also, Lawrence M. Friedman, *History of American Law* (New York: Simon and Schuster, 1985), 33.

10. The paradoxical curiosity of early modern Dutch culture was the theme of Schama's book, *The Embarrassment of Riches: An Interpretation of Dutch Culture in the Golden Age* (New York: Vintage, 1987).

11. Scholarly analyses of the Dutch golden age are numerous. Among recent studies are, Harold J. Cook, *Matters of Exchange: Commerce, Medicine, and Science in the Dutch Golden Age* (New Haven and London: Yale University Press, 2007); Maarten Prak, *The Dutch Republic in the Seventeenth Century: The Golden Age* (New York: Cambridge University Press, 205); Wayne E. Franits, *Dutch Seventeenth-Century Genre Painting: Stylistic and Thematic Evolution* (New Haven: Yale University Press, 2004); Hedley Bull, Benedict Kingsbury, and Adam Roberts, eds., *Hugo Grotius and International Relations* (Oxford and New York: Oxford University Press, 2002); Michael North, *Art and Commerce in the Dutch Golden Age*, trans. Catherine Hill (New Haven: Yale University Press, 1997); Jan de Vries and A. M. van der Woude, *The First Modern Economy: Success, Failure, and Perseverance of the Dutch, 1550–1815* (Cambridge and New York: Cambridge University Press, 1997); Jonathan I. Israel, *Dutch Primacy in World Trade, 1585–1740* (Oxford: Oxford University Press, 1989).

12. Zabin, "Women's Trading Networks," 291.

13. A. Agnes Sneller, "Reading Jacob Cats," in *Women of the Golden Age: An International Debate on Women in Seventeenth-Century Holland, England, and Italy*, ed. Els Kloek, Nicole Teeuwen, and Marijke Huisman (Hilversum: Verloren, 1994), 33.

14. Jacob Cats, *Huwelijk,* comp. Agnes Sneller and Boujke Thijs (Amsterdam: Querido, 1993), 72.

15. Lia van Gemert "The Power of the Weaker Vessels: Simon Schama and Johan van Beverwijck on Women," in Kloek, *Women of the Golden Age,* 39.

16. Johan van Beverwijck, *Van de Wtementhyt des Vrouwlicken Geslachts* (Dordrecht: 1643), quoted in Schama, *Embarrassment of Riches,* 419.

17. The seventeenth-century was a transitional period in Dutch society's perceptions of married women's roles. The changes appear evident in Dutch art and initial popularity then waning interest in Cats's *Huwelijk.* See, Martha Moffitt Peacock, "Domesticity in the Public Sphere," in *Saints, Sinners, and Sisters: Gender and Northern Art in Medieval and Early Modern Europe,* ed. Jan L. Carroll and Alison G. Stewart (Aldershot, UK and Burlington, VT: Ashgate, 2003), 44–68.

18. The quote in the paragraph is from, Schama, *Embarrassment of Riches,* 404; see also Joyce L. Irwin, trans. and ed., *Anna Maria van Schurman: Whether a Christian Woman Should be Educated and Other Writings from her Intellectual Circle* (Chicago and London: University of Chicago Press, 1998), 1–3.

19. Jonathan I. Israel, "The Intellectual Debate About Toleration in the Dutch Republic," in *The Emergence of Tolerance in the Dutch Republic,* ed. C. Berkins-Stevelinck, J. Israel, and G. M. Posthumus Meyje (Leiden: Brill, 1997), 3–36; Benjamin Kaplan, "Dutch Religious Tolerance: Celebration and Revision," in *Calvinism and Religious Toleration in the Dutch Golden Age,* ed. R. Po-Chia Hsia and Henk van Nierop (London and New York: Cambridge University Press, 2002), 8–26.

20. Irwin, *Anna Maria van Schurman,* 26.

21. Manon van der Heijden, "Secular and Ecclesiastical Marriage Control: Rotterdam, 1550–1700," in *Private Domain, Public Inquiry: Families and Lifestyles in the Netherlands and Europe, 1550 to the Present,* ed. Anton Schuurman and Pieter Spierenburg (Hilversum: Verloren, 1996), 57.

22. Peter R. Christoph, "The Colonial Family: Kinship and Power," in *A Beautiful and Fruitful Place: Selected Rensselaerwijck Seminar Papers,* ed. Nancy Anne McClure Zeller (Albany: New Netherland Project, 1991), 111–18; Julia Adams, *The Familial State: Ruling Families and Merchant Capitalism in Early Modern Europe* (Ithaca and London: Cornell University Press, 2005), 33.

23. Van der Heijden, "Secular and Ecclesiastical Marriage Control," 42; Adams, *Familial State,* 33.

24. Ibid, 41–43.

25. *RNA,* 335.

26. Ibid.

27. Ibid. A *mutjie* (*mutje, mutsje*) equaled fifteen fluid ounces, English measure. Peter R. Christoph, Kenneth Scott, and Kenn Stryker Rodda, eds., *New York Historical Manuscripts, Dutch: Kingston Papers,* 2 vols., trans. Dingman Versteeg (Baltimore: Genealogical Publishing, 1976), 765n1.

28. *RNA,* 335.

29. Ibid. The office of *schout* combined the duties charged to sheriffs and prosecuting attorneys in English jurisdictions. See, Jaap Jacob, *New Netherland: A Dutch Colony in Seventeenth-Century America* (Leiden and Boston: Brill, 2005), xvi.

30. *RNA,* 2: 338; Grotius, Jurisprudence of Holland, 29.

31. *RNA,* 2: 338; 4: 304.

32. Grotius, *Jurisprudence of Holland,* 29; Robert W. Lee, *An Introduction to Roman-Dutch Law,* 5th ed. (Oxford: Clarendon Press, 1953), 88–92; see also, Van der Heijden, "Secular and Ecclesiastical Marriage Control," 42–43. Van der Heijden maintained grounds for marital dissolution in Rotterdam included, "insanity, unchasteness, implacable hate, incurable disease, and being crippled or under-aged." Grotius included incapacity of a spouse that required appointment of a guardian among grounds for marital dissolution. (33).

33. Donald Haks, *Huewlijk en gezin in Holland in de 17de en 18de eeuw* (Assen: Van Gorcum, 1982), 178; Leonard Blussé, *Bitter Bonds: A Colonial Divorce Drama of the Seventeenth Century,* trans. Diane Webb (Princeton: Markus Wiener, 1997), 11.

34. *RNA,* 2: 335; 4: 328.

35. Ibid., 4: 304.

36. Ibid.

37. Ibid., 4: 328.

38. Ibid., 2: 335. Unfortunately, little other information about Joris and Boot relating to their backgrounds exists. Joris's testimony in the first hearing in February 1658 indicates they were not a young couple. In addition to asserting financial independence from her husband and his abuse, Joris informed the magistrates, "[I] have not slept with him in a long time, but were [I] a younger woman he would have more affection for [me]."

39. Ritchie, *The Duke's Province*, 22.

40. For use of 1685 as the closing date of the proprietorship of James, Duke of York see note 4 above.

41. Robert Oliphant and Nancy ver Steegh, *Family Law* (New York: Aspen Publishing, 2007), 5.

42. Friedman, *History of American Law*, 204; Hoffer, *Law and People*, 76–77; Lawrence Stone, *The Family, Sex, and Marriage in England, 1500–1800* (New York: Harper, 1977), 34. Although the Marriage Act of 1653 made marriage a civil act that required a ceremony before a justice of the peace, it did not address marital dissolution. See, Roderick Phillips, *Putting Asunder: A History of Divorce in Western Society* (Cambridge: Cambridge University Press, 1988), 130–31.

43. Spalletta, "Divorce in Colonial New York," 422–25. The magistrates granted a separation between Nicolaas Velthuysen and his wife, Aaltje Bickers, after only five months of marriage in November 1659. *RNA*, 3: 72–73. Several petitions for marital separation began under Dutch authority, but concluded during the proprietorship, though not always in the petitioner's favor.

44. Spalletta, "Divorce in Colonial New York," 425–34.

45. Morris, *Studies in the History of American Law*, 132.

46. Spalletta, 435.

47. Ibid., 427; Robert Bucholz and Newton Key, *Early Modern England, 1485–1714: A Narrative History* (Oxford: Blackwell, 2004), 165.

48. Charles P. Daly, *Historical Sketch of the Judicial Tribunals of New York, 1623–1846* (New York: Amerman, 1885), 25; Jacobs, *New Netherland*, 93.

49. Ritchie, *The Duke's Province*, 31.

50. Ibid., 32–34.

51. Introduced in 1665, but gradually and indiscriminately applied throughout the colony, the Duke's Laws were discontinued after 1691 following Leisler's Rebellion. See, Julius Goebel "The Courts and the Law in Colonial New York," in *Essays in the History of American Law*, ed. David H. Flaherty (Chapel Hill: University of North Carolina Press, 1969), 269.

52. Cornelia Hughes Dayton, "Was There a Calvinist Type of Patriarchy: New Haven Colony Reconsidered in the Early Modern Context," in *The Many Legalities of Early America*, ed. Christopher L. Tomlins and Bruce H. Mann (Chapel Hill: University of North Carolina Press, 2001), 348. Grouping the three law systems together does not imply the Dutch and New England law systems were the same. Ritchie, *The Duke's Province*, 34.

53. Continental reformers consulted by English clerics in the formative period of the Anglican Church did not include divorce among options for marital dissolution. See, Phillips, *Putting Asunder*, 21–24.

54. Lawrence Stone, *Road to Divorce: England, 1530–1987* (Oxford: Oxford University Press, 2002), 24–27; for reference to the debate over divorce among seventeenth-century scholars see, John Milton, *The Doctrine and Discipline of Divorce* (London: 1643). In the work, Milton argued in favor of expanding grounds for divorce beyond adultery and desertions, which were the only accepted grounds for divorce by secular and ecclesiastical authorities throughout Protestant Europe.

55. Stone, *Road to Divorce*, 141–48.

56. Henry Alan Finley, *To Have but not to Hold: A History of Attitudes to Marriage and Divorce in Australia, 1858–1975* (Annandale, NSW: Federation Press, 2005), 12–15.

57. David Thomas Konig, "Regionalization in Early American Law," in *The Cambridge History of Law in America,* ed. Michael Grossberg and Christopher Tomlins (Cambridge and New York: Cambridge University Press, 2008), 144.

58. Spalletta, "Divorce in Colonial New York," 434.

59. Amato and Irving, "Historical Trends in Divorce," 43; Riley, *Divorce: An American Tradition,* 14.

60. Shepherd Braithwait Kitchin, *A History of Divorce* (Clark, NJ: Lawbook Exchange, 2005), 92.

61. Royal Hinman, *The Blue Laws of New Haven Colony, Usually Called the Blue Laws of Connecticut: Quaker Laws of Plymouth and Massachusetts, Blue Laws of New York, Maryland, Virginia, and South Carolina* (Hartford,: Tiffany and Co., 1838), 174.

62. Riley, *Divorce: An American Tradition,* 12.

63. J. A. Doyle, "The Middle Colonies," in *English Colonies in America*, 5 vols. (New York: Henry Holt, 1907), 108.

64. Ritchie, *The Duke's Province,* 35–47; John M. Murrin, "English Rights as Ethnic Aggression: The English Conquest, the Charter of Liberties of 1683, and Leisler's Rebellion in New York," in *Authority and Resistance in Early New York,* ed. William Pencak and Conrad Edick Wright (New York: New York Historical Society, 1988), 56–94.

65. Charles Z. Lincoln, *The Colonial Laws of New York from the Year 1664 to the Revolution,* 5 vols. (Albany: J. B. Lyon, 1894), 46.

66. Ibid., 46–47.

67. George Elliot Howard, *A History of Marital Institutions: Chiefly in England and the United States,* 2 vols. (Chicago: University of Chicago Press, 1904), 294–96.

Chapter Thirteen

English Law Through Dutch Eyes

The Leislerian Understanding of the English Legal System in New York

David William Voorhees

The transformation from Dutch to English was accomplished at first with the stroke of a pen, but "on the ground" it was not abrupt. It began with the arrival of Col. Richard Nicolls with warships representing the English crown. He negotiated the "Articles of Capitulation on the Reduction of New Netherland" (August 27, 1664). With political astuteness, he agreed to generous terms for the colonists. English rule commenced at that point and was firmly reestablished in 1674, in the Treaty of Westminster, after the Dutch had recaptured New York in 1673.

In this chapter, David W. Voorhees points out that the Duke's Laws, a compilation of New England and Dutch law, were at first operative solely in New York's English communities on Long Island and were only gradually expanded to the rest of the province. Voorhees describes the Leislerian era and its interpretation of sovereignty based on Dutch Constitutional principles, concluding that throughout the eighteenth century, the constitutional theories of the Dutch Republic continued to inform New York's jurisprudence. No study of New York Constitutional theory, he maintains, can safely ignore Dutch-Roman law and practice in the Dutch Republic.

The constitutional ideals and legal theories of the seventeenth-century Dutch Republic, and in particular those of the state of Holland, shaped the development of modern New York legal thought. Indeed, laws of general obligations in New York are but one remnant of laws introduced by the Dutch into New Netherland, as are some of the general corporation laws of the state to this day.[1] Nonetheless, the influence of Dutch legal thought in New York after the 1664 English conquest of New Netherland is neglected. This is largely due to the successful imposition of English common law terminology and forms from the late seventeenth century onward. Therefore, in order to truly understand legal developments in New York one must look not only at English common law precedents but also to the laws and customs of the Dutch Republic and their introduction into the New World.

This chapter can touch only briefly on how Dutch legal thought modified English practices in New York after 1664. The main thrust of this paper is that the political turmoil of the Leislerian movement that swept the colony in the decades surrounding the turn of the eighteenth century was not a rebellion against English authority in itself, but the result of New Yorkers interpreting through Dutch legal traditions what they thought the English constitution should be. At the root of the Leislerians' interpretation was the issue of in whose hands—the sovereign's or the people's—final authority rested. Dutch theorists placed ultimate authority in the people, balanced by laws and institutions. Dutch legal and constitutional thought as interpreted by the Leislerian movement continued to modify New York law for generations thereafter and create a legal system unique among the American colonies.

On April 8, 1701, the New York City Mayor's Court adopted its first code of civil procedure. The code regulated through twenty-one rules the duties of the court, court officers, and other municipal officials. As the authors of *New York As an Eighteenth-Century Municipality* wrote in 1917, "Anyone who is interested could find much in our civil code that is traceable to this code of 1701."[2] The code, drafted by recently installed city recorder Abraham Gouverneur, not only regulated court procedures but also placed the court beyond the manipulation of colonial governors. Fifty years later, New York receiver-general Archibald Kennedy condemned New York's provincial legislators for their constitutional innovations. "They take upon themselves to be the sole judges," he wrote, and "insist . . . that no order for publick money shall issue, till their judgment has been obtained for it." Kennedy's charge reveals that the constitutional route that New Yorkers were following was a dramatic departure from English practice in the eighteenth century. Unlike England's Parliament, the New York legislature had captured control of the treasury, the establishment of the courts, and the role of adjudicating the public right to recompense.[3]

Historians have looked at the innovations of New York's colonial legal system in the terms of British law and legal theory. Christine Desan wrote, "Provincial legislators modeled their efforts explicitly on assertions of institutional authority made by their counterparts in the House of Commons."[4] Yet, as Douglas Greenberg noted in a study of colonial New York's criminal proceedings, "New York was, in many ways, unique among the British colonies in North America."[5] The uniqueness of colonial New York's legal developments is not so unique when the colony's Dutch origins are considered.

The Dutch West India Company established the legal system of New Netherland under the laws of the states of Holland and Zeeland. These laws reflected Germanic customary law, the Roman code of Justinian (*corpus juris*), canon law of the Roman Catholic Church, and the special corporate privileges granted by various medieval overlords.[6] Under the English, New York initially retained its Dutch forms of government, and no new changes were immediately introduced into the judicial administration as long as the magistrates "shall take the oath of allegiance to his majesty of England before they enter upon their office."[7] Because the English allowed the Dutch in New York to retain their customary laws and, because English imperial administration from London remained distant, the transition from Dutch to English legal culture was gradual. The Duke's Laws of 1665, written originally only for New York's English communities on Long Island, only gradually expanded province-wide. Moreover, the Duke's Laws contained a number of Dutch features. Among these were toleration in leaving the religious character of a community up to that community, plural nomination and partial retirement in public offices, and customary laws in inheritance, property, and family matters. The imposition of the English form of town government and expansion of the Duke's Laws in the Hudson Valley after 1675 thus did not represent a complete break with Dutch traditions. As late as the American Revolution, villages in the Hudson Valley were said to continue to follow "modes peculiar to the Hollanders."[8]

Ironically, the policies of James, as duke and king, reinforced the Dutchness of New York's political geography. In the seven Dutch states federated as the Republic of the United

Provinces, multiple jurisdictions overlapped between provinces, towns, and manorial estates. James's establishment in New York of counties in 1683 and of manors with administrative privileges, in addition to the confirmation of town patents, followed a pattern familiar to the Republic's political division into duchies, counties, and lordships—the latter a jurisdictional form that had been introduced into New Netherland with the patroonship in 1629 but had, with the exception of Rensselaerswyck, ultimately failed prior to 1664. As in the Netherlands, James's manorial grants gave their owners jurisdictional rights to adjudicate non-capital cases within their properties. The consequence was, as in the Dutch Republic, a tangled web of jurisdictions in New York.[9]

In the Netherlands, Hugo Grotius had in 1631 systematized the laws of the state of Holland in his *Inleydinge tot de Hollantsche rechtsgeleertheit* (*Introduction to the Jurisprudence of Holland*). The *Inleydinge,* brought to New Netherland, remained the standard legal text for customary law in New York long after the English takeover.[10] In addition to Grotius, New Netherland courts consulted the *Ordonnantie vande Policien Binnen Hollandt* (*Ordinances of the Police Within Holland*) (1580), which gave some uniformity to legal matters regarding marriage, succession, sales, leases, mortgages, and registration, Joost de Damhouder, *Practycke in Criminele Saecken* (*Practice in Criminal Procedures*) (1555) and *Practycke in Civile Saecken* (*Practice in Civil Procedures*) (1566), and Paul Merula, *Manier van Procederen in de Provintien van Holland, Zeeland ende West-Vriesland*

Figure 13.1. Jacob Leisler's residence on the Strand (now Whitehall Street). New York Public Library. Image ID 800017.210

(*Manner of Procedures in the Provinces of Holland, Zeeland, and West Friesland*) (1592). "Not only were these legal volumes available in the colony," Dr. Charles Gehring writes, "but also the uniformity and precision of the legal proceedings indicate that they were actively consulted."[11]

Joost de Damhouder (1507–1581) was particularly influential in New York civil law after 1664. A Flemish jurist, magistrate from Bruges, and commissioner of the Netherlands' treasury under Philip II from 1551 to 1581, Damhouder's manuals on criminal and civil law had been first published in Louvain (present-day Belgium) in Latin, and numerous Dutch editions appeared throughout the seventeenth century. Donna Merwick notes that these works "outlined procedures in criminal and civil cases" in New Netherland "and offered models for constructing legal instruments covering items such as ordinary contracts and conveyancing agreements."[12] Evidence of their continuing influence in New York jurisprudence after the English conquest may be found in their usage during the 1676 slander suit of Albany *domine* Nicholas van Rensselaer against Jacob Leisler. James, Duke of York, had appointed Van Rensselaer, ordained as an Anglican, to the Albany Dutch Reformed pulpit. The Roman Catholic duke's act outraged the Reformed Dutch, who held to the rule from the Synod of Dort that a minister must be ordained in the Reformed church and sent to a particular congregation by the classis.[13] In

Charles the Second by the grace

FIGURE 13.2. Duke of York's Charter from his brother King Charles II, granting him the colony of New York, 1664. New York State Archives. New York (State), Charter of the proprietary colony from Charles II to the Duke of York, 1664. Series B1371-93.

July 1676, Leisler, a New York City Reformed Church deacon, circulated a four-point glosse criticizing a sermon by Van Rensselaer on original sin. In Van Rensselaer's subsequent civil suit against Leisler, lawyers on both sides referred to Dutch customary law by citing Grotius and Damhouder, particularly the latter's *Practycke in Criminele Saecken,* in determining the legal definition of slander.[14]

For Damhouder, *jus non scriptum,* or customary law, meant the particular privileges, statutes, ordinances, customs, and manners that existed in each town or province according to the needs of the place. Grotius emphasized the corporate compact as the highest binding principle of law in his *ius civille* (civil law), a theory bolstered by Reformed Calvinisim.[15] Under the Dutch Republic, the ancient privileges and traditional liberties acquired by communities as corporate rights were tied to the welfare of the community. The towns, together with the *ridderschap* representing villages and the countryside, protected their rights in the representative provincial bodies, or estates, in which they collectively met. This meant that local communities participated directly in the government and that all decisions of provincial and national importance could only be made after referral back to, and concurrence by, the individual communities.[16]

The Dutch brought these legal and constitutional traditions with them to the New World. Under the English the Dutch influence is most evident, as will be seen, in New Yorkers' consistent communal resistance to centralizing tendencies in imperial authority. Moreover, the traditional liberties that the Dutch brought to the New World were incorporated into the complexities of the institutions they introduced. Within New York's communities, for example, special interest groups coalesced in Dutch fashion to pursue common goals. Individual rights were defended through the acquisition of communal privileges. In the Netherlands, trade guilds, for example, regulated and promoted specific craft interests within the community. Although the guild system never developed in New Netherland, beginning in the 1670s, New York's bakers, boatmen, butchers, cartmen, coopers, shoemakers, and tanners combined to protect their collective rights. Special interests thus, as in the Republic, became a fixture in colonial New York politics.[17]

James Stuart, as Duke of York and later King James II of England, was no friend of the Holland-style of decentralized representative government. During his twenty-five-year administration as New York's proprietor and sovereign from 1664 to June 1689, he only once granted New Yorkers a provincial assembly. This occurred in October 1683, when the duke, in dire need of money, allowed an elected assembly to convene for three weeks. During its short session, the New York Assembly managed a burst of legislation that included a judiciary act reorganizing the courts. This action, seemingly novel from an English perspective, followed Dutch practice. In the Republic, the estates, or provincial governing legislatures, oversaw judicial structures and appointments.[18] Following the decentralized Dutch example, the New York Assembly replaced a centralized court, the Court of Assizes, doing all the major legal business of the province, with local justices—petty courts for towns and county courts of sessions for non-capital felony cases. In addition to the formalization of local justice, the Assembly redefined the provincial high court. The Court of Assizes was abolished and replaced with a court of chancery for the entire province. Although the Assembly said the Chancery Court was to be the supreme court of the province, it had only an equitable jurisdiction. From the highest common law courts of the Assembly's creation, the courts of oyer and terminer, which heard capital cases, appeal could go directly to the king in council.[19] Thus, using English legal forms but following Dutch traditions, New York's legislature redefined New York's judicial structure.

Figure 13.3. The Duke of York's Charter. New York Public Library. Image ID 808252.

James, not surprisingly, took a dim view of the New York Assembly's actions. Using his constitutional change of status from proprietor to king with his accession to the English throne in 1685, James restructured New York's government and court system, now subsuming the Province of New York into the mega-colony of the Dominion of New England. Justice in New York, nonetheless, continued to be meted according to the outlines of the 1683 act until the province was formally joined to the Dominion in April 1688, at which point the Dominion's judicial system replaced the local courts. In actuality, however, the full effect of this action went

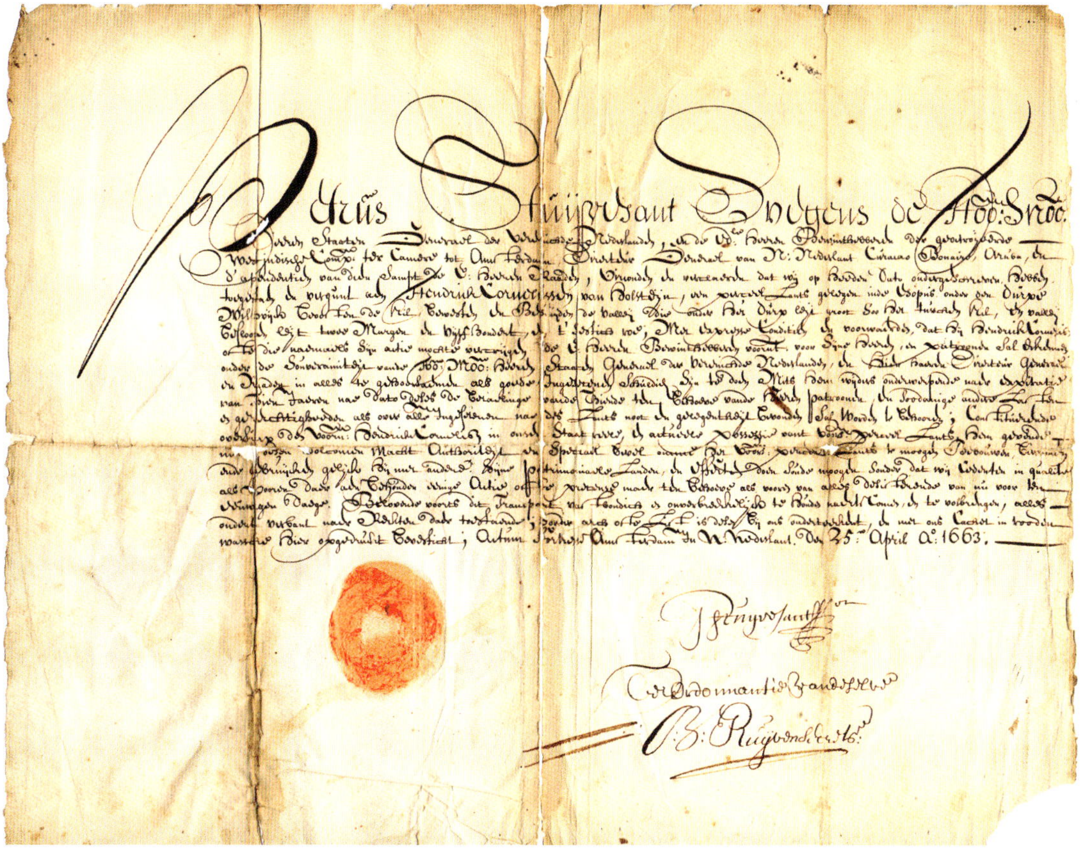

Figure 13.4. Dutch deed signed by Petrus Stuyvesant, granting land at Wildwyck (renamed Kingston in 1664), Apr. 25, 1663. The deed was presented to English Gov. Richard Nicolls to obtain confirmation of the Dutch grant, according to the Articles of Capitulation of 1664, which guaranteed Dutch land titles. New York State Archives, accession A0272, Applications for Land Grants ("Land Papers"), vol. 1, p. 7.

unrealized. In November 1688, William, Prince of Orange, stadholder of five of the seven Dutch provinces, and "defender of the Protestant faith," invaded England. New Yorkers learned of the Protestant prince's plans to invade England in December 1688, and by the following February they knew of the invasion's success and of James II's flight from the throne.[20]

Despite knowledge of England's so-called Glorious Revolution, it was not until May 31, 1689, that the New York militia seized control of New York City's fort from James's regular troops. It is important here to state that from first receipt of the news of the "unparalleled changes in England," New Yorkers' reactions reflected Dutch legal and political traditions. As an example, the Dutch nature of the New York uprising is clearly evident in the central role taken by the local militias. Indeed, a peculiar characteristic of colonial New York was the prominence in public affairs of the militia company, or burgemeester guard. In the Low Countries, citizens' militias, the *schutterijen,* traditionally played a pivotal role in civic life. In the Netherlands, civilian military units, created to maintain order within the towns and outside of city walls during times of crisis, increasingly acquired a more ceremonial role and active political capacity as the guardians of traditional liberties.[21] In similar fashion, the New York militia company served a more potent political role than that of a defensive unit. The English mocked the New York militia as a burlesque of militarism, but attempts by English governors to diminish the militias' autonomy through patronage in the appointment of officers were perceived by New Yorkers throughout the colonial period as a threat to traditional governmental balances.[22]

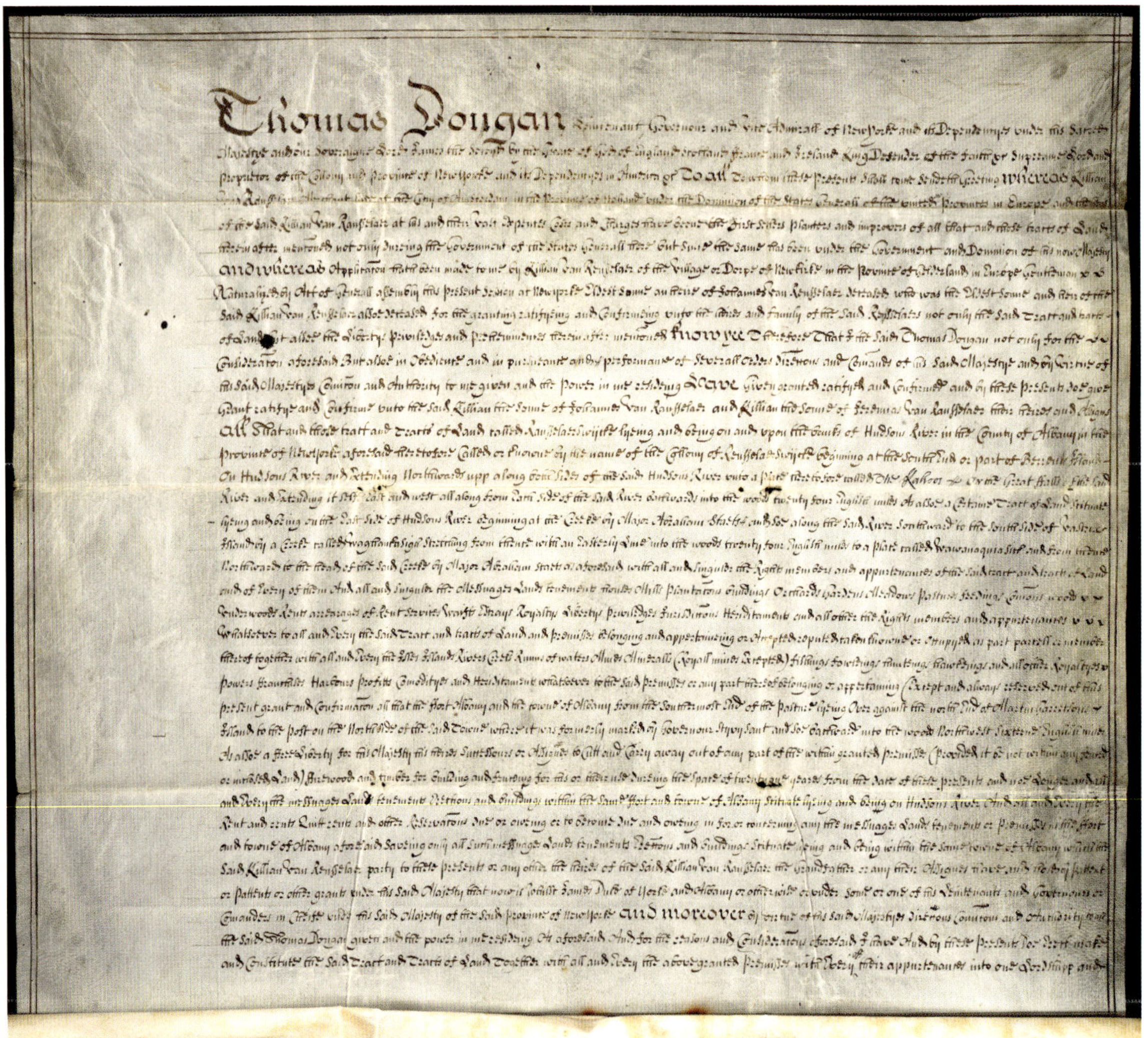
Thomas Dongan

FIGURE 13.5. Patent of the Manor of Rensselaerswyck, November 4, 1685, D. S. Thomas Dongan. New York State Library call number VSC7079 Item 2.

The militia companies, in their seizure of provincial control, believed that they were acting within a proper constitutional and legal framework. Prior to 1689, Holland's Orangist press, which promoted the political ambitions of William III, had churned out an enormous quantity of works aimed at the Dutch and English public stressing the threat of Roman Catholic "tyranny" to the "Liberties and Estates of Free Protestant Peoples."[23] Since William's successful military repulsion of French Roman Catholic King Louis XIV's invasion of the Republic in 1672, the prince had been seen by Dutch Reformed Protestants as the protector of traditional liberties and corporate privileges. The influence of Dutch Orangist propaganda is clearly evident in New Yorkers' justifications for revolt. Jacob Leisler, for example, claimed the New York government was seized "by the encouragement of the prince of Orange (now our gracious King) [and] his 3 declarations."[24] Leisler's reference is to William's *Declarations* of October 10 and 24, and November 28, 1688. The *First Declaration,* printed in Rotterdam in immense quantities in Dutch and English—sixty thousand copies in English alone—and probably the *Second,* reached Leisler in mid-March 1689, when he made them public. He had the *Third Declaration* by May 31, when Nicholas Bayard accused Leisler of plagiarizing it.[25]

In the *First Declaration,* confirmed by the *Second,* William justified his invasion of England "for Preserving of the Protestant Religion, and for Restoring the Law and Liberties of England." King James II, the declaration asserts, did "offer up the Laws, Rights and Liberties of a whole Nation" in order to establish the Papist religion and "thereby to enslave a Nation."[26] The *Third Declaration* called on magistrates to disarm Catholics and dispossess them of office. Catholics were given a clear warning: if they were found "with Arms" or holding any civil or military office "contrary to the known Laws of the Land," they and all who aided them would be treated as criminals and punished accordingly.[27] In New York, as in England, the *Third Declaration* had an electrifying impact. Ever since French King Louis XIV's 1672 invasion of the Republic, anti-Catholic hysteria had been building in the province, where many a settler's migration had been inspired by a fear of Roman Catholic violence.[28] King James II's appointment of Roman Catholics to New York's highest offices intensified apprehensions. "The adherents of popery (our Hon. Lord Governor being a papist) utilize all means for the advancement of the same," the Long Island consistory complained to the Amsterdam classis.[29] King Louis XIV's revocation of the Edict of Nantes in 1685, which had assured some rights to French Protestants (Huguenots), and his subsequent persecutions of them in France confirmed fears. "Hearing what greater success the Dragonnades in France had had," a New York letter recalls, "we could only know what was in store for us."[30]

Despite the three declarations' encouragement to rebel, New Yorkers were reluctant to act on them. Indeed, most of the militia captains as members of Lt. Gov. Francis Nicholson's expanded council, signed a declaration to defend the government at the uprising's outbreak against "meutanous and rebellious persons neare unto us."[31] This is because for those with a Dutch perspective the "defense of liberty was essentially based on a constitutional framework of fundamental laws and a balanced system of institutions."[32] The memory of these constitutional traditions restrained rebellion in New York and shaped its subsequent course. Political change had to follow legal principles. The captains, as the people's representatives, acted only *after* official confirmation of William's coronation had been received and only *after* the constituted magistrates continued to refuse to affirm it.

Dutch constitutional theory drew on sixteenth-century Huguenot thought to justify the Republic's own declaration of independence from Spain in 1581. Drawing on this thinking,

Hugo Grotius suggested that sovereignty rested with representative bodies, or, in the case of the Netherlands, as noted above, the provincial estates.[33] In the 1680s, English, French, and Dutch thinkers working in Rotterdam, such as John Locke and Pierre Jurieu, further expanded on this concept by reproducing the arguments of such sixteenth-century Calvinists as Theodore Beza, Francis Hotman, and Simon Goulart to prove that the "[s]overeign power is in the hands of the people and of assemblies composed of its deputies."[34] Goulart's popular *Mémoires de l'Estât de France sous Charles Neufiesme* (*Memoirs of the State of France under Charles IX*) (1576), for example, contained a number of revolutionary Calvinist political tracts such as Beza's *De jure magistratuum* (*The Right of Magistrates*) (1574), the anonymously written *La politique* (*The*

FIGURE 13.6. "In October 1683 the first New York Assembly established a 'Charter of Liberties' providing for trial by jury." Mural by Attilio Pusterla in the ceremonial courtroom at New York County Courthouse, 60 Centre Street, New York, NY, photographed by Teodors Ermansons.

Politician) (1574) and *Discours politiques* (*Political Discourses*) (1574), and Hotman's *Francogallia* (1576). Published in French, German, and Dutch editions, and frequently reprinted, Goulart's work was highly influential in popularizing in the late seventeenth century the compact theory of government and justification for resistance.[35]

Furthermore, by the late 1680s the discussion over the correct form of a state's constitution was taking place in the salons of the bustling Dutch port of Rotterdam. With a large Scots Presbyterian community, Rotterdam was in the 1680s a magnet for English, French, and other protestant dissenters in exile from Roman Catholic regimes. The resulting intellectual ferment produced by this melding of a network, called by modern historians a "Protestant International,"

created an explosion in republican political theory that drew heavily upon the theology of a pietist movement known as the *Nadere Reformatie,* or Further Reformation.[36] Gathering in salons, such as English merchant Benjamin Furley's "Lantern," were such English Whigs as John Locke, Charles Ashley Cooper, and Gilbert Burnet, such Huguenot theologians as Pierre Bayle and Pierre Jurieu, the Dutch Collegiants Frans Kuypers and Barent Joosten Stol, and Dutch jurist Lambert Velthuysen.[37] Also circulating among this group of thinkers in Rotterdam during the late 1680s were a number of New York merchants who would play a prominent role in New York's government after 1689. Foremost among these merchants were Jacob Milborne, Milborne's father-in-law Samuel Edsall, Benjamin Blagge, Jacob Mauritz, and Joost Stol.[38] The resulting constitutional theory emanating out of Rotterdam emphasized natural law and the compact theory of government.[39]

Following the principle of the compact theory and that they could not rule without the "People's Resolutions," the New York militia captains in June 1689 called for the representative convention "to act in the affairs." In late June 1689, an assembly of delegates from six New York counties and two East Jersey counties, known as the Committee of Safety, met in New York City. In doing so, they followed Dutch political traditions, where fundamental law, representative institutions, and popular sovereignty were important aspects of the political structure.[40] In June the convention elected senior militia captain Jacob Leisler commander of the fort, and in August commander-in-chief of the province.[41] The convention's election of Leisler as provincial commander-in-chief also followed Dutch precedents. In the Republic, when "ruling elites were discredited," historians note of political crises in the Netherlands, the "loss of legitimacy caused . . . a demand for changes of personnel in high offices, and a call for the restoration of the rights of local burgher communities."[42] Wealth, social prominence, and military expertise made Leisler a logical choice.[43]

Drawing on Calvinist thought as filtered through Orangist propaganda, Jacob Leisler and his party encouraged in New York a "Further Reformation"—a term they indeed used for their movement—for the "reestablishment and preservation of the true protestant Religion, liberty and property."[44] Bolstered by their connections to Rotterdam theorists, Leisler and his supporters sought to restore the traditional balances in the government by reclaiming the corporate rights of the people, the abolishment of monopolies, demands for no taxation without representation and the right of the people to bear arms unrestricted, and the devolution of governmental authority to local communities. In doing so, Jacob Leisler and his party followed Dutch Orangist arguments by intertwining true doctrine with the preservation of estates. Rotterdam theorists held that "nations give the supreme authority to their rulers only for the preservation of the property, lives, liberty, and religion."[45] By losing "their Laws and Religion," a Leislerian tract states, a people also lost "their Properties and their Souls."[46] Leisler thus sought a reformation to regenerate the Christian church from false creeds by securing civil control for "the preservation of our Religion."[47] Yet, just as he and his followers believed that they were regenerating the Christian church to its original evangelical fervor, their "Reformation" sought to restore the traditional balances of government. In the Dutch Republic, fundamental law, representative institutions, and popular sovereignty were important aspects of the Dutch constitution, enshrined in the *Union of Utrecht* (1579) and *Act of Abjuration* (1581).[48] The Leislerians thus sought to restore the traditional corporate rights of the people and to abolish monopolies so that "one place should have no more privileges than the other."[49]

In 1689, shortly after Jacob Leisler assumed control of the New York provincial government, he had an inventory made of the records in the office of the provincial secretary, and, beginning in September 1689, he attempted to codify New York's legal system.[50] Perceiving that England's Parliament had declared James II's government illegal, Leisler and his council voted on December 16 to restore the provincial government for "our Religion and lawes" as it stood prior to the Catholic James's accession. That form of government was the one established by the 1683 New York Assembly. The Judiciary Act of 1683 was thus restored as the foundation for a decentralized provincial legal system.[51] With this in mind, and the desperate need to raise revenues, the council then voted that the "Costumes and Accize be Collected according to an Act made by the Assembly for this province Anno 1683."[52]

On December 19, 1689, a *plakkaat* appeared in New York City condemning Leisler's resurrection of the 1683 act for raising revenues. Citing Magna Carta and statutes of English kings Edward I, Richard III, and Charles I, the authors (who turned out to be Leisler's wife's relations) declared "that no man thenceforth be Compeld to Make or yield any gift Loan benevolence tax or such Like Charge without Common Consent by act of [England's] parliament."[53] The following day, Leisler responded with a declaration against the "false construction on the wholesome Lawes of England" and concluded that the English constitution guaranteed New Yorkers that their "Supreame Legislative Authority under his Maties &ca shall for ever be & reside in a Governor, Councill & the People met in Generall Assembly."[54]

The dispute over the 1683 act highlights the Leislerian interpretation of sovereignty as based on Dutch constitutional theory. The New York debate, remember, occurred within a larger English constitutional crisis. At its root was the issue of in whose hands—the sovereign's or parliament's—final authority rested. Dutch theorists had placed ultimate authority in the people, balanced by laws and institutions.[55] It was within this framework that the Leislerians defined their regime. Moreover, the new sovereign was the Dutch *stadholder,* and it was logical to presume that his government would follow Dutch constitutional precepts. The Leislerians thus attempted to create a rational program for the political reality of an English New York on the legal principles as they understood them, or, as Leisler noted, out of "the [Dutch] Lawes of this our Province & the Lawes & Customes of our Kingdome of England."[56] Seeking a constitutional basis for their actions, the Leislerians determined that the 1683 New York Charter of Liberties validated the customs act, an act "created by the [people] represented in assembly."[57]

The events surrounding what came to be called "Leisler's Rebellion" on New York's political life cannot be overstated. Leisler's 1689–1691 administration deeply divided the population. The savage anti-Leislerian backlash in 1691 with the arrival of English governor Henry Sloughter, during which Jacob Leisler was executed, only further polarized the political camps and created an environment in which "judicial expropriation and execution of one's opponents was the stake in the lottery for political power."[58] As Leisler's government fell, the crown's appointed new governor called for elections for an assembly. This assembly, beginning in May 1691, reenacted some of the legislation of the 1683 Assembly but created a new judiciary act. This act, drafted by assembly speaker and former Dominion attorney-general James Graham, reestablished the provincial courts on a different basis from that of 1683. Instead, the 1691 act basically redesigned the Dominion's judicial structure for New York. The apex of the court system was now the Supreme Court of Judicature, consisting of a chief justice and two associate, or *puisne,* justices appointed by the governor. The Supreme Court, as the colony's highest court of law, had both original and appellate jurisdiction and exercised jurisdiction over "all pleas, Civill Criminall, and Mixt, as fully & amply to all Intents & purposes whatsoever, as the Courts of King's Bench, Comon Pleas, & Exchequer within their Majestyes Kingdome of England, have or ought to have."[59]

The foundation blocks of the New York court system were the justices of the peace. Considered the bastion of the English legal system, justices were to serve a similar function in New York. Yet, exactly how different in actual practice and popular perception justices were from the Dutch *commissarien* who had previously overseen the local administration of justice under the Dutch is open to question.[60] County courts of session were the central instrument of criminal justice. Criminal cases were brought before them as the result of a grand jury indictment, but the law also permitted the courts to hear cases resulting from personal complaint or information brought by one of the justices. The session courts guaranteed all defendants a jury trial before twelve peers. Many New Yorkers, however, distrusted the impartiality of juries and waived this privilege. In Dutch fashion they preferred court determination based on arbitration. In actual practice, then, customary traditions modified English forms. As Douglas Greenberg notes, the "system of criminal justice in New York was decentralized, and it granted extensive powers to local J.P.'s who were free to funding without supervision from the provincial authorities in New York City."[61]

The 1691 Judiciary Act became the basis for New York's legal system throughout the eighteenth century. The act, however, did not go unchallenged. England's official position was that courts could not be created by act of local legislatures. Rather, only governors, as delegates of the crown, could establish courts. The New York Assembly's 1691 Judiciary Act was thus not approved, and, according to historian Christine Desan, the "Supreme Court of New York, and all its acts, judgments, rules, and the titles to real estate and other property secured by its decisions, rested upon Ordinances issued by the Governor himself." To this position, in turn, no New York Assembly would explicitly concede.[62] Moreover, the 1691 Assembly had been elected by a small segment of the population, as Leislerians, under color of treason, were barred from voting.

The 1691 Act provided for no Chancery (Equity) jurisdiction, except so far as the Exchequer jurisdiction of the Supreme Court may have implied. It was in this area that New Yorkers began to reconstitute the 1691 judicial system according to their interpretation of constitutional principles from a Dutch perspective. As previously noted, in the Dutch Republic the states' legislatures, or estates, maintained control over both the treasury and judicial appointments. Beginning with the 1698 administration of Richard Coote, Earl of Bellomont, who was sympathetic to the Leislerian cause, Leislerians regained control of both local governments and the provincial assembly.[63] This was the political situation when Abraham Gouverneur, a leading Leislerian partisan and ideologue who had married Jacob Leisler's daughter Mary, wrote the code for New York City's courts.

It is in the area of judicial appointments at the expense of royal prerogatives that New Yorkers behaved most like their Old World Dutch counterparts. In the Republic, the judicial system was decentralized, local communities were given much autonomy in legal affairs, and there were no central courts of justice. Instead, the provincial estates acted in this capacity. Only in extraordinary cases, when the essential constitutional laws of the Republic were involved, was appeal made to the *Hoge Raad* (Supreme Court) in The Hague.[64] The continuing pressure by New Yorkers to retain a decentralized system can be seen when in 1711 English

ARMS OF THE STATE OF NEW YORK:
FAC SIMILE
of the Initial T, engraved on
A NEW YORK MILITARY COMMISSION
from Gov. G. Clinton,
of June 25, 1778.

FIGURE 13.7. Arms of the State of New York, 1778. Lady Justice is "draped in short gown and petticoat, according to the Dutch costume." Illustration and quote from Edgar A. Werner, Civil List and Constitutional History of the Colony and State of New York (1886). New York Court of Appeals Collection.

governor Robert Hunter revived the Chancery jurisdiction with himself as chancellor, and appointed officers of the court. The New York Assembly responded to this perceived threat to their traditional liberties with a denial of the governor's right to erect courts without its concurrence.[65] Thereafter, although English governors would employ equitable jurisdiction, New Yorkers' resistance to it would locate in and attack the legitimacy of the court. Increasingly New Yorkers pressed for the "establishment of courts by statutory enactment," albeit decentralized.[66]

The continuing impact of Dutch constitutional ideals upon New York is also seen in the wake of the Dutch Revolution of 1747, which placed Willem IV, prince of Orange, as *stadholder* in all seven provinces of the Republic. At the time of the 1747 revolution, the Dutch press turned out an enormous literature looking back to the traditional balances of good government and the corporate rights of the people. Following the example of the Netherlands, New Yorkers during this period also took a renewed interest in their Dutch constitutional heritage. Historian James Tanis convincingly argues that during the English imperial crisis of the 1740s and 1750s, New Yorkers resurrected their Dutch traditions. Citing numerous New York and New Jersey Dutch Reformed and Presbyterian sermons, the "Dutch example," he writes, "became an important symbol for the colonists at the time of the Albany Congress in 1754." For the population of the middle colonies, then, the sixteenth-century Dutch revolt against Spain and the actions of *stadholder* William III during the 1688 Glorious Revolution served as the "paradigm" of "union and independence."[67] As an illustration, during the 1750s, American Dutch-language almanacs, following the lead of the Netherlands' press, republished the 1581 Act of Abjuration, by which the Republic had declared its independence from Spain, and the 1579 Union of Utrecht, the Republic's basic federalizing document.[68]

The constitutional ideals and the legal theories of the Dutch Republic, and particularly those of the state of Holland, continued to play a prominent role in New York adjudication throughout the eighteenth century. These ideals were transmitted not only through custom and tradition, but also through the compilations of Grotius, Damhouder, and other legal theorists, which New Yorkers continued to consult. When, for example, John Jay, first United States Chief Justice, entered Kings College in New York City to prepare for law in 1764, Hugo Grotius remained the standard legal text and Damhouder remained a powerful influence in New York civil law.[69] Furthermore, it is stated that the New York Field Code of 1848, which merged law and equity actions and provided a uniform set of rules of pleading, was largely influenced by Edward Livingston's Louisiana Code of 1824–1833. Livingston was raised in a conservative Dutch cultural area of the Hudson Valley, educated in Reformed Dutch schools before entering Princeton, and studied for the bar in the Albany, New York, law firm of Dutchman John Lansing, where he became "strongly attracted" to the Code of Justinian, the basis for Dutch-Roman law.[70] In addition, the Dutch belief that statutes, ordinances, customs, and manners that exist in each town or province are according to the needs of the place had a profound impact on New York legal thinking. Thus, in order to understand the development of law and constitutional theory in New York, one must not only look to English common law traditions but to Dutch law.

NOTES

1. Robert Ludlow Fowler, *History of the Law of Real Property in New York* (New York: Baker, Voorhis and Co., 1895), 65–71. See Common Law: West's Encyclopedia of American Law, http://www.answers.com/topic/common-law.

2. Mayor's Court Minutes, April 8, 1701; Arthur Everett Peterson and George William Edwards, *New York As An Eighteenth-Century Municipality* (New York: Longmans, Green, 1917), 25.

3. Kennedy's quote is in Christine A. Desan, "Remaking Constitutional Tradition at the Margin of the Empire: The Creation of Legislative Adjudication in Colonial New York," *Law and History Review* 16 (Spring 1998): 257.

4. Ibid.

5. Douglas Greenberg, *Crime and Law Enforcement in the Colony of New York 1691–1776* (Ithaca and London: Cornell University Press, 1974), 25.

6. Charles T. Gehring, trans. and ed., *Laws and Writs of Appeal 1647–1663* (Syracuse: Syracuse University Press, 1991), xviii–xix.

7. The exact wording, though not substance, varied from community to community. The quote here comes from the terms for New Amsterdam. See Albert E. McKinley, "The Transition from Dutch to English Rule in New York," *American Historical Review* 6 (July 1901): 695.

8. Charles Z. Lincoln, *The Colonial Laws of New York from the Year 1664 to the Revolution,* 5 vols. (Albany: James B. Lyon, 1894), 1: 6–93; McKinley, 712–14; Milton M. Klein, *The Empire State: A History of New York* (Ithaca: Cornell University Press, 2001), 115–16.

9. Maarten Prak, *The Dutch Republic in the Seventeenth Century The Golden Age,* trans. Diane Webb (Cambridge: Cambridge University Press, 2005), 131–32; Henk F. K. van Nierop, *The Nobility of Holland: From Knights to Regents, 1500–1650* (Cambridge: Cambridge University Press, 1993), 199–207; Patricia U. Bonomi, *A Factious People: Politics and Society in Colonial New York* (New York and London: Columbia University Press, 1971), 28–55.

10. An English-language translation is Hugo Grotius, *The Jurisprudence of Holland,* Robert W. Lee, trans. (Oxford: Clarenden Press, 1896).

11. Gehring, *Laws and Writs of Appeal,* xviii–xix.

12. Donna Merwick, "A Genre of Their Own: Kiliaen van Rensselaer as Guide to the Reading and Writing Practices of Early Modern Businessmen," *The William and Mary Quarterly* 3rd series, LXV (October 2008), 4: 687.

13. Edmund B. O'Callaghan, *Documentary History of the State of New York,* 4 vols. (Albany: Weed, Parsons, 1848–1853), 3: 872–75 (hereafter cited as *DHNY*); Lawrence H. Leder, "The Unorthodox Domine: Nicholas Van Rensselaer," *New York History* 35 (April 1954): 166–76.

14. *Attestation of 12 Members, Van Rensselaer vs. Jacob Leisler and Jacob Milborne, Aug. 17, 1676,* GLC 3107, J. P. Morgan Library, New York City (translation, JLP No. 2472, Papers of Jacob Leisler, New York University); *Complaint of Nicholas van Rensselaer,* GLC 3107 (translation, JLP No. 2471); *Complaint of Nicholas van Rensselaer, July 17, 1676,* GLC 3107, Morgan Library (translation, JLP No. 2471).

15. Sir Johannes Wessels, Michael H. Hoeflich, *History of the Roman-Dutch Law* (Clark, NJ: The Lawbook Exchange, 2005), 204; Charles S. Edward, *Hugo Grotius The Miracle of Holland: A Study in Political and Legal Thought* (Chicago: Nelson-Hall, 1981), 110.

16. Jonathan Israel, *The Dutch Republic Its Rise, Greatness, and Fall, 1477–1806* (Oxford: Clarendon, 1995), 277–97.

17. Allan Tully, *Forming American Politics: Ideals, Interests, and Institutions in Colonial New York and Pennsylvania* (Baltimore: The Johns Hopkins University Press, 1994); Simon Middleton, *From Privileges to Rights: Work and Politics in Colonial New York City* (Philadelphia: University of Pennsylvania Press, 2006); Allison Gilbert Olson, *Making the Empire Work: London and American Interest Groups, 1690–1790* (Cambridge: Harvard University Press, 1992), 72–73.

18. Douglas Campbell, *The Puritan in Holland, England, and America: An Introduction to American History,* 2 vols. (New York: Harper and Brothers, 1892), 2: 451.

19. "An Act to settle Courts of Justice," November 1, 1683, Lincoln, *Colonial Laws of New York,* 1: 125–28.

20. News arrived in New York "of greater preparations in England" for war with Holland on December 3, 1688. See Francis Nicholson to Edward Randolph, December 3/5, 1688, and Stephen van Cortlandt to Edward Randolph, December 4, 1688, in Robert Noxan Toppan, ed., *Edward Randolph: Including His Letters and Official Papers from New England, Middle, and Southern Colonies in America and the West Indies*, 9 vols. (Boston: Prince Society, 1898–1909; New York, 1967), 4: 255–57. News that James had fled the throne arrived on February 5, 1689. See Francis Nicholson to Fitz-John Winthrop, February 16, 1689, in *Collections of the Massachusetts Historical Society*, 6th ser. (Boston: Massachusetts Historical Society, 1889), 3: 495.

21. Paul Knevel, *Burgers in het geweer: De schutterijen in Holland, 1550–1700* (Hilversum: Hist. Verlag Holland/Verloren, 1994); J. C. Grayson, "The Civic Militia in the County of Holland, 1560–81. Politics and Public Order in the Dutch Revolt," *Bijdragen en Mededelingen betreffende de Geschiedenis der Nederlanden* 95 (1980): 35–63.

22. Donna Merwick, *Possessing Albany, 1630–1710: The Dutch and English Experiences* (Cambridge and New York: Cambridge University Press, 1990), 273; Bonomi, *A Factious People*, 158–59.

23. W. P. C. Knuttel, *Catalogus van de pamfletten verzameling berustende in de Koninklijke Bibliotheek*, 8 vols. ('sGravenhage: Algemeene Landsdrukkerij, 1889–1920); G. O. van de Klashorst, W. H. Blom, and E. O. G. Haitsma Mulier, *Bibliography of Dutch Seventeenth Century Political Thought: An Annotated Inventory 1581–1710* (Amsterdam: APA-Holland University Press, 1986), 122–25. A selection of those tracts aimed at the English public is in *State Tracts: Being a Farther Collection of Several Choice Treatises Relating to the Government, From the Year 1660 to 1689*, 2 vols. (London: 1692; reprint, Wilmington, DE: R. Baldwin, 1973). Leisler often literally lifted passages from these works. For example, in 1690 he used the words of Charles Blount's *An Appeal from the Country to the City* (1679) to describe that year's devastating French and Indian February raid on Schenectady, well knowing the public was familiar with Blount's prophetic imagery of Catholic atrocities. See *State Tracts*, 1: 401–402, and Leisler to Maryland, March 4, 1689/90, *DHNY* 1: 307, and 2: 181–84.

24. Leisler to the Governor of Barbados, Nov. 23, 1689, *DHNY* 2: 40–42.

25. Robert Beddard, *A Kingdom without a King: The Journals of the Provisional Government in the Revolution of 1688* (Oxford: Phaidon, 1988), 29–31; Jonathan I. Israel, "The Dutch role in the Glorious Revolution," in *Anglo-Dutch moment*, 121–22. For Leisler's receipt of the declarations, see Deposition of Andries Greveraet and George Brewerton, December 31, 1689, CO5/1081, 223 Public Records Office, Kew Gardens, England (hereafter cited as PRO). Bayard wrote of Leisler's *Declaration of the Inhabitants Soldjers*, "Yet for want of some plausible cause these words were taken out of His Royall Highness The Prince of Orange's third Declaration in England." "Colonel Bayard's Narrative of Occurrences in New-York, April to December 1689," in *Documents Relative to the Colonial History of the State of New York*, 15 vols., ed. Edmund B. O'Callaghan, Berthold Fernow, and John Romeyn Brodhead (Albany: Weed, Parsons, 1853–1885), 3: 639–41(hereafter cited as *NYCD*).

26. *The Declaration of His Highness William Henry (by the Grace of God) Prince of Orange, &c. Of the Reasons inducing him to appear in Arms in the Kingdom of England, for Preserving of the Protestant Religion, and for Restoring the Laws and Liberties of England, Scotland and Ireland*, Oct. 10, 1688, *State Tracts* 2: 420–25.

27. *By his Highness William Henry, Prince of Orange, a Declaration* (or the *Third Declaration*), dated November 28, appeared in London on Decemeber 4, 1688. It later turned out to be a forgery, but William did not reveal this fact until after it had had the desired effect. *State Tracts* 2: 427–28; Beddard, *Kingdom without a King*, 30.

28. David Steven Cohen estimated that 54.5 percent of New Netherland immigrants were Calvinists fleeing Catholic persecutions in the Spanish Netherlands and France (17 percent) and the German states (37.5). "How Dutch Were the Dutch of New Netherland?" *New York History* 42 (1981): 43–60. With Louis XIV's 1685 revocation of the Edict of Nantes and subsequent persecutions of French Calvinists, "many French refugees were filling up the churches." New York *dominie* Henricus Selijns to Boston ministers

James Allen, Increase Mather, and Samuel Willard, May 8/18, 1683, in Charles W. Baird, *History of the Huguenot Emigration to America*, 2 vols. (New York: Dodd, Mead, 1885), 2: 397.

29. Long Island Consistory to the Amsterdam Classis, July 20, 1685, *Flatbush Church Records* 1: 169. In addition to governor Thomas Dongan, Roman Catholics appointed to high position in New York included Jarvis Baxter as commandant of the fort at Albany, Bartholomew Russel as commander at Fort James, Capt. Webb as commander of the kings forces on Staten and Long Islands, Matthew Plowman as collector of the port, James Larkin as overseer of the granary and custom house, James Cooley as official blacksmith, and Albany coroner Jan van Loon. See Peter Christoph, "The Time and Place of Jan van Loon: A Roman Catholic in Colonial Albany: Part I," *de Halve Maen* 60 (October 1987): 8–11, and "Part II" (December 1987): 9–12.

30. Members of the Dutch Church at New York to the Classis of Amsterdam, Oct. 21, 1698, in *Collections of the New-York Historical Society*, I (New York: 1868), 398.

31. Declaration of the Lieutenant Governor and Council, May 10, 1689, CO 5/1081, 9, Public Record Office, Kew, England.

32. Martin van Gelderen, *The Political Thought of the Dutch Revolt 1555–1590* (Cambridge: Cambridge University Press, 1992), 286.

33. Van Gelderen, *Political Thought of the Dutch Revolt*, 269–76; Hedley Bull, Benedict Kingsbury, Adam Roberts, *Hugo Grotius and International Relations* (New York: Oxford University Press, 1990), 102.

34. Herbert D. Foster, "International Calvinism through Locke and the Revolution of 1688," *American Historical Review* 32 (1926/27): 495.

35. *Memoires de l'estat de France sous Charles IX: contenans les choses plus notables, faites & publiees tant par les Catholiques que par ceux de la religion . . .* , 3 vols. (Middelbourg: Henrich Wolff, 1578). Goulart's work appears in the library of John Locke, see, Lord King's half of Locke's library cited in Foster, "International Calvinism," 495 note 19, and, see also, 492, 494–95. For discussion of the importance of Goulart's *Memoires* see Quentin Skinner, *The Foundations of Modern Political Thought*, 2 vols. (Cambridge/New York: Cambridge University Press), 2: 304–309.

36. Michiel Wielema, *Filosofen aan de Maas: Kroniek van vijfhonderd jaar wijsgerig denken in Rotterdam* (Baarn: Ambo, 1991), 25–87. Also see J. F. Bosher, "Huguenot Merchants and the Protestant International in the Seventeenth Century," *William and Mary Quarterly* 3d ser., 52 (January 1995): 77–100.

37. Augustus Charles Bickley, "Furley, Benjamin (1636–1714)," in *Dictionary of National Biography*, vol. 7 (Oxford: Oxford University Press, 1917), 770; Foster, "International Calvinism Through Locke and the Revolution of 1688," 482; Guy Howard Dodge, *The Political Theory of the Huguenots of the Dispersion: With Special Reference to the Thought and Influence of Pierre Jurieu* (New York: Columbia University Press, 1947); Wielema, *Filosofen aan de Maas*, 76–78.

38. The activities of New Yorkers in Rotterdam can be followed in Depositions of Benjamin Furley and others at the request of Jacob Milborne, May 28 and 29 and June 1, 1688, ONA 1397, fol. 365, June 1, 1688, ONA 1397, fol. 367, and July 27, 1688, ONA 1260, fol. 127, GAR; Deposition of Samuel Edsall, Henry Farr, and James Evetts on behalf of Jacob Milborne, February 15, 1689, ONA 1399, fol. 83, GAR. William Hull, *William Penn and the Dutch Quaker Migration to Pennsylvania* (Swarthmore, PA, 1935), 313–14. For Stol see Last Will and Testament of Lysbeth de Munnik, Feb. 24, 1680, ms. 1474.12, Gar; Wijnman, "Barent Joosten Stol," in *Nieuw Nederlandsch Biografisch Woordenboek*, 10 vols., ed. P. C. Molhuysen, P. J. Blok, L. Knappert (Leiden: A. W. Sijthoff's uitgevers maatschappij, 1911–1937), 5: 981–83; and Fix, *Dutch Collegiants*, 150–55, 174–76.

39. Michiel Wielema, *Filosofen aan de Maas: Kroniek van vijfhonderd jaar wijsgerig denken in Rotterdam* (Baarn: Ambo, 1991), 25–87; Rienk H. Vermij, *The Calvinist Copernicans: The Reception of the New Astronomy in the Dutch Republic, 1575–1750* (Amsterdam: Edita KNAW, 2002).

40. Circular to the Towns of Long Island, June 12, 1689, Charles R. Street, comp. and ed., *Huntington Town Records, Including Babylon, Long Island, New York*, 5 vols. (Huntington, NY: The Long Islander Print, 1887–88), 2: 31–32; *DHNY* 2: 11.

41. *NYCD* 3: 597; *DHNY* 2: 45.

42. Boone and Prak, "Rulers, Patricians, and Burghers," 119.

43. David William Voorhees, "The 'Fervent Zeale' of Jacob Leisler," *William and Mary Quarterly* 3rd ser., LI (July 1994), 3: 447–72.

44. Address of the Militia of New-York to William and Mary, June 3, 1689, *CDNY* 3: 583. For Leislerian use of the phrase "Further Reformation" see, for example, A Memoriall, 1689, *DHNY* 2:57, and Edsall et al. to Committee of Safety, Albany, Oct. 28, 1689, *DHNY* 2: 115.

45. Nobbs, *Theocracy and Toleration,* 209 (this page relates to Voetius's call upon a Christian civil rule to purge the church by force)]; Guy Howard Dodge, *The Political Theory of The Huguenots of the Dispersion with Special Reference to the Thought and Influence of Pierre Jurieu* (New York: Columbia University Press, 1947), 63.

46. "Loyalty Vindicated," in Andrews, *Narratives,* 389.

47. Address of the Militia of New-York to William and Mary, June 3, 1689, *NYCD* 3: 583.

48. Van Gelderen, *Political Thought of the Dutch Revolt,* 286. English texts of the Union of Utrecht and Act of Abjuration are in E. H. Kossmann and A. F. Mellink, eds., *Texts concerning the Revolt of the Netherlands* (Cambridge: Cambridge University Press, 1974), 166–73, 216–28. For the influence of these works on American constitutional development see James R. Tanis, "The Dutch-American Connection: The Impact of the Dutch Example on American Constitutional Beginnings," in *New York and the Union: Contributions to the American Constitutional Experience,* ed. Stephen L. Schechter and Richard B. Bernstein (Albany: New York State Commission on the Bicentennial of the United States Constitution, 1990), 22–28, and Stephen E. Lucas, "The Plakkaat van Verlatinge: A Neglected Model for the American Declaration of Independence" in *Connecting Cultures The Netherlands in Five Centuries of Transatlantic Exchange,* ed. Rosemarijn Hoefte and Johanna C. Kardux (Amsterdam: VU University Press, 1994), 187–207.

49. Act of Assembly, Apr. 24, 1690, *Colonial Laws* 1: 218. The abolition of monopolies and special privileges was an important aspect of Leisler's program.

50. See Gehring, *Laws and Writs of Appeal,* xix.

51. Commission to hold a Court of Oyer and Terminer, Jan. 18, 1689/90, *DHNY* 2: 61.

52. Minutes of Council, Dec. 16, 1689, ibid., 48–49.

53. Declaration of the English Freeman Regarding the 1683 Act of Customs, Dec. 19, 1689, PRO CO 5/1081, p. 203. Leisler in Council had ordered the customs and assizes to be collected according to the 1683 Act on Dec. 14, 1689, *DHNY* 2:49. The author of the declaration was Jacob de Kay, Sr., probably with Nicholas Bayard and William Nicolls. For the anti-Leislerian interpretation of this act see "A Modest and Impartial Narrative" (1690), in *Narratives of the Insurrections,* ed. Charles M. Andrews (New York: Charles Scribner's Sons, 1915), 340–44. Also see David S. Lovejoy, *The Glorious Revolution in America* (New York: Harper and Row, 1972; rept. Middletown, CT: Wesleyan University Press, 1987), 276; Robert C. Ritchie, *The Duke's Province A Study of New York Politics and Society, 1664–1691* (Chapel Hill: University of North Carolina Press, 1977), 210–11; and Charles Howard McCormick, *Leisler's Rebellion* (New York: Garland Press, 1989), 275.

54. *DHNY* 2: 50–51.

55. See, for example, Van Gelderen, *Political Thought of the Dutch Revolt,* 262–63.

56. *DHNY* 2: 61.

57. *DHNY* 2:51. See also Ritchie, *Duke's Province,* 210–11.

58. Eben Moglen, "Considering Zenger: Partisan Politics and the Legal Profession in Provincial New York," *Columbia Law Review* 94 (June 1994): 1498.

59. Lincoln, *Colonial Laws of New York* 1: 226–31; Martin L. Budd, "Law in Colonial New York: The Legal System of 1691," *Harvard Law Review* 80 (1967): 1757–72.

60. Dennis Maika, for example, argues that the similarities between Dutch and English commercial law made for an easy transition. Dennis J. Maika, *Commerce and Community: Manhattan Merchants in the Seventeenth Century* (PhD dissertation, New York University, 1995), 442–43. For the functions of the

commissarien at the local level see E. B. O'Callaghan, *Laws and ordinances of New Netherland, 1638–1674* (Albany: Weed, Parsons, 1868), 422–24.

61. Greenberg, 34–35.

62. Desan, "Remaking Constitutional Tradition at the Margin of the Empire."

63. Bonomi, *A Factious People,* 77.

64. J. L. Price, *The Dutch Republic in the Seventeenth Century* (New York: St. Martin's, 1998), 66, 68.

65. Mary Lou Lustig, *Privilege and Prerogative New York's Provincial Elite, 1710–1776* (Teaneck, NJ: Fairleigh Dickinson University Press, 1995), 24.

66. Bonomi, *A Factious People,* 124–27, 133.

67. James Tanis, "The American Dutch, Their Church, and the Revolution," in *A Bilateral Bicentennial: A History of Dutch-American Relations, 1782–1982,* ed. J. W. Schulte Nordholt and Robert P. Swierenga (Amsterdam: 1982), 116.

68. *De AMERICAANSE Almanak, Voo't Jaar na Christi geboorte 1754* (New York), Edelman, *Dutch-American Bibliography,* 56. English texts of the Union of Utrecht and Act of Abjuration are in E. H. Kossman and A. F. Mellink, eds., *Texts concerning the Revolt of the Netherland* (Cambridge: Cambridge University Press, 1974), 166–73, 216–28.

69. Landa M. Freeman, Louise V. North, and Janet M. Wedge, *Selected Letters of John Jay and Sarah Livingston Jay* (Jefferson, NC: McFarland, 2005), 291.

70. See, for example, C. H. van Rhee, "Mixed Legal System and Civil Procedure" (World Society of Mixed Jurisdiction Jurists Conference, University of Edinburgh, June 30, 2007); Charles Havens Hunt, George Bancroft, *Life of Edward Livingston* (New York: D. Appleton, 1864), particularly p. 41.

Contributor Biographies

ANNE-MARIE CANTWELL

Anne-Marie Cantwell is professor of anthropology at Rutgers University-Newark, specializing in ethnohistory and American archaeology. She has excavated sites in the Midwest and the Northeast and has published extensively on the archaeology of ancient American trade, ritual, and rise of complex societies; the archaeology of New Netherland; and issues relating to cultural property, indigenous peoples, and archaeological ethics. With Diana Wall, she co-authored "Unearthing Gotham: The Archaeology of New York City," which received the Society for American Archaeology's Book Award, and "Touring Gotham's Archaeological Past." She is currently working on the archaeology of both colonial societies, focusing on New Netherland, and the American Revolution.

PETER R. CHRISTOPH

Peter R. Christoph is the editor of fourteen volumes of historical records and has written some sixty articles, relating chiefly to colonial New York. For many years he was the head of Manuscripts and Special Collections at the New York State Library. He was the first director of the New Netherland translation project, and was elected a fellow of the Holland Society of New York. He has also served as archivist for First Lutheran Church in Albany and the Upstate New York Synod, and served on a church archives board for the northeastern states.

JOEP DE KONING

In 1998, Joep de Koning started a foundation seeking (1) political recognition of Governors Island as one of the three principal seventeenth-century European landing places on North America's east coast; (2) appreciation of the Island's national significance as the place on which the New World's first lawful expression of religious tolerance took place; (3) acknowledgment of the island as the authentic wellspring of the NY Tri-State region's unique legal-cultural condition of toleration as an individual right; and (4) support for visualizing the Island's symbolic worth to humanity and historic message vital to moral progress. After four years on Madison Avenue, Joep de Koning earned an MBA in finance from Columbia University in 1974—then worked on Wall Street until 1998.

WILSON C. FREEMAN

Wilson Freeman graduated from Case Western Reserve University in 2005 with a double major in political science and economics. After working for three years in economic consulting in Washington, D.C., he began law school at New York University in the fall of 2008, receiving his JD in 2011. His research interests include law and economics and procedure.

CHARLES GEHRING

Charles Gehring was born in Fort Plain, an old Revolutionary War and Erie Canal town in New York State's Mohawk Valley. After completing his undergraduate and graduate studies at Virginia Military Institute and West Virginia University he continued postgraduate work with assistance of a Fulbright grant at Albert-Ludwigs-Universität in Freiburg, Germany. There, he began his study of the Dutch language and first realized that his future research lay much closer to home. He eventually received a PhD in Germanic Linguistics from Indiana University with a concentration in Netherlandic Studies. His dissertation (1973) was a linguistic investigation of the survival of the Dutch language in colonial New York. He is presently director of the New Netherland Project (sponsored by the New York State Library). The Project is responsible for translating the official records of the Dutch colony and promoting awareness of the Dutch role in American history. He has been a fellow of the Holland Society of New York since 1979. In 1994 Her Majesty Queen Beatrix of the Netherlands conferred on him a knighthood as officer in the Order of Orange-Nassau. In 2004 he received gold medals from the Holland Society and the St. Nicholas Society of New York.

MICHAEL E. GHERKE

Michael E. Gherke is currently an associate professor of history at Glenville State College in West Virginia. He received his PhD in Early American history in 2001, following defense of his dissertation, "Dutch Women in New Netherland and New York in the Seventeenth Century." His interest in colonial Dutch-American history and Dutch contributions to early American culture continues to inspire his research efforts.

JOYCE D. GOODFRIEND

Joyce D. Goodfriend, professor of history at the University of Denver, is the author of *Before the Melting Pot: Society and Culture in Colonial New York City, 1664–1730* (Princeton University Press, 1992); the editor of *Revisiting New Netherland: Perspectives on Early Dutch America* (Brill, 2005); and the co-editor of *Going Dutch: The Dutch Presence in America 1609–2009* (Brill, 2008). She has also written a host of essays and articles on New Netherland, early New York, and the Dutch in America. She is the chair of the Hendricks Prize Committee for manuscripts on New Netherland and a member of the International Editorial Board of Urban History.

LEO HERSHKOWITZ

Leo Hershkowitz received a PhD degree from New York University and a Doctor of Humane Letters from the Hebrew Union College-Jewish Institute of Religion in 2006. He has taught American History and New York History as professor of history at Queens College, City University of New York, for many years. He has written numerous books and many articles on New York history. Among his many publications are *Tweed's New York: Another Look* (1977) and *Letters of the Franks Family, 1733–1748* (co-editor, 1968). In 2008, he received the Lee Max Friedman award for service to American Jewish History from the American Jewish Historical Society.

JAAP JACOBS

Jaap Jacobs (PhD Leiden, 1999) is a historian who has specialized in the history of the Dutch in the Americas in the early modern period. He has taught at Leiden University, the University of Amsterdam, Cornell University, The University of Pennsylvania, and Harvard University. He has published widely on New Netherland and New Amsterdam, including *The Colony of New Netherland: A Dutch Settlement in Seventeenth Century America* (Cornell University Press, 2009). He is currently working on a biography of Petrus Stuyvesant. He regularly gives lectures and presentations on Dutch New York.

TROY A. MCKENZIE

Troy McKenzie is associate professor of law at New York University School of Law. His research interests include bankruptcy, civil procedure, complex litigation, and the federal courts. McKenzie graduated in 1997 from Princeton University and received his law degree in 2000 from NYU, where he was an executive editor of the Law Review. He served as a law clerk to Judge Pierre N. Leval of the United States Court of Appeals for the Second Circuit and to Justice John Paul Stevens of the Supreme Court of the United States before working as a litigation associate at a New York City firm. He joined the NYU faculty in 2007.

WIJNAND W. MIJNHARDT

Wijnand Mijnhardt has been a professor of history at the University of Utrecht since 1976. He was a visiting professor at UCLA for a trimester each year from 2001–05 and since 2007 he has been director of the Descartes Centre for the History and Philosophy of the Sciences at UU. He published on the European Enlightenment and on the scientific infrastructure of the early modern period. He recently published, together with Lynn Hunt and Margaret Jacob, *The Book that Changed Europe: Picart and Bernard's Religious Ceremonies of the World* (Harvard University Press, 2010).

PAUL OTTO

Paul Otto is professor of history at George Fox University, Newberg, Oregon. His research focuses upon European-Native American relations in early America and is currently examining the evolution of wampum in the colonial northeast. His book, *The Dutch-Munsee Encounter in America: The Struggle for Sovereignty in the Hudson Valley,* won the Hendricks Award for the best volume in colonial Dutch studies. He has also been the recipient of a Mellon Fellowship and an Earhart Research Grant. In recognition for his work on New Netherland, he has been made a fellow of both the New Netherland Institute and the Holland Society of New York.

ALBERT M. ROSENBLATT

Albert M. Rosenblatt, a graduate of the University of Pennsylvania and Harvard Law School, teaches at New York University School of Law. He served as a Judge of the New York Court of Appeals, New York's highest court, from 1999 through 2006 and had been Chief Administrative Judge of the State of New York. He is president of the Historical Society of the Courts of the State of New York. His writings include *The Judges of the New York Court of Appeals: A Biographical History* and *Historic Courthouses of the State of New York*. He is affiliated with the law firm of McCabe and Mack in Poughkeepsie, New York.

JULIA C. ROSENBLATT

Julia C. Rosenblatt, a former professor at Vassar College, received her PhD from the University of Iowa. She is co-author of *Dining with Sherlock Holmes* and *Historic Courthouses of the State of New York*. She has written numerous articles about Sherlock Holmes and about skiing, including a regular column in the *Poughkeepsie Journal*. She and her husband, both members of the Baker Street Irregulars, live in the Mid-Hudson Valley. They have one daughter, Betsy, an attorney and law professor.

MARTHA DICKINSON SHATTUCK

Martha Dickinson Shattuck is an independent historian. She received her PhD from Boston University and has been the editor and researcher for the New Netherland Project since 1988. She has published various articles on New Netherland and is the editor of *Explorers, Fortunes and Love Letters: A Window on New Netherland* (New Netherland Institute, 2009), was the New Netherland and Colonial editor for *The Encyclopedia of New York State* (Syracuse University Press, 2005).

WILLIAM J. VANDEN HEUVEL

William J. vanden Heuvel has served as Deputy U.S. Permanent Representative to the United Nations and as U.S. Ambassador to the European Office of the U.N. He is an international lawyer and investment banker. Ambassador vanden Heuvel has served as president of the International Rescue Committee, as chairman of the United Nations Association, and as chairman of the New York City Board of Correction. He was editor-in-chief of the Cornell Law Review and later served as executive assistant to General William J. "Wild Bill" Donovan, special counsel to Governor Averell Harriman, and assistant to Attorney General Robert F. Kennedy. He is the founder and chair emeritus of the Franklin and Eleanor Roosevelt Institute.

DAVID WILLIAM VOORHEES

David William Voorhees is director of the Papers of Jacob Leisler Project at New York University and managing editor of *de Halve Maen,* a quarterly scholarly journal devoted to New Netherland studies. Formerly the managing reference history editor at Charles Scribner's Sons and a co-editor of *The Papers of William Livingston,* he received a PhD in history from New York University in 1988. His published works include *The Concise Dictionary of American History* (1983), *The Holland Society: A Centennial History 1885–1985* (1985), and *Records of the Reformed Protestant Church of Flatbush, Kings County, New York, Volume 1, 1677–1720,* and *Volume 2, Deacons' Accounts, 1654–1709* (1998, 2009). He was a New York State Council of the Humanities Speaker in 1996–98.

DIANA DIZEREGA WALL

Diana diZerega Wall is professor of anthropology at City College and the Graduate Center of the City University of New York. She studies the archaeology of American culture, including colonialism, slavery, gender, and the rise of capitalism in New York City. Currently she is working on two projects, one on Seneca Village, a nineteenth-century African American community in today's Central Park, and the other on the archaeology of New Netherland. In addition to numerous articles, she wrote *The Archaeology of Gender: Separating the Spheres in Urban America,* and co-authored *Unearthing Gotham, the Archaeology of New York City* and *Touring Gotham's Archaeological Past.*

Index

Note: Page numbers in *italics* indicate illustrations.

NOVA BELGICA sive
Quebecq
RIONALYS
Modus muniendi apud Mahikanensis
Maniere van Woonplaetsen ofte Dorpen der Mahicans
ende andre Natien haer geburen
Canomakers
Mackwaas
Armeomecks
t' Landt van Kats Kill
NEDER
Sennecaas.
Minnessinck ofte
t' Landt van Bacham
Modus apud Minnessincos
Gacheos
NIEUW
JORCK
Wappinges
Waranawankon
Waoranecks
Capitanasses
Matanac:
kouses
t' Hooge Landt
Weeke
Pachami
Siwanoys
Konekotays
PARS
Minquaas
t' Lange
Sanhicans
NIEU JARSEY
Sasquesahanough
Matovancous
Sauwan
Aquauachuques
Ermomex
Tockwoghs
Naraticons
Zuydt Rivier
Kuscara:
waoks